The Magic Cube of Ancient Chinese Poetry

This book focuses on the linguistic perspective of classical Chinese poetry and its changes and development in different historical periods. It offers a combination of theoretical analysis and aesthetic appreciation of exemplary poems.

The author discusses the following aspects of classical Chinese poetry: the relationships between background and meaning in the interpretation of a poem; how readers can deal with the tangle of linguistic approach and intuitive perception in interpreting poems; the engagement and disengagement of the poet's thought flow with and from the word order of the verse; the tonal and metrical schemes; and the three special features of classical Chinese poetry: the significance and role of allusions, "Xu Zi", and "Shi Yan". Last, the author analyses the development of Chinese poetry from the Vernacular Song Dynasty Style to the Vernacular Modern Style.

It will be a great read for students and scholars of East Asian studies, Chinese studies, linguistics, and those interested in Chinese poetry in general. The book aims to lead readers to discover a fresh and amazing world of classical Chinese poetry, a fantastic panoramic picture of its beauty and charm, and a poetic feast that the reader may not otherwise be privileged to enjoy.

Ge Zhaoguang is Distinguished Professor of Fudan University, Shanghai, China. He received his B.A. and M.A. degrees from Peking University in 1982 and 1984, respectively. He was Professor in the Department of History of Tsinghua University, Beijing, from 1992 to 2006. He then served as the Director of the National Institute for Advanced Humanistic Studies at Fudan University from 2007 to 2013. Professor Ge's fields of research include the intellectual, religious, and cultural history of East Asia and China. He was the first Princeton Global Scholar and winner of the Asia Pacific Award (2014, Japan), Paju Book Award (2014, South Korea), and Hong Kong Book Award (2015), among others.

China Perspectives

The *China Perspectives* series focuses on translating and publishing works by leading Chinese scholars, writing about both global topics and China-related themes. It covers Humanities & Social Sciences, Education, Media and Psychology, as well as many interdisciplinary themes.

This is the first time any of these books have been published in English for international readers. The series aims to put forward a Chinese perspective, give insights into cutting-edge academic thinking in China, and inspire researchers globally.

To submit proposals, please contact the Taylor & Francis Publisher for China Publishing Programme, Lian Sun (Lian.Sun@informa.com)

Titles in literature currently include:

Dual Narrative Dynamics
Dan Shen

Chinese Thought in a Multi-cultural World
Cross-Cultural Communication, Comparative Literature and Beyond
YUE Daiyun

Literature and Power
A Critical Investigation of Literary Legitimacy
Zhu Guohua

Fuzzy Language in Literature and Translation
Lu SHAO

The Magic Cube of Ancient Chinese Poetry
A Linguistic Perspective
Ge Zhaoguang

For more information, please visit www.routledge.com/China-Perspectives/book-series/CPH

The Magic Cube of Ancient Chinese Poetry
A Linguistic Perspective

Ge Zhaoguang

LONDON AND NEW YORK

First published 2023
by Routledge
4 Park Square, Milton Park, Abingdon, Oxon OX14 4RN

and by Routledge
605 Third Avenue, New York, NY 10158

Routledge is an imprint of the Taylor & Francis Group, an informa business

© 2023 Ge Zhaoguang

Translated by Chen Hengshi

The right of Ge Zhaoguang to be identified as author of this work has been asserted in accordance with sections 77 and 78 of the Copyright, Designs and Patents Act 1988.

All rights reserved. No part of this book may be reprinted or reproduced or utilised in any form or by any electronic, mechanical, or other means, now known or hereafter invented, including photocopying and recording, or in any information storage or retrieval system, without permission in writing from the publishers.

Trademark notice: Product or corporate names may be trademarks or registered trademarks, and are used only for identification and explanation without intent to infringe.

English Version by permission of Fudan University Press

British Library Cataloguing-in-Publication Data
A catalogue record for this book is available from the British Library

Library of Congress Cataloging-in-Publication Data
Names: Ge, Zhaoguang, 1968– author.
Title: The magic cube of ancient Chinese poetry : a linguistic perspective / Ge Zhaoguang.
Description: Abingdon Oxon ; New York, NY : Routledge, 2023. | Series: China perspectives | Includes bibliographical references and index.
Identifiers: LCCN 2023000994 (print) | LCCN 2023000995 (ebook) | ISBN 9781032522890 (hardback) | ISBN 9781032522999 (paperback) | ISBN 9781003405993 (ebook)
Subjects: LCSH: Chinese poetry—History and criticism. | LCGFT: Literary criticism.
Classification: LCC PL2307 .G4 2023 (print) | LCC PL2307 (ebook) | DDC 895.11009—dc23/eng/20230404
LC record available at https://lccn.loc.gov/2023000994
LC ebook record available at https://lccn.loc.gov/2023000995

ISBN: 978-1-032-52289-0 (hbk)
ISBN: 978-1-032-52299-9 (pbk)
ISBN: 978-1-003-40599-3 (ebk)

DOI: 10.4324/9781003405993

Typeset in Times New Roman
by Apex CoVantage, LLC

Contents

	List of Figures	*vi*
	Acknowledgements	*vii*
1	Background and meaning: a retrospective on the tradition of interpretation of poetry in ancient China	1
2	Linguistic approach and intuitive perception: a tangle that ancient Chinese poetry critics had to unravel	21
3	Thought flow and word order: seeming disengagement of thinking from verse	39
4	Tonal and metrical schemes: a analysis of the patterns of ancient Chinese poetry	62
5	Allusion: one special aspect of ancient Chinese poetry	99
6	"Xu zi" words or phrases: a second special aspect of ancient Chinese poetry	122
7	Shi yan: a third special aspect of ancient Chinese poetry	140
8	Development of Chinese poetry from vernacular Song Dynasty style to vernacular modern style: inheritance of the spirit of vernacular Song Dynasty poetry	157
	Index	*193*

Figures

4.1	The Pattern of Tonal and Metrical Schemes	70
4.2	The Pattern of Tonal and Metrical Schemes	72
4.3	The Number of Poems With Various Numbers of Verses by Xie Lingyun, Xie Tiao, and Yu Xin Here	88

Acknowledgements

It took nearly two years for me to translate this book into English. Its translation also involved Zhang Shaolan, who played the indispensable role of a careful and effective coordinator; Tu Yungen, who devoted much of his time to compiling the bibliography for its English version; Danilo R. Briones and Erik Li, who proofread its English manuscript; and Li Xinyi, who took care of its editing.

I am grateful for their contributory effort.

My thanks go also to Guilin Tourism University, where I work, which has encouraged and facilitated my translation.

Chen Hengshi, translator of this book, 2022

1 Background and meaning

A retrospective on the tradition of interpretation of poetry in ancient China

When reading a poem, one is inclined to associate it with this or that background. One tends to ask, for example, "What is the background against which the poem was composed?" or "What is the background with which the poet lived at the time?" Background is also an important factor when it comes to looking at part of the history of poetry: What could a period be like when a certain poetic style was in vogue? In fact, it is safe to say that this is also the mindset of almost every poetry critic. Few of them will begin to doubt the justification of "background" as a prerequisite for understanding a poem, not to mention thinking twice about it.

According to some linguists, 背景 in Chinese (pronounced as *bei jing* in pinyin) is a term loaned from the Japanese kana はいけい, a Japanese version of the English "background". Basically, "background" has a threefold meaning: the circumstances in which an event takes place; the backdrop of a drawing, a photo, or the like; and the patron or patronage that is a backup. Undoubtedly, the first meaning is what a poetry critic uses. As for the second meaning, it, if rightly exploited, also applies to critique of poetry without any glitch, for, from another perspective, the background of a poem can be likened to that of a photo or a drawing. As recorded in the twenty-first chapter, which is about skill and art, of *A New Account of Tales of the World* by Liu Yiqing of the Song period of the Southern Dynasties, Gu Changkang (348–409), a Jin Dynasty painter, used both mountains and a river as the background for the portrait of Xie Kun (281–324), an official also of the Jin Dynasty, for, in the eyes of the painter, only such a background could best set off Xie's comportment. Likewise, the meaning of a poem is believed to have much to do with a certain background as well, so the latter is supposed to direct explanation of the former. In his *Introduction to Main Currents in the Nineteenth Century Literature*, George Brandes, using photographic viewing as an analogy, says that "the scientific view of literature provides us with a telescope of which the one end magnifies and the other diminishes; it must be so focused as to remedy the illusions of unassisted eyesight". But a problem thus arises such that a change in focus will result in blurring the foreground or rather the main figure or object and highlighting the background, analogous to what the reverse will cause, as in the case of Gu Changkang's portrayal of Xie Kun, where the landscape could overshadow the person. Then what if "background" should be taken as the one and only clue to interpretation of the meanings of a poem?

2 Background and meaning

One's certain approach is guided by a certain notion on one's mind, regardless of when the certain notion is committed to paper. This argument is supported, indirectly, by Quentin Skiner in his *Hermeneutics and the Role of History*, where he says that an approach to determination of the background can best facilitate comprehension of what one is reading is already on one's mind. Indeed, a certain notion determines a certain approach on the one hand; on the other hand, a certain approach mirrors a certain notion, be they right or wrong, like what a road-map is to a road. When it comes to background and meaning with respect to poetry, which is comparable to the lens' focus and the object being photographed, if a background is rightly determined, the meaning of a poem will correspondingly be interpreted, as in the interpretation by Qian Qianyi of the Qing Dynasty of "dong lai luo tuo man jiu du (Camels coming from the east were seen everywhere around the former capital)" (from Du Fu of the Tang Dynasty's poem entitled "Lament for the Princes") as a scene of plunder, which truly describes what was occurring in the crisis of the An Lushan-Shi Siming Rebellion when the rebels drove many camels to transport the loot out of the then capital (see *The Biography of Shi Siming*). But, if a background is wrongly determined, the meaning of a poem will consequently be distorted, as in the misleading interpretation presumably by Wang Zhu and Zhao Cigong of the Song Dynasty of Du Fu's poem entitled "Looking at the Mounts Below", which was written actually before the rebellion, as a lament over the fate of Emperor Xuanzong of the Tang Dynasty, who was forced to flee from the capital when the rebel army was approaching and of one of its verses "yi lan zhong shan xiao (My sweeping view from its summit reveals how all other mountains are dwarfed)", against this mistaken background, as metaphorically caricaturing the despicable rebels. There are also other instances where either the relationship between background and meaning is, though not explicit, traceable by one or another cue offered by the poet, as in the elucidation by Qiu Zhaoao, a poetry critic between the end of the Ming Dynasty and the beginning of the Qing Dynasty, in his *Copious Notes on Du Fu's Poetry*, of Du Fu's poem entitled "The Gaunt Horse: A Ballad" as a recounting of a past event because its verse "qu nian ben bo zhu yu kou (Last year in a rushing wave they chased the last rebels)" implies when, where, and why this poem was composed or wherein the poet gives no cue about the background against which his poem was written, so it depends on the reader to discover the background, which, unfortunately, could turn out to be arbitrarily far-fetched, as in the explication by Yao Wenxie of the Qing Dynasty in his *Annotated Li He's Poems*, of Li He of the Tang Dynasty's poem entitled "Li Ping at the Vertical Harp" as promotion of a national treasure that ought to be well preserved and passed down, actually a wrong conclusion drawn from his wilful misinterpretation of two Chinese characters (中国, pronounced as *zhong guo* in pinyin) as "China" rather than "within the capital", which is correct, as well as of a record in *The Book of Tang*.

These instances show that, apart from disparities on the part of poetry critics in knowledge of history and capacity for literary appreciation, notion of "background" being the one and only approach to interpretation of the meaning of a poem should also be to blame, when interpretation is erroneous, shouldn't it? As the previous indicates, unfortunately, each of those poetry critics seems convinced that his approach is the "panacea" for unravelling the mysteries of a poem. As a matter of fact, there is no panacea-like approach that can get at all the implications of even one poem, for any approach is neither perfect nor dominant, not to mention that a poem is so involved. Remember what Alexander Pope, in his "Essay on Criticism", says:

> Tis with our Judgments as our Watches, none Go just alike, yet each believes his own.

A "background", after all, has its limits.

1.1. Is background-based interpretation a skeleton key that opens all locks?

This world itself has no such absolute distinction as periphery versus centre, background versus foreground, and so on. In this sense, it is indefinite. For one, however, there is distinction of this nature, relative to his or her vision. For, if one, as the centre, focuses on something around him or her, then that something is foregrounded, with the rest relatively backgrounded. In this sense, this world is definite. As one only focuses on what he or she intends to, with the rest around it, from his or her perspective, being out of focus, so a poetry critic who tends to use a certain background to interpret a certain poem, will, from his or her perspective, decide on what should be such background; worthy of mention is, in this sense, that such background actually is "foregrounded", is it not?

But even certain backgrounds used by certain prestigious ancient Chinese poetry critics, however they argue for them, however their arguments are enshrined by those who study the poetics or the history of Chinese poetry at the very beginning of their works, are still, like focusless panoramas, suspected of being one-size-fits-all, too general for the reader to apply to interpretation of a specific poem. For example, there are such backgrounds as those concerning either politics (related to times) or thoughts (related to scholarship); they are regarded by some ancient Chinese critics as the ultimate references. In fact, those inclusive backgrounds, which concern the nature of humankind, the impact of social circumstances and vicissitudes on literature, and so forth, however overwhelming the arguments for them can sound, are basically of little or no use for interpretation of a specific poem, which, after all, demands not just specific but, more importantly, pertinent backgrounds (see *The Works of Mencius·Wan Zhang Part One*; *The Literary Mind and the Carving of Dragons* by Liu Xie of the Southern Dynasties; *The Grand History of the Chinese Literature* by Xie Wuliang, a modern Chinese literature theorist; *A Preface to "The History of the Chinese Literature* by Tong Xingbai, a modern Chinese literature theorist; *The Literature of the Wei of the Han Dynasty and the Six Dynasties* by Chen Zhongfan, a modern Chinese literature theorist; *The Outline of the Tang Poetry* by Su Xuelin, a modern Chinese literature theorist, etc.). For a time, new notions of a background concerning environment, ethnicity, economy, or social stratum were introduced from Japan and Europe, including

Russia. To be fair, these notions not just enrich but also modernize the repertoire of knowledge of the "background" theoretically and empirically. Nonetheless, such a repertoire, albeit ample and inclusive, is not necessarily an improvement in terms of specificness and immediate pertinence. Therefore, in application, there can be this scenario: a "background" from it, used with a view to helping to interpret a poem, ends up being to no avail. Even so, nonetheless, its user can be reluctant to give it up. Usage of such background in the interpretation of a poem is analogous either to the besieging of a fortress by an army without attacking and successfully capturing it or to a technique of design by which a landscape external to a garden is exploited in the hope of its lending to the view of the garden but without avail or to an art of slaying a dragon that is enviable yet not practicable. Worse, if such a background should be used as a recourse to understand both a poet or one of his poems, it would, as a result of its generalness, impair their intrinsic individualities, just as Tzvetan Todorov, in his *Critique de la critique: Un Roman D'apprentissage*, derides by alluding to darkness in which the multiple colours of multifarious cats are reduced to one colour: grey. In fact, as poets are individual, so are their poems, even if against a certain common background. Evidence for this argument is in poems by such poets as Wang Wei, Li Bai, and Du Fu during the prime of the Tang Dynasty.

Also, if a general background is used in interpretation of both a poet and a certain poem, it, being open to interpretation, can be manipulated arbitrarily by the interpreters as they see fit. That is, for example, why William Shakespeare's plays, in the eyes of Staël and Schlegel, though commonly against the "the northern spirit" background, carry different qualities: the qualities of Northern ignorance (by the former) versus the qualities in the later civilized North (by the latter). Thus, although often much space of this or that work on critique of poetry can be devoted to the affirmation of such a general background, it is still a specific and pertinent background that, in practice, is favoured in interpretation of a poet or his poem. Such a preference is mentioned by Chen Yinque, a modern Chinese scholar, as follows (see his *On Yuan Zhen and Bai Juyi's Poems*) (Yuan Zhen and Bai Juyi, poets of the Tang Dynasty):

> Today's compilers of literary history tend to collate as many works by the then literati as they can, in order of dates and localities, into a compendium, just as chroniclers do. Readers of such compendium can undoubtedly draw on it so as to meet their own specific needs.

What is to be discussed is just about such a specific "background", which is widely used by ancient Chinese poetry critics to interpret ancient Chinese poems.

The previous quotation actually has a precursor in *The Chronicle of Han Yu of the Tang Dynasty's Life* by Lv Dafang of the Song Dynasty, which says that "Chronicling his life enables us to know approximately when he wrote his works". This proves that, at least as early as back in Lv's time, a specific instead of general background was preferable when it comes to literary critique, which is embodied by the then-emerging chronological collection or anthology of literary works and chronicles of a writer's life. Application of a background as such eventually matures with the development of meticulous exact attestation of historical events and the poets' life. Indeed, a specific and pertinent background not only provides an ancient Chinese poetry critic with reliable clues but also circumscribes the meaning of a targeted poem. For example, to annotate Du Fu's poem "Lament for the Princes", Qian Qianyi referred to *The Old Book of Tang* and *History as a Mirror*, both of which respectively record what happened to Emperor Xuan Zong of the Tang Dynasty, his offspring, and his other subjects when the rebellious armies were closing in upon the capital, and this commotion happened to be witnessed by Du Fu. With knowledge of such a background, Qian could naturally understand Du's "jin bian zhe duan jiu ma si (The gilded riding crop snapped and his nine horses died)/gu rou bu de tong qu chi (He did not wait for his flesh and blood to gallop away with him)/yao xia bao jue qing shan hu (A precious jue was ringing at his waist of blue coral)/ke lian wang sun qi lu yu (A pitiable young prince was weeping at the roadside)". In his annotation on Li Shangyin (also known as Li Yishan or Yuxisheng) of the Tang Dynasty's poem entitled "Return from Hanzhong by Way of Fenshuiling (literally Watershed Ridge) to the North", as in his *Annotations on the Collected Poems of Li Yishan*, Zhu Heling, a poetry critic between the end of the Ming Dynasty and the beginning of the Qing Dynasty, infers from its title that Fenshuiling must have been located at the Han River; that the man by the name of Ling-hu Chu was governor in charge of civil and military affairs in the region where Hanzhong was centred according the historical records; and that the poet was a minion under Ling-hu Chu according the chronicle of Li Shangyin's life, eventually to conclude that, on his way from Hanzhong back to the north, the poet wrote this poem, whose "na tong ji mu wang (I strained my eyes to see the distant watershed ridge)/you zuo duan chang fen (Where the flow of water is sadly separated)/zheng yi lai sui ji (I had arrived at Zhenyi, a postal station, in good time)/yan tai ku bu wen (Now I was shedding tears, but my cry was going unheard)" thus vents the poet's grief over the demise of Ling-hu Chu. Wang Wengao of the Qing Dynasty, in his *A Collection of Su Shi's Poems with Annotations*, interprets the eight poems composed by Su Shi of the Song Dynasty within a particular month in virtue of the documented happenings to the poet at the time; his knowledge of this specific pertinent background leads to his conclusion that, for example, in the verses of the poet's eight poems, "lao ren xin shi ri cui tui (Day by day I, an ageing man, is being worn out by preoccupations)" expresses the poet's utter hopelessness, "zhi wo kong tang zuo hua hui (Imagine that, seated in my empty hall, I was scratching the ashes with a poker)" the poet's desperate loneliness, and "yue shu jia tong hao shou shi (I asked my valet to pack up for departure)/gu shan li zao dai gui lai (The pears and dates on my hometown hills were awaiting me to pick)" the poet's gnawing homesickness.

Knowledge of a specific and pertinent background, rather than a general and irrelevant nonsensical one like "the vast land" in "human beings on the vast land" or "the deep sea" in "fishes in the deep sea", is indispensable if one wants to accurately interpret a poem. That is why certain ancient Chinese poetry critics preach to their followers this belief: your adequate knowledge of what background a poem was created against ensures an accurate understanding of the poem. Such a belief is reminiscent of using a key to open a lock. However, at the same time, a question arises: If the meaning of a poem is compared to the lock, while a certain specific and pertinent background is a key, is a background of this nature a skeleton key that is capable of opening locks?

1.2. The three conundrums facing background-based interpretation

The first conundrum is that whether a certain background is the one against which a poem was composed is hard to verify. This is because, first, supposedly pertinent documentation may, over time, not be as pertinent as it is supposed to be; second, there is little authorized pertinent documentation about poets and their poetry. Consequently, to chronicle an anthology or a collection of poems, one has to turn to the selected poems themselves, in terms of their topoi and the implications of their words, for some background information. The problem is to what extent the clues of this kind are true to the past reality and who is authoritative enough to claim that his or her interpretations based on such clues (which actually can be dubious) are convincing. To be fair, there were, in ancient China, many poetry critics who endeavoured to chronicle the lifetimes of Chinese poets before them, as well as their poems, as specifically and accurately as possible. Due to the scarcity or simply a lack of true-to-life historical records, however, their endeavour was, on the one hand, like answering riddles that actually may have no definite answer; on the other hand, they could, even among themselves, disagree on a certain piece of documentation about a certain poet or a certain poem. So, in the end, many disputable questions are left unanswered. What's worse, there were some ancient Chinese poetry critics who had the audacity to associate a poem arbitrarily with what they felt was its pertinent background.

Let us look first at a part of Du Fu's poem "Yu Hua Gong (The Yuhua Palace)": "bu zhi he wang dian (Which king ordered construction of this palace)?/yi gou jue bi xia (Its relics are still seen under the precipitous cliffs)/yin fang gui huo qing (With the bluish spectral flickers on and off in the desolate chambers)/huai dao ai tuan ji (Alas, the roads have been eroded by the racing currents)". Obviously, this is the poet's lamentation. But when did he lament over what? Does it have the same tone as that of his aforementioned "Lament for the Princes", the time of whose composition should be evident in its "qie wen tian zi yi chuan wei (I heard that His Majesty has passed his throne over to the crown prince)/sheng de bei fu nan chan yu (The King of the Southern Hun State has submitted himself to our new monarch of divine morality)"? In his *Assiduous Annotations on Du Fu's Poems*, Pu Qilong of the Qing Dynasty sets it in lunar August of the second lunar year of the Zhide Reign (757) of the Tang Dynasty, asserting that it is Du's "heartbroken lamentation over the worsening situation after the An Lushan-Shi Siming Rebellion" that caused "sighs and tears". But one fact is that the Yuhua Palace had been downgraded to a temple as early as back in the second lunar year (651) of the Yonghui Reign of the Tang Dynasty and that Du Fu had passed it long before he composed this poem.

Why had he not *then* vented such emotions? Another fact is that, since almost all ancient Chinese poets characteristically express such emotions at the sight of any dilapidated old building, not necessarily inspired by what has come of a rebellion, it is likely that Du Fu wrote "Yu Hua Gong" in his earlier instead of later years. If so, is not Pu Qi Long's interpretation of this poem totally false?

Let us look next at the aforementioned Li Shangyin poem "Return from Hanzhong by Way of Fenshuiling to the North". What if this poem, which has adequate background information to interpret, including its title as well as the pertinent geographic, historical, and biographical information to refer to, had no such evidence, as in the case of his "Titleless" poem series, which is understood by some ancient Chinese poetry critics to metaphorize the bonds between the poet and a politician or as the poet's recollection of the cursed love between himself and a Taoist priestess? Would his "you zuo duan chang fen (Where the flow of water is sadly separated)" be taken to mean a man's departure for ever from his lover or vice versa? Would his "yan tai ku bu wen (Now I am shedding tears, but my cry is going unheard)" be associated with a young lady, confined in her boudoir, grieving over the absence of her lover? These questions have been bewildering, and the attempts to solve such bewilderment often end in being thwarted.

As mentioned, there is also this occasion: Ancient Chinese poetry critics tend to dispute over a certain poem by a certain poet; thus their annotations of it differ, only to confuse the reader. Such examples are many. Take *A Catalogue of Collected Li Bai's Poems in a Chronicle* by Huang Xigui, a poetry critic between the end of the Qing Dynasty and the beginning of the Republic of China, and *A Collection of Li Bai's Poems in a Chronicle* by the modern-day scholar Zhan Ying: The two works have far more divergences (over 70 up to even 80 percent) than convergences (less than 30 or even 20 percent) on the same foci. As for when Li Bai wrote the poem "Bidding Farewell to Song Zhiti at Jiangxia", there are at least three different arguments for the first year of the Shangyuan Reign (760), the first year of the Qianyuan Reign (758), and the twenty-ninth year of the Kaiyuan Reign (741) of the Tang Dynasty. But which of them is true? As to the meaning of the eighth of Li He's thirteen-poem series under the title "Southern Garden", which reads "chun shui chu sheng ru yan fei (Young swallows are learning to swoop over spring waters)/ huang feng xiao wei pu hua gui (Bees with golden tiny tails are flying back from feeding pollen and nectar)/chuang han yuan se tong shu huang (The distant vista framed by the window seems to be presenting itself in the studio)/yu yong xiang gou jin shi ji (Around a jutting rock in the water are swarming fishes for a scented bait on a hook)", due to a lack of specific and pertinent background information, it is open to interpretation: the poet's sensibility in reclusive leisure, the scornful caricature by the poet of an imperial counsellor who, tempted by personal gain in the officialdom, discontinued his life as a hermit, analogous to being tempted to bite bait on a hook, as observed by Wang Qi of the Qing Dynasty in his *Annotation on the Selected Annotations on Li He's Poems*, and so on.

As to the second conundrum, that is, just because one has adequate knowledge of the specific and pertinent background against which a poem was composed does not necessarily mean that one thus can claim, on behalf of the poet, that such a background is what the poet intended to represent in his poem. Most ancient Chinese poets do not have the habit of jotting down what inspired or affected their versification; as a result, a later poetry critic does not have this kind of information that he or she can refer to when interpreting their poems, most of which are expressions of sentiments or depictions of scenery. The poetry critic may, from his or her perspective, relate a certain background to a certain poem to guess at what the latter can mean. But, at any rate, a guess is a guess, no matter how precise it is claimed to be. So it should not be well grounded to accept such background-related interpretations of a poem as true, unless the poet himself should come back to life to nod his head in affirmation. For, first, a given background is a reconstruction by a poetry critic, as mentioned, from his or her perspective, so as to meet certain needs for interpretation of a poem; second, such a reconstructed background probably is not what actually was true, including a poet's state of mind and the happenings to the poet back then, after the lapse of a long time; and, third, what a poetry critic has for reconstruction of a certain background is, at best, the poem itself and the reconstructions by others of what they believe must concern the poem and its author. In his *Tropics of Discourse*, Hayden White says that the so-called historical facts may not be true; they, tailored to certain needs, may be distorted and even charged with a certain person's, like a recorder's and/or his follower's, sentiment and valuation to dictate what direction the reader should think. Or, as Michel Foucault says (see his *The Archaeology of Knowledge*), the background reconstructed by a poetry critic may be preposterous brainwork. To concede, even if a certain reconstructed background can be close to what a poet intended his poem to mean, "close" does not equal "the same", so even a "close" background does not provide *the* window on what a poet truly intended when he composed a poem, which can be complicated and elusive; in that case, how can it be simple to equate even a "close" background, not to mention one that may not be so "close", with what a poet intended his poem to mean? But why is this or that background so valued by some ancient Chinese poetry critics in their interpretation of ancient Chinese poems? This could be because they have too much trust in a background, insofar as it is believed to be indispensable, especially when poetry in ancient China was taken as an instrument of reproof and admonition. So Pu Qilong, in his *A Catalogue of the Chronicled Collection of the Poems by Du Fu*, an introductory part to his *Assiduous Annotations on Du Fu's Poems*, maintains that

> If chronicling is untrue, then facts thereof are untrue; if untrue facts are provided, true interpretations cannot possibly be achieved; and, without true interpretations, the minds of a poet and the meanings of his verses cannot possibly be known. All this will lead to corruption of their poems. And vice versa.

Pu's idea can be understood, in a sense, to echo earlier Liu Xie's over-trust, supposedly against this or that background (see *Times and Literature*, a chapter of his *The Literary Mind and the Carving of Dragons*): "Discovery of what begins and what ends will guarantee full knowledge of the trends of literature even over a hundred generations". But Liu's over-trust is most likely to breed "intentional fallacies", which William K. Wimsatt and Monroe C. Beardsley warn of (see *A Collection of New Criticism Papers* compiled by Zhao Yiheng), unless a poet's poems are truly inspired by the vicissitudes of his time. The fact is, however, that, of the poems by an ancient Chinese poet, few are truly historical records; on the contrary, many are improvised on the spur of the moment, such as at a waning crescent moon or a sad chime, or on a given subject, such as to honour a host who threw a dinner party. In that case, the poem has little if not nothing to do with, say, the then political or social background, doesn't it? Still, the trust in this or that background persists. For one example, Li He's "Extreme Northern Cold" was written during the reign of Emperor Dezong of the Tang Dynasty; this temporal background leads Chen Benli of the Qing Dynasty to infer that Li composed this poem to reprove Emperor Dezong for his many misconducts in governance, that its verse "huang he bing he yu long si (The Yellow River was iced over and the fishes and dragon got stuck and died)" alluded to Emperor Xiaozong's partiality to his queen consort, his trust in a wicked minister, his execution of the crown prince, and his removal of the incumbent emperor from the throne who was later honoured with the nominal title of Grand Emperor, and that its verse "hui dao bu ru mi meng tian (The sword was being wielded, but it could not cut through the smoky haze in the sky)" censured an opinionated emperor who had blamed anything not in his favour on the Mandate of Heaven (see his *To Discover the Profundities of Poems*). But is his inference true concerning Li's poem really means? Should the answer be yes, Li He would be regarded as a commentator with an encyclopaedic knowledge of history on political issues and his poem as his comment on historical events (see Jin Kaicheng and Ge Zhaoguang's *Detailed Annotations on Quintessential Ancient Chinese Poems*). For another example, ancient Chinese poetry critics agree that Li Shangyin's "A Ballad on the Sea" was composed when he was a ministerial secretary during the Dazhong reign of the Tang Dynasty (847). Still, their annotations on this poem differ: Zhu Heling, in his *Annotations on the Collected Poems of Li Yishan*, claims that he can read into it the pursuit of immortality; Feng Hao of the Qing Dynasty, in his *Annotations on Yuxisheng's Poems*, holds that it implies demotion of two high-ranking Tang government officials; and Zhang Caitian, a scholar between the end of the Qing Dynasty and the beginning of the Republic of China, in his *Annotations on the Chronicled Poems by Yuxisheng*, pronounces his empathy with the poet's frustration with his unfulfilled career. As for its verses, such as "gui shui han yu jiang (The water of Gui Sea feels colder than that of a river)/yu tu qiu leng ye (The Jade Rabbit makes no sound shivering with the autumnal chill)", to some ancient Chinese poetry critics, who base their interpretation on what they believe is the pertinent historical background, these hint at the then-current political situation, and their interpretation is endorsed even by Ye Jiaying, an eminent modern Chinese scholar (see her *An Assemblage of Criticisms on Classical Ancient Chinese Poems*), What, then, causes these differences in interpretation of even the same poem, given that its temporal background cannot be more verified? The third example is Du Fu's "A New Crescent". This poem certainly was written after the Tang Dynasty Emperor Suzong's ascendancy. What remains to be answered is whether it is about the moonlight or about a political event. According to *Copious Notes on Du Fu's Poetry* by Qiu Zhaoao, it deals not with politics but with a moonlit yet misty night under a new crescent at Qinzhou, whereas other scholars before him, like Cai Mengbi of the Song Dynasty and Wang Sishi of the latter Ming and early Qing dynasties, argue, from their perspectives, that the temporal background can be discerned in this poem; thus its verse "wei sheng gu sai wai ([The new crescent] hardly started to rise beyond the ancient fortification)" refers implicitly to Emperor Suzong's ascendancy at Lingwu, its verse "yi yin mu yun duan (When it already disappeared behind the evening clouds overhead)" to Emperor Suzong's being prevented by his queen consort and his most trusted minister from being informed about what was occurring without his imperial palace; its verse "he han bu gai se (The colour of the Milky Way does not change)" to the constancy of mountains and rivers; its verse "guan shan kong zi han (Mount Guan stands alone and desolate in the cold)" to the poet's despair; and its verses "ting qian you bai lu (In sight are the white dews at the front of the courtyard)/an man ju hua tuan (Which dim the flowering heads of daisies)" to not just the chilly milieu at night but, more profoundly, to the evil element's having had the upper hand of those worthy people. Piecing together their various interpretations would portray Du Fu more as a commentator who foresaw the political situations than a writer who just indulged in reciting verses about the moonlight (see *A Sequel to 'The Criticisms by the Qing Dynasty Critics on Poetry'* compiled by Shanghai Classics Publishing House). To this, Wu Leifa of the Qing Dynasty, in his *A Discourse in Bits and Pieces on Poems*, responded as follows:

> A poem should be profound and subtle. But such poem can be a hard nut to crack, especially for those who are thick-witted. When they interpret an ancient poem, prestigious poetry critics will try to find out about when and where it was composed, as well as what could transpire vis-à-vis it. They then will arbitrarily piece those things together to determine which verse refers to whom and which verse to what.

Indeed, this kind of practice is popular with ancient Chinese poetry critics for, to them, a certain background is to the meaning of a certain poem what a key is to a lock, if one hopes to grasp the meaning of the poem or, metaphorically, to discover the treasures therein; otherwise, one is likely to be stupidly misled, as observed by Xue Xue (also known as Yipiao) of the Qing Dynasty in his *Yipiao's Remarks on Poetry*. True, an ancient Chinese poem should be scrutinized for its author's intent (see Wu Qiao of the Qing Dynasty's *Talks about Poetry around the Hearth*), but, if such scrutiny is guided by the knowledge of this or that irrelevant background that is arbitrarily related by a poetry critic to the poem, should he or she not ask if he or she is ridiculously opinionated and if he or she feels guilty of having probably distorted the meaning of the poem? In fact, the state of mind of a poet in composing a poem can be incredibly intricate, and the meaning of a poem can be incredibly broad and profound, so the reader cannot possibly get at, either particularly or generally, what the poet may think and what the poem may mean simply by way of this or that background, whether it is a political event or a social issue. Given this, if a poetry critic should insist on the monopoly of the knowledge of this or that background over interpretation of a poem, does he or she respect or disrespect the poet and his poem?

The third conundrum is: Even though the background offers the pertinent clues necessary for interpretation of a poem, what, then, will result? A poem is for the reader to appreciate in terms of its aesthetic appeal. But its specific and pertinent background may unsympathetically ruin it as a work of art, the way an x-ray machine scans someone beautiful only to photograph their skeleton or the way a chemical analysis breaks down a flower into its constituents. If a certain background is used as the one and only way of interpreting a poem, the poem may then be turned into, at best, a readable historical record whose subject matter, in that case, would mainly be about wars or arts of war. If a poem is so reduced, what else but something like a dispatch will impinge on the reader?

Let us read two examples.

The third and fourth verses, "jin xiang qing geng qie (My uneasy heart was beating faster and faster as I was approaching nearer and nearer to my home-place)/bu gan wen lai ren (I dared not inquire any of my fellow folks I had met on the road about what had happened at home)", from Song Zhiwen of the Tang Dynasty's poem "Ferrying across the Han River" evidently convey "my" anxiety on the way homeward after a long separation both about "my" kin's well-being and about their attitude towards "me", mixed with pleasant excitement. Such a mix of thrill and uneasiness on the part of a man separated long from home is a universally shared sentiment. According to those ancient Chinese poetry critics so obsessed with this or that background, however, Song's poem is his description of a part of his experience as an exile when he crossed the Han River sometime to Luoyang during the second year of the Shenlong Reign (706) of the Tang Dynasty. In this light, its penultimate verse describes the psychology of the escaped man on the road, while its last verse shows his alertness when running covertly for his life. Thus interpreted, it is deprived of the returned man's good mood. The third and fourth verses, "luo yang qin you ru xiang wen (When my family or friends out there in Luoyang inquire you about me)/yi pian bing xin zai yu hu (Kindly tell them that my heart is still as crystal as ice and it lodges still in the pot of jade)", from Wang Changling of the Tang Dynasty's poem "Seeing Xin Jian Off at the Hibiscus Tower" boast the beauty that is in any exquisite poem, and its fourth verse in particular strikes the reader as pure and translucent. But, according to some ancient Chinese poetry critics, who derive their viewpoints from Yin Fan of the Tang Dynasty's *A Collection of the Poems by the Quintessential Poets of the High Tang Dynasty*, which says of Wang that "he paid no attention to what he thought was trivial in his conduct, thus such ignorance caused an uproar of slanders", this poem doubtless is his request that Xin Jian as his friend kindly help clear him of any defamation when Xin Jian arrives in Luoyang, then the capital, as his smeared reputation could have been spread to his kin and other friends. Admittedly, there is some sense in their interpretation. But if this poem is scrutinized against such a background, "Kindly tell them that my heart is still as crystal as ice and it lodges still in the pot of jade" can be understood to be an attestation of the poet's overindulgent self-praise as well as his unconvincing self-defence, in light of which one will read into this poem more an insipid appeal to the imperial court than an engaging rhyme.

1.3. Distortion of the meaning of a poem as a result of referring only to a supposedly pertinent background

An opinion held by ancient Chinese poetry critics is that a poem can be understood by virtue of its pertinent background and vice versa. This is comparable, though maybe not exactly, to what an actor is both on stage and off stage.

To grasp the meaning of a poem through a certain background, to learn about a certain background by way of the meaning of a poem has a longer history, which originated as early as in an ancient Chinese ritual that

> His Majesty or the Son of Heaven inspected his land and his people every five years. . . . When His Majesty arrived at a place, the ritual supervisor would be ordered to have its poems chanted for His Majesty, who would thus learn about its customs.

Confucius is said to have summarized it in *The Analects* in one sentence: "Poetry serves as the mirror (of local customs)". The earliest evidence of putting his notion to use may be what is recorded in *Zuo Qiuming's Commentaries on the Spring and Autumn Annals* (Zuo Qiuming, a historian at the end of the Spring and Autumn Period) about how Ji Zha, an aristocrat from the State of Wu, appreciated the Zhou Dynasty royal tunes played by the state of Lu musicians (see Fang Xiaoyue's *Literary Criticism in China*). In fact, it is not until *A Preface to the Book of Songs*, whose author is controversial, appeared that this notion was widely applied to the critique of poetry. A great many ancient Chinese poems have undergone such scrutiny.

For one example, into Tao Yuanming of the Eastern Jin Dynasty's poem "Narration for Wine" is read his mourning over the assassination of Emperor Gong of his time, which thus is alleged to be what its verses "liu lei bao zhong tan (Shedding tears and sighing a sorrowful sigh deep at heart)/qing er ting si chen (All ears to the crow of a rooster)", a mournful depiction of the moment when the emperor was anticipating his death, are about; another of Tao's poems, "Motionless Aggregated Clouds", is seen as a commendation of a man who remained loyal to the overthrown dynasty by refusing to submit himself to the ruling one, in stark contrast to others who were servilely currying favour with the reigning monarch, as implied by its verses "jing yong xin hao (They are vying to bloom)/yi yi yu qing (My heart is so pleased)", which actually are a pungent attack on those servile office seekers. Tao has the habit of dating his writings, which span the end of the Eastern Jin period and the beginning of the Song period of the Southern Dynasties, a period of the thriving of Zen Buddhism. Against this temporal background, which itself is not quite verified, Tao's bucolic poems could be interpreted by some Song Dynasty poetry critics as his vows of allegiance; thus he, who actually is a self-conscious poet yearning for a reclusive life away from the madding crowds, is hailed simply as a loyalist to the monarch of the Eastern Jin Dynasty even if he lives under a new one. (see *Annotations on Tao Jingjie* [Tao Yuanming is also known as Tao Jingjie]*'s Poems* by Tang Han of the Song Dynasty and *Annotations on the Collected Works by Tao Yuanming* by He Mengchun of the Ming Dynasty).

For another example. "Fifty-Nine Poems in Ancient Style" was composed by Li Bai at random over a time. They concern emotions, Taoist seclusion, rectification of wrongs in the world, and so on. In the eyes of Chen Jin of the Qing Dynasty, however, Li's poems belong in what he produced later in exile about the political climate; moreover, they indicate that the poet was worried about the chaotic situation, as he had perceived the culprit, but he was afraid of bluntly exposing it for fear of being slandered or even persecuted. Li Bai's actually random poems are thus elevated to the status of a purposeful series believed to aim at continuing what characterizes the elegant poetry of remote antiquity, and Li Bai himself, a man of fantasies and boasts, is transformed into the incarnation of fidelity and love, an equal in this respect even to Du Fu.

There are far more verses singled out from poems than poems treated as a whole that are arbitrarily associated with far-fetched backgrounds. For example, two verses, "chi tang sheng chun cao (The pond is lush with vernal grasses)/yuan liu bian ming qin (The garden willows nestle chirping birds)", from "Ascending the Pavilion by the Pond" by Xie Lingyun, a poet between the Eastern Jin Dynasty and the Song period of the Southern Dynasties, are interpreted as respectively indicating that the royal grace ran out because the poet metaphorizes the drying up of a pond only to allow growth of grasses and that the political climate changed because, likewise, the poet metaphorizes the twittering of birds perched on the willow branches, which implies different monarchs. In Wang Wei's poem "Mount Zhongnan", "tai yi jin tian du (Mount Taiyi stands near the celestial capital)/lian shan jie hai yu (It extends, range after range, to seashores)/bai yun hui wang he (I looked back to see white clouds gathering into a mass)/qing ai ru kan wu (I lost myself in the mists emerging from the mount)/fen ye zhong feng bian (The peak divides the region into two areas, east and west)/yin qing zhong he shu (One has its own climate in its own valleys, different than the other)/yu tou ren chu su (I was keen to find a household where I'd put up for a night)/ge shui wen qiao fu (Across a rivulet was a woodcutter from whom I'd ask for information)" are questionably linked respectively with those powerful and domineering elites, their hypocrisy, their abuse of power, and their buying as many followers as possible by any means and the poet's predicament of having nowhere to turn. In a word, Wang's poem is alleged to imply the situation of political corruption and unfair treatment at the time. Such an improbable linkage should have been taken as a recipe for how to understand a Tang Dynasty poem (see Wu Qiao's *Talks about Poetry around the Hearth*). Han Hong of the Tang Dynasty's poem *Cold Food* is about a custom observed in the capital, and its verses, like "chun cheng wu chu bu fei hua (Into spring flowery petals are seen drifting all over the town)", depict the scene; nonetheless, there is an opinion that "wu hou (the nobles)" betrays its background, namely

14 *Background and meaning*

the culprits in the fall of the Tang Dynasty were the eunuchs who had, under the authority of Emperor Daizong, controlled the armies. This poem was composed at the early years of Jianzhong, one of the periods of the reign of Emperor Dezong, so, naturally, it is related back to what had transpired during the reign of Emperor Daizong. Such relation is insinuated through 'wu hou (the nobles)', the way *The Spring and Autumn Annals* is done.

Thus, Wang's poem could turn out to be not a sketch of a local ritual observance but a serious record of historical occurrences. Han Wo of the Tang Dynasty's "Reflection on Falling Flowery Petals" is an expression of the poet's pensiveness at the sight of petals falling from their flowers, the way a sentimentally delicate young lady, usually in ancient China, who would collect and bury fallen flowers, would feel, but its verses, for example, "yan xun pian pian sui liu qu (I saw petals falling, piece by piece, on a stream that carried them far away)/hen man zhi zhi bei yu qin (My heart grieved over flowery shoots that were being ruined by rain)", to some Qing Dynasty poetry critics, hint respectively at Emperor Zhaozong's fleeing the capital and at the execution of his princes; "zong de tai zhe you wei yi (That petals fell on a layer of lichen could, after all, assuage my grief to some degree)/ruo jiao ni wu geng shang xin (As it felt much better than their otherwise being soiled by filthy mud)" could imply two generals, Li Keyong and Wang Shifan, having come to the rescue of their monarch and Tang Dynasty warlord Han Jian's mutiny that debilitated the sovereignty of Emperor Zhaozong, respectively; and "lin xuan yi zhan bei chun jiu (At the window I was drinking wine from a goblet, lamenting over passage of spring)/ming ri chi tang shi lv yin (The pond down there would the morrow be reflecting greenery only)" is taken as a sad allusion to the assassination of Emperor Zhaozong by Zhu Wen, a general of the Latter Tang Dynasty, and the latter's usurpation. Such interpretations portray Han Wo, a poet of literary sensibilities tinged with melancholy, as a man of allegiance and righteousness, on the one hand, and, on the other hand, turn this ingenious sentimental poem into a colourless political account. But the most distorted are the verses from poems by Du Fu, whose vow of allegiance to his monarch seems to have offered the pretext under which a great many ancient poetry critics would, regardless of what is actually in his poetry, relate almost any one of them to the background of the An Lushan-Shi Siming Rebellion. Thus, for example, his verse "sha shang fu chu ban mu mian (On sand a young wild duck clinging to its mother is having a sound sleep)" (from his "Nine Five-Word-A-Verse Jue Ju Poems Composed with Motions"), a depiction of a scene of serenity and affection, is interpreted as a hint at a liaison between An Lushan, the commander of the rebellious army, and Yang Yuhuan, the then-emperor's concubine, as in *Jiangzhai's Commentaries on Poetry* by Wang Fuzhi (also known as Jiangzhai, a philosopher between the end of the Ming Dynasty and the beginning of the Qing Dynasty); "shei lian yi pian ying (Who would pity that lonely shadowy wild goose)/xiang shi wan chong yun (It has flown stray from the flock who have disappeared far beyond clustered clouds)" (from his "A Stray Lonely Wild Goose Left Behind the Flock") as a reference to worthy gentlemen dispersed into desolation; and "du he gui he wan (A solitary crane returned so late)/hun ya yi man lin (Crows in dusk had already occupied all the perches of the woods)" (from his "An Outlook at the Wilderness") as scoffing at raucous wicked men. To sum up, these interpretations of the verses feel as if the verses were arbitrarily treated not as the embodiment of sentiment and vitality but as lifeless bodies under an autopsy. Thus their authors are reduced simply to the recorders, by verse, of the given backgrounds. And, as a result, the verses mean nothing but operate only as the means of showing the backgrounds.

Those ancient Chinese poetry critics so stress this or that background for a reason. Part of their reason is that, due to the symbolic meanings of some words in some ancient Chinese poems, those words are automatically linked with certain backgrounds. For example, "vanilla" and "beauty" were utilized by some ancient Chinese poets to symbolize a certain political background. Ever since then, whenever those special words are either intentionally or inadvertently employed any other ancient Chinese poems, they, to an ancient Chinese critic, should be so interpreted. "Han Wu", which literally means Emperor Hanwu of the Han Dynasty, was once used to refer analogously to the Tang Dynasty emperors; henceforth, the appearance of "Han Wu" in any later ancient Chinese poem is related to the Tang Dynasty. In his poem "A Concubine Who Soon Lost Favour", Li Bai, through the short-lived romance between Emperor Hanwu and one of his concubines, expresses his sympathy with any beauty who is now in favour yet can be out of favour anytime soon. But, in his *The Supplementary Categorical Annotations on Li Bai's Poems*, Xiao Shiyun of the Yuan Dynasty believes that Li's usage reveals Emperor Xuanzong of the Tang Dynasty's reluctance to favour his wife, against which this poem was composed, ignoring the fact that it actually happened 20 years earlier than Li Bai's poem. "Niu lang" and "zhi nv", a shepherd boy and weaving girl in an ancient Chinese myth, are used to allude to Emperor Xuanzong and his favourite concubine by the name of Yang Yuhuan, so the two mythical personae that appear in any ancient Chinese poem ever since are understood to have something to do with Emperor Xuanzong's Tianbao Reign period; thus "niu nv nian nian du (The Herd Boy and the Weaving Girl ferry across it every year)/he ceng feng lang sheng (When has one ever seen it billowing with waves or roaring with winds)?" in Du Fu's "The Milky Way" is interpreted as an indirect rebuke to Emperor Xuanzong who indulged in love with Yang Yuhuan such that it caused a rebellion that plunged the country into chaos. Such a connection finds a supporter in Li Diaoyuan of the Qing Dynasty, whose style name was Yucun, who, in his *Yucun's Remarks on Poetry*, argues that it is well grounded because Emperor Xuanzong and his favoured concubine avowed their undying love for each other in the Palace of Eternal Youth on the seventh evening of the seventh lunar month of the lunar calendar. But the truth is that their such avowal, even if ever made, would be rumoured and become public decades later than Du's poem.

Still, those ancient Chinese poetry critics seem obsessed with such an approach, because it enables them to effortlessly identify the meanings of the verses of a poem. So, prior to interpretation of an ancient Chinese poem, they would, most of the time, look into what could be the background of the poem. For example, as aforementioned, they already learned about the period of tumult between the

Eastern Jin Dynasty and the Song period of the Southern Dynasties, as well as the attendant zeal for the Buddhist Zen, which Tao Yuanming had experienced; about the An Lushan-Shi Siming Rebellion and the attendant turbulences, a part of Li Bai's life experience; about the loss of royal grace and the change of political climate when Xie Lingyun had happened to write "Ascending the Pavilion by the Pond"; about the abuse of power by a cohort of high-ranking officials while Wang Wei produced his "Mount Zhongnan"; about the eunuchs' control of the army at the time Han Hong had penned his "Cold Food"; and about the imminent collapse of the Tang Dynasty when Han Wo authored "Reflection on Falling Flowery Petals". Equipped with this prior knowledge of the background, those ancient Chinese poetry critics would instantly conjure up what they believed to be the right linkage between a certain word or phrase, once used symbolically, in a verse and background from their repertoire of backgrounds to get at what they believed to be the right meaning of the verse, regardless of the fact that such a linkage had actually been pre-established rather than being discovered by scrutiny of the verse. This is reminiscent of a man's presupposition that his neighbour must have stolen his hatchet so that the latter looks every inch the thief, which, in the case of a poem, means that each of its verses must correspond to a certain background. But, according to David Couzens Hoy, interpretation of a poem by way of "a certain background directs at a certain meaning and vice versa" is a form of circular reasoning which should not be deemed ill founded, as expounded in his *The Critical Circle: Literature, History and Philosophical Hermeneutics*; besides, according to the hermeneutics, either the critic or the reader cannot possibly avoid presupposing a certain background which in turn directs their interpretation of such as a poem, as defended by Jürgen Habermas, a German philosopher. Even so, interpretation of this nature is not convincing, thus hard to accept. In his *Practical Criticism*, I.A. Richards introduces this experiment: thirteen poems, without any background information, such as their authors and the dates of their composition, and even without any titles, were given to students selected from Cambridge University for their judgment, and a mess resulted in that the mediocre poems were judged superb and the superb ones mediocre. What if judgment of the aforementioned ancient Chinese poems were subjected to such as experiment? A similar embarrassing mess would be most likely. Another interesting thing happened to Qian Xuantong, a modern Chinese scholar, and his peers. According to his *Record of Motions*, he, as well as a few of his peers, felt that the author of a *ci poem* (i.e., a variant of ancient Chinese poetry) must have been an official with the past imperial court because of the alleged hint of "gu guo tui yang (The slanting sunlight that is fading and the dynasty which is a thing of the past)/huai gong fang cao (The dilapidated palace and luxuriant grasses)" and that the official must have dreamed of restoring the lost dynasty, given the alleged hint of "he nian cui nian chong gui (When will the imperial carriage be seen again on the road to the palace)?", and the poem contained what they believed to be the symbolic words that they would associate with what they believed to be pertinent backgrounds. Ironically, however, the truth, as they later found out, contradicts their presupposition: the author actually is "a veteran revolutionary" who joined in toppling the imperial government. Qian's anecdote proves that one's pre-established

Background and meaning 17

knowledge of the pertinence of either a certain background to a certain word or vice versa can lead to fallacy in interpretation of a poem.

1.4. Is a poem an independent literary text or a background-based equivalent of a historical dossier?

Background-based interpretation of a poem, as discussed, concerns H.G. Gadamer's hermeneutic circle, which requires one to play either the role of a historian or that of a poetry critic when one either uses a certain background to interpret a poem (as a historian) or uses the meaning of a poem to identify a certain background (as a poetry critic) (see David Couzens Hoy's *The Critical Circle: Literature, History and Philosophical Hermeneutics*). And this is a circle that will not end with a definite solution. The cause of formation of such a circle is the notion of the meaning of the word or phrase of a verse relating to a certain background and vice versa. In the case of ancient Chinese poetry critics, this notion compelled them to identify a certain background for interpretation of the verse(s) of a poem and/or a poem in entirety, even if in a far-fetched manner. In that case, why not break the circle to have a way out? As for a certain historical background, it has actually become an account by historians, one after another, over a long time, of what was true at a point in history. And such an account may be not factual anymore, but, as Martin Heidegger, in his *Being and Time*, points out, personal and interpretational, which may not be as reliable as it is supposed to be. In contrast, a poem itself, a personal creation or a work of subjectivity, has remained as it was, despite the elapsing of a long time. So a poem is, to a considerable extent, independent of this or that background. Background-based interpretation is merely one of the approaches rather than *the* approach to interpretation of a poem. After all, what matters in terms of the meaning of a poem is not what it meant to the "then" reader but what it means to the "now" reader. In that case, the allegedly ironclad bond between background and meaning, when it comes to interpretation of a poem, begs the question: is a poem an independent literary text or a background-based equivalent of a historical dossier?

The answer is evidently negative.

It is definitely an independent literary text, for it is a work of art which is composed of the poetic language that is a medium of conveying feelings and meanings, although this type of text is considered a patchwork of allusive words or phrases, which actually is also true of other types of text, as noted by Julia Kristeva in her *Sèméiotikè: Recherches pour une sémanalyse*. Of a poem, a certain background, if embedded in it, is, at best, only a part of the allusive words or phrases. In fact, a great many poems, without being embedded with any background-related word or phrase, still speak fully for themselves, especially in the case of those ancient Chinese poems which are neither about a historical event nor about a custom but express what is universally shared by humankind, such as love of freedom, philosophy of existence, affinity with nature, and emotional attachment to a person. Those poetic elements easily strike a chord with the reader. To interpret such poems, arbitrary reference to a certain background, which is not immune to personal discrimination, will jeopardize the otherwise judicious interpretation of them. That is why Nietzsche, in his *The Use and Abuse of History*, urges one to learn to forget, for dependence on too many memories will impair one's own creativity. Indeed, so it is with interpretation of ancient Chinese poetry: one's submission to his or her knowledge of an omnipresent background will forbid him or her from freely and reasonably interpreting a poem. For one example, when one of Li Shangyin's poem series under the title of "Titleless" is interpreted by some ancient Chinese poetry critics, who associate it with the privacy of a maidservant or a Taoist priestess, their interpretations deprive it of its perpetual appeal as a work of art, for it is downgraded to a mere recounting of personal affairs. This background may be true but at the cost of "beauty" and even "goodness" in the poem. For another example, Wang Wei's "Birds Chirping in the Canyon" and "The Valley of Magnolia" are set by some ancient Chinese poetry critics in what they believe is the pertinent background, which is the aftermath of the An Lushan-Shi Siming Rebellion, when the poet was demoted, thus the poet's otherwise inner tranquil indifference, not without vivacity, is imperiously scratched off, and instead they interpret the work as the gloomy mood of the poet as a worried escapee from venomous slander, only to reduce these two poems to the poet's confession or a diagnosis of his latent mental abnormality, only in the guise of a poem. The point is that one reads a poem not to learn about this or that historical background but for aesthetic appreciation. A poem, though an independent text, as discussed, does not necessarily rule out a historical background that is at best fictional. But this absolutely does not mean that a certain historical background should direct interpretation of a poem as an independent text.

Since a poem is a work of art composed in a particular language, it, apart from conveying what a poet means, imparts how he feels. The latter can be extremely intricate, considering the historical, social, political, academic, geological, ethnic, economic, or simply cultural influence over one. Such an influence has to undergo what is called a process of displacement, which naturally involves reformation and even distortion caused by a poet's temperament, personality, state of mind, and so on, before zigzagging into a poem, only to end up there with the slightest possible vestige of it. Thus: are both a poet's transient poetic epiphany and unlimited poetic imagination put forth by Lu Ji of the Western Jin Dynasty in his *Remarks in the Style of an Ode on Literary Creation* inspired just by the background he is situated against? This question also concerns Liu Xie's notion of versification that "At a poet's heart resides the spirit which is commanded by both his will and his internal vitality; external matters are perceived through his ears and/or eyes and his rhetoric is the key to giving expression to such perceptions" (see his *The Literary Mind and the Carving of Dragons*). A positive answer is hard to accept. Indeed, background-based interpretation of a poem is so simple-minded an approach that even those ancient Chinese poetry critics who attached great importance to the affinity between poetry and society would not nod their approval. This is also echoed by such Western literary theorists as Tzvetan Todorov (see his *Critique De La Critique: Un Roman D'apprentissage*). As the history of poetry shows, just because a poet lives in a prosperous era does not necessarily mean that his poetry sings the praises of such prosperity and vice versa. So, understandably, Tao Yuanming, who is better known for his idyllic and reclusive poems, also writes poems like "A Song for Jing Ke" (Jing Ke, a heroic assassin during the Warring States Period who failed his mission of murdering Ying Zheng, Lord of the State of Qin, and was killed by the latter) and "An Ode to My Fair Lady" (about the poet's aspiration to win over a fair lady, which ended in failure); Du Fu, who focuses mainly on his people's hardships, can also shift to distractions. When reference to a certain background is necessitated in interpretation of a poem, this is because, first, the otherwise involved process of versification is oversimplified to a mode of involuntary stimulus-response or simply pull action, only to make a puppet of a poet and deprive his poem of vitality, and, second, focus on what is thought to be the background puts the worth of the poem, as an idiosyncratic meaningful work of art with its linguistic charm and aesthetic appeal, into oblivion, to name just a few problems with this approach.

Given that versification involves the intricate feelings of a poet, how can it be that background-based interpretation, which is at best one of the approaches to interpretation of a poem, should crowd out the other ones? True, background-based interpretation has its role to play, especially when the subject matter of a poem relates closely to a certain historical background; nevertheless, background-based interpretation of a poem cannot possibly take the place of the appreciation of it on the part of the reader, for, after all, the meaning of a poem lies in its text itself, which depends on the reader to discover. Moreover, a poem, a liberal world, is open to any access. In his *Development of Shakespeare's Imagery*, Wolfgang Clemen points out that it is a weird blunder to relate a certain poem to a certain historical background, the way a certain dovecot is compartmented for a certain dove, with each labelled, in the hope of having an ultimate understanding of the poem, because doing so will deny the reader his or her right to feel the poem on his or her own, which will in turn leave its spellbinding nuances and profundities unappreciated. So it is with ancient Chinese poetry. A certain background functions not as a label but as a cue on a certain poem. And it, as a cue, has to be pertinent. Remember to avoid the snare of determinism, which is to say one must not take it for granted that a certain background is the only access to interpretation of a poem, with many other accesses excluded, only to let "a historian" override "a poet" on what he intends his poem to mean.

Finally, when it comes to interpretation of a poem, a poetry critic should follow this aphorism: "There is more than one way to the world of poetry". It may weaken his or her valued exclusive authority, but will give him or her much more freedom.

References

1. Brandes, George. *Shijiu shiji wenxue zhuliu* 十九世纪文学主流 (Main Currents in the Nineteenth Century Literature), translated by Daozhen Zhang 张道真. Beijing: People's Literature Publishing House, 1980.
2. Chen, Benli 陈本礼. "Xielü gouxuan" 协律勾玄(To Discover the Profundities of Poems). In *Lidai shiwen yaoji xiangjie* 历代诗文要籍详解 (Detailed Annotations on Quintessential Ancient Chinese Poems), edited by Kaicheng Jin 金开诚 and Zhaoguang Ge 葛兆光. Beijing: Beijing Publishing House, 1988.

3. Chen, Yinke 陈寅恪. *Yuanbai shijian zhenggao* 元白诗笺证稿 (On Yuan Zhen and Bai Juyi's Poems). Shanghai: Shanghai Classics Publishing House, 1982.
4. Chen, Zhongfan 陈钟凡. *Hanwei liuchao wenxue* 汉魏六朝文学 (The Literature of the Wei Period of the Han Dynasty, the Jin Dynasty, and the Southern Dynasties). Shanghai: The Commercial Press, 1931.
5. Fang, Xiaoyue 方孝岳. *Zhongguo wenxue piping* 中国文学批评 (Literary Criticism in China). Shanghai: The World Book Company, 1936.
6. Heidegger, Martin. *Cunzai yu shijian* 存在与时间 (Being and Time), translated by Jiaying Chen 陈嘉映 and Qingjie Wang 王庆节. Beijing: SDX Joint Publishing Company, 1987.
7. Hoy, David Couzens. *Piping de xunhuan* 批评的循环 (The Critical Circle: Literature, History and Philosophical Hermeneutics), translated by Jinren Lan 兰金仁. Shenyang: Liaoning People's Publishing House, 1987.
8. Li, Diaoyuan 李调元. "Yucun shihua" 雨村诗话 (Yucun's Remarks on Poetry). In *Qing shihua xubian* 清诗话续编 (A Sequel to the Poetic Discourses of the Qing Dynasty), edited by Shaoyu Guo 郭绍虞. Shanghai: Shanghai Classics Publishing House, 1983.
9. Nietzsche, Friedrich. *Lishi de shiyong yu lanyong* 历史的使用与滥用 (The Use and Abuse of History), translated by Tao Chen 陈涛 et al. Shanghai: Shanghai People's Publishing House, 2005.
10. Richards, Ivor Armstrong. "Shiyong piping" 实用批评 (Practical Criticism). In *Beiping chenbao* 北平晨报 (Peking Morning). Beiping: Beiping Morning Office, 1934.
11. Skiner, Quentin. "Hermeneutics and the role of history". *New Literary History*, 7(1), 1975.
12. Todorov, Tzvetan. *Piping de piping* 批评的批评 (Critique De La Critique: Un Roman D'apprentissage), translated by Dongliao Wang 王东亮. Beijing: SDX Joint Publishing Company, 1988.
13. Wang, Fuzhi. 王夫之. "Jiangzhai shihua" 姜斋诗话 (Jiangzhai's Commentaries on Poetry). In *Qing shihua* 清诗话 (The Poetic Discourses of the Qing Dynasty), edited by Fuzhi Wang 王夫之. Shanghai: Shanghai Classics Publishing House, 1978.
14. Wang, Qi 王琦. *Lichangji geshi huijie* 李长吉歌诗汇解 (Annotation on the Selected Annotations on Li He's Poems). Shanghai: Shanghai Classics Publishing House, 1978.
15. Wu, Qiao 吴乔. "Weilu shihua" 围炉诗话 (Talks about Poetry around the Hearth). In *Qing shihua xubian* 清诗话续编 (A Sequel to the Poetic Discourses of the Qing Dynasty), edited by Shaoyu Guo 郭绍虞. Shanghai: Shanghai Classics Publishing House, 1983.
16. Yin, Fan 殷璠. "Heyue yinglingji" 河岳英灵集 (A Collection of the Poems by the Quintessential Poets of the High Tang Dynasty). In *Tangren xuan tangshi shizhong* 唐人选唐诗十种 (Ten Tang Versions of an Anthology of the Tang Poetry), edited by Jie Yuan 元结. Shanghai: Shanghai Classics Publishing House, 1958.

2 Linguistic approach and intuitive perception
A tangle that ancient Chinese poetry critics had to unravel

2.1. Linguistic approach and intuitive perception: a hard-to-unravel tangle

In a book review, I mentioned the complex tangle of one's linguistic approach and one's intuitive perception, which I believe poses a challenge to those ancient Chinese poetry critics who attempt to establish an objective system of poetry critique exclusively through their linguistic approach. But can they make it without their intuitive perception?

A general consensus is that ancient Chinese poetry critics prioritize their intuitive perception over their linguistic approach. This tradition with a long history has its root in the notion that "Language is incapable of conveying all on one's mind" and is upheld by ancient Chinese poets and poetry critics alike. Examples are many. Chen Yuyi of the Song Dynasty, through one of his "Two Poems Composed on a Spring Day", which reads "zhao lai ting shu you ming qin (Early in the morning in the courtyard trees perched chirping birds)/hong lv fu chun shang yuan lin (Interspersed red flowers and green plants adding to spring sprawled as far as to a distant forest)/hu you hao shi sheng yan di (On the spur of the moment I would improvise an ingenious poem)/an pai ju fa yi nan xun (Alas, it evaporated into thin air after I had considered its wording and composition)", seems, by its third and fourth verses, to imply that attention to wording is the culprit for the loss of an otherwise genius impromptu poem. Gong Xiang of the Song Dynasty, in one of his two poems "Learn to Compose a Poem", which runs "xue shi hun si xue can chan (Learning to compose poetry is like learning to attain the Buddhist Zen in meditation)/yu ke an pai yi mo chuan (Words chosen for composition does not necessarily convey the meaning)/hui yi ji chao sheng lv jie (To convey the meaning is to transcend the constrictions of tonal and metrical scheme)/bu xu lian shi bu qing tian (There is no need for smelted stones to mend the broken blue sky)", sees the tonal and metrical schemes and the "smelt stones" (analogous to words), which are to him the mundane devices, as encumbrances to transcendence to the nirvana of meaning. This can evoke a picture of one discarding his fishing net of bamboo (i.e., a fishing device in ancient China) after having netted fishes. Notions held by other ancient Chinese poetry critics, such as "Words are incapable of conveying meanings that are beyond them" (see *Liuyi's Commentaries on Poetry* by

Ouyang Xiu, also known as Liuyi Ju Shi, i.e., the Layman Buddhist of Six Ones, of the Song Dynasty) and even "Words surely do not generate meanings" (see *Jianzhai's Remarks on Poetry* [Jianzhai, Zhang's style name] by Zhang Qianyi of the Qing Dynasty), as good as decouple poetry and its language. According to them, it seems that, without linguistic help, the subtleties and profundities of a poem can still be attained. Even if words are not denied their role in a poem altogether, they are deemed, at best, minor players, as likened by Wang Fuzhi, as in his *Jiangzhai's Commentaries on Poetry*, and Yuan Mei of the Qing Dynasty (Suiyuan, a part of his two other names), as in his *A Sequel to 'Critique of Poetry'*, to privates or maid-servants insofar as anyone who shows overdue respect for them should punitively be labelled provincial and myopic. In the eyes of ancient Chinese poetry critics, the language has to give way to the intuitive perception. And the latter involves the reader's (including the poetry critic) feelings and knowledge. Their critique of poetry, including its linguistic aspect, is very abstract, which is no more than the description of their intuitive perception. For example, in his *Remarks on Poetry in Reclusion on the Han River*, Wei Tai of the Song Dynasty, comparing "zhong song *jie zuo lao* long lin (Planted pine trees have all grown to look like old dragon scales)" and "zhong song *jie lao zuo* long lin (Planted pine trees have all grown old and looked dragon scales)", two versions of Wang Wei's verse, only notes in an abstract way that the latter is "much better" than the former without elaborating concretely on why "jie zuo lao (all grow old)" beats "jie lao zuo (all old and grow)" in terms of the effect of just changing the word order. Feng Ban of the Qing Dynasty says, economically and indefinitely, of "yi ge chen sha dao li qian (It looks as if being aloof a thousand li away from the dusty world down below" and "fen fen liu su shang shi xian (Lo and behold, those snobbish crowds are still being keen on the pursuit of immortality)", two verses of Wang Anshi of the Song Dynasty's poem "Ascending the Top of Mount Damao", that they are "unnaturally crafted". Small wonder that Wei's or Feng's critique only befuddles their readers. To be fair, a poetry critic, also as a poetry reader, may count on intuitive perception. But, at the same time, the reader of the critique may demand his elaboration on how much intuitive perception is formed on and beyond a text in proportion.

In his *Appreciation, Like Smelling Aroma, of the Poetry by Xu Yuantan*, Qian Qianyi quotes a recluse as saying "When it comes to appreciation of poetry, I prefer using my nose to using my eyes". Huang Ziyun of the Qing Dynasty, also known as Yehong, in his *The Yardsticks by Yehong for Critique of Poetry*, proposes that "We should harness our heart to feel what is hidden in obscurity" in this respect. Obviously, such perception, either through "nose" or "heart", of poetry is conducted characteristically beyond what a poem itself offers. A problem thus arises as to what extent the perception of this nature can be sourced from a poem itself and how well it can be understood. For one example, Ji Yun of the Qing Dynasty's opinion of Zhu Qingyu of the Tang Dynasty's two verses "chong si jiao ying xi (The fine shadows of spiders and gossamers look as if more than insubstantial)/ten zi zhui sheng you (The gentle falling of vines sounds as indistinct as from the deepest recess)" that they are wonderfully minute and dainty is confusing: is it about their language, their grammatical structure, or their meanings? For another example,

Shi Buhua of the Qing Dynasty, in his *A Garrison Secretary's Talk about Poetry*, only cites Du Fu's "lv chui feng zhe sun (Green dangling, wind-snapped bamboo shoots)/hong zhang yu fei mei (Red split, rain-fattened plums)" as a contrast to "shi ya sun xie chu (Even if under the pressure of rocks emerge bamboo shoots)/yan xuan hua dao sheng (Despite overhanging cliffs sprout blooming flowers)" with an abstract comment that the latter is "close to unnaturalness", which certainly baffles the reader: why does the former supersede the latter in terms of, in Shi's words, "choice of words and tinges"?

Evidently, those ancient Chinese poetry critics' dependence on their intuitive perception does not necessarily yield convincing interpretations of a poem. First, their intuitive perception can lead them to self-assuredly understand, for example, a word in a verse superficially and thus interpret it, and, second, their intuitive perception can lead them to inject into a poem their own conjectures about, for example, its background and its author's personality and intent. To rectify the problem caused by those ancient Chinese poetry critics' intuitive perception, some linguistic devices are thus needed. But the linguistic devices here differ from what the linguistic researchers use. So far, in China, a line has been drawn between the linguistics and the literature, either like two neighbours divided by a fence, which they occasionally mend, or like two withdrawn strangers who keep off each other's borders. Thus, a linguist focuses only on things such as semantics, phonetics, grammar, and rhetoric. This is manifest in works by such modern Chinese linguists as Wang Li (see his *The Chinese Prosody*) and Jiang Shaoyu (see his *A Study of the Language of the Tang Dynasty Poetry*) even when they touch upon aspects of poetry. So their works have so far been deemed studies on the Chinese language rather than on the language of the Chinese poetry; thus they have not been classified under the category of critiques of Chinese literature. Otherwise, they would run counter to the notion of poetry being a literary form with its own features and thus created by its own criteria. Indeed, a poem, at the hands of these linguists, is no more than a body under autopsy, with its author's personality, psychology, sentiments, and the like ignored altogether, or a poem is to them as an ox is to a legendary chef in ancient Chinese folklore: as the chef could dissect an ox skilfully and precisely, so they can analyse a poem as well, but they both give no consideration to what lives in the dissected or the analysed, which, in the case of a poem, inspires the reader. This more or less conforms with what William Kurtz Wimsatt and Monroe Curtis Beardsley, in their *The Affective Fallacy*, state: that a poem as a text and the outcome of appreciation of it should by no means be mixed to avoid the snare of either intuitive perception or a relativist approach. Their statement should not be applied to poetry critique. Otherwise, what could one learn about a poem? As a house is not a building merely of brick, mortar, and beams, so a poem is more than a work of words, verses, and grammatical structure. When one attempts to interpret a poem, his or her intuitive perception will inevitably be involved in the interpretation, and his or her interpretation will inevitably not be limited to the pure linguistic aspects of the poem. A case in point is one of Li Shangyin's "Titleless" poem series. Its verse "chun can dao si si fang jin (Spring silkworms keep spinning silk till they die)" certainly does not mean what it literally means; if a linguist says it uses a metaphor and a pun (as "死 [die/death]" and "丝 [silk]" here are two homophonic Chinese words), then what are the metaphor and the pun about? If one answers that they are about love, then his answer involves his or her appreciation, and if he or she further points out that they are about an *unrequited* love, then this engages his or her intuitive perception, which can be an amalgam of his or her knowledge of the poet's life, empathy with the poet's feelings, view of love, and so on. The linguist cannot help it if he or she appreciates the verse as a *poetic* verse. So it is with its symmetrically antithetical verse "la ju cheng hui lei shi gan (Candles' tear-like melted wax starts to dry when they burn up)", which, likewise, is about more than a physical phenomenon. If a poetry critic is advised to, for the sake of objectivity, interpret a poem linguistically without engaging intuitive perception, such advice is not practicable, for, after all, the poetry critic is a reader too; given this, how can it be that he or she should be free from the tangle of linguistic approach and intuitive perception when the language he or she has to deal with is poetic?

Indeed, neither an ancient Chinese poetry critic, who favours his intuitive perception, nor a modern Western New Criticism theorist, who advocates the linguistic aspects, can escape this kind of tangle if they only interpret a poem. In his *Questions and Answers on Poetry at Gu Fu Yu Pavilion*, Wang Shizhen of the Qing Dynasty maintains that the meaning of a poem is primary, whereas its wording is secondary, and versification is for a poet to convey meaning. In his *Jianzhai's Remarks on Poetry*, Zhang Qianyi asserts that "Wording itself surely does not generate meanings" but at the same time concedes that wording, though a matter of form, is where the spirit of a poem is. Indirectly they admit that interpretation of a poem is the symbiosis of engaging one's intuitive perception and looking at the linguistic aspects of the poem. This is also the case of literary criticism beyond the borders of China. The advocates either of Russian Formalism or of the Anglo-American New Criticism both emphasize the scientific and objective properties of literary criticism while de-emphasizing such theories established by nineteenth-century literary critics as impressionistic appreciation, historiographic hermeneutic, and contrastive realism, as listed in René Wellek's review of the leading trend in literary criticism in the twentieth century; still, their attempt is thwarted at removing anything to do with the intuitive perception by relieving poetry of the yoke of symbolism, as observed by Terence Hawkes in his *Structuralism and Semiotics*. Even among themselves, critics argue pro and con in this respect. For example, while Elder Olson, criticizing William Butler Yeats' poetry, harshly denounces the trend of poetry critique that the reader's association inspired by a particular word should be the centre of attention, Cleanth Brooks, a torchbearer of New Criticism, in his *The Well-Wrought Urn: Studies in the Structure of Poetry*, urges both the reader and the critic, by the example of interpretation of John Donne's poem "The Canonization", to feel a poem, for he believes that to appreciate a poem is not to break it down into what may be likened to chemical elements, which will not just reduce its poetic beauty but end to no avail.

Either as a reader or as a critic of a poem, one will converse with its author through its language. Most of the time, it is impossible for the reader or the critic of the poem to solicit its author for help. Thus its language is the only indicator of its author's intention, as well as the only medium by which this conversation, in defiance of time and space, is conducted. So the poetry critic in particular is obliged to justify the significance of, but at the same time, circumscribe the extent of, its language in interpretation of the poem. This is one thing. The other thing is that, in these circumstances, the poetry critic is not allowed to say what is actually not in the poem in the name of its author. On the other hand, its linguistic world, which embodies its author's thoughts and feelings, is like a stockhouse under no lock and key for its reader, who is free, if he or she chooses, to bring his or her own stock inside. So, if the reader happens to be a critic, the critique of the poem will unavoidably be imbued with his or her intuitive perception. Whether this intuitive perception is right is almost impossible to verify, unless the author of the poem comes forward with substantial evidence for or against it, and if this does not happen, then it holds true. At any rate, it is hard to interpret a poem purely in terms of its language without involving its critic's intuitive perception. The question is to what extent such intuitive perception should be involved.

2.2. Case study in terms of semantics and phonology

According to *Liunan's Desultory Notes* by Wang Yingkui (Liunan as his style name) of the Qing Dynasty, ancient Chinese love to recite poems on snowfall, and it contains this story: one day, a Buddhist Zen master, boating on a lake, was thus inspired to improvise a quatrain: "shuo feng zhen zhen han (Freezing north winds are sweeping from time to time/tian gong da tu tan (God of Heaven is expectorating his flake-size mucus)/ming zhao hong ri chu (Next morning will rise a red sun)/ bian shi hua tan wan (A ball of wonder that will melt and evaporate the mucus aground)"; at the time, whoever read it could not help but admire the master's genius. From the linguistic perspective, "da tu tan (expectorating his flake-size mucus)" and "hua tan wan (a ball of wonder)", respectively, metaphorize the falling snowflakes and the rising sun, and such metaphors are apt in their own right. Moreover, metaphorization as such for the first time ever, even if it sounds incorrect, should conform with what Victor Shklovsky, a Russian Formalist literary critic, defines as linguistic "defamiliarization". In the eyes of most readers back then, nonetheless, it is too lowbrow for a poem. In the early period of the Republic of China, the modern Chinese scholar Hu Shi's vernacular verses "liang ge huang hu die (Two yellow butterflies)/tian shang tai gu dan (It was so solitary in the sky)/ bu zhi wei shen me (I didn't know why)" were criticized by his contemporary Qian Xuantong (see his *My Objections to the So-Called Literary Revolutionization*), who feels that "liang ge huang hu die (two yellow butterflies)" should be modified to "shuang fei huang hu die (A pair of yellow butterflies in flight)" and "tian shang (in the sky)" to "ling xiao (high up to and beyond clouds)". Linguistically speaking, there should be little discrepancy between Hu's original version and Qian's modification, as their words, which both are representative devices only, describe one and the same thing. Even so, in the eyes of Qian, the latter is more refined, more elegant, and more poetic. But Liu Bannong, Qian's peer, thinks less of Qian's proud modification.

26 Linguistic approach and intuitive perception

Old Chinese linguistics has terms such as allegory, exaggeration, inheritance, and inspiration particularly for the art of poetic language. New Chinese linguistics has also introduced such terms as tension, irony, and ambiguity in this respect. Both the old and the new ones, plus those such as intension and extension, particularly for formal logic, still cannot help one distinguish between vulgarity and refinement when it comes to poetic language. This notwithstanding, the difference between words in taste is still there, and one can intuitively feel it. For example, Ji Yun bluntly dismisses "xu mao (a silk floss hat)" and "tong zheng (a bronze percussion instrument)" used by Su Shi in one of his two poems under the title of "On the Way to Xincheng", which reads "ling shang qing yun pi xu mao (Fine clouds cover the peaks of mounts as if they were wearing silk floss hats)/shu tou chu ri gua tong zheng (The sun rising above the canopy of trees looks as if a bronze percussion instrument were hanging overhead)", as a disappointment, for they are not elegant at all. By the same token, Zhou Liangpei, a modern Chinese poetry critic, in his *Epilogue to the Collection of Xu Zhimo's Poetry* (Xu Zhimo, a modern Chinese poet) disapproves of Xu's metaphorizing blood with either rose or peony in one of his poems, "An Ode to Captives", and entitling another poem "Don't Pinch Me; It Hurts" in that Xu blurs what is hideous and what is beautiful in the former and mistakes the intimate arousing murmur of one in love for an interesting utterance in the latter; hence Zhou judges that Xu's words are of low taste. Evidently, hitherto, the aforementioned terms, either old or new or logical, are incapable of explaining those critics' discrimination. Then is such distinction in taste semantically intrinsic to the poetic language? The answer should be negative. For example, Du Fu, in his poems, uses language that the commoners, like vendors and errand boys, of his time habitually used in their everyday life, such as "wu gui (turtles)", "huang yu (yellow croakers)", "ge (apiece)", and "chi (tuck away)", of which Zhang Jie of the Song Dynasty, in his *Notes on Poetry Written in the Pine and Cypress Studio*, says that, though apparently vulgar, they actually epitomize refinement and plainness. Ironically, it is still Zhang who treats "bu ji liu dun han (Such a complete moron is he)" and "qi wan chi bu de (The seventh bowl of tea is more than enough)", two verses from the identically styled poem by Lu Tong of the Tang Dynasty, simply with a diametrical attitude, harshly criticizing them for an utter lack of poetic taste, due allegedly to the poet's brainless flippancy. Shi Buhua and Zhang are poles apart in judgment of the aforementioned Du's poetic language, with Shi, in his *A Garrison Secretary's Talk about Poetry*, speaking scornfully of it as evidence of distasteful vulgarity, which thus does not deserve emulation, despite Du's prominent status as a poet. Such contradictions are also seen in the respective judgment by Wang Shizhen and Weng Fanggang, also of the Qing Dynasty, of "hong (red)" and "fei (fattened)" in "lv chui feng zhe sun (Green dangling, wind-snapped bamboo shoots)/hong zhang yu fei mei (Red split, rain-fattened plums)" from Du Fu's poem "Escorting Zhen Guangwen in a Tour of the He Clan's Forested Mountain", in that, by Wang's standards, "hong (red)" and "fei (fattened)" are crass and naturally not a good model for later poets, even though they are highly acclaimed, which is, on the other hand, argued against by Weng, who insists that the two words are not unrefined and that Wang's verdict does not make any sense. And Weng goes on to taunt Wang for his addiction to so-called unique genius words (see his *The Commentaries on Poetry at the Rocky Edge of an Islet*).

These instances, in a way, prove that a word or a phrase, not to mention a poetic word or a poetic phrase, as in the previous poems, has what is beyond semantics, such as taste, which differs with different readers or critics. But arguments in this regard persist. For example, Mao Chunyuan of the Qing Dynasty, also known as Shenyuan, in his *Shenyuan's Remarks on Poetry*, believes that words themselves are intrinsically distinct in taste, suggesting that words of good taste should repel those of bad taste the way a cohort of highbrows refuse to admit any lowbrow to their club; on the contrary, again Wang Shizhen, according to He Shiqi of the Qing Dynasty's *A Record of the Remarks by a Burning Lamp*, holds that words themselves do not intrinsically differentiate in taste and that their difference, if there were any, would be caused by what is external, by comparing a word to a woman, who remains as she was however she is dressed or wears her makeup. Then, how does a poetry critic tell one word from another in terms of taste?

Nuances of this nature are perceived in the words of the language of a nation and, what's more, in the words, which mean nearly the same, of the languages of two nations. In his *The Sense of Beauty*, George Santayana lists pairs of such words as English "bread" and Spanish "pan" and English "God" and Greek "Dios", noting that "bread" does not connotate humanity, which is in "pan", and that "Dios" lacks what is sublime in "God". Michael Kohn Ackermann, in his *The German-Chinese Dictionary*, points out that the nuances of two German adjectives "sinnlich" and "erotisch" cannot be rendered satisfactorily into Chinese, and, worse, their Chinese renditions confuse which is derogatory and which is laudatory. Likewise, in the case of "yuan tian (园田)" in Chinese, which means an ideal home for Tao Yuanming, "countryside" in English hardly matches it in nicety, for Tao's "yuan tian (园田)", to a Chinese person, feels warm, comfortable, and secure. "Gui(归)" in Chinese can be rendered in English as "return", as one reads in the ending part of J.H. Payne's "Home, Sweet Home", but the "return", to a Chinese person, does not connotate what "gui"(归) in ancient Chinese poems does: one's homecoming eagerness and thrill, the reunion of a married woman with her parents, the return of cattle and sheep to their pens and of poultry back to their roosts, as described in *The Book of Songs*: the earth being back where it is meant to be, Laozi's philosophy of "All in the universe will end where they originated", one's sheer bliss of life back to nature after being frustrated with the mundane world where genuineness is a rarity, or finding a home for one's homeless soul. And, as Zhou Zizhi of the Song Dynasty says, each of Tao Yuanming's poems either contains or connotates "gui (归)", which, to later generations, is evocative and whose evocativeness, so subtle and so profound over a long time that it is beyond description, can only be felt instead.

According to H.S. Canby, rhetoric cannot tackle what concerns complicated emotions or thoughts (see his *The Elements of Composition*). His denial of the role of linguistic devices, when it comes to interpretation of a work of literature, should also express what is on poetry critics' minds when it comes to interpretation of a poem. But it does not mean that poetry critics are inclined to despise linguistic devices. It is just that linguistic devices often fail in dealing satisfyingly with what concerns a poem in terms of not only a word or a phrase in a verse, as aforementioned, but also a verse which is to be discussed. When it comes to interpretation of the verse of a poem, linguistic devices, such as ellipsis and transposition for ancient Chinese poetry critics, modern syntactic analysis, the Western collocations of semantic codes, and so on, have proved almost futile. For example, "xiang dao zhuo yu ying wu li (verbatim: Aromatic rice grains pecked leftover parrots) (The rice grains are the leftovers after parrots have pecked their fill)" by Du Fu in one of his eight-poem series written on the spur of the moment about an autumnal view and "hai ri sheng can ye (verbatim: The sea sun rose the remnant night) (The sun was rising above the sea while night was waning)"/jiang chun ru jiu nian (verbatim: The southern side of the lower reaches of the Yangtze River spring entered the old year) (Spring fell on Jiangnan even before the old year passed)" by Wang Wan of the Tang Dynasty, in his "Mooring at the Foot of Mount Beigu", can certainly be syntactically be analysed, but such syntactic analysis does not at all bring out what is truly in and beyond the *poetic* verses. Take Li Shangyin's "chun can dao si si fang jin (Spring silkworms keep spinning silk till they die)/la ju cheng hui lei shi gan (Candles' tear-like melted wax starts to dry when they burn up)" for another instance. Grammatically, Li's pair of verses reads like two simple statements. Actually, they signify more. As John Donne similizes romantic love in his "The Canonization", a part of which reads "Call's what you will, we are made such by love/Call her one, me another fly/We're tapers too, and at our own cost die", so Li, through the pair of verses, metaphorizes romantic love, because the words like "love" and "her and me" which appear in John Donne's verses do not appear in Li's. Since this pair of verses is deemed metaphoric, they are like an open-ended riddle without any cue for, say, a poetic critic, who has to interpret, for example, why Li metaphorizes romantic love by virtue of both his or her knowledge, for example, of Li's life and other ancient Chinese poets' similar verses, such as "wei zhu zhi zi fen yi zhi yong (Candles burn themselves to illuminate darkness)/yi you sha shen yi cheng ren (Virtuous men sacrifice their lives for a just cause)"(from "An Ode to Candles" by Fu Xian of the Western Jin Dynasty) and "chun can bu ying lao (A spring silkworm is tiring herself out)/zhou ye chang huai si (Spinning her silk cocoon day and night)/he xi wei qu jin (She is taking no care of her fatigued tiny body)/chan mian zi you shi (Simply for a short moment of romantic indulgence)" (from "Spinning a Silk Cocoon", a ballad of the Liang period of the Southern Dynasties) and his or her intuitive perception. If he or she further deduces that Li's metaphorized romantic love is unrequited, he or she must remember such verses as "tou shen tang shui zhong (I am eager to be plunged into hot water)/gui de gong cheng pi (As it is a rare occasion of you and me together meeting to make a piece of fabric)" (ibid.), an expression of desperate resoluteness; "bai si chan zhong xin (As if numerous silk filaments were entangling my heart)/qiao cui wei suo huan (I am languishing day by day for my beloved)" (from "Nahe Shoals", a ballad of the Southern Dynasties), an expression of emotional attachment; "yi ti liu xi shang (In recollection my tears are dropping down on my laps)/zhu yan luo hua zhong (While the candle flame is guttering, its wax melting into flowery patterns)" (from "Reflection on Candle in Reply to the Poem by the Prince in Charge of Xiangdong Citadel" by Monarch Jianwen of the Liang period of the Southern Dynasties), an expression of mournful pensiveness; and "la zhu you xin hai xi bie (Even the candle does not have the heart to watch the farewell scene)/ti ren chui lei dao tian ming (Its melting wax flowing like tears do all the way till daybreak)" (from one of Du Mu's, also known as Fanchuan, of the Tang Dynasty's two poems under the title of "Lamenting the Departure"), an expression of grief over pending separation. All in all, the interpretation of Li's pair of verses is far beyond what a sheer objective linguistic analysis is capable of.

Interpretation of Li's pair of verses, one may argue, should also be credited to contextual factors. This argument seems to hold water, and it can find support in I.A. Richards' *The Philosophy of Rhetoric*, which says that words are interpreted based both on the text wherein they appear and on their context or, in other words, whatever externally concerns the words to be interpreted. Even so, such an interpretation is not necessarily purely linguistically objective.

Let us look at *The Pale Toll* by Wang Duqing, a modern Chinese poet, which should be contextless:

"cang bai de zhong sheng shuai fu de meng long
(Pale toll decadent mist)
shu san ling long huang liang de meng long de gu zhong
(Dispersing delicate desolate misty vale)
... shuai cao qian chong wan chong
(... withered grasses layers upon layers)
ting yong yuan de huang tang de gu zhong
(Hark eternal bizarre ancient toll)
ting qian sheng wan sheng
(Hark resonance upon resonance)"

Obviously, in this poem, the toll is the focus, and the other words are used to reinforce its effect. Each part of speech of the verses can be analysed to learn about how it strikes, how loud it sounds, and how far it is from the listener, which should, from the perspective of rhetoric, have implications, including even emotional ones. Indeed, but a reader, not to mention a poetry critic, of this poem should read into it more than this: he or she will also feel a peculiar forsakenness and otherworldliness, although such a feelings is beyond its words. And the feeling of this nature, as if with the rippling of the toll, diffuses the whole poem. This is, as Wang Duqing says in his essay "A Discourse on Poetry", what a true poem should be like: it can either be like a wave vibrating along the reader's nerves, which can be either visible or invisible and either tangible or intangible, or like a remote sound in a dense fog, which can be either audible or inaudible, an analogy to such feelings in a poem as can be either expressible or inexpressible. But Wang's observation begs the question: if the feelings as such are inexpressible, how can they be known by the reader? If they are expressible, which word, phrase, or verse of a poem expresses such feelings? For an answer, we need to look not just at but beyond the words. Here, worthy of mention as proof, is that a Chinese person, when listening to a chime, habitually keeps a distance from it, for being close to it can make its otherwise pleasant sound disagreeable, as if it were a piece of thunderous grating metal, which would certainly torment the listener to madness, whereas a distant tolling can evoke a feeling of tranquillity and vastness and can also arouse and set free its listener's association and imagination, as in the case of such verses as "xi shang yao wen jing she zhong (The chime from the temple afar can be heard out here at the creek)" (from "Looking Southward to the Cypress Forest Buddhist Temple" by Lang Shiyuan of the Tang Dynasty), "que ting shu zhong yi cui wei (I turned my head only to hear the sporadic chimes that evoked the image of those lush mountains)"(from "Recalling with a Friend the Mountains Back at Home One Night in Chang'an" by Zhao Gu of the Tang Dynasty), "zhong sheng ge pu wei (Heard across the river, the chimes weakened to faint sounds)"(from "Starting Out at Daybreak" by Yao Hu of the Tang Dynasty), "yuan si ting zhong xun (The Chimes led me to their far temple)" (from "In the Midst of the Mountains" by Mi Yan of the Song Dynasty poet), "ge wu wen zhong jue si shen (The chimes beyond the col make a listener feel as if the temple lies afar)"(from "An Inscription on Li Shinan's Painted Folding Fan" by Cai Zhao of the Song Dynasty), and Lu You of the Song Dynasty's "shu zhong ge wu wen (The sporadic chimes beyond the col were heard)", which all describe the listeners' or rather the poets' feeling of serenity and peace with distant, and perhaps indistinct, chimes. And this kind of feeling would be shared by Chinese people of the time. So "An Impression" by Dai Wangshu, a modern Chinese poet, starts with "shi piao luo shen gu qu de (As if wafting down to a canyon)/you wei de ling sheng (Were dim chimes, to my ears)", wherein it is the poet's feeling that the reader has to look beyond the words and verses to empathize with.

Likewise, even a branch that reaches over a courtyard wall in spring will arouse a particular feeling, as in Du Fu's "wei wen nan xi zhu (Pray, the Bamboos flanking the southern stream)/chou shao he guo qiang (Why is one of your branches projecting beyond the wall)?" and "lv zhu ban han tuo (The tender green bamboo stems are being wrapped at their lower parts in layers of shells)/xin shao cai chu qiang (One of their new branches is shooting just over the wall)", Wu Rong of the Tang Dynasty's "yi zhi hong yan chu qiang tou (A twig of brightly red apricot flower was jutting beyond a wall", Li Jianxun of the Tang Dynasty's "yu bian shei zhi chu qiang zhi (Someone was pointing a fine whip at a twig of plum blossom over a wall)", Madam Wei of the Song Dynasty's "ge an liang san jia (Across the river are scattered a couple of households)/chu qiang hong xing hua (Beyond one of their walls is extending a twig of red apricot flower)", and Lin Bu of the Song Dynasty's "wu yan xie ru yi zhi di (Over the inclined eaves and beyond the wall overhangs low a twig of plum blossom)", wherein a single shoot of bamboo, a single twig of apricot blossom, or a single branch of plum flower poking over a wall should be so touching and inspirational, in contrast to a grove or a cluster of things in kind, for example, growing outside a wall, to which the poets would be indifferent. The answer to why it is so will have to be found not through linguistic analysis of the verses but by looking into their authors' intuitive perception, which involves their aesthetic bent developed through their life experience.

Back to linguistic interpretation of poetry, it involves elements such as cadence, rhyme, and tone. In his *Descriptive Linguistics, An Introduction*, Winfred P. Lehmann even concludes that, from the perspective of linguistics, literature means a work that is composed of the linguistic elements that are qualified. As regards poetry, its qualified linguistic elements are the ones that are selected to meet the requirements of tonal and metrical scheme. They concern, among others, the metrical iambus, the tonal stress, the sound duration, and the like, as in the case of the Western poetry, and the level (平, *pin* in pinyin; hereinafter referred to as "l") and the deflected (仄, *ze* in pinyin; hereinafter referred to as "d") tones and symmetrical antitheses, as in the case of, for example, Recent Style poetry. They work together to make a melodic poetic pattern, as observed by Wolfgang Kayser in his *Das Sprachliche Kunstwerk-Eine Einführungin die Literaturwis-senschaft*. This kind of melodic poetic pattern serves the purpose of not just producing a sound and cadence effect as expected but also hinting at what is beyond such pattern, including a poet's feelings, just as Philip Sidney, in his *The Defence of Poetry*, argues for the workings of the iambus, a device that he believes can vividly express all sorts of passions. His view is echoed by Roman Jakobson, a Russian literary critic, also an advocate of Formalism, who says that meticulous arrangement, such as recurrence, of metrical foot, alliteration, antithesis, homophone or otherwise, tonal length, and so forth helps remarkably in perception of what can be behind verses. In the event, these physical aural poetic elements have become things for one to mentally perceive. And this certainly involves one's intuitive perception or one's sensibility. Without it, how could one perceive something idyllic, heroic, or intimate in the tonal and metrical scheme of a poem, given that, for example, tones themselves, like musical notes (staves or numbers), are the most abstract, thus carrying the least perceived meaning or sentiment? The truth is that a certain feeling can be aroused by a certain tone in one the way a musical note does. This certainly should not be ascribed simply to things such as pitch and beat, which cannot explain why the same tone varies, in terms of impact, with various listeners. It is safe to say that their intuitive perception should be credited for it. So it is with the tonal and metrical schemes of, for example, Recent Style poetry.

> [In versification,] the same consonant parts of the syllables should be shunned; the same vowel parts of the syllables should alternate; the stressed tones and the unstressed tones should properly be arranged; the voiced and the voiceless tones should not be confused; in a word, whatever concerns the tonal (and metrical) schemes demands circumspection.
> (see Wang Yingkui's Liunan's Desultory Notes)

These rules and regulations are formulated neither for a crossword-wise game of using the right words within a tonal and metrical scheme nor for a show of one's mastery of this kind of craft. To ancient Chinese poetry critics, elements such as the sub-genre of four tones under the genre of the "l" and the "d" ones in the Chinese language have their own implications, including one's sentiments. For example,

"A voiceless tone can imply Heaven, whereas a voiced one Earth"; the "l" tone, because of its property of clearness and gentleness, feels peaceful and harmonious, whereas the "d" one sounds heavy and rapid and is thus that of despondency and anxiety (see *Annotated Commentary of Liezi*). According to Mao Chunrong (under the style name of Shenyuan) of the Qing Dynasty's *Shenyuan's Poetic Discourse*, "The 'l' tone is slow and circuitous while the 'd' one rapid and abrupt". *Elucidation of Musical Notes* of *Conforming to or Nearing Elegance* (the first canonical Chinese dictionary) says of the tones, which are actually the ancient five musical notes, namely 宫 in Chinese (gong in *pinyin*), 商 (shang), 角 (jue), 徵 (zhi), and 羽 (yu), that each of them has its own connotation. Hao Yixing of the Qing Dynasty's *Annotations on the Classical Annotations on 'Conforming to or Nearing Elegance'* echoes the conception of the musical notes being not just phonological but, more importantly, perceptional, which is that "gong" feels resonant and orotund, "shang" light and swift, "jue" mellow and lingering, "zhi" vibrating and rippling, and "yu" flat and unemphatic. As for the sub-genre of four tones under the genre of the "l" and "d" ones, the "l" tone is claimed to sound steady, the rising tone elevating, the rising-falling tone diminishing, and the entering tone urgent. In a word, these descriptions of the tones or musical notes are seemingly about their properties, which result naturally from one's intuitive perception. That is why Xie Zhen of the Ming Dynasty, with Siming (i.e., a "sea-in-the-four-direction recluse") as his literary name, in his *A Sea-in-the-Four-Direction Recluse's Remarks on Poetry*, concludes that it is one's intuitive perception that feels what the four tones carry. In this sense, the tonal and metrical schemes of poetry and one's intuitive perception are closely interrelated, a mere reader will use his or her intuitive perception to feel, and a poetry critic will not just use intuitive perception to feel but have to rightly describe what these phonological poetic elements can produce in terms of impression.

A few more words about the conception of the modern Chinese linguists in this regard. Xie Yunfei, in his *Rhymes and Tones vis-a-vis Literature*, details the feeling, such as of gloom, frustration, and flippancy, which he thinks is aroused even by the way the different component parts of Chinese characters are pronounced. His conception, though disputable, still finds what can be seen as evidence in modern Chinese linguists' works such as *A Partial Discourse on the Correspondence between Designation and Denotation* by Liu Shipei and *A Manuscript about the History of the Chinese Language* by Wang Li, whose case studies on rhyming Chinese words vis-a-vis their meanings in a way support Xie's argument.

As a conclusion to this section, let us look at this pair of verses, which are believed to epitomize the style of Meng Jiao of the Tang Dynasty, of one of his fifteen-poem series under the title of "Reflection in Autumn": "leng lu di meng po (verbatim: Cold dew dropped dream broken) (Drops of cold dew fell only to shatter my dream)/qiao feng shu gu han (verbatim: Freezing winds combed bones chill) (Freezing winds felt like combing my bones, sending chill through them)". The five Chinese words of the first verse, all in the "d" tone, especially due to "fell" (滴 *di* in pinyin) in the entering tone, a sub-genre tone under the genre of the "d" tone, startle one with a sensation of drops of cold dew striking vehemently; "freezing" (峭 *qiao*) and "comb" (梳 *shu*) in the second verse describe respectively the bone-chilling air and the sensation of it, the effect produced by way of pronunciation of the consonant parts of the two words, like a ceramic piece scratching across the bottom of a ceramic bowl, intensifying the sensation of bitter cold. Moreover, the first verse contrasts with the second one in that the former's scheme, mainly in the "d" tone, which feels like running briskly, indicates the short sound of dropping dew, while the latter's scheme, mainly in the "l" tone, which moves at a slower cadence, suggests the abiding torture of cold (compare them with "suan 酸" [poignant] and "she 射" [penetrate] in the verse "dong guan suan feng she mou zi [verbatim: The eastern gate poignant winds penetrated eyeballs] [The poignant winds through the Eastern Gate penetrated his eyeballs]" of Li He's poem entitled "A Song for the Golden Statue of the Immortal Cast in Bronze which will Leave the Han Palace"). Hitherto, it should be evident that a feeling, whatever it may be, is one's intuitive perception of what tones can carry, which should certainly partly be ascribed to the meanings of intoned words as well. Imagine what the tonal (and metrical) scheme of a poem would communicate to a poetry critic without involvement of his intuitive perception in interpretation of it.

2.3. What is the right intuitive perception?

Needless to say, there are limits to one's intuitive perception when one interprets a poem by virtue of it. For example, one must not be driven by intuitive perception to fancifully interpret a poem. In other words, one's interpretation of a poem must be based on its language so that the interpretation is well founded and well accepted.

Let us learn lessons from the history of poetry critique and shun three kinds of intuitive perception that are misleading.

The first kind, which has a long history and seems dominant, is that based on a seemingly pertinent yet actually far-fetched background. This can be sourced to one of Mencius' beliefs, namely, "to learn about one's background in order to learn about his personality". Since then, ancient Chinese poetry critics would base their perception of a poem on a certain background. This inclination thus subjects a poem to its alleged background, and, worse, the meaning of the poem can thus be misinterpreted. If a poetry critic depends on such background-based intuitive perception, all he or she would do is turn simply to a naive or even faulty historical textbook, not to mention well-documented historical archives, for help in interpretation of a poem. In fact, either such a textbook or such an archive is really seen by some ancient Chinese poetry critics as a key to unlocking the door or as a must to access the world of a poem. Thus interpretation of a poem is oversimplified: a poem, if composed in a time of turmoil, must satirize the politics; vanilla and beauties must analogize a monarch and his ministers. For example, Xie Lingyun's "chi tang sheng chun cao (The pond is lush with vernal grasses)" thus must suggest "the pond of grace from the sovereign ruler dried up", and also Xie's "yuan liu bian ming qin (The garden willows nestle chirping birds)" thus must hint at a transformed era, as annotated by Pan Deyu of the Qing Dynasty in his *Remarks on Poetry at Yangyi Studio*; Liu Changqing of the Tang Dynasty's "xian hua luo di ting wu sheng (Dead flowers dropped down to the ground still)" thus must allude to his demotion; Han Wo's "yan sui pian pian yan liu qu (I saw petals falling, piece by piece, on a stream that carried them far away)" thus must refer to Emperor Zhaozong of the Tang Dynasty fleeing the imperial capital; Wang Changling's two poems under the title of "Songs of the Noble Mansion", actually each an appreciative description of a grand spectacle, thus should arbitrarily be explicated as denunciation of extravaganzas outweighing military affairs, and another of his poems, "The Song of the Frontier", actually a depiction of the expansive and bleak frontier, a recollection of a bloody battle, and an extolment of the valour of the garrisoned troops, thus is interpreted by some so-called delving ancient Chinese poetry critics as ridiculing the commanders; Li Bai's "What a Trek to Shu", inspired by the spectacle of geological precipitousness prior to the An Lushan-Shi Siming Rebellion, to those poetry critics who know of the history of the Tang Dynasty, thus is a mockery of Emperor Xuanzong, who fled to Sichuan, and an allegory of the rebellion and its ramifications, so Li Bai is transformed into a sagacious prophet; Song Zhiwen's "Ferrying across the Han River", in the eyes of those ancient Chinese poetry critics who scrutinized what was allegedly the pertinent background, is thus the record of the psychology of Song who, an exile, sneakily escaped homeward, and his "jin xiang qing geng qie (My uneasy heart is beating faster and faster as I am approaching nearer and nearer to my home-place/bu gan wen lai ren (I dare not inquire any of my fellow folks I have met on the road about what has happened at home)" show the state of mind of the escaped. So, it is true that one's background-based intuitive perception, to some extent, helps in interpretation of what is beyond a poem, but, most of the time, it is also the culprit in misinterpreting a poem and depriving it of what it as a poem should have.

The second kind is based on the personality of a poet. Its precursor is seen in *The Book of Change*, which says: "Those who will defect tend to speak remorsefully; those who are confused tend to speak equivocally; those who are kind and virtuous tend speak succinctly; and those who are impetuous tend to speak ramblingly". Indeed, ancient Chinese poetry critics either, by virtue of the language of the poetry of a poet, guess at what type of personality he might have or, by virtue of the personality of a poet, interpret why he used a certain language in his poetry. The notion of one's language embodying one's personality, as a tenet, is seen in Yang Xiong of the West Han Dynasty's *Exemplary Sayings*. By this, for example, almost every one of Du Fu's poems is considered to reflect his personality as a loyalist to his sovereign; into nearly all Tao Yuanming's poems can be read his reclusive personality. And, by the same token, but conversely, to presuppose a poet's personality is to presuppose the meanings, and even the taste, of his poetry. (see Xuzeng [also known as Eran]'s *Eran's Remarks on Poetry*) For example, Bai Juyi's poetry is deemed amiable because of his allegedly amicable personality; Wang Anshi's allegedly uncongenial personality predetermined the uncongeniality in his poetry (see Yuan Mei's *Suiyuan's Remarks on Poetry*). Such personality-based intuitive perception of poetry, to digress, could also apply to appraisal of, for example, Cai Jing's (one of the Song Dynasty prime ministers) calligraphy, which is rated as not worthy of a look altogether, because of his allegedly unworthy personality; thus to pigeonhole his works is a wise decision (see Li Diaoyuan's *Yucun's Remarks on Poetry*). Back to poetry, the previous instances point to one thing: a personality-based intuitive perception of a poem is legitimized. But there are opponents to it. In his *Remarks on Poetry at Yangyi Studio*, Pan Deyu argues that one's personality and poetry should be scrutinized separately or, in other words, just because one has a perverse personality does not necessarily mean that one's poetry is also perverse. To be fair, his objection is not just fair but insightful.

The third kind is based on a poet's intent. In his *Yipiao's Remarks on Poetry*, Xue Xue famously says that "To understand a poem, the reader must discern what its author intended". Actually, prior to Xue, Wu Qiao, in his *Talks about Poetry around the Hearth*, suggests that, "The reader must closely scrutinize a poem, above all, its author's intent". Further back, Liu Xie's observation that "Although people are separated by a long distance only not to see one another in person, one can tell what is on another's mind by perusing his writings" (see his *The Literary Mind and the Carving of Dragons*) could be the precursor to the preceding arguments about the poet's intent-based intuitive perception of poetry. In modern China, some poetry critics still maintain that the standards for poetry critique must be based on poets' intent that compelled their creation, although this affirmation is derided by New Criticism advocates.

Those advocates for the poet's intent-based intuitive perception of a poem are opinionated. As regards a poet's intent, they should bear in mind that they are not in a position to, in a poet's stead, claim what his intent is behind his poem. In actuality, however, they are inclined to impose their intent on the mind of a poet, equating it with the meaning of his poem. In the event, for one thing, they confuse a poet's intent, which actually is their conjecture, and the meaning of his poem, which could have resulted from their scrutiny; thus they are snared in not just erroneous but absurd circular reasoning. A case in point is the aforementioned Qian Xuantong's fallacy, and the most absurd example is Wang Sishi's interpretation, in his *Explication of Du Fu's Intentions in His Poetry*, which is curiously claimed as the most incisive analyses of poets' minds, of one of Du's poems, "The Press-Gang at Shi Hao Village", that the poem was intended to laud the heroine, the elderly lady, for her manly performance by which her plaintive account actually disguised her deliberated decision, and, rather than being the victim of woeful separation from her family for military service in her children's stead, she was a shrewd woman who knew how to deal foxily with the press-gang.

Different from the three types of intuitive perception of poetry previously, the language-based intuitive perception of poetry is recommendable. A word or a phrase, to the Buddhists, is a denomination. As *Verses on the Treasury* teaches, a denomination inspires one's imagination or recollection. Such imagination or recollection entails denotations, which in turn give rise to sensations. For example, denotations of sugar and red bayberry stimulate sweet and sour sensations, respectively. Certainly, the effect of the denotations of specifically the word or phrase and generally the language of the verse(s) of a poem on one is more complex and more delicate. Oblique words and their irregular arrangement in a verse differ with different readers in terms of meaning, analogous to the effect produced by the bright moon as described in *Annotations on "Flower Garland Sutra"*:

> The moon was shedding its brilliance on a pellucid river. Three people separately on board three boats were looking up at it. To one on board the stayed boat, the moon also stayed; to one on board the southbound boat, the moon was moving southward as far as a thousand li; to one on board the northbound boat, the moon was moving northward as far as a thousand li.

On three different lookers. This is one thing. The other thing is that the language used by a poet at a point in history in his poetry can be strange to a later reader or poetry critic. The poetry critic, let us say, has to try every means to reconstruct the context where the poet used the language in order to decode it, on the one hand; on the other, he or she cannot help but inject some new aspects into the interpretation, as noted by Zhong Xing of the Ming Dynasty in his *A Treatise on Poetry*: "Poetry lives. . . . There have been any number of poetry explicators generation after generation, whose explications can differ . . . and such difference is relative. In a word, that explication of a poem changes from time to time is normal". This certainly involves the poetry critic's intuitive perception, which is not limited to but based on the language of a poem. In his *The Literary Mind and the Carving of Dragons*, Liu Xie says that "One feels a poem through its language". Michel Foucault, in his *The Archaeology of Knowledge*, suggests the language-based decoding of what one needs to learn about. Indeed, either a poetry reader or a poetry critic should depend on their language-based intuitive perception to feel a poet's feelings in his poem, for its language contains and insinuates what was involved in the process of its creation. After all, considering that a poet may already have passed away, and taking into account that his poetry embodies his feelings, and since the language of his poetry is an important access to his feelings, his reader or critic has to base their intuitive perception, if they count on it, on the language of their poetry, whose historical cues and insinuations should enable them to truly feel his feelings in his poetry.

To sum up, interpretation of a poem should centre around its language. This certainly does not exclude its critic or reader's language-based intuitive perception. To centre around its language is to find out about the meanings of its words back then and their evolution over a period of time. This is what exegesis is about. At the same time, to engage its critic or reader's language-based intuitive perception is for them to feel the feelings of its author by virtue of what is in its words that concerns the ethos and aesthetic principles back then. Both, necessary for interpretation of a poem, do not preclude the other but, on the contrary, work hand in hand to build an affinity between the poet and his critic or reader. Or, in other words, neither pure linguistics nor pure intuitive perception can fully interpret a poem, so, to fully interpret a poem, they must combine. Here, let us keep in mind what Roman Jakobson, in his *Closing Statement: Linguistics and Poetics*, says: "All of us here, however, definitely, realize that a linguist deaf to the poetic function of language and a literary scholar indifferent to linguistic problems and inconversant with linguistic methods are equally flagrant anachronisms", which apparently may sound not suitable but essentially applies here.

References

1. Brooks, Cleanth. *The Well-Wrought Urn: Studies in the Structure of Poetry*. New York: Harcourt, Brace, 1947.
2. Hawkes, Terence. *Jiegouzhuyi yu fuhaoxue* 结构主义与符号学 (Structuralism and semiotics), translated by Tiepeng Qu 瞿铁鹏. Shanghai: Shanghai Translation Publishing House, 1987.
3. Huang, Ziyun 黄子云. "Yehong shidi" 野鸿诗的 (The Yardsticks by Yehong for Critique of Poetry). In *Qing shihua* 清诗话 (The Poetic Discourses of the Qing Dynasty), edited by Fuzhi Wang 王夫之. Shanghai: Shanghai Classics Publishing House, 1978.
4. Jakobson, Roman. "Yuyanxue yu shixue" 语言学与诗学 (Closing Statement: Linguistics and Poetics). In *Wenxue jiegouzhuyi* 文学结构主义 (Structuralism in Literature: An Introduction), edited by Robert Scholes, translated by Yu Liu 刘豫. Beijing: SDX Joint Publishing Company, 1988.
5. Jiang, Shaoyu 蒋绍愚. *Tangshi yuyan yanjiu* 唐诗语言研究 (A Study of the Language of the Tang Dynasty Poetry). Zhengzhou: Zhongzhou Ancient Literature Publishing House, 1990.
6. Kayser, Wolfgang. *Yuyan de yishu zuopin* 语言的艺术作品 (Das Sprachliche Kunstwerk-Eine Einführungin die Literaturwi−senschaft), translated by Quan Chen 陈铨. Shanghai: Shanghai Translation Publishing House, 1984.
7. Lehmann, Winfred P. *Miaoxie yuyanxue yinlun* 描写语言学引论 (Descriptive Linguistics, An Introduction), translated by Zhaoxiang Jin 金兆骧 and Xiuzhu Chen 陈秀珠. Shanghai: Shanghai Foreign Language Education Press, 1986.
8. Li, Diaoyuan 李调元. "Yucun shihua" 雨村诗话 (Yucun's Remarks on Poetry). In *Qing shihua xubian* 清诗话续编 (A Sequel to the Poetic Discourses of the Qing Dynasty), edited by Shaoyu Guo 郭绍虞. Shanghai: Shanghai Classics Publishing House, 1983.
9. Lieh Tzu 列子. *Liezi jishi* 列子集释 (Annotated Commentary of Liezi, edited by Bojun Yang 杨伯峻). Beijing: Zhonghua Book Company, 1983.
10. Mao, Chunrong. 冒春荣. "Shenyuan shihua" 葚园诗话 (Shenyuan's Poetic Discourse). In *Qing shihua xubian* 清诗话续编 (A Sequel to the Poetic Discourses of the Qing Dynasty), edited by Shaoyu Guo 郭绍虞. Shanghai: Shanghai Classics Publishing House, 1983.
11. Ouyang, Xiu 欧阳修. "Liuyi shihua" 六一诗话 (Liuyi's Commentaries on Poetry). In *Lidai shihua* 历代诗话 (The Commentaries by the Critics of the Past Dynasties on Poetry), edited by Wenhuan He 何文焕. Beijing: Zhonghua Book Company, 1981.
12. Pan, Deyu 潘德舆. "Yangyizhai shihua" 养一斋诗话 (Remarks on Poetry at Yangyi Studio). In *Qing shihua xubian* 清诗话续编 (A Sequel to the Poetic Discourses of the Qing Dynasty), edited by Shaoyu Guo 郭绍虞. Shanghai: Shanghai Classics Publishing House, 1983.
13. Qian, Qianyi 钱谦益. "Xiangguan shuoshu Xu Yuantan shi hou" 香观说书徐元叹诗后 (Appreciation, like Smelling Aroma, of the Poetry by Xu Yuantan). In *Muzhai you xueji* 牧斋有学集 (The Collection of the New Works by Muzhai), by Qianyi Qian 钱谦益. Shanghai: Shanghai Classics Publishing House, 1996.
14. Qian, Xuantong 钱玄同. "Wenxue geming zhi fanxiang" 文学革命之反响 (My Objections to the So-Called Literary Revolution). *Xinqingnian* 新青年 (The New Youth), 4, 1918.
15. Richards, Ivor Armstrong. *The Philosophy of Rhetoric*. London: Oxford University Press, 1936.
16. Santayana, George. *Meigan* 美感 (The Sense of Beauty), translated by Lingzhu Miu 缪灵珠. Beijing: Social Sciences Academic Press, 1982.
17. Shi, Buhua 施补华. "Xian yong shuoshi" 岘佣说诗 (A Garrison Secretary's Talk about Poetry). In *Qing shihua* 清诗话 (The Poetic Discourses of the Qing Dynasty), edited by Fuzhi Wang 王夫之. Shanghai: Shanghai Classics Publishing House, 1978.

18. Wang, Fuzhi 王夫之. "Jiangzhai shihua" 姜斋诗话 (Jiangzhai's Commentaries on Poetry). In *Qing shihua* 清诗话 (The Poetic Discourses of the Qing Dynasty), edited by Fuzhi Wang 王夫之. Shanghai: Shanghai Classics Publishing House, 1978.
19. Wang, Li 王力. *Hanyu shilüxue* 汉语诗律学 (The Chinese Prosody). Shanghai: Shanghai Educational Publishing House, 1979.
20. Wang, Shizhen 王士禛. "Shiyoushi chuanxulu" 诗友诗传续录 (Questions and Answers on Poetry at Gu Fu Yu Pavilion). In *Qing shihua* 清诗话 (The Poetic Discourses of the Qing Dynasty), edited by Fuzhi Wang 王夫之. Shanghai: Shanghai Classics Publishing House, 1978.
21. Wang, Yingkui 王应奎. *Liunan suibi* 柳南随笔 (Liunan's Desultory Notes). Beijing: Zhonghua Book Company, 1983.
22. Wei, Tai 魏泰. "Lin han yinju shihua" 临汉隐居诗话 (Remarks on Poetry in Reclusion on the Han River). In *Lidai shihua* 历代诗话 (The Commentaries by the Critics of the Past Dynasties on Poetry), edited by Wenhuan He 何文焕. Beijing: Zhonghua Book Company, 1981.
23. Weng, Fanggang 翁方纲. "Shizhou shihua" 石洲诗话 (The Commentaries on Poetry at the Rocky Edge of an Islet). In *Qing shihua xubian* 清诗话续编 (A Sequel to the Poetic Discourses of the Qing Dynasty), edited by Shaoyu Guo 郭绍虞. Shanghai: Shanghai Classics Publishing House, 1983.
24. Wimsatt, William Kurtz and Monroe, Curtis Beardsley. "Ganshou miujian" 感受谬见 (The Affective Fallacy), translated by Hongxi Huang 黄宏熙. In *Xinpiping wenji* "新批评" 文集 (An Anthology of the New Criticism Theories), edited by Yiheng Zhao 赵毅衡. Beijing: Social Science Academic Press, 1988.
25. Xie, Zhen 谢榛. "Siming shuhua" 四溟诗话 (A Sea-in-the-Four-Direction Recluse's Remarks on Poetry). In *Lidai shihua xubian* 历代诗话续编 (A Sequel to the Commentaries by the Critics of the Past Dynasties on Poetry), edited by Fubao Ding 丁福保. Beijing: Zhonghua Book Company, 1983.
26. Xu, Zeng 徐增. "Eran shihua" 而庵诗话 (Eran's Remarks on Poetry). In *Qing shihua* 清诗话 (The Poetic Discourses of the Qing Dynasty), edited by Fuzhi Wang 王夫之. Shanghai: Shanghai Classics Publishing House, 1978.
27. Yang, Xiong 杨雄. "Fayan" 法言 (Exemplary Sayings). In *Ershierzi* 二十二子 (A Collection of Twenty-Two Ancient Chinese Classics), edited by Suoyin Zhejiang shuju huikeben 缩印浙江书局汇刻本 (A size-reduced block-printed edition by Zhejiang Book Company). Shanghai: Shanghai Classics Publishing House, 1986.
28. Yuan, Mei 袁枚. *Suiyuan shihua* 随园诗话 (Suiyuan's Remarks on Poetry). Beijing: People's Literature Publishing House, 1960.
29. Yuan, Mei 袁枚. "Xu shipin" 续诗品 (A Sequel to "Critique of Poetry"). In *Qing shihua* 清诗话 (The Poetic Discourses of the Qing Dynasty), edited by Fuzhi Wang 王夫之. Shanghai: Shanghai Classics Publishing House, 1978.
30. Zhang, Jie 张戒. "Suihantang shihua" 岁寒堂诗话 (Notes on Poetry Written in the Pine and Cypress Studio). In *Lidai shihua xubian* 历代诗话续编 (A Sequel to the Commentaries by the Critics of the Past Dynasties on Poetry), edited by Fubao Ding 丁福保. Beijing: Zhonghua Book Company, 1983.
31. Zhang, Qianyi 张谦宜. "Jianzhai shi tan" 絸斋诗谈 (Jianzhai's Remarks on Poetry). In *Qing shihua xubian* 清诗话续编 (A Sequel to the Poetic Discourses of the Qing Dynasty), edited by Shaoyu Guo 郭绍虞. Shanghai: Shanghai Classics Publishing House, 1983.
32. Zhou, Liangpei 周良沛. "Xu Zhimo shiji bianhou" 徐志摩诗集·编后 (Epilogue to the Collection of Xu Zhimo's Poetry). *Xinwenxue luncong* 新文学论丛 (Theses on the New Literature), 4, 1980.

3 Thought flow and word order

Seeming disengagement of thinking from verse

There is no need to explain what the word order of the verses of a poem is about. Then what is a poet's thought flow? The notion of thought flow is not conceived ad hoc; on the contrary, it has a long history. Liu Xie (see his *The Literary Mind and the Carving of Dragons*) and later ancient Chinese poetry critics used such notions as the thread of meaning, the vein of blood, the movement of word, the meridian, the flow of energy, and so forth. They can be seen as the precursors to the notion of the thought flow of a poet in his poem.

Traditionally, ancient Chinese poetry critics seem not to bother to define, and thus delimit, the meaning of a notion. So interpretation of a notion can be either too broad or too narrow in the case of poetry. Besides, ancient Chinese poetry critics tended to confuse the meaning of the notion of a poet's thought flow. For example, on one occasion, it was related to, in the words of those ancient Chinese poetry critics, a vein of blood, which was believed to enliven a poem the way the veins of blood do to a human, while, on another occasion, it was related to a logical link, without which they believed a poem would end up being an incoherent mess (see Wu Hang of the Song Dynasty [also known as Master Huanxi because he lived as a hermit at Huanxi]'s *Poetic Commentaries at the Huanxi Quarters*). Such indefiniteness and confusion may correspond with the Taoist tenet of "The Way of Heaven can be defined, but, at the same time, the Way of Heaven changes too much to define", and allows ancient Chinese poetry critics, especially those who are either indolent or obsessed with elusiveness, to use the notion to refer to concepts such as, apart from what has been mentioned, energy (气 *qi* in pinyin), the Way (道 *dao*), and appeal (韵 *yun*), which are metaphysical, and subtle (含蓄 *han xu*), abandoned (放荡 *fang dang*), detached (冲淡 *chong dan*), and natural (自然 *zi ran*), which are descriptive, at will. Using such indefinite notions widely in interpretation of poetry naturally causes disputes among Chinese literati over its definition.

So, before using the notion of the thought flow of a poet, let me define it as follows:

> A poet's thought flow is a process in which the meaning of a poem unfolds or a dynamic continuous process in which the reader perceives the meaning of a poem.

40 *Thought flow and word order*

In this chapter, we will discuss the relationships between a poet's thought flow and the word order of the verses of his poem, that is, how the thought flow in a poem engages with and disengages from the movement of its verses at different points of the development of ancient Chinese poetry.

3.1. A new perspective on the word order of the verses of a poem

Speech tells what is on one's mind, or one's language gives expression to one's thought. Indeed, when one speaks, one certainly is speaking their mind, unless they deliberately gloss over their speech or tell a lie. So both speech and thought flow should agree. In this regard, James H-Y Tai asserts:

> The word order of the ancient Chinese language is not an arbitrary mechanism about semantics and syntax. Rather, it corresponds with the thought flow in a genuinely natural way.

Compared to the word order in Noam Chomsky's universal grammar for the Western languages, in my opinion, the word order of the Chinese language should more naturally conform more to what James H-Y Tai calls "the principle of temporal sequence", which is believed to be followed by one who speaks or writes in a certain language. There are other arguments. For example, a sentence in the Chinese language, unlike that in any of the Western languages, which is constructed in the order of subject plus predicate plus object, is constructed in the order of the degree of emphasis on words, which is that more emphasized words precede less emphasized ones, so the Chinese language can be called one of topicalization, as mentioned by Winfred Philip Lehmann in his *Descriptive Linguistics: An Introduction*.

It should be pointed out that the Chinese language studied either by James H-Y Tai or by Winfred Philip Lehmann is that used by Chinese people in their daily life. Whether their notion of the Chinese language is true depends on the linguists of this field of expertise to verify. Nonetheless, one thing is certain: their notion does not apply globally to the Recent Style poetry. Indeed, not only these linguists' efforts but also so many other linguists' efforts prove to no avail when it comes to the language of this style of Chinese poetry. By analogy, they have the keys, but none of their keys can open the lock on the door to its linguistic mansion, or they want to use their bank's universal credit card in an old tribe where people barter with one another and find out that such cards are useless. This is because the word order of the language of the Recent Style poetry is neither of temporal sequence nor of topicalization. Take this pair of verses: "han zhu yi gu yan (verbatim: cold islet one solitary goose) (The chilly islet in the midst of the river, a lonely wild goose)/ xi yang qian wan shan (verbatim: setting sun thousands of mounts) (A setting sun and range upon range of mountains)" of Liu Changqing's "A Poem Composed at a Riverside Pavilion in Late Autumn", for instance. Do these juxtaposed images, like the ones in "ku teng lao shu hun ya (Dry veins, ancient trees, and crows in twilight)" in Ma Zhiyuan of the Yuan Dynasty's aria-wise poem, appear in the order a "topicalization sequence" dictates? The answer is negative. Another example is Du Fu's "lv chui feng zhe sun (verbatim: Green dangling winds snapped bamboo shoots) (Green dangling, wind-snapped bamboo shoots)/hong zhang yu fei mei (verbatim: Red split rain fattened plum) (Red split, rain-fattened plums)", which does not run in the customarily syntactic word order, much less in keeping with the "temporal sequence": did the poet first perceive "green", then "dangling", then "winds", then "snapped", and finally "bamboo shoots"? The answer is negative too. Evidently, any "universal" rule for the word order does not apply here.

That said, there must be something, whatever it may be, for the word order of the Recent Style poetry. Only by virtue of this something can a Recent Style poet communicate successfully with the reader and vice versa. Otherwise, their communication will get nowhere. Then what is it?

Before answering this question, let us look at a few more examples, such as "ke bing liu yin yao (verbatim: The guest sick stays for medication) (I, far away from home, had to stay because of my illness and need for medication)/chun shen mai wei hua (verbatim: Spring deep bought for flowers) (Deep in spring, I bought a garden to grow flowers)" (in Du Fu's "A Small Garden"), "xi cao wei feng an (verbatim: Fine grasses, gentle breezes, banks) (Fine grasses along the banks were swaying in gentle breezes)/wei qiang du ye zhou (verbatim: A high mast, a lonely night, a boat) (My boat with its high mast was moored, alone, at night.)" (in Du Fu's "Reflection One Night on my Home-Bound Journey"), "bai hua yan wai duo (verbatim: White flowers, over the eaves, in clusters) (White flowers are blooming, in clusters, over the eaves)/qing liu jian qian shao (verbatim: Green willows, before the banister, in lashes) (Green willows are lashing, like whips, before the banister)" (in Du Fu's "An Inscription on Beiqiao Tower at Xinjin"), "ri zhao hong ni si (verbatim: sunshine rainbow resemblance) (In the sunshine waterfalls appeared as brilliantly colourful as rainbows)/tian qing feng yu wen (verbatim: Sky clear wind rain hear) (A rainstorm seemed to be heard even if the skies were cloudless)" (in Zhang Jiuling of the Tang Dynasty's "Looking Out from Hukou at the Mount Lu's Waterfalls"), and "liu se qing shan ying (verbatim: Willow tinge green mounts reflect) (The tinge of willows was reflecting the greenness of luxuriant mounts)/li hua xi niao cang (verbatim: Pear blossom set sun birds hide) (Birds back in twilight were hiding themselves among flowery pear trees)" (in Wang Wei's "Composed at a Buddhist Temple on a Spring Day"). As is obvious, these verses are, in terms of syntactic structure, transposed and elliptical, and they have no customary word order to speak of. This, however, neither surprises nor confuses the reader, who not only takes it for granted but can well understand them. Why? "xiang dao zhuo yu ying wu li (verbatim: Aromatic rice grains pecked leftover parrots) (The rice grains are the leftovers after parrots have pecked their fill)/bi wu qi lao feng huang zhi (verbatim: Leafy Chinese parasol trees nestle old a phoenix branch) (The Leafy Chinese parasol tree is the one on whose branch an old phoenix has perched for rest)" (in one of Du Fu's eight-poem series entitled "Inspired by the Autumnal View") have no word order to speak of either, but Wang Sishi sees them as natural. He feels that "the impetus inherent in the poem calls for it, should the verses run smoothly and coherently". In other words, this is just how they should be ordered, however asyntactical they appear. According to Rudolf Arnheim's *Visual Thinking*, "Verbal language is a one-dimensional string of words because it is used by intellectual thinking to label sequences of concepts". Therefore, unlike a painting, which simultaneously displays various images on one surface, and unlike a duet or quartet, which is made for the simultaneous performance of multiple instruments or voices, a poetic verse should "be combined in succession. . . . Language is used linearly because each word or cluster of words stands for an intellectual concept, and such concepts can be combined only in succession". But the verses in question, due to transposition and/or ellipsis, read like no more than a disarray of words, which should make it hard to tell how they are logically coherent and what their author's thought flow is. The actuality is, however, that such asyntactical word order poses no problem to ancient Chinese poetry critics. Shen Kuo and Zhao Cigong of the Song Dynasty do not consider this asyntactical word order an impediment to their interpretation of the verses constructed as such. So when it comes to interpretation of Du Fu's verses, they do so effortlessly. Then what is "this something" that facilitates their effortless interpretation? Is it ellipsis and/or transposition, which, albeit asyntactical, they are used to and grasp; thus they do not see it as a challenge?

Some Chinese linguists argue thus, and they include transposition and ellipsis in the family of grammar. Some Chinese poetry critics have no answer in this regard but simply one-size-fits-all empty platitudes. The former attempts at expanding the territory of grammar. The latter try to trick their way around what they deem unanswerable. Both fail to get at *the* right answer. In that case, why not let us look into the nature of the relationships between the deep linguistic structure and the surface linguistic structure, which may eventually yield the solution?

According to Chomsky, the deep linguistic structure, which reflects what is basically and truly on one's mind, is common to all languages, whereas the surface linguistic structures, because of the different transformative (from the deep linguistic structure to a surface linguistic structure) mechanisms, differ with different languages. The deep linguistic structure is about one's initial impression of either still or motional concrete objects in the external world around them. This external world presents itself in various forms and colours, and the initial impression of it is images simultaneously juxtaposed on one's mental screen. Allen Ginsberg, the epitome of the Beat Generation, once described this kind of impression, though he sounded like a deranged man. His description was indirectly confirmed by Johann Gottfried Herder, except that, although the latter's external world is complicated, messy, and dynamic, its images projected on one's mental screen, according to the latter, will be simplified into order, a result of the process of transformation from the external to the internal. (See his *On the Origin of Language*.) At any rate, the external objects perceived by one will be internalized into subjective or rather mental images. In the process, one's focus can change, and the perceived objects will be sifted. The processed results are what one decides are the images of the meaningful objects. And they are the initial impression of the external world around one. This impression constitutes the deep linguistic structure. The deep linguistic structure, by way of a thought-language transformative mechanism, is transformed into a surface linguistic structure, or rather a sentence, whose order, on many occasions, is regulated by certain grammatical rules and whose meaning is already predetermined by the deep linguistic structure, as noted by Rudolf Arnheim and Chomsky.

Transformation of the linguistic deep structure, which is out of word order, to a surface linguistic structure, which is in word order, has two aspects that are worthy of note. One is about its evolution. To Chomsky, this aspect has to do with the evolution of one's language acquisition faculty that is responsible for organizing a sentence in word order. Evidenced by the relevant studies by anthropologists and historians, the farther the surface linguistic structure is traced back, the simpler and more fragmentary it is grammatically, as demonstrated by what is represented in Egyptian hieroglyphs, Chinese oracle bone inscriptions, or a primitive tribal language. The other is about representation by a surface linguistic structure of the deep linguistic structure. This aspect is a process of transforming what is represented by the deep linguistic structure into what is represented by a surface deep structure in a linear word order as syntactically required. Such a word order demands not just appropriate placement of such words as nouns, verbs, and adjectives but also clear logical relationships in terms of time, space, and cause and effect, which thus needs the interspersion of function words like conjunctional, propositional, and adverbial ones. Only at this point can such a transformation be completed. As mentioned, surface linguistic structures differ due to different transformative mechanisms. That is why different languages have different traits. But, however a language is, those who use it as their native language have no difficulty in communicating in it with one another among themselves, as, first, as mentioned, they share the same deep linguistic structure, which predetermines the meaning of what they speak or write about; second, they have developed the same habit of using their native language; and, finally, their sense of their native language is deep rooted in their souls.

Thus, we have the following inferences:

First, a certain set of grammatical rules is not independent of but an intrinsic part of a certain language itself. They are discovered, extracted, abstracted, and formulated by grammarians. There is no one-size-fits-all grammatical rule for any aspect of a language. So there is no telling, by this or that grammatical rule, whether a sentence pattern or rather the word order of a sentence is right, not to mention the deep linguistic structure, whose poetic embodiment, such as Recent Style poetry, can contradict a linguist's grammatical analysis in terms of word order.
Second, the deep linguistic structure, that is, the juxtaposed images in the sentential form of content word, as a result of its having been transformed into or represented by a certain surface linguistic structure, is equivocal. Such equivocality, which is caused by ellipsis, transposition, and a lack of logical coherence in terms of time, space, cause and effect, subject and object, and so on, is the very effect that the language of, let us say the Recent Style poetry should aim at.
Third, in the process of the deep linguistic structure or rather juxtaposed images being transformed into a certain surface linguistic structure or ordered line of words, the more syntactic such an order is, the farther removed it is from what

the deep linguistic structure truly is, or, in other words, the more ellipses and transpositions, the closer to the deep linguistic structure. The deep linguistic structure in question refers here to what is represented in the form of a Recent Style poem: a poet's initial impression of the externalities around him. And this he expects the reader to appreciate.

The way of ancient Chinese thinking is said to be closest to the deep linguistic structure. This does not mean disparagement or acclaim of any kind. The ways of thinking are equal and benefit one another. This explains why Lucien Levy-Bruhl's famous *Primitive Mentality* is inspired by the Chinese *Records of the Historian*, and *The Book of Change* is credited partly for Carl Gustav Jung's discovery of the principles of, for example, cause-effect and synchronization, as in his *Psychology and Literature*. Back to the aforementioned way of ancient Chinese thinking, when it is embodied in the Recent Style poetry, the latter thus features:

First, pictorialness. A Recent Style poem is a picture of objects, because, as Leonard Robert Palmer understands, the Chinese language is a simplified system that represents imagery by its own rules, or, as in the eyes of amazed Ezra Pound, a Chinese word itself is a vivid meaningful picture, which a Western language may lack.
Second, thus, self-evidence in meaning of its words. This trait enables each Chinese content word, wherever it is placed in a verse, and with no need for contextual reference, to convey its meaning effectively to the reader.
Third, thus, retainment of the simplicity of the deep linguistic structure, which is shared by the Chinese reader, who can understand verses composed as such, depending partly on his or her own brain-work to collocate their words, whose meanings are already predetermined and circumscribed.

Here, let us listen to what Li Jinxi, a modern Chinese scholar, says:

> When it comes to a sentence in Chinese, its emphasis is laid more on feeling than on form. Besides, in terms of form, a sentence in Chinese is not so grammatically complete as that of a Western language, so the pictorialness of the Chinese words helps in comprehension of the meanings embodied in them, without which their meanings can be elusive.
> There is no limit to how the rhetoric of a literary work in Chinese should be used only if its logical relationships are clear.

Li's remarks seem to echo Wilhelm von Humboldt's opinion of the Chinese language.

Their perspectives further show that Chinese words are free to be transposed and that the verses thus constructed are syntactically simple (as a result of ellipsis); structurally flexible; and, on the part of the poet, arbitrary. This should, in a way, differentiate the language of Recent Style poetry from a Western language, in that the former should more closely reflect the deep linguistic structure.

It is a linguist's duty to judge the merits and demerits of the Chinese language. Here I want to point out that it is thanks to its features that the Chinese language should perfectly meet the needs for composition of Recent Style poetry. First, it enables a Recent Style poet to naturally and vividly represent his or her initial impression of the world around him or her in a diverse, colourful, and vigorous, rather than a logical, abstract, and cold, manner. Second, a poet is said to think like a child, who does much less illogically than spontaneously; this should also be the case of a Recent Style poet's way of thinking, and it perfectly embodies such thinking. Third, it enables a Recent Style poet to create a poetic world that is misty and mystic. And, finally, it can equivocate what a Recent Style poet means in his or her verses, which will in turn inspire the reader's meditation, imagination, and association, and this should be what a Recent Style poet expects of the reader.

Take for instance the celebrated pair of verses "ji sheng mao dian yue (verbatim: Rooster crow, thatched inn, moon) (The crow of roosters around the thatched inn in the moonlight)/ren ji ban qiao shuang (verbatim: Human footprints, plank bridge, frost) (A few human footprints in the frost covering the bridge of plank)" of Wen Tingyun of the Tang Dynasty's poem "Early Departure from the Inn at the Shang Mount":

This pair of verses can be divided into six noun phrases, each of which represents either an aural or a visual image. The six juxtaposed individual images together make a poetic panorama, whose ambience can instantly be perceived by the reader. The ellipses in this pair of verses are obvious. If the same panorama is presented in the vernacular modern Chinese, more words have to be added: "(I heard) rooster crow, (being informed about daybreak) (and I looked up and saw well above the) thatched inn the moon/(I lowered my head and spotted) a few human footprints (on) the plank bridge (for it was covered by) frost". And, on top of the addition, there may be an unuttered ejaculation: "How weary I as a wayfarer could be". Back to the original. Composed economically of content words merely for both the aural and visual images, they perfectly reflect the deep linguistic structure, as previously discussed, which lacks any function word as the indicator of any logical relationship therein, in the poet's mind. But who would deny that these images themselves already represent, probably equivocally yet semantically circumscribed, what the poet intended to mean and that the poet's thought flow can be followed through these images? That is why this pair of verses earned Li Dongyang of the Ming Dynasty's acclaim (see his *Litang's Remarks on Poetry*).

To sum up, when it comes to the word order of, for example, Recent Style poetry, it is the reflection of the deep linguistic structure in the poet's mind or rather the way of thinking. The traits of the Chinese language, which should be consummate for versification, should be credited for the formation of such word order. The word order of this nature, despite ellipsis and transposition, still poses no problem to the Chinese reader, because he or she is mentally equipped with the same deep linguistic structure. So, a Recent Style poet depends totally on this deep linguistic structure and these features of Chinese words to devise and create a poetic world almost at will, believing that the reader can fully appreciate this poetic world.

Let us review what Fan Wen of the Song Dynasty (also known as Qianxi) in his *Qianxi's Perspective on Poetry*, says:

> The ancient "lv shi" poems (i.e., tonally and metrically regulated five-word-a-verse or seven-word-a-verse eight-verse poems, one of the two types of the Recent Style poems which matures in the Tang Dynasty) are wonderfully structured. Their verses seem out of order, but their meanings are clear and the poets' thought flow in them is as coherent as a string of beads.

Indeed, the syntactic disorder of this nature, or rather the mere juxtaposed imagery, is the nature of Recent Style poetry, which stands for a type of art.

3.2. Seeming disengagement of a poet's thought flow from the word order of his verses as a result of defamiliarization of the familiar poetic language

In all fairness, ancient Chinese literati did not always communicate in a disordered and confusing manner which would lead to much guesswork; they did, probably unconsciously, obey what are now termed grammatical rules so that their readers would not be confounded by their otherwise ungrammatical writings. Among them, those earliest ancient Chinese poets did not resort to techniques such as ellipsis and transposition, the way their successors deliberately did, in versification.

Until it was realized that there should be a special language for poetry, until practical purposes gave way to belles lettres, had ancient Chinese poetry linguistically been prosaic or vernacular, which is that a poet's thought flow in his poem back then had been transparent, smooth, and easy to grasp and that the word order of his poem had been syntactically complete and customary. The differences, if there were any, between poetry and prose at the time were that the former could be rhymed and the latter unrhymed; that the former could use fewer function words than the latter; and that the former's verses could be symmetrized, whereas the latter's sentences were not symmetrized. The reason a poem as such should have been taken as a poem was that the reader back then presupposed it was a poem, so he or she would recite it with a poetic cadence, not the way he or she would read a piece of prosaic writing.

Specifically, *The Book of Songs* features the use of such auxiliary function words as 之 (zhi), 乎 (hu), 焉 (yan), 也 (ye), 者 (zhe), 云 (yun), 矣 (yi), 兮 (xi), and 而 (er). Liu Xie, in his *The Literary Mind and the Carving of Dragons*, defends this feature, saying that those function words "seem useless in terms of elucidation; in fact, such usage is ingenious". But Hong Mai of the Song Dynasty discerns the similarities between the poems of *The Book of Songs* and ancient Chinese prose, observing in his *Five Notes from the Tolerant Studio* that "So far prose writers have also used these function words". Fei Gun, also of the Song Dynasty, does not discern what Hong Mai does, although he, in his *Notes of Liangxi*, points out that "Too many function words in a poem weaken its charm as a poem".

One case in point is "guan guan ju jiu (Kuan-Kuan sounds an osprey)/zai he zhi zhou (On the islet in a river)/yao tiao shu nv (A modest, retiring, virtuous, young lady)/jun zi hao qiu (For our prince a good mate she)" (from *The Book of Songs*). As the verses indicate, the perspective of the probable observer shifted naturally from an osprey on the islet in a river that was sounding "kuan-kuan" to a fair young lady who was regarded as a perfect match for a prince; the word order of these verses is no different from that in the pre-Qin people's daily communication: natural, normal, and complete with the necessary parts of speech, such as the attribute and adverbial, which are rightly placed. Is there any distinction between, for example, "An osprey that is sounding 'kuan-kuan' is on the islet in a river and a young lady who is modest, retiring, and virtuous is a good mate for our prince", a prosaic version, and the previous original, except for a few more insignificant words in the former?

Another case is the four concluding verses of "A Long Song" in the collection of Han Yue-Fu's poems: "bai chuan dong dao hai (All rivers flow eastward and eventually into the seas)/he shi fu xi gui (Whoever ever sees them running back westward)/shao zhuang bu nu li (Strive for the better when you are young)/lao da nai shang bei (Or you shall lament over the past when old)". Likewise, just as the addition of a few unimportant words will turn it into a prosaic piece: "All rivers flow eastward and eventually into the seas. Tell me whoever among you ever sees them running back westward? Listen to me, let's strive for the better when you are young; or else, mark my words, you shall lament over the past when you are old".

There are many other similar cases, such as the poems in "A Collection of Nineteen Ancient Poems". They, extolled by Zhong Rong of the Southern Dynasties as the best of the ancient Chinese poems ever composed before his time, and regarded by Jiao Ran, a Buddhist monk-poet of the Tang Dynasty, as the epitome of the Eastern Han Style poetry, are "linguistically simple and plain yet connotatively subtle and profound . . . and betray no trace of human exertion. They read, in every way, like daily communication, thus natural", as noted by Kobo Daishi, an ancient Japanese Buddhist monk, in his *Treatise on the Secret Treasury of Literary Mirror*.

These examples show that there was less than an iota of dissimilarity between poetry and prose back then. Here, let us cite Xie Zhen's remarks in his *A Sea-in-the-Four-Direction Recluse's Remarks on Poetry* as a further proof: "Those poems are so simple and plain with no vestige of artificiality. They give the impression that a scholar is having a natural small talk with one of his friends".

But no distinction between poetry and prose back then would eventually harm the former. This is because the prosaic word order, the transparent poet's thought flow, and the simple and clear meaning of the former, though natural and intimate, would make poetry, which should have been idiosyncratic, read much less like poetry, and, worse, if this style had continued, poetry of such style would have eventually lost its appeal to the reader, for he or she would have eventually felt fed up with such a style of poetry, just like a child will feel sick after playing for a long time with an unchallenging and unexciting toy or how eating too much of one soup can also ruin one's appetite. In that case, the need for a language particular to poetry became urgent so that poetry would differ totally from prose or daily speech.

In this regard, Xie Lingyun, as well as his peers and successors, contributed remarkably, which led to the birth of the Yongming Style (Yongming, the title of the reigning period of Emperor Wu of the Qi period of the Southern Dynasties) or rather the nascent Recent Style poetry, which developed and matured around the early years of the Tang Dynasty. This part of the history of the development of the language of ancient Chinese poetry is that of, in the term used by Viktor Shklovsky, a major representative of the Formalism critic school in Russia, "defamiliarization", that is, the pursuit of a language particular to poetry. Xie Lingyun took the lead in this movement. His poetic language, not as plain and natural as that of the past poetry, read as more refined and more literary. Interestingly, this poetic language was criticized later by Yan Yu, popularly known as Yan Canlang, of the Song Dynasty, for having altogether discarded the past well-established linguistic standards for poetry, saying that the language of Xie's poetry, contrary to that used by the poets between the reign of Jian'an and the end of the East Han Dynasty, which had plainly and directly expressed what they had seen and how they had felt, focused too much on wording. To be fair, however, it was just Xie's heresy that started the reformation of the language of past poetry (which will be discussed in detail): fewer and fewer function words, more and more symmetrical antitheses, attention to tonal and metrical schemes, weighed and elegant wording, and the like. And his contemporaries such as Yan Yanzhi and Xie Zhuang also joined in his endeavour. Thus a new poetic language emerged and prevailed. Later, as a reinforcement, Shen Yue, Xie Tiao, Zhou Yong, and Liu Hui, poetry critics and/or poets, also of the Southern Dynasties, in the course of "the pursuit of the utmost sophistication", theorized about the "Eight Defects", which quickened the pace of the divergence of poetry, in linguistic terms, from prose or daily speech. The characteristics of such poetic language are, to borrow the epithets used by Viktor Shklovsky in his *Theory of Prose*, "difficult", "laborious", "impeding", and "distorted", because, also in the words of Viktor Shklovsky, "the aim of poetry is to reverse that process, to defamiliarize that with which we are overly familiar, to 'creatively deform' the usual, the normal, and so to inculcate a new, childlike, non-jaded vision in us". Indeed, when the language, certainly including its word order, of ancient Chinese poetry started to bore the reader as a result of having been confused with that of prose or daily speech, the time came when it needed reforming to keep alive the appealing novelty of ancient Chinese poetry.

René Wellek and Austin Warren, in their *Theory of Literature*, say that "the intellectual content of most poetry . . . is usually much exaggerated. If we analyze many famous poems admired for their philosophy, we frequently discover mere commonplaces concerning man's mortality or the uncertainty of fate". They talk about the content of poetry. By extension, their opinion also applies to the language of poetry or rather ancient Chinese poetry. In fact, even in terms of content, ancient Chinese poetry before the Southern Dynasties or rather the time of Xie Lingyun also mainly concerns "intellectual" "commonplaces", such as individuals and their societies in terms of moral integrity and noble deeds, man and nature in terms of mortality and immortality, and person-to-person relationships in terms of love and feuds, not to mention its prosaic or simply vernacular language. And there were signs back then that this would threaten the survival of ancient Chinese poetry. So, presumably aware of such a threat, Xie Lingyun, as well as other contemporary poets, began to reform past Chinese poetry by blending reflection on what concerns life and sentiment into descriptions of scenery and, more importantly, by exploring the uncharted territory of poetic language. Here, let us focus on how they reformed poetic language. Xie Zhen, in his *A Sea-in-the-Four-Direction Recluse's Remarks on Poetry*, after lauding "A Collection of Nineteen Ancient Poems" for their reading "like chit-chats without any vestige of exertion on wording", comments, not without a note of contempt, that

> The language of the poems of the Wei, Western Jin and Eastern Jin dynasties was half vernacular and half literary. Into the Qi and Liang periods of the Southern Dynasties, the poems were written, without an exception, in the literary language. It saves a poet much trouble to exploit the vernacular whereas it can rack a poet's brains to employ the literary language. And the vernacular sounds natural while the literary language feels affected.

Indeed, a coterie of poetry critics of the Ming Dynasty, with Xie Zhen at the helm, directed by their unjustified opinion of "naturalness", favoured the poetry before the emergence of Recent Style poetry. But, from the perspective of development, should seemingly affected and unnatural poetic language not be regarded as part of the pursuit of linguistic defamiliarization by poets of and since the Southern Dynasties? Poetry, by nature, is not an effortless genre, so the poet is compelled to work hard on even a single verse for some astounding effect. Plainness and naturalness are not defects, but to enshrine them in versification is a defect; otherwise, why not simply scribble doggerel? True, the vernacular language sounds familiar and intimate, but, as endless repetitious chit-chat can bore one, so the vernacular language can make the reader jaded when it is invariably pervasive in poetry. So, that is why the poets of the Southern Dynasties, who might have been aware of what the language of past Chinese poetry had or would have resulted in, started a campaign of linguistic reformation in versification: to juxtapose images; to minimize function words; to use a new word order, if it could be so called; to devise demanding intra- and intertextual tonal and metrical schemes; and so forth. Eventually, they distinguished poetry from either prose or daily speech, thus developing a new set of aesthetic standards for versification and appreciation, of which ellipsis and transposition are important parts.

As for ellipsis in versification since the Southern Dynasties, subject pronouns like "I" and "you"; spatial prepositions like "in", "at", "on", and so on; defining copulative words like "is"; auxiliary words like "zhi" (roughly an English equivalent of "of"); end-stopped interjections (no such English equivalent) like "hu", "ye", and "yan"; and so forth are left out.

Ellipsis as such in nascent and mature Recent Style poetry does not prevent the Chinese reader from comprehending it. The Chinese reader can use, for example, their intuitive perception to find out about what is left out and what it may mean; thus a poet's thought flow in his poem, even if not as transparent as in poetry before the Southern Dynasties, can still be discerned and followed throughout. And this should also be credited partly to the aforementioned self-evidence in meaning of Chinese words, as well as to their shared deep linguistic structure.

Ellipsis has these benefits. It helps both to antithetically symmetrize verses of a poem within a scheme of tone and meter and to juxtapose its images. Also it helps to subtilize a poem, which is due to ellipsis of adverbs and prepositions, which in turn obscures temporal and spatial relationships, and of subjects, which in turn multiplies the otherwise one and only perspective.

Let us look next at transposition. As a result of ellipsis, for example, of function words, the chain-like verse of a poem is broken loose; thus the words in the verse are free to be transposed. Free transposition of words in a verse makes it open to interpretations. Thus a poem as such, which is already subtle because of ellipsis, is further subtilized.

Here are two pairs of verses respectively by He Xun and Jiang Zong of the Southern Dynasties:

bai nian ji si shu (verbatim: A hundred years accretion dead trees)/qian chi gua han teng (verbatim: A thousand-chi [chi, a Chinese measurement unit of length, width, height, etc.] hang cold vines)
                    (in He Xun's "When I Ferried across Lianqi")

feng chuang chuan shi dou (verbatim: Winds through a hole in a rock)/yue yong fu shuang song (verbatim: Moon/Moonlight casement caress frost pines)
                    (in Jiang Zong's "When I lodged in the Buddhist
                                Monk's Residence at Longqiuyan")

Ellipsis is obvious in the verses. This can lead to free transposition (here mainly free collocation) of the words in them. And they combine to equivocate the meanings. Who can interpret exactly what the verses mean? For example, does He's "bai nian ji si shu" mean "A hundred years have seen accretion of dead trees" or "For a hundred years have settled those accreted dead trees"? Does Jiang's "yue yong fu shuang song" mean "Moonlight is caressing pines covered with a film of frost outside the casement" or "Moonlight is shining through the casement upon the pines covered with a film of frost"? Which of them is appropriate depends on how the reader, by his or her aesthetic experience, collocates the images juxtaposed in the verses.

Such open-ended verses make up a large portion of the corpus of the Recent Style poetry of the Tang Dynasty, such as "guan kan bin ke er tong xi (verbatim: Habitually see visitors children happy) (His children have got used to welcoming visitors with smiles)/de shi jie chu niao shou xun (verbatim: Gain food steps birds beasts tamed) (There is always food scattered on the steps so that birds are even domesticated flocking there)" (in Du Fu's "Our Southern Neighbour") and "sheng zao ji xian zhi ye duan (verbatim: Crow early rooster first know night short) (Roosters crowing at daybreak are the first to be aware that night is shortening)/se nong liu zui zhan chun duo (verbatim: Colour deep willows take up the most spring) (Willows turning dark green have more share of spring than all others on earth" (in Bai Juyi's "Recollecting Weizhi in Early Spring").

Here "xi cao wei feng an (verbatim: Fine grasses, gentle breezes, banks)/wei qiang du ye zhou (verbatim: A high mast, a lonely night, a boat) (in Du Fu's "Reflection One Night on my Home-Bound Journey") is worthy of a special mention. This pair of verses are composed of sheer noun words and phrases or, in other words, just juxtapose these perceived images (i.e., the representation of, as previously discussed, the poet's deep linguistic structure): "xi cao (delicate grasses)", "wei feng (faint winds)", "an (banks)", "wei qiang (a stark mast)", "du ye (a lone night)", and "zhou (a boat)", between which the poet uses neither connective words that otherwise should have indicated spatial and possessional relationships nor even verbs. Thus, as with the previous instances, their resultant equivocality allows for more than one interpretation (the very poetic appeal), such as either "Faint winds are swaying delicate bank grasses/The stark mast on a boat is standing upright alone at night", "Faint winds are blowing across the banks overgrown with delicate grasses/A boat with an upright mast is moored alone at night", "Delicate grasses on the banks are being swayed by faint winds/The stark mast on a boat is standing upright alone at night", and "Delicate grasses, faint winds across the banks/Stark mast, a lone night boat". However they are interpreted, the poet's thought flow thereof corresponds and can be perceived and followed all the way by the reader. Ouyang Xiu, in his *Liuyi's Commentaries on Poetry*, annotates Mei Shengyu of the Song Dynasty's annotations on Wen Tingyun's "ji sheng mao dian yue (verbatim: Rooster crow, thatched inn, moon) (The crow of roosters around the thatched inn in the moonlight)/ren ji ban qiao shuang (verbatim: Human footprints, plank bridge, frost) (A few human footprints in the frost covering the bridge of plank)": "A poet attains such by heart, his reader feels it by telepathy, and this kind of feel is beyond description". Indeed, even if the reader may deviate from the so-called authorized interpretation of a poem, the deviation is still within the scope of meaning circumscribed by the images of the poem and thus one of its multifaceted interpretations, a result of combination of his or her own aesthetic experience and what can be represented in the poem. This is what a poem is intended to achieve, as Terence Hawks, in his *Structuralism and Semiotics*, says: "The poet thus aims to disrupt 'stock responses', and to generate a heightened awareness: to restructure our ordinary perception of 'reality'".

3.3. Importance of disengagement of a poet's thought flow from the word order of his verses

Ancient Chinese poetry critics have various arguments about relationships between a poet's thought flow and the word order of his poem. In his *The Literary Mind and the Carving of Dragons*, Liu Xie succinctly observes that "The external pattern of a poem should be colourful whereas its author's thought flow should lurk beneath". Sikong Tu of the Tang Dynasty, in his *Twenty-Four Poems on Poetry*, likens a poet's thought flow to a zigzagging path and the word order to his movements on it. But this analogy may not be as apt as that used by Jiang Kui, otherwise known as Baishidaoren, a Taoist by the name of White Rock, his predecessor of the Southern Dynasties, that a poet's thought flow should be as fluid as blood circulating in the veins and as hidden as the veins of blood. (See his *Baishidaoren's Poetic Discourse*.) In his *Illuminating Chatters*, Fang Dongshu of the Qing Dynasty likens a poet's thought flow to a trace left by a snake when it wriggles across a grassy land or by a thread when it is trailed through stove ashes, either of which is barely perceptible, or to an allegedly indistinct yet felt divine being; he maintains that the word order, whatever it is, does not clog a poet's thought flow; he further asserts that "When one exercises his discernment, he shall discern the poet's thought flow in his poem. It runs smoothly and vigorously there, and it also feels as if cast there by God. In a word, it is simply divine", and, to describe the relationship between the word order and the poet's thought flow, Fang uses this pair of interesting verses: "mei ren xi yi yun tie ping (A beauty smooths out her dress with great care)/feng cai mie jin zhen xian ji (A tailor contrives to leave no trace of his stitches)"; a poetic imitation of the Tang Dynasty monk-poet Jiaoran's analogy in his *Styles of Poetry: Poets' Active and Strenuous Mental Work*: "Like passing a needle and making a loop of thread in sewing, it seems to stop at one stitch and yet continue to the next one".

These analogies are too elusive. But those ancient Chinese poetry critics love to so elusively describe what concerns poetry. As a result, one can sense something in their description, on the one hand, but, on the other hand, one cannot determine exactly what it should mean. So it is with judgment of a poem. According to Chen Shan, a scholar of the Song Dynasty, in *New Discourses by Approaching Annoying Problems*, Wang Anshi once suggested that "fei qin ying (flying birds)" and "zhe zhu sheng (snapping of bamboos) in Du Xunhe of the Tang Dynasty's "jiang hu bu jian fei qin ying (No flying bird is in sight, over the lake and the river)/yan gu wei wen zhe zhu sheng (Only snapping of bamboos is heard up on cliffs and down in a ravine)" (in his poem "Snow") would be better rewritten as "qin fei ying (birds flying)" and "zhu zhe sheng (bamboos snapping)" and that the first verse of "ri xie zou ba 'chang yang fu' (The sun is descending westwards, with recitation of 'The Rhapsody to the Hunting at Changyang' to the music done)/xian fu chen ai kan hua qiang (Idly, I am appreciating the drawings on the wall, dusting my common garment)" (in his contemporary Wang Zhongzhi's "Poem Composed When I Sought a Post in the Imperial Academic Office") as "ri xie zou fu chang yang ba (With the sun descending westwards, I've rhapsodized the hunting at Changyang to the music)"; as to why, his answer was simply "so it is robuster". In his *Litang's Remarks on Poetry*, Li Dongyang cites such verses from Du Fu's poems as "feng lian zi shang gou (verbatim: Winds curtains by themselves onto hook) (Winds are raising curtains onto the hook as if curtains did so by themselves)", "feng chuang zhan shu juan (verbatim: Winds window unroll scrolls) (Winds going in and out of the window, my scrolls are being unrolled)", and "feng yuan cang jin zhu (verbatim: Winds mandarin ducks hide near islet) (Winds are forcing mandarin ducks to find a shelter on a near islet)" as a perfect example of transposition for "a feel of potency" and "feng jiang sa sa luan fan qiu (verbatim: Winds river whistle unfurl sails autumn) (Winds whistling across the river are wildly driving autumn sails)" as the cream of the cream for being "the pithiest".

But by what standards should those ancient Chinese poetry critics judge those verses? Obviously, it should be impossible to turn to their comments, nor should it be possible to turn to such modern theories as impressionism and symbolism, for an answer. Such an answer, in my opinion, should be acquired by virtue of the relationships between the poet's thought flow and the word order of the verses of his poem.

First, the judgment of the verses should be ascribed to juxtaposition of imagery as a result of ellipsis and transposition, which in turn causes the seeming disengagement of a poet's thought flow from the word order of the verses of his poem. In his *The Act of Reading: A Theory of Aesthetic Response*, Wolfgang Iser says that "The process of assembling the meaning of the text . . . mobilizes the subjective disposition of the reader"; "mobilizes the subjective disposition of the reader" means that the reader, in the case of a poem, mentally receives its images in order of its words or phrases that represent them. This is the psychology of the reader in the course of appreciating a poem: he or she is anticipating, usually within the periphery of already acquired relevant knowledge, the next while reading the present, just as R. Ingarden, in his *The Cognition of the Literary Work of Art*, says: "readers who are absorbed into a flow of thought tend to anticipate similar continuation after a sentence is comprehended". When anticipation is rightly met, the reader feels good; thus the process of appreciation goes on in a smooth and easy way; otherwise, displeasure is most likely to result. Usually, the reader feels comfortable with the prosaic or vernacular language and the customarily syntactic word order, as in the case of ancient Chinese poetry prior to the birth of the Recent Style poetry. For example, "ke cong yuan fang lai (From afar a visitor came to see me)/wei wo shuang li yu (He gave me as a gift two carps)/hu tong peng li yu (I told my young attendant to have them cooked)/He was surprised to see a lengthy letter in it)", according to Xie Zhen's *A Sea-in-the-Four-Direction Recluse's Remarks on Poetry*, read like chit-chat exchanged between a scholar and one of his friends. Its word order is regular, uninterrupted, and complete, and the poet's thought flow therein is transparent and unclogged. According to French poet Paul Valery, however, "a common and familiar language tends to negate itself". In other words, if the language of a poem is effortlessly understood, if a poet's thought flow in his poem is as clear as day, each particular image represented by the language is consequently passed easily without focusing the reader's attention and fades just as they do into oblivion, as he need not ponder hard over what the poet's thought flow is by virtue of the images and their associations. When ellipsis and transposition permeate a poem, it will be a different story. As previously discussed, ellipsis of words such as conjunctions, prepositions, and even verbs in a poem leads to unrestricted transposition of either its words or phrases, such unrestricted transposition leads to juxtaposition of its images represented by either its words or phrases, and such juxtaposition of its images leads to the otherwise transparent poet's thought flow being obscured. When the poet's thought flow is obscured, the reader will focus on the juxtaposed images, which are thus highlighted, and all their possible associations, with a view to in this way clarifying the poet's thought flow for comprehension of his poem. In this sense, the juxtaposed images are comparable to stepping stones by way of which the reader can walk to the other side, which can be likened to a poet's thought flow or rather the meaning of the poem, like a stream.

Verses to such effect are many. Du Fu's "feng chen san chi jian (A three-foot sword in dust of war)/she ji yi rong yi (An altar of Earth and Grain, one man in armour)" (in his "On Passing by Zhaoling Once Again"), obviously derived from Yu Xin of the Southern Dynasties' "zhong feng san chi jian (A three-foot sword was put in the sheath and hung up in the end)/chang juan yi rong yi (A folded armour would no more be worn by its owner for the rest of his life" (in his "The Song of the Zhou's Ancestral Temple"), omits such words as "zhong (in the end)", "feng (was put in the sheath and hung up)", "chang (for the rest of his life)", and "juan (folded)", and the images of a sword that collected dust, an altar of Earth and Grain, and an armoured man are juxtaposed and highlighted, to become the centre of attention, which the reader shall contemplate to follow the poet's thought flow or rather find out what the pair of verses means. In his *A Random All-Inclusive Record by the Owner of 'Being Capable of Self-Rectification' Study*, Wu Zeng of the Song Dynasty compares "yu chu qing bo pao kuai yu (Perches from limpid waves, cooked in fillets, rare delicacies)/ju han han lu jiu fu jin (Chilly dews glistening on daisy petals, mellow wine glittering like gold)" (by Lv Jifu of the Song Dynasty) and "li ze lu fei ren kuai yu (Diners have an appetite for filleted full-grown Taihu Lake perches, rare delicacies)/dong ting ju shu ke fen jin (Visitors crave for segments of ripe Dongtin Hill tangerines, golden in appearance)" (by Su Shunqin, also of the Song Dynasty), judging that the former surpasses the latter, for, because of "ren (diners)" and "ke (visitors)", Su's pair of verses runs in the customarily syntactic word order, their images are scattered, and his thought flow is there for all to see, as a result of which the reader is deprived of the pleasure of laborious yet rewarding contemplation of what the associations of the images could be and what they could mean. According to *Chips of Precious Jade Collected from the Treasury of Remarks on Poetry* by Wei Qingzhi of the Song Dynasty, Han Zicang, also of the Song Dynasty, once substituted "zhong (in the midst of)" and "li (inside)" in "bai yu tang zhong ceng cao zhao (In the imperial academy I drafted decrees)/shui jing gong li jin ti shi (In the moonlight I just scribbled poems)", a pair of verses by his contemporary Zeng Jifu, with "shen (deep)" and "leng (chilly)", respectively; thus "bai yu tang shen ceng cao zhao (Deep is the imperial academy where I once drafted decrees)/shui jing gong leng jin ti shi (The chilly moonlight just saw me scribbling poems)", which is, Wei comments, "far better than the original", for Han's modifications, as aforementioned, juxtapose and highlight the images separately in the two verses, which in turn focus the reader's attention and compel contemplation.

Xie Zhen's *A Sea-in-the-Four-Direction Recluse's Remarks on Poetry* contains this anecdote. A father and his son sought Xie Zhen's advice on the art of versification. Xie told them to improve Li Jianxun's "wei you yi ye meng (I have never slept through a single night)/bu gui qian li jia (Without dreaming of returning to my home a thousand li away)". This pair of verses was thus condensed respectively into "gui meng wu xu ye (I have spent no night without dreaming of returning to my home afar)" and "ye ye xiang shan meng mei zhong (Mounts back at home mounts appear in my dream every night)", to Xie's satisfaction. Still they wondered why, and Xie explained that Li Jianxun's verses, though in pair, pointed at the same thing, that is, "I haven't slept through every night without dreaming of going back to my far homeplace". So they needed syncopating to have their images juxtaposed and highlighted so that the reader's attention would be concentrated and the reader would be compelled to contemplate the significance of the images. Xie metaphorically termed this improvement "suoyinfa", literally, a technique of refining silver. And he was proud of it.

Qiu Zhaoao comments on Du Fu's "ri yue long zhong niao (Days and months [Sun and moon], a bird in a cage)/qian kun shui shang ping (Heaven and Earth, a duckweed on waters)" (in his "Seeing Off Censor-in-Chief Li Mian on His Way to Guangzhou") (note: "ri" and "yue" are two homophonic Chinese words, with "ri" denoting either "day" or "sun" and "yue" either "month" or "moon"), saying that

> Du Fu's other verses, like 'qian kun wan li yan (Heaven and Earth are like eyes that see thousands of leagues)/shi xu bai nian xin (The cycle of seasons remains constant over centuries)' and 'shen shi shuang peng bin (Tangled hair at the temples is all I've gained all my life)/qian kun yi cao ting (Between Earth and Heaven there is nothing I can claim but a thatched shelter)', are lucid in meaning. In contrast, this pair of verses are not so explicit. To clarify them, addition of extra words to them is necessary.

But what words? This is Wang Sishi's solution: "Sun and moon (shine and) (I liken myself to) a bird (confined) in a cage/(Between) Heaven and Earth (I have been roaming like) a duckweed on waters (adrift) (note: the plight of a man on his last leg)". Indeed, the addition of these words both bares the poet's thought flow and elucidates the meaning of the verses. But the original is far more subtle and poetic, just because of its juxtaposed images as a result of ellipsis.

It is safe to say that poetic juxtaposition of imagery results from the development of a poetic language. As Zhong Rong, in his *Critique of Poetry*, says of poems by such poets as Yan Yanzhi, Xie Zhuang, Xie Lingyun, Xie Taio, Ren Fang, Wang Rong, and Shen Yue, also of the Southern Dynasties, in comparison with the vernacular or rather plain, natural, and syntactically loose Chinese poetry prior to Recent Style poetry, their poems are distinctly densified by cutting out things such as function words, just because they, especially Xie Lingyun, are, averse to the style of the past Chinese poetry in terms mainly of language, and their experiment with a new linguistic style can slightly compromise their poems, as in the case of poems by Xie Taio. Zhong's criticisms, whether justified or not, indirectly indicate that juxtaposition of the images, like a montage of scenes, in the current poetry and attendant concealment of the poet's thought flow therein as a result of ellipsis, such as ellipsis of such function words as determinants of time, position, affiliation, and so on, and/or transposition, such as assignment of the words or phrases that represent images to wherever a poet sees fit within his verse, became a trend at the time, and a poem thus composed naturally is open to reasonable *interpretations*.

Second, seeming disengagement of a poet's thought flow in his poem from its verses that seem out of order as a result of ellipsis and transposition enables a poem as such to carry more than, for example, one before the Southern Dynasties which was composed in the vernacular or prosaic language, does. This "more" is what is termed "tension".

The world built by a poet of his poetic language, different from that both of science and of mundane life, is mainly of sentiment. As John Crowe Ransom, in his *The New Criticism*, points out, the world of science which is treated in a scientific discourse is a reduced, emasculated, and docile one, and plebs' realistic and pragmatic considerations and pursuits reduce their world to a vulgarized one. In contrast, the world that a poet intends to build is one that, as previously discussed, embodies the deep linguistic structure: a denser and more refractory one which has originally been projected on the poet's mental screen but is perceivable. If a poet treats this world in nonpoetic language, his poem as such shall convey nothing but *the* unequivocal meaning. For this language lacks what poetic language has that can inspire the reader's association and imagination or, in other words, that can give a poem "tension".

As a stutterer is frustrated when he has exerted himself or herself, only to have spoken little of what he or she is keen to say, so, into the Southern Dynasties, ancient Chinese poets would sigh over how language had failed them when they wanted so much to express themselves in it. To enable a poem to express more than what the words of the poem literally expressed, some ancient Chinese poets back then, apart from turning to those metaphysical ways that had been promulgated by ancient Chinese sages, which, nonetheless, could be impractical, began to reform the language used in past Chinese poetry. The reformed poetic language featured ellipsis and transposition. It led to the juxtaposition of images, asyntactic word order, and a poet's thought flow, as well as the poet as the subject being in obscurity and thus his thought flow seemingly disengaging from the verses in a poem. As a result, the new poetic language acquired the same charm as the Zen Buddhists' seemingly illogical yet witty interlocutions; a poem composed in it, like Pablo Picasso's abstract paintings, can be interpreted by different readers from their different perspectives, just as Su Shi uses "heng kan cheng ling ce cheng feng (seen from its front, it is a long range while from its side a lofty peak)" to describe the various aspects of Mount Lu. Ji Xianlin, a contemporary Chinese scholar, once made this analogy when criticising flowery yet meaningless writings: they are like a torn-apart "Ba Bao Lou Tai (a glorious tower)", whose bits and bobs can bear no scrutiny. From another perspective, however, these "bits and bobs" can be reassembled by various people into various "Ba Bao Lou Tai". This also applies to, say, a Recent Style poem: thanks to its new poetic language, the reader, who is all too ready to interpret it, is allowed to reassemble the parts of it, as he or she sees fit, into his poetic worlds.

For example, "ri zhao hong ni si (verbatim: sunshine rainbow resemblance)/ tian qing feng yu wen (verbatim: Sky clear wind rain hear)" (in Zhang Jiuling's "Looking Out from Hukou at the Mount Lu's Waterfalls") can, without suggestion of the title, be understood to mean either "The sun is shining as beautifully as a rainbow/Winds are whistling and rain is pattering, though under a clear sky" or "A rainbow is as red as the radiant sun/Winds are so weak and rain so light, giving a delusion of no wind and no rain under a clear sky" or "A rainbow in the sunlight looks like [something]/Under a clear sky winds and rain sound like [something])". "Zhu xuan gui huan nv (verbatim: Bamboo din return washer-maids/lian dong xia yu zhou (verbatim: Lotus sway underneath fishing boat"(in Wang Wei's "A View of the Autumnal Evening Near My Mount Villa") is traditionally understood to mean "Din from the bamboo grove is made by the washer-maids who are returning" and "The lotuses are swaying because a fishing boat is passing underneath them", but can they not be understood also to mean "Din from the bamboo grove foretells that washer-maids are returning" and "The swaying lotus betrays a fishing boat that is passing underneath"? The two interpretations of each of these two verses vary finely in that the former is an objective or rational description and the latter an anticipation which has, more or less, a tinge of the reader's sensibility. Of another of Wang Wei's pair of verses "liu se chuan shan ying (verbatim: Willow[s] hue vernal mountain[s] reflection[s])/li hua xi niao cang (verbatim: Pear blossom set sun birds hide)" (in his "Composed at a Buddhist Temple on a Spring Day"), the second one, whose meaning would be crystal clear should "dusk birds" hide themselves *among* "pear tree blossoms", nevertheless neither unequivocally indicates the spatial relationship between bird and blooming pear tree nor the number of birds and pear trees; in addition, juxtaposition of the images as a result of ellipsis and transposition allows free collocation. Therefore, the reader is given free rein to imagine that either a shadowy bird was dotting a white blooming pear tree at dusk; birds were flying into white blooming pear trees at dusk; or a grove of white blooming pear trees stood there in contrast with a flock of birds, both silhouetted, at dusk or dusk was hastening birds to their nestles hidden in blooming pear trees; and so on. Evidently, it is the particular poetic language that gives the verse such "tension".

Third, ellipsis and/or transposition, which lead(s) to juxtaposition of images, demolish(es) what can prevent one from accessing the deep linguistic structure, the true reflection of the external world, which is embodied in poetry thus composed.

That Martin Heidegger was enthusiastic about the poetry by Hölderlin astounded and puzzled those around him: why did he take so much interest in poetry? His *Hölderlin and the Essence of Poetry* gives this answer. Poetic and non-poetic language differ. A world constructed of the latter, though rationally conceptualized and logically coherent, is not the original and genuine world that one should have perceived and felt with heart and soul and retained in the form of the deep linguistic structure. The so-called rational and logical world totally manipulates one's cognition by non-poetic language whose designation and/or direction can be deceiving and misleading, like the descriptive appellations by which one learns, rather superficially than naturally, about an advertised product represented by them. In these circumstances, a philosopher is obliged to find language that can represent the original and genuine world which has projected itself on one's mental screen, as just mentioned, in the form of the deep linguistic structure. And poetic language is the one for this purpose, because, as Martin Heidegger says, "Indeed, the pursuit of poetry often looks like little more than play. Without responsibility, it invents a world of images; lost in thought, it remains within an imaginary realm. Such play evades the seriousness of decisions". Wolfgang Stegmüller, in his *Hauptstromungen der gegenwartsphilosophie*, also says that a "des Transzendieren über die Welt (transcendental world)" has to be created through "tearing-down mental activities" in the form of antithesis, circular reasoning, and declassification, thus flashing up. His "tearing-down mental activities" should include versification. A poet will thus refuse to subject himself to such logical restrictions as cause and effect and time and space but rather, intuitively, sense a world as it is, unsusceptible to the constrictions imposed by a surface linguistic structure.

This is the case with Recent Style poetry. Let us look at the worlds shown in such Recent Style verses as "jie qian duan cao ni bu luan (verbatim: Before the steps short grasses muddy not messy) (The short grasses before the steps are muddy but not messy)/yuan zhong chang tiao feng zha xi (verbatim: In the courtyard long willows winds abruptly weak) (Winds are abruptly becoming weaker on long courtyard willows)" and "juan lian can yue ying (verbatim: curtain break moon shadow) (The curtains shattered the otherwise pool-like moonlight)/gao zhen yuan jiang sheng (verbatim: High pillow distant the river's noise) (Supporting my head on an elevated pillow distanced me from the splashing river)" (respectively in Du Fu's "Relentless Raining" and "Reflection Far Away from Home on a Night View"), "shuang shuang gui zhe yan (verbatim: Pairs return winter swallows) (Winter swallows, in pairs, fluttering back to the warm/yi yi jiao yuan qun (verbatim: One one scream apes group) (Apes, in couples, screaming at the top of their lungs)" (in Han Yu's "Moored at Jiangkou for a Night"), "yu pu nan ling guo (verbatim: Fishing bay outskirts Nanling Town) (Lo and behold, there stretches the fishing bay around the outskirts of Nanling Town)/ren jia chun gu xi (verbatim: Households spring ravine stream) (Along a ravine where runs a stream are scattered households)" (in Wang Wei's "Seeing Zhang Wuyin off back to Xuancheng"), Sikong Shu of the Tang Dynasty's "yu zhong huang ye shu (verbatim: In the rain yellow leaves trees) (I feel like a tree, its leaves yellowing on rainy days)/deng xia bai tou ren (verbatim: Under a lamp a grizzled person) (A lantern is shedding dim light on me, a doddering grey-haired man)" (in his "Happy to Have Received My Cousin Lu Lun Who Stayed at My Home for a Night"), Liu Changqing's "han zhu yi gu yan (verbatim: cold islet one solitary goose) (The chilly islet in the midst of the river, a lonely wild goose)/xi yang qian wan shan (verbatim: setting sun thousands of mounts) (A setting sun and range upon range of mountains)" (in his "A Poem Composed at a Riverside Pavilion in Late Autumn"), and Lu You's "lou chuan ye xue gua zhou du (verbatim: War boats night snow Guazhou ferry) (War boats, a snowy night, Guazhou Ferry)/tie ma qiu feng da san guan (verbatim: Iron horse autumnal wind Dasan Pass) (Armoured war horses, autumnal winds, the Dasan Pass)" (in his "A Wrathful Poem"), to choose just a few. As is manifest in these verses, the poets take advantage of ellipsis and transposition in their poetic language to juxtapose images, which should exactly represent the deep linguistic structure or rather their intuitive perception of the genuine externalities, and present it without any rationally logical constrictions in terms of temporal, spatial, causal, effectual, or other relationships. And the poets' thought flow, obscured as a result of the poets, who should have been the subjects, having faded into oblivion, is still there to be perceived. Such are the worlds as they are, which the reader can access through this poetic language without being deceived or misled by distortions and delusions caused by so-called rational and logical non-poetic language.

In his *After Babel: Aspects of Language and Translation*, George Steiner says that "In modern hermeneutics the poetry, letters, and translations of Hölderlin occupy a privileged place. Heidegger's ontology of language is partly based on them". For

> (Hölderlin) used such devices as hyperbaton, the separation of object from predicate, the isolation of epithets either preceding or following on their substantive, the asymmetry of predicates and attributes, in order to produce a 'German-Greek' intelligible to German speakers.

This is Hölderlin's poetic language.

Imagine what Heidegger would say if he read the language of the Recent Style poetry. All its salient characteristics, as previously discussed, enable a Recent Style poem to carry more than it literally does, but it still is intelligible to the Chinese reader. What a Recent Style poem represents is the external world that impresses its author via his intuitive perception. Such a world is essential and genuine and, what's more, can also be perceived by the Chinese reader. Is a world of this nature not a "des Transzendieren über die Welt (transcendental world)", one that Heidegger, as well as other Western philosophers of the twentieth century, hoped to reach? And it would also be what a twentieth-century Western poet was keen on.

These three aspects that have been discussed may well explain, for example, why Wang Anshi claimed "so it is robuster" when he commented on Du Xunhe's "Snow" as mentioned.

Let us conclude this chapter by quoting Thomas Stearns Eliot:

> Our civilization comprehends great variety and complexity, and this variety and complexity, playing upon *a refined sensibility*, must produce various and complex results. The poet must become more and more comprehensive, *more allusive, more indirect*, in order to force, to *dislocate,* if necessary, language into his meaning.
>
> (see his The Metaphysical Poets)

References

1. Arnheim, Rudolf. *Shijue siwei* 视觉思维 (Visual Thinking), translated by Shouyao Teng 滕守尧. Beijing: Guangming Daily Publishing House, 1987.
2. Eliot, Thomas Stearns. "Xuanxuepai shiren" 玄学派诗人 (The Metaphysical Poets). In *Ailuete wenxue lunwenji* 艾略特文学论文集 (Theses on the Works by Thomas Stearns Eliot), translated by Funing Li 李赋宁. Tianjin: Baihua Literary and Art Press, 1994.
3. Fan, Wen 范温. "Qianxi shiyan" 潜溪诗眼 (Qianxi's Perspective on Poetry). In *Song shihua jiyi* 宋诗话辑佚 (The Recovery of Lost Song Dynasty Poems), edited by Shaoyu Guo 郭绍虞. Beijing: Zhonghua Book Company, 1980.

4. Fang, Dongshu 方东树. *Zhaomei zhan yan* 昭昧詹言 (Illuminating Chatters). Beijing: People's Literature Publishing House, 1961.
5. Fei, Gun 费衮. *Liangxi man zhi* 梁谿漫志 (Notes of Liangxi). Shanghai: Shanghai Classics Publishing House, 1985.
6. Hawkes, Terence. *Jiegouzhuyi yu fuhaoxue* 结构主义与符号学 (Structuralism and Semiotics), translated by Tiepeng Qu 瞿铁鹏. Shanghai: Shanghai Translation Publishing House, 1987.
7. Herder, Johann Gottfried. *Lun yuyan de qiyuan* 论语言的起源 (On the Origin of Language), translated by Xiaoping Yao 姚小平. Beijing: The Commercial Press, 1998.
8. Hong, Mai 洪迈. *Rongzhai wubi* 容斋五笔 (Five Notes from the Tolerant Studio). Shanghai: Shanghai Classics Publishing House, 1996.
9. Ingarden, R. *The Cognition of the Literary Work of Art*. Evanston: Northwestern University Press, 1973.
10. Iser, Wolfgang. *The Act of Reading: A Theory of Aesthetic Response*. London: Routledge and Kegan Paul, 1978.
11. Jakobson, Roman. "Yuyanxue yu shixue" 语言学与诗学 (Closing Statement: Linguistics and Poetics). In *Wenxue jiegouzhuyi* 文学结构主义 (Structuralism in Literature: An Introduction), by Robert Scholes, translated by Yu Liu 刘豫, Beijing: SDX Joint Publishing Company, 1988.
12. Jiang, Kui 姜夔. "Baishidaoren shi shuo" 白石道人诗说 (Baishidaoren's Poetic Discourse). In *Lidai shihua* 历代诗话 (The Commentaries by the Critics of the Past Dynasties on Poetry), edited by Wenhuan He 何文焕. Beijing: Zhonghua Book Company, 1981.
13. Jung, Carl Gustav. *Xinlixue yu wenxue* 心理学与文学 (Psychology and Literature), translated by Chuan Feng 冯川 et al. Beijing: SDX Joint Publishing Company, 1987.
14. Kobo, Daishi. *Wen jin mi fu lun* 文镜秘府论 (Treatise on the Secret Treasury of Literary Mirror). Beijing: People's Literature Publishing House, 1980.
15. Lehmann, Winfred P. *Miaoxie yuyanxue yinlun* 描写语言学引论 (Descriptive Linguistics, An Introduction), translated by Zhaoxiang Jin 金兆骧 and Xiuzhu Chen 陈秀珠. Shanghai: Shanghai Foreign Language Education Press, 1986.
16. Li, Dongyang 李东阳. "Litang shihua" 麓堂诗话 (Litang's Remarks on Poetry). In *Lidai shihua xubian* 历代诗话续编 (A Sequel to the Commentaries by the Critics of the Past Dynasties on Poetry), edited by Fubao Ding 丁福保. Beijing: Zhonghua Book Company, 1983.
17. Lvy-Bruhl, Lucien. *Yanshi siwei* 原始思维 (Primitive Mentality), translated by You Ding 丁由. Beijing: The Commercial Press, 1981.
18. Ouyang, Xiu 欧阳修. "Liuyi shihua" 六一诗话 (Liuyi's Commentaries on Poetry). In *Lidai shihua* 历代诗话 (The Commentaries by the Critics of the Past Dynasties on Poetry), edited by Wenhuan He 何文焕. Beijing: Zhonghua Book Company, 1981.
19. Ransom, John Crowe. "Xinpiping" 新批评 (The New Criticism), translated by Tingchen Zhang 张廷琛. In *Xinpiping wenji* "新批评" 文集 (An Anthology of the New Criticism Theories), edited by Yiheng Zhao 赵毅衡. Beijing: Social Sciences Academic Press, 1988.
20. Sikong, Tu 司空图. "Ershisi shi pin" 二十四诗品 (Twenty-Four Poems on Poetry). In *Lidai shihua* 历代诗话 (The Commentaries by the Critics of the Past Dynasties on Poetry), edited by Wenhuan He 何文焕. Beijing: Zhonghua Book Company, 1981.
21. Stegmuller, Wolfgang. *Dangdai zhexue zhuliu* 当代哲学主流 (Hauptstromungen der gegenwartsphilosophie), translated by Bingwen Wang 王炳文 et al. Beijing: The Commercial Press, 1986.

22. Steiner, George. *Tongtianta: wenxue fanyi lilun yanjiu* 通天塔—文学翻译理论研究 (After Babel: Aspects of Language and Translation), translated by Yichuan Zhuang 庄绎传. Beijing: China Translation Corporation, 1989.
23. Wei, Qingzhi 魏庆之. *Shiren Yu Xie* 诗人玉屑 (Chips of Precious Jade Collected from the Treasury of Remarks on Poetry). Shanghai: Shanghai Classics Publishing House, 1978.
24. Wellek, René and Austin Warren. *Wenxue lilun* 文学理论 (Theory of Literature), translated by Xiangyu Liu 刘象愚 et al. Beijing: SDX Joint Publishing Company, 1984.
25. Wu, Hang 吴沆. *Huanxi shihua* 环溪诗话 (Poetic Commentaries at the Huanxi Quarters). Beijing: Zhonghua Book Company, 1988.
26. Xie, Zhen 谢榛. "Siming shuhua" 四溟诗话 (A Sea-in-the-Four-Direction Recluse's Remarks on Poetry). In *Lidai shihua xubian 1* 历代诗话续编 (A Sequel to the Commentaries by the Critics of the Past Dynasties on Poetry), edited by Fubao Ding 丁福保. Beijing: Zhonghua Book Company, 1983.
27. Zhong, Rong 钟嵘. "Shipin" 诗品 (Critique of Poetry). In *Lidai shihua* 历代诗话 (The Commentaries by the Critics of the Past Dynasties on Poetry), edited by Wenhuan He 何文焕. Beijing: Zhonghua Book Company, 1981.

4 Tonal and metrical schemes
A analysis of the patterns of ancient Chinese poetry

Talk of the tonal and metrical schemes can be associated with three things. One is the law. In his *Liunan's Desultory Notes*, Wang Yingkui says that "The rules for the tonal and metrical schemes, comparable to laws, through a poem, dictate usage of each word and each antithetical symmetry to ensure a consummate pattern". Thus a poet is, to a degree, limited, the way a fettered man is confined to a cramped cell. Against such circumstances, Ye Mengde of the Song Dynasty, in his *Tales and Critique of Poetry at Shilin*, bitterly protests that "Since the Recent Style poetry of the Tang Dynasty, poets have felt as if shackled". Even Wen Yiduo, a modern Chinese poet, in his *The Tonal and Metrical Schemes of Poetry*, compares versification to a poet dancing with his ankles shackled.

Another is the pattern. Wolfgang Kayser, in his *Das Sprachliche Kunstwerk-Eine Einführungin die Literaturwis-senschaf*, asserts that "the significance of a tonal and metrical scheme is that it constitutes the pattern of a poem". Actually, similar notions are also read in such ancient Chinese literary works as Lu Ji's *Remarks in the Style of an Ode on Literary Creation*, which draws a parallel between aural and visual effect, noting that "Musical tones undulate harmoniously in pitch, just as five colours set off one another to form a beautiful palette". Ouyang Xiu's *The Biography of Song Zhiwen* of his *New Tang Book*, which recommends a beautifully fabricated pattern to regulate verses so that a poem is immune to any tonal and metrical defect, a suggestion that would be closer than Lu Ji's to the concept of "pattern". And t

The third is the architecture. Wen Yiduo seems to be the first one who used, as in his *The Tonal and Metrical Schemes of Poetry*, this term, but actually a similar idea was propounded far earlier by, for instance, Liu Xie, who, in his *The Literary Mind and the Carving of Dragons*, says that

> A good poem, comparable to a perfectly shaped timber that has been cut along the ink-marked lines into what is desired to be, is ingeniously crafted so that its ending corresponds to its beginning and its composition is logically structured

and, more aptly, Fan Wen, who, when commenting on Du Fu's poetry in his *Qianxi's Perspective on Poetry*, feels that "All are arranged in their right places, as

DOI: 10.4324/9781003405993-4

in a government office, a mansion, a main hall, or a chamber wherein everything is placed where it should be", an analogy that could be patented for being the first to be the closest to "architecture". Thereafter, whenever critiquing either paintings, arias, dramas or fictions, ancient Chinese critics tended to use Fan's analogy for concrete elucidation. For example, Wang Jide of the Ming Dynasty, in his *A Comprehensive Study of Arias and Dramas*, compares "the rules and regulations for composition of arias" to "the layout meticulously designed prior to construction of a palace"; in the Chinese classical novel entitled *The Story of the Stone*, Xue Baochai, one of its heroines, deliberated on how to deal with the relationships between far and near, open and dense, primary and secondary, and high and low to draw a picture of a grand garden; Li Yu of the latter Ming and the early Qing dynasties, in the part of *The Structure of Lyrics and Arias* of his magnum opus *Spontaneous Glimpses in Leisure*, uses the analogy of not just the location of its main hall and doors but its entire layout that has to be carefully considered before a house is constructed, with a view to advising poets to think twice before putting to paper what they intend to compose; to digress, an anonymous literary critic, reviewing the thirty-third chapter of *The Scholars*, a Chinese classical novel, said that

> When one writes a book, remember to do the way an architect builds a house: he has to definitely set out its halls, its bedrooms, its study, its kitchen, its pen of livestock, and the like prior to its construction

and Ye Xie of the Qing Dynasty, an eminent poetry critic, in his *A Probe into the Essence of Versification*, reiterates that the poetry of the Kingdom of Wei of the Han Dynasty read like the framework of a house; the poetry of the Six Dynasties like a house complete with its windows, its rails, and its columns; and the poetry of the Tang Dynasty like chambers furnished with curtained beds and other necessities such as vessels, so his advice is that a poet should compose a poem the way an architect constructs a house, having a clear picture of what is needed where it best fits.

Specifically, Recent Style poetry, which developed from the Qi and Liang periods of the Southern Dynasties through the Tang Dynasty to the Song Dynasty, and which differs from the ancient Chinese arias, paintings, short tales, and fictions, as well as some, albeit rhymed, Western poems, has its own sophisticated tonal and metrical schemes in the form of the pentasyllabic or heptasyllabic quatrain, which is termed "jue ju", and the pentasyllabic or heptasyllabic eight-verse, which is termed "lv shi". These schemes, sets of rules, and regulations for tone, meter, and form in versification, which can affect meaning, are as rigid and as demanding as laws, patterns, or architecture. A Recent Style poet has to obey them in every particular. But here arise two questions: Are they the acme of perfection, like palaces such as the Forbidden City, which is constructed in a symmetrical layout along the axis into an imposing, uncompromisingly arrayed complex? Do they result naturally from the evolution of the ancient Chinese poetry? If the answers are negative, why should so many ancient Chinese poets, who loved naturalness, accept such brass-bound unnatural schemes? If the answers are positive, do such

4.1. From the Yongming Style to the Recent Style in terms of tonal and metrical scheme

A poem is not just a meaningful entity of words but also a meaningful one of tonal and metrical schemes. The workings of the tonal and metrical scheme of a poem affect both its aesthetic appeal and the communication between the poet and the reader. Rhymed ancient Chinese poetry started as early as in the Pre-Qin period. Rhyming is a part of the tonal and metrical schemes. As the terminal words of the verses of a poem at a regular interval are rhymed, the poem thus has an intertextual cadence and recurrent echo-wise effect in correspondence, but, intratextually, the other words of its verses are not tonally and metrically schemed, which can mar the tonal and sound effect of the poem as a whole. So, into the Southern Dynasties, especially during the reign of Emperor Wu (Yongming) of the Qi period of the Southern Dynasties, ancient Chinese poets began to pursue tonal and metrical musicality and harmony both in particular and in general. In this respect, they drew from what their predecessors since the Kingdom of Wei of the Han dynasty had achieved and the Sanskrit phonetic and rhyming system that, along with Buddhism, had been introduced to China, by virtue of the characteristics of Chinese words, to devise their tonal and metrical schemes for poetry, with a view to ensuring the intraverse, interverse, and even intercouplet tonal and metrical harmony in diversity. The result is their "Four Tones" and "Eight Defects", a set of criteria for versification in terms of tone and cadence.

Key to understanding these criteria are two quotations respectively from *The Biography of Xie Lingyun* of *The History of the Song Period of the Southern Dynasties* by Shen Yue of the Liang period of the Southern Dynasties and *The Biography of Lu Jue* of *The History of the Southern Dynasties* by Li Dashi and his son Li Yanshou of the Tang Dynasty:

> As the beautiful palette of five colours set off each other, so the musical instruments made of eight materials produce harmonious tunes. This is because they fit together. So it is with poetry: its various tones and pitches should alternate. For example, if a tone is gentle and circuitous, the tone that follows immediately on it should be loud and curt. Moreover, tones and pitches not only within a verse but also between verses should alternate. Having attained this, one can claim to have composed a good poem.
>
> (Shen Yue)

> Poets at the time would seek musical effect by virtue of the "Four Tones", namely, the level tone, the rising tone, the falling tone, and the entering tone. But, at the same time, arose the "Eight Defects": in the case of a pentasyllabic poem, the first and second words of the two verses of the couplet correspond to each other in the identical tone, which is called "ping tou"; the

terminal words of the two verses of the couplet have the identical tone, which is called "shang wei", unless the terminal words as such are rhymed; the second word and the terminal word within a verse have the identical tone, which is called "feng yao"; and the terminal words separately in the first verses of the adjacent couplets are identically intoned, which is called "he xi". To avoid such "Eight Defects", in the case of a pentasyllabic poem, both the words within a verse and the words between the verses of a couplet and even between couplets should undulate in tone.

(Li Dashi and Li Yanshou)

This is believed to be the incipient conception by such poets during the reign of Emperor Wu of the Qi period of the Southern Dynasties as Shen Yue, Wang Rong, Xie Tiao, and Zhou Yong of the tonal and metrical schemes for versification. In fact, the "Four Tones", as already mentioned, had already permeated people's daily speech. Nonetheless, to give credit where credit is due: it is those previously mentioned poets who discovered, classified, and standardized the four tones for versification. Their work, to be fair, is significant in the history of Chinese linguistics. But discovery of the four tones only started the exploration for new tonal and metrical schemes. It was not until conception of the "Eight Defects", the other four of which, apart from the four previously mentioned, in the case of a pentasyllabic poem, refer respectively to "da yun" and "xiao yun", both of which, generally, concern avoidance of words that are identical both in tone and in rhyme in a couplet, and "zheng niu" and "pang niu", both of which concern avoidance of words that are identical in the initial consonant radicals of their syllables, with the exception of words in antithetical symmetry whose vowel radicals are identical in a couplet in which the tonal and metrical schemes for versification were formulated. Such schemes, analogous to an architect's plan by which timbers, bricks, tiles, and the like are used to construct a house, were intended to attain harmony in diversity in terms of musical effect.

Here, before talking further about the "Eight Defects", let us look briefly at what had happened prior to the discovery of the "Four Tones". As is known, the increasing awareness since the Han Dynasty of the sound effect of a Chinese word deepened knowledge of its pronunciation, and first matured into a way of pronunciation called "fanqie", which is using the first consonant and the second vowel respectively of two Chinese words to pronounce a third Chinese word. Still, the idea of "tone" was not so clear. It is not uncommon to see in some ancient Chinese literature instances of using musical notes, namely the five ones represented separately by five Chinese words, which are Gong (宫), the equivalent of 1 in numbered musical notation; Shang (商), the equivalent of 2; Jue (角), the equivalent of 3; Zhi(徵), the equivalent of 5; and Yu (羽), the equivalent of 6, either to allude to objects or to represent sensibilities. This may be seen as evidence that what could approximate tones was noticed back then. But, at any rate, they are still not tones, for the five musical notes concern pitch and do not correspond literally to the "Four Tones". True, Li Deng, of the Kingdom of Wei of the Three Kingdom period of the Han Dynasty, compiled a book entitled *Classification in Order of the Five Musical*

Notes of the Initial Consonants of Chinese Words; Lv Jing, of the Jin Dynasty, discussed the five musical notes respectively in five separate chapters which make up *The Collection of the Second Vowels of Chinese Words*. But to use musical notes to illustrate tonal harmony in poetry was an expedient approach which was far from sophisticated and thus lacking the aptness and accuracy required of categorization and description of tones in actual practice. That is why Shen Yue so confidently affirmed that "All the past classical books, including the past historical records, touched upon, if any, not the 'Four Tones' but the five musical notes". Chanting by Buddhist monks of scriptures might, in terms of aural sensation, sound similar to recitation of poetry; nonetheless, that sensation had not been sublimed into something like a tonal and metrical scheme to purposely regulate versification for a certain aesthetic effect. That also explains why Shen Yue boasted that "Qu Yuan did not discover the 'Four Tones'; no one else ever since has discovered them either". So discovery and classification by Shen Yue and his peers of the "Four Tones" is the breakthrough in this regard, and all Chinese words would, by tone, be distinctly categorized as well. In his *The Gist of the Four Tones*, Liu Shanjing of the Sui Dynasty says: "All sounds fall under the categories of the 'Four Tones', in one of which any of the Chinese words is intoned".

Thus far, tone was distinguished from pitch and sound. This laid the foundation on which Shen Yue and his peers' "Eight Defects" for versification were conceptualized, and the "Four Tones" and the "Eight Defects" combine to form tonal and metrical schemes.

These tonal and metrical schemes originally concerned pentasyllabic poetry. For such poetry to produce a diversified yet harmonious musical effect by these tonal and metrical schemes, each word within the verse of a poem of this kind should vary tonally; the verses of each couplet of the poem should, word to word, antithetically and tonally correspond. Such tonal and metrical schemes restrictively stipulate how a pentasyllabic poem is tonally regulated. All in all, according to Kobo Daishi's *Treatise on the Secret Treasury of Literary Mirror*, such tonal and metrical schemes are aimed at shunning any tonal repetition and monotony.

To learn more about such tonal and metrical schemes, let us look specifically at their regulations, as in the case of a pentasyllabic poem.

First, the five words in each verse must avoid the aforementioned "feng yao" to attain the effect of diversity. For example, with "du (secretly)" and "shi (embellish)" both in the entering tone in "qie *du* zi diao *shi* (I secretly began to embellish myself)", and "bu" (pace) and "chu" (out) in the falling tone in "xu *bu* jin men *chu* (Walking out of the gold gate at a slow pace)", such tonal repetition must be avoided.

Second, the verses of a couplet must avoid the aforementioned "ping tou", as in the case of "*jin ri* liang yan hui (What a banquet for today)/*huan le* ju nan chen (It can be hard to detail its happiness)", where "jin (this)" and "huan (felicity)" have the same level tone and "ri (day)" and "le (felicity)" the same entering tone, and "shang wei", as in the case of "xi bei you gao *lou* (To the northwest erupts a grand tower)/shang yu fu yun *qi* (It stands so tall as to reach [the height of] overhanging clouds)", where both "lou" (tower) and "qi" (reach the height of) are in the level tone, to diversify the tonal effect by virtue of antithetical symmetry.

Third, the aforementioned "he xi" must be avoided, as in the case of "ke cong yuan fang *lai* (From afar arrived a visitor)/wei wo yi shu zha (Who brought me a letter)/Shang yan chang xiang *si* (It began with expression of abiding lovesickness)/xia yan jiu bie li (It ended with grieving over long separation)", wherein "lai (arrived)" on the level tone and "si (lovesickness)", also on the level tone, are identically intoned. According to Shen Yue and his peers, "he xi" would mar the fluency and give the reader a sensation of "playing in darkness an untuned zither or walking at night on a bumpy road", to the point of debilitating the poetic aesthetic appeal. This regulation applies, by extension, to the terminal words of the first verses respectively of any other two adjacent couplets.

As for "da yun", "xiao yun", "pang niu", and "zheng niu", refer back to the previously mentioned.

These are roughly what the "Four Tones" and "Eight Defects" are about. Kobo Daishi's *Treatise on the Secret Treasury of Literary Mirror*", as well as works by those who specialize in the history of the modern Chinese literature, provide more comprehensive and more detailed perspectives on them. What I want to stress here is that, although the "Four Tones" and the "Eight Defects", especially the latter, which regulate versification from the negative angle, are excessively intricate and thus impractical, they definitely grasp the tonal features of Chinese words and set the trend of the development of ancient Chinese poetry in terms of tonal and metrical scheme, just as Shen Yue said:

> When a poet is adept at executing the "Four Tones" and avoiding the "Eight Defects", his pentasyllabic poetry will, in a fascinating manner, produce a melodious and gripping effect.

But the "Four Tones" and the "Eight Defects" do not necessarily materialize, any more than the design of a building necessarily becomes real or a screenplay necessarily turns into a movie. There is a long way in between to go. The reason such tonal and metrical schemes as devised by Shen Yue and his peers turn out to be impractical is that they ignore two things, which proves fatal. The Chinese reader of an ancient Chinese poem does not feel its tones the way the audience does a piece of music, which, due to its particularity as a sheer acoustic work of art, can concentrate the attention of its audience on its tempo, its pitch, and its duration, whereas the reader has to pay attention at the same time both to the meaning of the poem he or she is reading and its tones, so he or she cannot focus only on such tonal intricacies as dictated by the "Four Tones" and the "Eight Defects" but only perceives tonal alternations by antithetical tonal dichotomy, which has its root in the ancient Chinese notion of the universe being dichotomized, as in the case of division of tone into, for example, light, sounding as if rising up to the skies, and heavy, feeling as if plummeting down to the ground, despite the meticulous analysis by Shen Yue and his peers of the "Four Tones". In fact, even Shen Yue himself saw this (see his *Biography of Xie Lingyun*), not to mention other ancient Chinese poetry critics such as Liu Xie (see his *The Literary Mind and the Carving of Dragons*) and Jiang Hong (see his "Praising a Singsong Girl") of the Liang period of the Southern Dynasties. This is one thing. The other is that Shen Yue and his peers must not have anticipated so many attacks on their overly sophisticated tonal and metrical schemes. For example, Yin Fan, in his *A Collection of the Poems by the Quintessential Poets of the High Tang Dynasty*, objects by asserting that "A poet need not stringently abide by what the 'Four Tones' and the 'Eight Defects" dictate to produce the most eloquent effect. Even though he breaks those regulations, such breach does not necessarily result in any fault in his poem"; less politely than Yin Fan, Jiaoran, in his *Styles of Poetry: Poets' Active and Strenuous Mental Work*, accuses Shen Yue of having

> judged the poetry arbitrarily by the yardsticks of the "Eight Defects" and intoned a poem fastidiously with the "Four Tones", insofar as it was deprived of almost all its elegance and flavour; and later poets of an average order in aptitude and perception, having fallen under the spell of Shen Yue's advocacy, followed it, so blindly and so obsessedly that they did not for a second think of disobeying it.

Interestingly, even poems by the founders and/or advocates of the "Four Tones" and the "Eight Defects" are held up to ridicule for contradiction of their own tonal and metrical schemes, such as "A Newly Completed Palace Named Tranquility and Peace" by Yin Keng (of the Liang and Chen periods of the Southern Dynasties), which, commended by Hu Yinglin of the Ming Dynasty for being the epitome of the consummate tonal and metrical schemes according to the "Four Tones" and the "Eight Defects" and the precursor to the Recent Style poetry, is scoffed at for its defect of "feng yao", as, in its first stanza, the second words "gong (palace)" and "pian (flap)" separately and the fifth words "zai (an interjectional word, an equivalent of "oh", expressing surprise)" and "lai (come)", respectively, in the first and the fourth verses, that is, "xin *gong* shi zhuang *zai* (How magnificent the newly completed palace looks)" and "lian *pian* he yan *lai* (Congratulatory swallows in succession are flapping to come here)", are found incongruous with the regulation that the two pairs of words must not be tonally identical (the level tone in this case), not to mention Shen Yue's "A Slow Tempo Song" and "A White Horse".

Anything improves through development. While arguments, both in speech and in writing, for the tonal and metrical schemes by the "Four Tones" and the "Eight Defects" enjoyed a vogue at the time, their faults also appeared, so efforts to rectify them had to be made. Into the Tang Dynasty, such complicated and rigid tonal and metrical schemes were incrementally simplified to a simpler and more relaxed "level", like the previously mentioned "l", and "deflected", like the previously mentioned "d" tonal and metrical ones. Such dichotomization of the tonal and metrical schemes led to liberation of ancient Chinese poets from their otherwise shackled plight when it came to poetic tone.

The question as to exactly when the "l" and "d" tones which apply in versification replaced Shen Yue and his peers' "Four Tones", which is more linguistic than poetic, is yet to be answered. *The Biographies of the Eminent and Learned Monks* by Hui Jiao, a monk-poet of the Liang period of the Southern Dynasties, contains such phrases as "aside tune" and "leveling-off tune"; Li Shan of the Tang Dynasty, in his annotation, quoted from Shen Yue's *The History of the Song Period of the Southern Dynasties* on the poem "Pacing to Chanting" by Xie Lingyun in *Selections of Refined Literature* by Prince Xiao Tong of the Liang period of the Southern Dynasties, and used such phrases as "the first horizontal tune" and "the fifth aside tune". From these instances, some ancient Chinese poetry critics inferred that the notion of "l" and "d" tones must have been accepted as early as the Qi or Liang period of the Southern Dynasties. Such an argument based on what is supposed to be evidential literature can be plausible, but, at the same time, can also be implausible, for words such as "aside tune", "leveling-off tune", and "horizontal tune" may not necessarily be identified with the "l" or "d" tones, on the one hand, and, on the other hand, how can it be that Shen Yue and his peers should have highlighted the "Four Tones" while de-emphasizing the simpler and more workable "l" and "d" ones if the latter had already been there? Let alone that musical "tune" and poetic "tone" should not be confused, or else, not Shen Yue and his peers but Lv Jing, the author of *The Collection of the Second Vowels of Chinese Words*, and Li Deng, the author of *Classification in Order of the Five Musical Notes of the Initial Consonants of Chinese Words*, should have been regarded as the originators of the "Four Tones". Other ancient Chinese poetry critics, on the grounds that Liu Xie and Shen Yue exploited pairs of words, such as "rising and falling", "low and high", "light and heavy", and "loud and gentle", to contrast tones deduced that those contrasting words had not been termed but de facto approximated the "l" and "d" tones during the Qi and Liang periods of the Southern Dynasties. To be fair, this theory more or less holds water. But, all the same, just because there was a tonal dichotomization with a view to contrasting tones, which could be suspected to be a trend towards the "l" and "d" tones, does not necessarily mean that Liu and Shen already had the notion of tones being dichotomized into "l" and "d", for there is as yet no substantial evidence in this regard. After all, a hypothesis does not equal a truth; otherwise, shouldn't men of letters of the Han Dynasty such as Sima Xiangru, who suggested alternation between "gong" and "shang", two Chinese words in pinyin for musical notes as mentioned, in composing a rhapsody; Gao You, who differentiated "leisurely cadence" from "speedy cadence" in his annotation on "*Huainanzi*"; and He Xiu, who compared "circuitous speech" and "curt speech" in his annotation on *Gongyang Commentary* have been deemed the expounders of the precursors of the "l" and "d" tones? In fact, it is not until the Middle Tang Dynasty, it is believed, that the notion of the "l" and "d" tones was formulated. But, in reality, the use of the de facto "l" and "d" tones started as early as in the incipient Recent Style poems by Yu Xin and Jiang Zong of the Southern Dynasties or later in the mature Recent Style poems by Emperor Taizong, Li Baiyao, and Shangguan Yi of the early years of the Tang Dynasty. Whether they did so knowingly remains unproved due to a lack of relevant literature. The earliest literature that concerns this could be Yin Fan's *A*

70 *Tonal and metrical schemes*

Collection of the Poems by the Quintessential Poets of the High Tang Dynasty and Kobo Daishi's *Treatise on the Secret Treasury of Literary Mirror*, both of which respectively contain the following words:

> The poems respectively by Cao Cao (the first monarch of the Kingdom of Wei of the Han Dynasty) and Liu Zhen (a scholar of the Kingdom of Wei) were plain and direct, not regulated by any rigid tonal scheme: either the five words in a verse should run all on the "d" tone or all the ten words in a pair of verses should be intoned with the "l" tone.
>
> (Yin Fan)

> Of a pair of verses, if the first one is intoned with the "l" tone, the second one is intoned with the rising, falling, or entering tone; if the first one is intoned with the rising, falling, or entering tone, the second one is intoned with the "l" tone. This kind of tonal scheme alternates till the end of the poem.
>
> (Kobo Daishi)

Yin Fan's exposition may not be as clear as Kobo Daishi's. Kobo Daishi actually echoes the advocacy by the poets of the Tang Dynasty, specifying the tonal schemes that the poets of the Early and the High Tang Dynasty used for their Recent Style poems. His specification informs us about simplification of the "Four Tones" into the "l" tone and the other three, specifically, rising, falling, and entering tones as a tonal unit and about alternation between the "l" tone and any one in the three-tone unit.

This, in a specific and positive way, responds to Shen Yue's aforementioned proposition. Also, it realizes "harmony in diversity" in terms of tone in the incipient Recent Style poetry, which thus attains more aesthetic appeal.

In light of this tonal scheme, the incipient Recent Style poetry should tonally be arranged as follows:

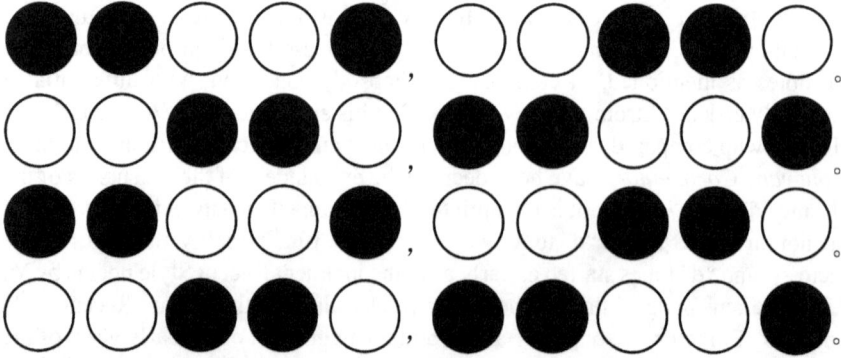

Figure 4.1 The Pattern of Tonal and Metrical Schemes

As the figure shows, the 'l' and "d" tones within a verse alternate, and the "l" and the "d" tones between the two verses in a couplet, and even between the two couplets of a stanza, are antithetical, thus forming a quatrain of symmetrically antithetical tonal mosaic.

However, the disparities are obvious between these tonal schemes and those for mature Recent Style poetry. The scheming of the "l" and "d" tones in the latter, for cadence and rime, across "jue ju" or "lv shi" poetry is further improved, as observed by Wang Li in his *The Chinese Prosody*, which theory, it should be pointed out, does not quite apply in more flexible practice. At any rate, however, the figure sketches the tonal and metrical schemes for mature Recent Style poetry, which is that the "l" and "d" tones within a verse alternate and, between the two verses of a couplet, are antithetical.

As has previously been discussed, ancient Chinese poetry before the Southern Dynasties counts on the recurrent same rhyme on the terminal words of its verses for meter. Herein arises a glitch, in that the meter of this nature does not feel quick paced, just because only the terminal words of this style of poem, at intervals, are identically rhymed, thus producing a lasting echo-like effect and playing down the other words of the verses in terms of tone and meter, as in the case of this Han Dynasty poem:

hui che jia yan mai (I turned my chariot to move to a far destination) /
you you she chang *dao* (From then on my journey stretched long ahead) /
si gu he mang mang (I looked around only to see an endless wilderness) /
dong feng yao bai *cao* (Swaying vernal winds had given grasses a new lease on life) /
suo yu wu gu wu (All grasses in sight along the way were a new growth) /
yan de bu su *lao* (It is irresistible that men age as fast as grasses wither) /
sheng shuai ge you shi (Men naturally have their apex and nadir of life) /
li sheng ku bu *zao* (So you may regret not having early established yourself) /
ren sheng fei jin shi (men are not so hard as metal and solid as stone)/
qi neng chang shou *kao* (Even the greatest longevity will inevitably come to its end) /
yan hu sui wu hua (Men cannot possibly escape the destiny of passing away) /
rong ming yi wei *bao* (So waste no time to strive to attain treasured fame and office).
[Note: the italicized terminal words are identically rhymed.]

As mentioned, a tonal and metrical scheme of this kind has room for improvement. To overcome a dull recurrence in rhyme and boring drag in meter, ancient Chinese poets thought of transitional rhymes. This rhyming technique, according to *The History of the Qi Period of the Southern Dynasties*, was initially used by the poets of the Han Dynasty in their poems, wherein the transitional rhyming occurred at the interval of, usually, eight verses or, rarely, two or three verses. Fu Xuan of the Western Jin Dynasty shortened the long transitional interval. Wang Shaozhi of the Eastern Jin Dynasty and Yan Yanszhi of the Song period of the Southern Dynasties fixed the transitional interval at every four verses. All they hoped to achieve by doing so was to quicken the meter of a poem, and they succeeded, to some extent. But, at the same time, a problem arises that if the terminal-word rhyme within a

72 Tonal and metrical schemes

poem changes too often, the role of a rhyme as a regulator is weakened, and, as a result of a lack of the aforementioned lasting echo-like effect, the wholeness of a poem as such is liable to be jeopardized. On top of this, frequent change in the terminal-word rhyme of a poem actually has little effect on each word within a verse; thus the meter of a poem is still unfavourably affected. So the Recent Style poets of the Tang Dynasty paid attention not just to the terminal-word rhyme but also to assignment of the "l" and "d" tones to each word of a poem, in line with the aesthetic principles. As a result, each word tonally contrasts its (horizontally and vertically) adjacent words, thus attaining sonorous resonance and a brisk meter. This is comparable to a row of high- and low-rise buildings, each of which appears distinct due to their disparities in height, in contrast to a string of beads of a size, each of whose beads thus loses its individuality. To illustrate this, let us take "A Prisoner's Reflection on Buzzing Cicadae" by Luo Binwang of the Tang Dynasty, for instance:

> xi lu chan sheng chang (Into late autumn cicadae keep buzzing) /
> nan guan ke si qin (A prisoner [note: the poet's self-reference] is being beset by homesickness) /
> na kan xuan bin ying (It is a torment to see cicadae fluttering their wings) /
> lai dui bai tou yin (Buzzing on and on in the direction of a grey-haired me) /
> lu zhong fei nan jin (They will find it hard to fly high in such a dewy autumn) /
> feng duo xiang yi chen (The sound of gusts of wind easily drown cicadae's buzz) /
> wu ren xin gao jie (None would believe cicadae are insects of integrity) /
> shei wei biao yu xin (Who would plead the case for me a man of innocence)?

This poem, it should be pointed out, is not typical of Recent Style poetry, but, nonetheless, it differs from the previous poem of the Han Dynasty, in that, in contrast to the latter, which moves at a relatively sluggish meter as a result of its merely counting on its repetitious terminal-word rhyme for rhythmic effect, the former has all its words schemed, contrastively and alternately, vertically and horizontally, in the "l" and "d" tones; hence it undulates on, falling versus rising, long versus short, and heavy versus light, at a musical meter. A poem with such antithesis and symmetry naturally arouses, psychologically and physiologically, a sense of rhythmic modulation in the reader, whose heart beats with the poetic impact quite the way the tide rises and ebbs by turns.

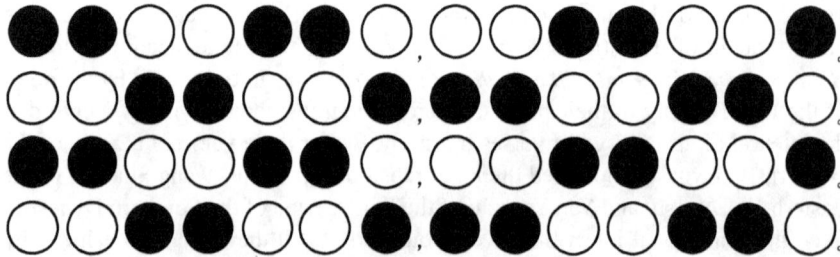

Figure 4.2 The Pattern of Tonal and Metrical Schemes

4.2. Significance of antithetically symmetrical or symmetrically antithetical verses

Not just tone but form affects the conveyance of the meaning of a poem. In the case of Recent Style poetry, the form of antithetical symmetry is typical of almost all its poems.

The form of antithetical symmetry was not adopted exclusively by the Recent Style poets of the Tang Dynasty. Such a form, according to modern Chinese scholar Hu Xiansu's *A Critical Look at Hu Shi's "Attempts at Composing Poetry in the Vernacular"* (published during the May Fourth Movement of 1919 in China), had already appeared in the classics by Laozi and Zhuangzi, two ancient Chinese philosophers, as early as back in the Zhou Dynasty. If this is not convincing enough, let us look further at the proof given by earlier Chinese scholars. Xu Shizeng of the Ming Dynasty, in his *An Anthology of All-Time Critics' Remarks on Poetry*, cited "gou min ji duo (Afflictions are numerous)/shou wu bu shao (Humiliations are countless)" in "The Ballads from the State of Bei of The Book of Songs" to attest to the long history of antithetical symmetry. Even farther back, Liu Xie, in his *The Literary Mind and the Carving of Dragons*, pointed out that documents of remote antiquity such as *Gao Yao's Counsels on Governance* had already contained instances of antithetical symmetry.

The reason for this is that, since a long time before, ancient Chinese began to see the world as one of two opposite elements, that is, Yin (negative or feminine) versus Yang (positive or masculine), and this notion has directed Chinese people in their judgment and appreciation. So it is natural that they, voluntarily or involuntarily, use antithetical symmetry in their speech or writing because of its formal beauty. This well explains why ancient Chinese poets, especially the Recent Style poets of the Tang Dynasty, preferred this kind of poetic form. After all, the form of a poem is used not just for tonal and metrical schemes but to embody what is deep down in a poet's heart. Apart from those poets, even a layman can realize the importance of antithetical symmetry. For example, in *The Story of the Stone*, in the thirty-first chapter subtitled "A Torn Fan Wins a Smile from a Maid/A Pair of Unicorn Suggest a Match", a servant maid named Cuilv, though illiterate, is able to talk, more or less to the point, about antithesis between Yin and Yang. But, in the case of the poems, which contain pairs of verses in antithetical symmetry prior to the emergence of Recent Style poetry, according to Shen Yue, they only demonstrate their writers' intuitive pursuit of formal beauty rather than their awareness of antithetical symmetry as a beautiful form. Ye Mengde, in his *Tales and Critique of Poetry at Shilin*, noted that the poets between the Kingdom of Wei and the Jin Dynasty had not known what was later known as antithetical symmetry, but antithetical symmetry was still used in their verses, as recorded in the anecdotes about men of prestige of the time, such as Lu Shilong or Lu Yun and Xun Minghe or Xun Yin, who had, one in response to the other, chanted witty verses, like "ri xia xun ming he (Under the sun is Xun Minhe)" and "yun jian lu shi long (among the clouds lives Lu Shilong)", and Xi Zaochi and Shi Daoan, who had smartly greeted each other separately with "si hai xi zao chi (Across the four seas spreads the fame of Xi Zaochi)" and "mi tian shi dao an (Up to the heavens reaches the reputation of Shi Daoan)", proving that antithetical symmetry could be intrinsic rather than contrived by such poets as Shen Yue. Ye is, at most, partly right about the history of antithetical symmetry. This is because he does not realize that usage of antithetical symmetry being out of a poet's awareness of it or not draws a significant line in terms of critique of poetry between, for example, the poetry of the Kingdom of Wei of the Han dynasty and farther back and that of the Southern Dynasties and henceforth.

"Ling qian fu lv shui (Waternuts and pods are floating on limpid water)/fu rong fa dan rong (Lotuses are sprouting into red blossoms)" (from the founder of the Wei Dynasty Cao Pi' s "A Poem Composed on the Xuanwu Embankment"), though eloquent in seeming antithetical symmetry, lacks the beauty of the antithetical symmetry that is intended. So it is with Cao Pi's contemporary poet Wang Can's "bai ri ban xi shan (The white sun is descending half behind the western mounts)/sang zi you yu hui (The tips of the branches of mulberry and catalpa trees are tinged with twilight)/xi shuai jia an ming (Crickets along the river sides keep chirping their notes)/gu niao pian pian fei (A single bird over the river is flapping its wings)" (from his "Five Military Life Poems"), a stanza of two couplets, which are only symmetrical in terms of meaning and the number of words. So, Xie Zhen, in his *A Sea-in-the-Four-Direction Recluse's Remarks on Poetry*, said of the poems by Cao Pi, Cao Zhi, Ruan Ji, Zhang Hua, Zuo Si, Zhang Xie, Pan Yue, and Lu Ji, of the Wei and Jin dynasties, that they did contain verses in, more or less, antithetical symmetry, but they still must not be considered part of the genre of the Recent Style, which did not develop until Xie Lingyun and Xie Tiao, two epitomes of the poet community of the Southern Dynasties, began to reform the past poetic language.

This development is chronicled in *The History of the Qi Period of the Southern Dynasties*: "A trend of versification in the Southern Dynasties that whatever was written, either for an account or for an analogy, would use antithetical symmetry for the sake of beauty of form and tone began to develop".

Here are a few extracts from poems by the poets of the Southern Dynasties:

tong ling ying bi jian (Hills in bronze hue are reflected in the crystal-clear stream in the dale)/shi deng xie hong quan (Red-tinged spring water is cascading down the steps chiselled on the rock)

(Xie Lingyun)

ting ting ying jiang yue (The moon high up is reflected in the river)/liu liu chu gu biao (The limpid water is racing out of the dale)

(Xie Huilian)

lv ye ying lu zi (Green leaves welcome dewy moisture)/zhu bao dai shuang run (red buds await frosty damp)

(Shen Yue)

yuan shu nuan qian qian (Distant leafy trees look like intense shadows)/ sheng yan fen mo mo (Mists are spreading into gossamer haze)

(Xie Tiao)

shan cui yu yan ji (Girdling lush mountains are lingering hazy mists)/chuan ping wan zhao shou (Over an expansive plain is a setting sun in sight)

(Xiao Jun)

ji feng luan huan niao (Gusts of wind disrupted the flight of returned birds)/ qing han jing mu chan (A chill in the air silenced dusk cicadae)

(Zhu Chao)

ba chuan ben ju he (Rapids from eight rivers are racing to meet in an enormous valley)/wan qing yi cheng bo (Billowing pure waves are overflowing so expansive a range)

(Yin Keng)

In each pair of these verses; their words are refined; they sound melodic; they run smoothly in meter; and they are structured, word to word, meaning to meaning, in antithetical symmetry, to make an impressive contrast.

The tonal and metrical schemes and antithetical symmetry are both held to be the basic constituents of Recent Style poetry. In *The New Book of Tang*, of whose author-compiler team he was a member, Ouyang Xiu looked back over the development of Recent Style poetry thus:

In versification, Shen Yue and Yu Xin pursued tonal delicacy and structural symmetry; later, Song Zhiwen and Shen Quanqi improved the past poetic tone and structure to lend more to a poem which would appeal like a beautiful piece of brocade.

Wang Shizhen of the Ming Dynasty, in his *Random Talk from the Garden of Art*, remarked that Towards the end of the Southern Dynasties . . . poets were more careful with the tonal and metrical schemes and the antithetical symmetry in versification for a more robust and more euphonic effect. Their poems thus composed actually were the embryos of the Recent Style poetry. The Recent Style poetry in its truest sense came to fruition at the inception of the Tang Dynasty and Shen Quanqin and Song Zhiwen were credited for its perfection.

Since tonal and metrical schemes and antithetical symmetry are the salient features of Recent Style poetry, to discuss antithetical symmetry, it is advisable to look first at how the pioneers of Recent Style poetry looked at it.

In the event, however, past theories, if they are about this respect, can be disappointing: intricate, unsystematized, and inconsistent with one another. According to Wei Qingzhi's *Chips of Precious Jade Collected from the Treasury of Remarks on Poetry*, as early as the Early Tang Dynasty, Shangguan Yi sorted out, by nature, six and eight types of antithetical symmetry. As Kobo Daishi's *Treatise on the Secret Treasury of Literary Mirror* records, into the Middle Tang Dynasty, with the maturation of Recent Style poetry, antithetical symmetry was classified more meticulously, insofar as there were as many as twenty-nine types. These types certainly should be intended to meet all the requirements of the Recent Style poetry and set up standards for poets of later generations, but, in reality, they did not work as anticipated, just because, paradoxically, they were too inclusive on the one hand and, on the other, too particular. For example, the twenty-ninth type, as recorded by Kobo Daishi, termed "non-antithetical antithesis", an absurd type indeed, would slacken otherwise rigid antithetical strictures, to the point that even an otherwise non-antithetical couplet should be accepted as antithetical and a poem as such should be deemed ingenious, much to one's confusion.

In that case, let us revert to some earlier opinions to learn about antithetical symmetry. Liu Xie's *The Literary Mind and the Carving of Dragons* should attract our attention with the following succinct and unmistakable remarks:

> As for antithesis, it has four types. The first one is the antithesis between words, which should be the easiest. The second one is the antithesis between allusions, which can be the most difficult. The third one is the heterogeneous antithesis, which needs encouraging. The fourth one is the homogeneous antithesis, which must be avoided.

Liu Xie advises that a poet should adopt the second and third types if he wants to prove his ingenuity and enhance the readability of his poetry. His advice, admittedly, smacks of being opinionated and fastidious. But, to be fair, of his four types, his contrastive heterogeneous type and his non-contrastive homogeneous type are the most distinct and fundamental classification of antithetical symmetry. So, here, let us focus on these two types, setting aside the second, which will be discussed in Chapter 5, and the first, which concerns rhyming compounds, which are beyond the scope of this book.

Homogeneous antithetical symmetry, according to Liu Xie, means that "each verse of a couplet seems to have different references but naturally one repeats the other in meaning". To illustrate it, he cited "han zu xiang fen yu (Hanzu [Emperor Hanzu, the founder of the Western Han Dynasty] missed Fenyu [his homeplace]/ guang wu si bai shui (Guanwu [Emperor Guangwu, the founder of the Eastern Han Dynasty] recollected Baishui [his birthplace]" (from Zhang Zai of the Western Jin Dynasty's poem series entitled "Seven Lamentations"). Three more examples in this regard can be cited. The first one is Tao Yuanming's "ji niao lian jiu lin (A caged bird will dream of its native woods)/chi yu si gu yuan (A fish confined to a pond will recall its old deep waters)", an imitation of "hu ma yi bei fen (A horse from the north will like the north wind)/yue niao chao nan zhi (A bird from the south will perch on a southward branch)". The two verses, despite their different wording, convey the same sentiment, that is, a displaced person's homesickness, thus giving the reader a sensation of repetitiousness, monotonousness, and aridity, just as Guan Shiming of the Qing Dynasty analogized: "Two verses actually refer to one thing, feeling like stationing guards in front of an already guarded carriage" or, as Zen Buddhists say of recourse to more than mana, which is redundant, for meditation (see *A Sequel to "The Criticisms by the Qing Dynasty Critics on Poetry"*). The second one is "chan zao lin yu jing (The more cicadas' buzzing, the more hushed the woods)/niao ming shan geng you (The louder birds' chirping, the more tranquil the mounts)" by Wang Ji of the Liang Period of the Southern Dynasties. The two verses, each being an exemplary depiction of a peaceful ambience though, entail dreariness due to their repetitiousness in meaning. That is why Cai Juhou of the Song Dynasty, also known as Cai Kuanfu, in his *Cai Kuanfu's Remarks on Poetry,* regretted such defects in a pair of verses despite their antithetical symmetry and individual ingenuity. Cai's remarks were echoed by Wang Shizhen, who, in his *Random Talk from the Garden of Art*, commented:

Although "niao ming shan geng you (The louder birds' chirping, the more tranquil the mounts)" is not as good as its ancient precursors, it still can be rated ingenious. But, coupled by "chan zao lin yu jing (The more cicadas' buzzing, the more hushed the woods)", its poetic beauty is thus impaired due to the aforementioned repetitiousness.

And the third one is the first pair of verses "mu chan bu ke ting (As it is distressing to hear dying cicadae buzzing)/luo ye qi kan wen (So the sight of leaves falling can be an agony)" (in Lang Shiyuan's poem "To Bid Adieu to Qian Da at Zheng Yi's Residence in Zhouzhi County"). They were commended by Gao Zhongwu of the Tang Dynasty in his *The Anthology of the Poetry of the Resurgent Period of the Tang Dynasty* for "being well crafted from the very beginning", yet, in the eyes of the poetry critics of the Ming and Qing dynasties, had little craft to speak of or rather, in the eyes of Wang Shimao of the Ming Dynasty, even deserved scorn and thus, as Mao Xianshu of the Qing Dynasty judged, were not worth emulation, due to their dull monotonousness as a result of expression by the two verses of the same meaning, which was not inspiring.

Heterogeneous antithetical symmetry, according to Liu Xie, means that one of a pair of verses seemingly differs from but essentially complements the other in meaning. To exemplify this, he cited Wang Can's pair of verses "zhong yi you er chu zou xi (Zhong Yi, though prisoned, still played his home tune on his zither)/zhuang xi xian er yue yin (Zhuang Xi, though ennobled, still spoke his native dialect)" in his "Rhapsody on Ascending Maicheng Tower". Strictly speaking, his citation does not apply here, because, first, it is not from a poem, the subject in question, but from a rhapsody; second, it is antithetical but not symmetrical; and, third, it better exemplifies homogeneous antithesis than heterogeneous antithesis. Given that, let us look for other examples, such as "min jie shi qian shou (A thousand poems spring out of your quick brain)/piao ling jiu yi bei (In exile you gulp down your loneliness with a cup of wine)" (in Du Fu's "The Absence"), in which "min jie (quick brain)" and "piao ling (in exile)", "qian shou (a thousand poems)" and "yi bei (a cup of wine)", the two pairs in striking contrast, sketch accurately the persona of the poem, a solitary Li Bai, Du Fu's friend, who experienced ups and downs or woe and weal in his singular eventful life, and such heterogeneous antithesis imbues the two verses with subtle nuances.

78   *Tonal and metrical schemes*

Here is the suggestion: heterogeneous antithetical symmetry should be broadly understood; that is, any pair of verses which separately project various images, convey various meanings, arouse various feelings, and so forth should fall under this category, for example, Wang Wei's "qing gu lin shui ba (Green cane shoots stand tall over waters)/bai niao xiang shan fan（White birds are fluttering up towards mounts）", wherein "qing (green)" versus "bai (white), "gu (cane shoots)" versus "niao (birds)", and "lin shui (over waters) versus "xiang shan (towards mounts)", in contrast, create an image of expansive space; Lang Shiyuan's "chan sheng jing kong guan (The singing of cicadae quietened the empty lodge)/yu se ge qiu yuan (The mist of rain screened the autumnal field)" shifts between near and far, interior and exterior, and sound and hue; Wei Yingwu of the Tang Dynasty's "mo mo fan lai chong (Sails are approaching in smoky vapour)/ming ming niao qu chi (Birds are receding in hazy twilight)" contrasts nearing sails on water with disappearing birds in the air in terms of space and movement; and Du Fu's "wan li bei qiu chang zuo ke (The autumnal vistas saddened me, a traveller thousands of miles away from home)/bai nian duo bing du deng tai (I, suffering all my life from ailments, ascended a highly raised terrace by myself)" contains as many as eight pertinent references which, antithetically symmetrized separately in two seven-word or hepta-syllabic verses, give vent to the poet's pent-up feelings (see *Jade Dew in the Crane's Forest or Tales of the Men of Letters of the Song Dynasty* by Luo Dajing of the Song Dynasty).

As these examples show, heterogeneous antithetical symmetry helps to expand the horizons of a poem in many aspects. Ancient Chinese poetry critics, who were not adept at definitely conceptualizing its function, turned to impressionistic description, as in the Qing Dynasty poetry critic Zhu Tinzhen's (also known as Xiaoyuan) *Xiaoyuan's Remarks on Poetry*: "A pair of verses in antithetical symmetry must contrast with each another . . . by near versus far, aural versus visual" or as in Mao Chunrong's *Shenyuan's Poetic Discourse*: "Commotion versus quietude, high versus low, vertical versus horizontal, more versus less, etc."

In modern terms, heterogeneous antithetical symmetry enables a pair of verses to attain (1) visual openness and contrast, as in Wang Zhihuan of the Tang Dynasty's "bai ri yi shan jin (A fading sun is setting beyond mounts)/huang he ru hai liu (The Yellow River is flowing towards seas)" and Wang Wei's "da mo gu yan *zhi* (A plum of smoke on a vast barren desert was rising like an upright column)/chang he luo ri *yuan* (A sun descending against a long river appeared even rounder)"; (2) temporal shift and overlapping, as in Lu You's "xiao lou yi ye ting chun yu (Outside my low-storeyed house the spring rain was heard falling all night)/shen xiang ming zhao mai xing hua (Along deep alleys peddlers would be selling apricot flowers the next morrow)"; (3) nuanced and contrastive conveyance of meaning, as in Li Shangyin's "shen wu cai feng shuang fei yi (Although you and I, unlike the phoenix, have no wings to fly together)/xin you ling xi yi dian tong (We both have the magic-horn-like sensibility to understand each other at a slight touch)"; and (4) the reader's empathy with the description of physical externalities, as in Lin Bu's "shu ying heng xie shui qing qian (Limpid shallow water was reflecting obliquely sprayed thin plum blossoms)/an xiang fu dong yue huang hun (At dusk under the moon in the air was lingering an aroma)".

The advantage of heterogeneous antithetical symmetry over homogeneous antithetical symmetry lies in that it enables what is asynchronous to be concurrent in terms of imagery, sensation, and the like, wherein contrast, intensification, and transformation imbue pairs of verses with more than what they literally carry, as in "bai ri yi shan jin (A fading sun is setting beyond mounts)/huang he ru hai liu (The Yellow River is flowing towards seas)", in which a setting sun and undulating mountain ridges to the west, on the one hand, and the racing Yellow River and an extensive wilderness to the east, on the other, are artistically compressed into one frame of imagery against the infinite universe; in "da mo gu yan zhi (A plume of smoke on a vast barren desert was rising like an upright column)/chang he luo ri yuan (A sun descending against a long river appeared even rounder)", in which a horizontal plain versus a meandering river and a rising pillar of smoke versus a sun coursing down a trajectory, offer the reader a far more expansive perspective; and in "xiao lou yi ye ting chun yu (Outside my low-storeyed house spring rain was heard falling all night)/shen xiang ming zhao mai xing e hua (Along deep alleys peddlers would be selling apricot flowers the next morrow)", whose second verse represents only the poet's vision, which could be provoked by actual pattering spring rainfall, of peddlers hawking their white apricot flowers with drops of spring rain, in which two images, the image of rain pattering right now at night and apricot flowers being sold on the morrow, overlap.

This is why heterogeneous antithetical symmetry supersedes homogeneous. Indeed, the former features variousness and complementariness, whereas the latter strikes one as repetitious and monotonous; more importantly, the former inspires the reader's imagination much more than the latter. And a pair of verses, heterogeneously in antithetical symmetry in every aspect, looks far removed from each other in terms of reference and separate in space but actually are concurrent in meaning, and they together project a montage of images which compel the reader to contemplate, as in the case of "xie feng chui bai ye (Sideway winds were sweeping away scattered leaves)/han zhu zhao chou ren (A burning candle in cold was shedding light on a plaintive wayfarer)" (in Du Xunhe's "Lodging in a Mountainous Tavern in the Fall"), which compels the reader to ponder what the images in the different perspectives can metaphorically mean, by dint of:

1 fallen leaves being swept by sideway winds and a plaintive wayfarer in the light of a burning candle at a cold night;
2 the outdoor scene and the man inside the tavern; and
3 sideways winds and a burning candle on a cold night, as well as scattered fallen leaves and the plaintive wayfarer.

By way of such contemplation affinities shall be found between this pair of antithetically symmetrical verses, in terms not just of tone and meter but even of meaning, thus they are linked closely with each other and combine to produce a powerful impact. On the other hand, they are antithetical, after all, in terms of perspective, wording, reference, and so on, so there is "tension" between them that can strike the reader as sharply contrastive, as in Jia Dao of the Tang Dynasty's "niao su chi bian shu (Birds perched on the trees by the pond)/seng qiao yue xia men (In moonlight a monk was tapping at the door)" (in his "Reflection on Having Not Visited with Li Ning at his Reclusive Abode"), wherein "tension" between quietude and noisiness and darkness and light is strongly felt by the reader, who will first have two separate and then overlapping visual and aural images in the course of appreciation, also as in Jiao Dao's "du xing tan di ying (The Pond reflected him, a lonely wayfarer)/shu xi shu bian shen (He leaned many times on trees for a rest)" (in his "To See Off Revered Monk Wu Ke"), whose symmetrical antitheses are not just between different locations, that is, on the side of the pond versus by the trees along the journey, but between indefinite time of solitary travel and definite times of rest, as well as between moving versus static; thus the reader will have to discern such antitheses and scrutinize them separately before integrating them into a meaningful whole, just as in the case of Du Xunhe's "Lodging in a Mountainous Tavern in the Fall", which we have just discussed, in stark contrast to a pair of verses in homogeneous symmetrical antithesis between which each squarely overlaps the other.

The advantage of heterogeneous antithetical symmetry was also detected by Wang Yingkui, who, in his *Liunan's Desultory Notes*, criticized Feng Wu of the early Qing Dynasty's "zhu yuan hua shang lu (Dews scattered on flowers appear as round as pearls)/yu sui cao tou shuang (Frost covering grass blades look like bits of broken jade)", though symmetrical, for being ingenuous, as a result of homogeneous antithesis, which disagreed with the notion of

> Of a pair of verses in good antithetical symmetry, the first verse does not give to the second one any clue, to acquire which, the reader will have to think hard but often can end up in frustration. This happens only in the case of the heterogeneous antithetical symmetry.

Of a pair of verses in heterogeneous antithetical symmetry, one verse seemingly differs, in every corresponding aspect, from the other, so absence of one of the two verses would make it an unbeatable challenge for the reader to conceive what it could be, even though he has read the other, because such a pair, unlike that of homogeneous antithesis, rejects square overlapping altogether. This is comparable to a duet that is performed at once in diversity and in harmony. At this point, a conclusion can be reached that, as beauty is taken as something that arouses a sense of equilibrium in its appreciator, so heterogeneous antithetical symmetry effects aesthetic appeal through its two kinds of apparently conflicting yet naturally reconciling powers inherent in a pair of verses which operate together to intensify expressiveness. Zhu Tingzhen of the Qing Dynasty, also known as Xiaoyuan, in his *Xiaoyuan's Commentaries on Poetry*, observed that "A pair of verses as such seem poles apart but, in nature, breathe the same breath". Indeed, and, what's more, the tension therefrom enriches their meanings and broadens their horizon.

That said, there is an obstacle that can defy an ancient Chinese poet to overcome. As far as they are concerned, pairs of verses in antithetical symmetry are the brainchildren of poets rather than growths out of nature, no matter how delicately crafted and no matter what aesthetic appeal they can have. Any vestige of artificial contrivance, in the eyes of ancient Chinese poets, tarnished what they enshrined as the holiest tenet: naturalness. Antithetical symmetry is contrived, so it certainly is unnatural. Then, how to naturalize unnaturally contrived pairs of verses in antithetical symmetry?

One may turn to Liu Xie's "When the Creator created human beings, He endowed them with pairs of limbs to their torsi"; to the ancient Chinese philosophy of Yin and Yang; to the physical world, where "there are laws that govern the relationships between Heavens and Earth. So there are laws for pairs of verses in antithetical symmetry. A poem in antithetical symmetry is comparable to a bird who is born with a pair of wings"; or to the earliest oracular indication as "shui liu shi (water flows to a wet depression); huo jiu zao (fire spreads toward a dry area); yun cong long (clouds drift when a dragon moans); feng cong hu (winds blow as a tiger roars)", to choose just a few, for evidence that antithetical symmetry in versification, though seemingly an unnatural contrivance, came into being naturally. Still, such evidence is far from convincing, for there is no escaping the fact that the Recent Style poetry which started from the Southern Dynasties and matured in the Tang Dynasty is full of exquisitely *crafted* verses in antithetical symmetry. Such unnatural "crafted" work certainly is what the poets who upheld naturalness renounced. But simple renunciation of artificial contrivance for sheer naturalness should not be a way out, for simple and plain versification is natural yet at the expense of the aesthetic appeal of a poem. So, a workable alternative should be striking a balance. But how? Jiao Ran, in his *Styles of Poetry: Poets' Active and Strenuous Mental Work*, seemed to be directing a way out, saying that

> there are laws that govern composition of pairs of verses in antithetical symmetry, as there are laws that govern the relationships between Heaven and Earth, between monarch and minister, and between father and son. They all are preordained, which is manifestation of natural laws. In the case of versification, any vestige of artificiality goes against the tenet of naturalness. Unnaturalness certainly is not what the poet intends.

But, actually, his remarks sound like a kind of observation or rather suggestion that antithetical symmetry in versification should be crafted so naturally that no vestige of unnaturalness would be detected, like a woman's skilled needlework that looks smooth and seamless or like a woman's delicate facial make-up that defies the keenest eyes looking for any trace of cosmetics. The emphasis of his advice can be understood to be laid on this: craftiness is needed, but, at the same time, this craftiness must not be detected; in other words, a poet should pursue naturalness in unnaturalness.

To practice this suggestion, ancient Chinese poets had to shift their focus from the rigid form, eventually, to their natural sensibility and the vitality of their poems. In his *Canghai's Commentaries on Poetry*, Wu Ke, also known as Canhai Lay Buddhist, of the Song Dynasty, maintained that "If a poet should focus on the rigid antithetical symmetry, it would devitalize his poetry. Thus, a poet should let the vitality of his poetry take precedence over the rigid antithetical symmetry". This viewpoint, to some, sounded arbitrary, so they retorted, "Isn't it ridiculous to blame on antithetical symmetry for its having devitalized a poem that itself is weak in vitality?" Interestingly, there were poets such as those with the Jiangxi Poetry Society who chose not to craft pairs of verses in antithetical symmetry lest their antithetical symmetry should, if not well crafted, betray their unskillfulness or, if over-crafted, reveal their unnaturalness. Their fear was scoffed at by Ge Lifang of the Song Dynasty, who, in his *Ge Lifang's Commentaries on Poetry*, criticized them for their lack of audacity. But neither Wu nor Ge contributed substantially to how to deal naturally with antithetical symmetry.

In that case, we would do well to listen to what other ancient Chinese poetry critics said about antithetical symmetry:

"willows" is used to contrast "flowers", which is too conventional. An antithetical symmetry as such actually is not a good one, thus deficient.
(*Baishidaoren's Poetic Discourse* by Jiang Kui)

For a pair of verses in antithetical symmetry, robust is preferable to delicate, unskillful to skillful, and plain to adorned. Nevertheless, conventionality and coarseness must be shunned.
(*Techniques of Versification* by Yang Zai of the Yuan Dynasty)

Evidently, Jiang Kui cautioned poets against readily copying their predecessors' antitheses, which would entomb their own creativity and originality; Yang Zai recommended plainness in embellishment, which would strike the reader as natural speech. To exemplify Yang Zai's recommendation, let us look at Ye Mengde, Yang's predecessor, commenting, in his *Tales and Critique of Poetry at Shilin*, on Du Fu's two verses "xi yu yu er chu (In misty drizzles fishes were leaping out of water)/wei feng yan zi xie (Against gentle breezes swallows were flying obliquely overhead)": they were composed with ingenuity yet without a vestige of artificiality, for each of the five words of each verse of this couplet, which seemed effortlessly harnessed, actually was a painstaking result of aptness and accuracy, insofar as none could be dispensable. Du's ingenious contrivance in the guise of ease and naturalness certainly is beyond the capacity of a mediocre poet, who can only, at best, spawn such an uninspiring unnatural antithetically symmetrical couplet as "yu yue lian chuan pao yu chi (A fish leaping out of a ribbon-like river looks like a ruler of jade)/ying chuan si liu zhi jin suo (An oriole flying through willow twigs seems to be a passing golden shuttle)". Thus, another criterion for a pair of verses in antithetical symmetry is that they should be concocted so ingeniously as to show no vestige of concoction. This is a much more demanding criterion.

Then, what exactly is it that should be done to meet this high criterion? Any specific answer has not been found as yet in what ancient Chinese poets or poetry critics ever theorized about. For, after all, it is something that is too metaphysical for verbal description but has to be mentally perceived. Even so, what ancient

Tonal and metrical schemes 83

Chinese poets or poetry critics themselves did or felt about versification could be a revelation. So let us look at Ye Mengde's *Tales and Critique of Poetry at Shilin*:

> In his last leg of life, Grandee Wang Anshi was stricter than ever before with any of his couplets. He would not allow for any redundant word in each verse. Moreover, his wording, which should represent his intention, thus must agree with it, and vice versa. In a word, his couplet is a crafted yet natural one of symbiosis. For example, his "han feng ya lv lin lin qi (In breezes greenish waters are rippling in glitter)/nong ri e huang niao niao chui (In sunlight yellowish willows are swaying their slender twigs)" and "xi shu luo hua yin zuo jiu (I sat a long time for having counted fallen blossoms)/huan xun fang cao de gui chi (I returned late for having spent much time seeking orchids)" hide his hard-earned antithetical symmetry behind ease and leisure and attain subtlety and profundity through indiscernible chosen diction.
>
> The poetry by Grandee Ouyang Xiu shows that he was the first one to rectify the defects of the Xikun School poetry (the poems by a school of poets, the name of whose style alludes to the west of Mount Kunlun, a legendary mountain where immortals were believed to reside). His poetry focuses on spirit, thus most of his poetic words are plain, simple, and unrestrained. His pairs of verses can seem lacking in antithetical symmetry. Even so, this is not what he cared about. He cared only about whether what he intended to express would have been perfectly expressed. . . . But his poetry boasts more than this merit. Take for instance his pair of verses from his "Reflection on the Inscription Left by Princess Chonghui of the Tang Dynasty" which read "yu yan zi gu wei shen lei (Ever since remote antiquity any beauty would suffer from her such endowment)/rou shi he ren yu guo mou (Who among those of high rank or status ever has ever considered the destiny of his country)?" They are his observations on a historical interlude and a political climate. This pair of heptasyllabic verses undulates in tone. Into them one can read euphony and power. They run, word for word, in such antithetical symmetry that even the best of the Xikun School poets would marvel at it. Their diction and intention so consummately fuse into one that it should be deemed the acme of perfection.
>
> In versification, allusions must not far-fetchedly be exploited. Allusions must not be exploited unless their exploitation is necessary. This ensures blending of allusions into verses to form a natural whole. Su Shi's pair of elegiac verses "qi yi ri xie geng zi hou (Imagine that the sun descended across the sky a while ago)/hu jing sui zai si chen nian (Yet, taken aback, I had the illusion that ages had passed)" exemplify how a pair of verses in antithetical symmetry are naturally composed, which shows no poet's exertion. But the antithetical symmetry in Wen Tingyun's pair of verses "feng juan peng gen tun wu ji (Although the imperial army is stationed along the frontier where winds sweep off even rooted grasses)/yue yi zhuo ying shou geng shen (One

can't lay his heart at rest as the moon drifts and shadows keep distorting)" is much inferior, as the symmetrical antithesis between the allusions separately in each of his two verses are contrived merely for the sake of symmetrical antithesis . . . thus the allusions are far-fetched.

The first quotation is mainly about a poet's intention, whose pivotal role takes precedence over wording and antithetical symmetry. What a poet should do is, first and foremost, pervade his poem with what and how he feels about something. He then weighs words and devises his antithetical symmetry to represent it. His pair of verses as such thus read naturally both in wording and structure.

The second quotation highlights spirit to attain naturalness. Doing so sidelines wording and antithetical symmetry, opposed to which is the practice by the Xikun School poets, who exerted themselves to word, rhyme, and symmetrize their pairs of verses and embed them with allusions for the sake of allusion at the cost of genuineness, coherence, and fluidity, which is also the case in the third quotation. For example, for the sake of antithetical symmetry, Wen Tingyun unnaturally paired "geng shen", which metonymically means "one can't lay his heart at rest", and "wu ji", which metonymically means "the imperial army is stationed along the frontier". That is why He Shang of the Qing Dynasty, in his *A Discourse on Poetry at Zaijiu Garden*, dismissed it as an awkward contrivance, which, seemingly ingenious, makes little sense but, worse, affects fluidity. Another case is Xu Hun of the Tang Dynasty's "xi yun chu qi ri chen ge (Panxi is being abruptly clouded, with the sun falling beyond the temple)/shan yu yu lai feng man lou (Winds roaring through the tower is heralding imminent rain from mounts)", whose antithetical symmetry feels artificially strained, because the first verse of this couplet is coupled, for the sake of antithetical symmetry only, with the second one and thus a forced antithetical symmetry.

All in all, as far as the previous is concerned, when it comes to whether antithetical symmetry in versification is natural, it is a matter of either-or: to attain natural antithetical symmetry, intention and/or spirit must be put before wording, tone, meter, allusion, and so on and not the other way around. But doing so should in turn benefit what is secondary, that is, wording, tone, meter, allusion, and so on, which should in correspondence come naturally to a poet's mind.

But for a poet to reach this high level really is a huge challenge. Who of ancient Chinese poets is adept at dealing with his intention and/or the spirit of his poetry: the primary thing(s), on the one hand, and, on the other hand, for example, antithetical symmetry, the secondary thing, so ingeniously yet naturally, without the tiniest imperfection? In fact, one would be achieved, more or less, at the cost of the other. He Yisun of the Qing Dynasty, in his *The Raft of Poetry*, likened antithetical symmetry in versification to either a string of pearls, each shining on the other, or a round piece of jade, rolling unimpeded, effortlessly and naturally. This certainly is ideal but, in actuality, a dream that may never come true. Like the rockeries in one's garden and the mountains in the wild, certainly, the former will always be artificial, however they can be made, whereas the latter natural just because of their crudeness. In a sense, to antithetically symmetrize a pair of verses in a crude yet clever way can be an insurmountable obstacle for a poet. How to surmount it and to what extent depends on his aptitude and wisdom. That is why Jiaoran, in his *Styles of Poetry: Poets' Active and Strenuous Mental Work*, lamented: "When it comes to antithetical symmetry, if plainness is emphasized over daintiness, it leads to sacrifice of intriguing contrivance; if meaning is emphasized over wording, it leads to sacrifice of refined elegance". Indeed, this is the conundrum that can defy the effort of a poet to find a solution both for ingenuity and naturalness. Regardless, ancient Chinese poetry critics such as Ge Lifang, Jiangkui, and Zhang Biaochen, of the Song Dynasty, still theorized, in the hope of finding an equilibrium, about what they assumed to be a solution, like "While a poet prizes deliberation, he should also guard against artificiality; while a poet prizes straightforwardness, he should also guard against coarseness" (in *Ge Lifang's Commentaries on Poetry*); "Craftiness should not impede permeation of vitality and embellishment should not harm naturalness. Bear it in mind that roughness results from a lack of ingenuity and no embellishment causes ruggedness" (in Jiang Kui's *Baishidaoren's Poetic Discourse*); and "Versification should prioritize deep-rooted naturalness over superficial craftiness" (in Zhang Biaochen's *A Miscellany of Insightful Remarks on Poetry and Other Subjects*), which actually smack of a bias. And, in reality, their solutions are theoretical only. There is no denying that there are epitomes of this equilibrium such as the aforementioned Du Fu's pair of verses and also his "liang ge huang li ming cui liu (A pair of orioles are chirping through green wickers)/yi hang bai lu shang qing tian (A flight of egrets are soaring up to the azure)". But how many ancient Chinese poets could have ever achieved what Du Fu did? And how many more pairs of verses even by Du Fu himself could have attained such divine equilibrium as the two pairs of verses in question?

4.3. Change in the number of couplets within a poem in the development of Recent Style poetry

Recent Style poetry is the epitome of ancient Chinese poetry. Its fundamental feature is its antithetical symmetry between the odd-numbered verse and the even-numbered one that immediately follows it. Recent Style poetry became more poetic than past poetry mainly because of its antithetically symmetrical couplets, which ensured aspects such as regular alternation between tones, musical cadence, juxtaposition of imagery, shifting perspectives, contrasts, overlapping in temporal and spatial descriptions, and so forth, or, in other words, these aspects sustained the pattern of antithetical symmetry. Eventually, nevertheless, a flaw in early Recent Style poetry shows itself. Just as a piece of music, however melodious, can bore its audience if it lasts, as if it has no limit, repetitiously, so it is with early Recent Style poetry, no matter how euphonic each couplet might be, as it should be rolling on too many such couplets. So the number of couplets needs to be limited, and this is an evolutionary process.

86 *Tonal and metrical schemes*

True, compared to past poets, the poets of the Southern Dynasties began to pay far more attention to antithetical symmetry, of which the tonal and metrical schemes are the key part; thus they, by virtue of this, started composing what is known as Recent Style poetry, even if back then, it was nascent. But, at the same time, they were obsessed with the tonal euphony and metrical beauty of pairs of verses in antithetical symmetry and would repetitiously and tediously overuse such couplets in their poems, to the point of boring their readers. This flaw is obvious in early Recent Style poems by even major, not to mention minor, poets:

Take the major poets' poems, for instance:

hun dan bian qi hou/shan shui han qing hui.
(Weather varies from dawn to dusk/Mounts and waters bask in shimmery effulgence.)
qing hui neng yu ren/you zi dan wang gui.
(Such a light-hued view was pleasant to me, a sightseer/Who, so indulging it, was reluctant to return home.)
chu gu ri shang zao/ru zhou yang yi wei.
(The sun was still high up in the sky when we went out of the valley/By the time we got on board the boat the twilight had diffused.)
lin he lian ming se/yun xia shou xi fei.
(Duskiness shrouded the woods and vale altogether/Billowing glowing clouds had by then disappeared.)
ji he die ying wei/pu bai xiang yin yi.
(Waternut and lotus in the lake set off one another/Cattail and weeds grew together like good companions.)
pi fu qu nan jing/yu yue yan dong fei.
(I parted the grass along the access to my doorway/In the eastern chamber I happily lay down on my back.)
lv dan wu zi qing/yi qie li wu wei.
(The less worried about gain or loss, the more indifferent to externalities/The more satiation of one's heart, the less violation of the canon for longevity)
ji yan she sheng ke/shi yong ci dao tui.
(Take my advice, my folks, if you hope for good health/This should be the way you practice for well-being.)
            ("Returning to my Shibi Study by Way of the Lake" by Xie Lingyun)

jiang lu xi nan yong/gui liu dong bei wu.
(I have embarked on a long journey south-westward on the river/While the river is racing north-eastward into the sea.)
tian ji shi gui zhou/yun zhong bian jiang shu.
(Returning boats on the distant horizon can still be distinguished/So be the hazy trees afar on the river.)
lv si juan yao yao/gu you xi yi lv.
(My rocking boat, my tiring journey, makes me feel drowsy/Lonesome is my journey, but I have experienced many like this.)

ji huan huai lu qing/fu xie cang zhou qu.
(I have gratefully enjoyed His Majesty's grace and ensuing benefits/But reclusion at a far undisturbed place is a greater bliss.)
xiao chen zi zi ge/shang xin cong ci yu.
(Ever since I will have isolated myself from noise and dust/What an opportunity, an honour generously bestowed on me.)
sui wu xuan bao zi/zhong yin nan shan wu.
(Incomparable to a mythic wise leopard who evaded perils/Still I can hide in fogs in southern mounts as my guardians.)

    ("A Poem Composed from Xinlinpu to Banqiaopu on the Journey
            to Xuancheng Magistracy" by Xie Tiao)

shi ce qian jin ma/lai deng wu zhang yuan.
(Why not ride your pedigree steed/To ascend up to Wuzhang Highland?)
you cheng reng jiu xian/wu shu ji xin cun.
(For the outlook of towns/the sight of woods, the view of hamlets.)
shui xiang lan chi po/ri xie xi liu yuan.
(Streams ending in the fair lake/Slender wickers lacing a descending rounder sun.)
he zhu tong sha lu/han qu se shui men.
(A sandy path in the dry river linking the islet/A ditch frozen all the way to where it originates.)
dan de feng yun shang/he xu ren shi lun.
(When there is such a view for you to relish/How relieved you shall be of those worldly concerns.)

   ("A Poem Composed for the Outlook of the Countryside" by Yu Xin)

It must be acknowledged that the three poems in question offer a few genius verses. But, nonetheless, each of them, as a whole, smacks more or less of monotony, insipidness, and dullness. This is because, as a close look indicates, first, the pairs of verses in antithetical symmetry run throughout, with almost every two verses end-rhymed homophonically; second, all the couplets but the ending ones that preach a moral describe views; and, third, they are overlong and crammed with too many identically patterned verses. Thus who as a reader will not eventually lose interest in a poem of this kind, especially when he or she is compelled to follow its writer from scene to scene and, in the end, listen to his abrupt preaching? And, as these three poems demonstrate, this characterizes the nascent Recent Style poetry of the Southern Dynasties. The poets at the time enjoyed shifting their perspectives with their changing itineraries, their thought flow thus corresponding, without caring about whether their approaches would suit the reader, who, after all, should be allowed, metaphorically speaking, some warm-up, preparing mentally and physically for such an arduous hike. But the reader bumps, at the very beginning, into scenery and, before having the leisure of appreciating it, is overwhelmed by dazzling descriptions, one pair after another, of more scenery. He or she is led, involuntarily, to this or that scenery and feels as if such a tour would be lengthy when he or she is stopped by an abrupt end which preaches a moral. And the better part of such a poem runs short of either climax or anticlimax, with its ending pair and others disconnected. So small wonder that Zhong Rong, in his *Critique of Poetry*, deplored such flaws in poems by Xie Lingyun, Yan Yanzhi, and Xie Tiao. Even Emperor Jianwen of the Liang period of the Southern Dynasties, according to *The History of the Southern Dynasties*, detected in Xie Lingyun's poems flaws such as being "unrestrained and lacking in correspondence between beginning and end". As late as the Qing Dynasty, Huang Ziyun, in his *The Yardsticks by Yehong for Critique of Poetry*, warned against emulation of aspects of poems by the poets of the Southern Dynasties such as "over-length" and "too many antithetically symmetrical pairs of verses for a single poem".

But, to be fair, poets, like Xie Lingyun, Xie Tiao, and Yu Xin, from the beginning to the end of the Southern Dynasties, no matter whether they were aware of this, eventually de facto limited and reduced the number of antithetically symmetrical pairs of verses in their scenery poems. Actually, the three previous poems can, though not very obviously, demonstrate this trend. Indeed, the statistics, in terms of length, about all the poems (exclusive of the poems modelled on the style of Yuefu Poetry or Ballads) by Xie Lingyun, Xie Tiao, and Yu Xin further prove it:

	Xie Lingyun	Xie Tiao	Yu Xin
Number of verses		Number of poems	
16 and more	50	28	28
14	5	6	15
12	2	1	15
10	2	16	42
8	4	36	70
6	1		3
4			53
Total	64	87	226

Figure 4.3 The Number of Poems With Various Numbers of Verses by Xie Lingyun, Xie Tiao, and Yu Xin Here

Tonal and metrical schemes 89

As the figure shows, the bulk of Xie Lingyun's poems are long ones (sixteen and more verses for a poem), Xie Taio's long and short poems are almost equal in proportion, and the percentage of short poems (ten and fewer verses for a poem) of Yu Xin's poems remarkably increases. Both the decrease in the number of long poems and the increase in the number of short poems could be the outcome of evolutionary selection, for a poet is believed to have the spontaneity, rather than the awareness, of improving his poetry in every aspect, certainly including optimization of its length, to attain more aesthetic appeal. Optimization of this nature, in case of the Recent Style poetry, continued until the early years of the Tang Dynasty when it matured, as we see today, set in one of the basic forms (another of which is "jue ju"), that is, "lv shi".

Then why become set in the form of a "lv shi" poem, or rather one of eight verses, instead of six or ten per poem? This question, as with that of golden section, might be unanswerable. For it is often about, as said previously, one's spontaneity that is there but hard to describe verbally. But, given that annotations and commentaries on "lv shi" poems abound, we may well, by virtue of these, as well as of my inference, which may be liable to be somewhat assumptive or arbitrary, identify an answer.

For a Recent Style poem, the "l" and "d" tones should alternate intratextually and contrast intertextually. A pair of verses as such constitute one unit of tonal pattern. According to ancient Chinese poets, who had the notion of, as mentioned, Yin and Yang or dichotomy, which was believed to complete a cycle, another pair of verses, that is, another unit of tonal pattern, symmetrically antithetical to the preceding one, should thus be needed. The two units of tonal pattern make a cycle. Take, for instance, the first two pairs of verses in a Du Fu's "lv shi" poem entitled "Spring Outlook":

guo po shan he zai /
(Tone: d d l l d)
(The country remains intact, despite destruction of its capital /)
cheng chun cao mu shen.
(Tone: l l d d l)
(Within the capital, wild grasses and trees are overgrowing with arrival of spring.)
gan shi hua jian lei /
(Tone: l l l d d)
(The sight of desolateness moves me to tears dropping on untended flowers /)
hen bie niao jing xin.
(Tone: d d d l l)
(My heart should be more agitated by even a bird's shrill when I'm departing.)

The two tonal patterns contrast to make a tonal cycle.

Another example is Wang Wei's first two pairs of verses in his "lv shi" poem entitled "A View of the Autumnal Evening near my Mount Villa":

kong shan xin yu hou /
(Tone: l l l d d)

90   *Tonal and metrical schemes*

(Fresh rain has just fallen on untrodden quiet mountains /)
tian qi wan lai qiu.
(Tone: d d d l l)
(Towards evening an autumnal chill is being felt.)
ming yue song jian zhao /
(Tone: d d l l d)
(A bright moon is shedding its brilliance through pine trees /)
qing quan shi shang liu.
(Tone: l l d d l)
(A stream of clean crystal spring water is gurgling down over vale boulders.)

Also, the two tonal patterns antithetically and symmetrically make a tonal cycle.

Worthy of note is that such a tonal cycle is how a "jue ju" poem is tonally schemed. A "lv shi" poem consists of two "jue ju" poems or two quatrains. Let us look respectively at the other quatrains of Du Fu's "Spring Outlook" and Wang Wei's "A View of the Autumnal Evening near my Mount Villa":

feng huo lian san yue /
(Tone: d d l l d)
(When war fire has been burning as long as three months/)
jia shu di wan jin.
(Tone: l l d d l)
(A family letter can be as valuable as a gold nugget.)
bai tou sao geng duan /
(Tone: l l l d d)
(Scratching thinned my thinner grey hair /)
hun yu bu sheng zan.
(Tone: d d d l l)
(Not to be tufted to hold a hairpin.)

                                                    (by Du Fu)

zhu xuan gui huan nv /
(Tone: l l l d d)
(Din from the bamboo grove foretells that washer-maids are returning /)
lian dong xia yu zhou.
(Tone: d d d l l)
(The swaying lotus betrays a fishing boat that is passing underneath.)
sui yi chun fang xie /
(Tone: d d l l d)
(Let vernal blossoms and grasses be as it may eventually be /)
wang sun zi ke liu.
(Tone: l l d d l)
(In autumn I'd choose to stay here to live a reclusive life.)

Obviously, in terms of tonal pattern, the second parts or quatrains of Du's and Wang's "lv shi" poems repeat their first parts or quatrains or, in other words, a "lv

Tonal and metrical schemes 91

shi" poem, whatever it may be, universally consists of two basically identical tonal cycles.

But why is a "lv shi" poem tonally devised like this? This should not be understood to be simply a "refrain". As mentioned, the poets of the Southern Dynasties began to reduce the number of pairs of antithetically symmetrized verses. Their reduction also involved putting in intervals so that not all pairs of verses were antithetically symmetrized, or else a "lv shi" poem would feel jammed as a result of repetition of the same pattern. Such intervals should also be in the form of pairs of verses which, strictly speaking, were not antithetically symmetrical. For example, Yin Keng's first pair of verses "ke xing feng ri mu (Twilight began to greet me a traveller)/jie lan wan zhou zhong (I moored my boat at Wuzhou towards evening)" and the last pair of verses "yao lian yi zhu guan (Lo and behold, that column-like sight afar)/yu qing qian li feng (It seems to aspire to flight on breezes over a thousand miles)" of his poem entitled "Moored at Wuzhou for a Night" are not antithetically symmetrized, except for its middle two pairs of verses "shu lou yin kan xian (The garrison tower erected on a precipice looks hazardous)/cun lu ru jiang qiong (The hamlet path comes to an end where the river flows)" and "shui sui yun du hei (The waters gloomed while clouds darkened)/shan dai ri gui hong (Mountains reddened with the glow of a setting sun)". So it is also with the first and last pairs of verses of Jiang Zong's poem entitled "Using the Old Verse 'Hand in Hand upon the Venue of Departure' to Entitle the Poem Composed in Response to the Decree by His Majesty", which read "zao qiu tian qi liang (Early autumn air feels chilly)/fen shou guan shan chang (Mountains ahead will stretch, from where we depart, range after range)" and "qin chuan xin duan jue (Qinchuan is where our hearts can break)/he wu shi he liang (How has it ever occurred to us that this should be the venue of departure?)" and the middle two pairs of verses, which read "yun chou shu chu hei (Patches of melancholic clouds look gloomy)/mu luo ji zhi huang (Leafless trees retain a few bare yellow boughs)" and "niao gui you shi lu (Even a returned bird knows its direction)/liu qu bu zhi xiang (A roamer is at a loss for where he is bound)". And a third similar example is Li Juren of the Sui Dynasty's "Using the Old Verse 'Whitish Waters Contained in the Square Pond' to Entitle My Poem":

bai shui yi fang tang /
(Whitish water fills the square pond to the full /)
miao miao su bo yang.
(It thus is heaving with whitish waves.)
die lang qing fu ying /
(Swelling with waves are dexterous wild ducks /)
lian yi xie yan hang.
(Ripples are reflecting flights of wild geese.)
chang di liu se cui /
(Willows along the long embankment are greening /)
jia an xing hua huang.
(Flanking the banks are sprouting yellow flowers.)
guan yu zi you le /
(Seeing fishes swimming here is a happy thing /)

92 *Tonal and metrical schemes*

he bi zai hao liang".
(No need to do so on the bridge over the Hao River.)

These "lv shi" poems are formed into "two couplets (which are not strictly antithetically symmetrical) or let us say two-couplet interval + two pairs of antithetically symmetrized verses + two pairs of antithetically symmetrized verse + two-couplet interval". This form coincides with the tonal scheme, that is, two identical tonal cycles, required of a "lv shi" poem. Obviously, eight verses, at a minimum, are needed to achieve this arrangement, or we could say that it is this kind of formal and tonal arrangement which is intrinsic to a "lv shi" poem that has an already predetermined minimum number of verses: eight.

"Lv shi" poetry during the Early and High Tang periods, it should be pointed out, did not conform rigidly with what has been discussed. But, after all, formal and tonal coincidence have virtues. For example, in terms of cadence, the four pairs of verses of a "lv shi" poem, comparable to four musical movements, move slowly on the first pair, which serve as a lead-in, then more and more rapidly over the middle two pairs, which project, juxtapose, and montage the images of externalities, and slowly again on the last pair, which can be either enlightening or inspiring. Because of such virtues, the embodiment of the formal and tonal coincidence and the finalized, antithetical, yet symmetrical, diverse yet harmonious, structure of "lv shi" poetry became more and more popular and was enshrined as an inviolable model.

Such poems are numerous. For example:

dong gao bo mu wang /
(Towards evening, at a reclusive place, I looked out /)
xi yi yu he yi.
(Loitering, I did not know where I'd return to.)
shu shu jie qiu se /
(Trees, each and every one, were painted in autumanl hues /)
shan shan wei luo hui.
(Ranges and ranges of mounts were shone by a setting sun.)
mu ren qu du fan /
(A herdsman was driving his cattle on the way homeward /)
lie ma dai qin gui.
(A hunter with his games was riding past where I stood.)
xiang gu wu xiang shi /
(We, unacquainted, greeted one another without a word /)
chang ge huai cai wei.
(How I wanted to, with abandon, sing as a recluse among mounts.)
                    ("The Outlook of a Countryside" by Wang Ji of the
                                      Early Tang period)

du you huan you ren /
(It is only the man who has been appointed to office far away from home /)

pian jing wu hou xin.
(Who is particularly sensitive to any change in flora and climate.)
yun xia chu hai shu /
(Morning clouds glowing over seas are heralding an imminent sun-rise /)
mei liu du jiang chun.
(Across the river plum flowers are reddening and willow wickers are greening.)
shu qi cui huang niao /
(Orioles keep chirping as if at the urge by warm vernal breezes /)
qing guang zhuan lv ping.
(Bright sunshine is making duckweed look much greener than ever before.)
Hu wen ge gu diao /
(I did not expect that you would have chanted such an old-style poem /)
Gui si yu zhan jin.
(At which my homesickness is surging, and my tears are shedding on my garment.)

("In Response to Lu Cheng, Native of Jinling,
Who Wrot.e for Me a Poem Entitled "An Early Spring Excursion"
by Du Shenyan of the High Tang period)

Also there are seven-word-a-verse eight-verse "lv shi" poems by other Tang poets, like Shen Quanqi's "A Poem Using an Ancient Title for Ballads", Su Ting's "In Response to the Decree by His Majesty Who Has Marked His Inspection on a Good Spring Day of Wangchuan (Relishing Spring) Palace by Composing a Poem", and Chu Guangxi's "Ten-Thousand-Year-Long Tower". They all adopt this form and have the same effect on the reader and his or her heart, in response with great relish, and beat with the undulation of the musical cadence.

Although the form of "lv shi" poetry is the product of the poet's spontaneity, later ancient Chinese poetry critics endeavoured to theorize about it in every aspect. Yang Zai, in his *Techniques of Versification*, characterized it with four words: "qi (opening)", "cheng (development)", "zhuan (transition)", and "he (conclusion)", expounding that its first pair of verses, as a starter, struck the reader as abrupt and commanding; its second pair of verses followed both coherently and naturally; its third pair of verses varied from yet were connected to its second one; and its ending pair of verses transcended to compel the reader's imagination and association. Yang's exposition is not off the mark but may read as pedantic; he seems to have paid more attention to coherence in content than change across the form itself, hence not to the effect of saying thus: "The first pair of verses are particularly hard to compose, for they must be lofty in meaning"; "the middle two pairs of verses must be as fluid as circulation of blood in the veins and antithetically symmetrized both in tone and in wording"; and "the last pair of verses must transcend the preceding ones and compel its readers to think further". Hu Yinglin, in his *Thickets of Criticism*, said of a five-word-a-verse eight-verse "lv shi" poem that "As a rule, its first pair of verses open a subject while its last pair of verses conclude it; and of its middle two pairs of verses, one describes sceneries while the other express sentiments". Such a view, though seemingly flawless, is still not to the point. As has been discussed, either "qi (opening)", "jing (sceneries)", "qing (sentiments)", and "jie (ending)" or "qi (opening)", "cheng (development)", "zhuan (transition)", and "he (conclusion)" not only concern the content of a "lv shi" poem, which certainly contributes to finalization of the form of the poem, but, apart from this, its finalized form also involves the pursuit of antithesis and symmetry. In this sense, the following quotation from *Random Talk from the Garden of Art* by Wang Shizhen, though somewhat enigmatic, could be comprehensive and accurate:

> A "lv shi" poem should have both a starter and an ending, both relaxation and tension, both a call and an answer, both folding and unfolding, both rising and falling, and correspondence between image and meaning. This is a rule that must not be violated.
>
> Correspondence between opening and conclusion, alternation between words and between verses, these should be perfectly organized. This is the law for composition of a "lv shi" poem.

Wang's perspective on the content (the first quotation) and the form (the second quotation) of a "lv shi" poem could further explain why completion of this kind of poem requires, at a minimum, eight verses. Such a form, the product of the poet's spontaneity or rather the poet's aesthetic intuition, happens to, as practice attests, epitomize the acme of perfection with respect to a "lv shi" poem, for it ensures the symbiosis of tone, cadence, content, meaning, and the like via antithetical symmetry.

4.4. A mysterious correspondence with the Way of Heaven

The Recent Style poetry, including "jue ju" and "lv shi", believed to best represent the ancient Chinese poetry in every aspect certainly results from the new poetic language, the new tonal and metrical schemes, the new poetic forms, the resultant antithetical symmetry and juxtaposition of imagery, and so on.

As an old saying goes, it is birds like swans and orioles that taught man to sing, so the features of Recent Style poetry, like antithetical symmetry in tone, are, as mentioned, not the brainchild of ancient poets simply through their sheer rationalization but through their intuitive perception of what ancient Chinese enshrined as the Way of Heaven, based on their mental and physical experience, by virtue of linguistic devices and by certain aesthetic principles. Worthy of note here is the significance of the Way of Heaven. Let us digress to review what *The Book of Rites* and Aristotle's *Poetics* say about tune: any tune originates from the human heart (according to the former); the sense of tune and cadence is part of human nature (according to the latter). Both telepathically agree and should support the deep-seated ancient Chinese notion that poetic tones derive from human sounds, which contain musical tunes which develop from human intrinsic vitality (see Liu Xie's *The Literary Mind and the Carving of Dragons*). And "human intrinsic vitality" is believed to correspond naturally with the Way of Heaven. So "Music is created by Heaven" (see *The Book of Rites*), "Music reflects the way of Heaven and Earth and the nature of all" (see *On Music* by Ruan Ji of the Three-Kingdom period of the Han Dynasty), and "Heaven and Earth join to grow all . . . which manifest themselves in five colours and make themselves heard in five tunes" (see *On the Absence of Sentiments in Music* by Ji Kang of the Three-Kingdom period of the Han Dynasty).

Back to poetic tones. As the universe consists essentially of Yin and Yang, so poetic tones show antitheses between, for example, unstressed and stressed, rising and falling, long and short, but in a harmonious manner, which is in conformity with Yin and Yang.

Such conformity, I would say, must come from an enigmatic divine revelation. *The Book of Change* says that "Heaven is high up whereas Earth lies underneath, so the overall order, the status of the noble and the ignoble, the state of the motion and the motionless, the property of the hard and the soft, etc., in the universe are preordained". This is the Dao, the Way of Heaven, or Yin and Yang. According to *Laozi*, a Chinese classical book of philosophy, the Dao gives birth to the one, the one contains Yin or negative energy and Yang or positive energy, the two kinds of energy constitute the state of equilibrium, and this state generates all in the universe. This philosophy reveals the unification of the two contrary yet complementary elements, and this relationship permeates and manipulates all in the universe, which even a heroine and a maid of *The Story of the Stone* could understand. Indeed, poetic elements such as tone and cadence are certainly also part of them. This explains why ancient Chinese poetry critics dichotomized tone and cadence into what they believed to be euphonic, one of two antithetical yet harmonious aspects. This is reminiscent of Pythagoras' view that music is the result of unification of conflicting factors, of harmonization of diversified factors, or of reconciliation of unreconciled factors (see *A History of Western Aesthetics* by Zhu Guangqian, a modern Chinese aesthetician) and also of Liu Xie's observation that, when different tones complement one another, harmonization is attained; when identical tones echo one another, rhyming is attained. (See his *The Literary Mind and the Carving of Dragons*.) These feature antithetical yet euphonic tonal and metrical schemes, which relate closely to conveyance of meaning for Recent Style poetry.

Presumably, it is because the notion of dichotomization in a contrastive yet harmonious manner was so deeply rooted in the mind of ancient Chinese poets that they applied it, in the way of antithetical symmetry, to tonal and metrical schemes, the composition of a verse, the form of a poem, and even conveyance of the meaning, which, by virtue of the unique traits of Chinese words, were constructed into the magnificent edifice of Recent Style poetry. Chen Mengjia, a modern Chinese scholar, in his preface to his *A Selection of the Poems by the New Crescent School Poets*, says that "Chinese words are monosyllabic; they are intoned either in the 'l' tone or the 'd' tone, so the cadence of a Chinese poem depends primarily on the number and the array of Chinese words in its verses". But he seems to have ignored the other two attributes of a Chinese word, namely being visual and *meaningfully* monosyllabic, which matter semantically. It is thanks to these attributes that the verses of a Recent Style poem can be antithetically symmetrized. When comparing ancient Chinese poetry and Western poetry in his *On New Poetry*, Ye Gongchao, another modern Chinese scholar, maintains that

> Western poets also use antithesis and symmetry in their poems, but less effectively than Chinese poets, whose advantage over their Western counterparts is that, in addition to their visual effect, Chinese words are *meaningfully* monosyllabic and take up equal space, so they are easy to be arrayed in antithetical symmetry in its truest sense.

Indeed, it is these traits that facilitate integration of the tonal and metrical schemes (one facet of the multifaceted antithetical symmetry), the pattern of composition, and the conveyance of meaning into a Recent Style poem, which makes a mosaic of short versus long, stressed versus unstressed, high versus low, and so on in tone; dark versus bright, heavy versus light, and so on in colour; unfolding versus folding in structure; scenery versus sentiment; and so on. And all these ultimately should, as discussed previously, correspond occultly with the Way of Heaven.

References

1. Cai, Kuanfu 蔡宽夫. "Caikuanfu shihua" 蔡宽夫诗话 (Cai Kuanfu's Remarks on Poetry). In *Song shihua jiyi* 宋诗话辑佚 (The Recovery of Lost Song Dynasty Poems), edited by Shaoyu Guo 郭绍虞. Beijing: Zhonghua Book Company, 1980.
2. Fan, Wen 范温. "Qianxi shiyan" 潜溪诗眼 (Qianxi's Perspective on Poetry). In *Song shihua jiyi* 宋诗话辑佚 (The Recovery of Lost Song Dynasty Poems), edited by Shaoyu Guo 郭绍虞. Beijing: Zhonghua Book Company, 1980.
3. Ge, Lifang 葛立方. "Yunyu yangqiu" 韵语阳秋 (Ge Lifang's Commentaries on Poetry). In *Lidai shihua* 历代诗话 (The Commentaries by the Critics of the Past Dynasties on Poetry), edited by Wenhuan He 何文焕. Beijing: Zhonghua Book Company, 1981.
4. He, Shang 贺裳. "Zaijiuyuan shihua" 载酒园诗话 (A Discourse on Poetry at Zaijiu Garden). In *Qing shihua xubian* 清诗话续编 (A Sequel to the Poetic Discourses of the Qing Dynasty), edited by Shaoyu Guo 郭绍虞. Shanghai: Shanghai Classics Publishing House, 1983.
5. He, Yisun 贺贻孙. "Shifa" 诗筏 (The Raft of Poetry). In *Qing shihua xubian* 清诗话续编 (A Sequel to the Poetic Discourses of the Qing Dynasty), edited by Shaoyu Guo 郭绍虞. Shanghai: Shanghai Classics Publishing House, 1983.
6. Hu, Xiansu 胡先骕. "Ping changshi ji" 评尝试集 (A Critical Look at Hu Shi's "Attempts at Composing Poetry in the Vernacular"). In *Zhongguo xinwenxue daxi wenxue lunzheng ji* 中国新文学大系·文学论争集 (The Schools Part of the Anthology of New Chinese Literature), edited by Jiabi Zhao 赵家璧. Shanghai: Liangyou Book Company, 1935.
7. Hu, Yinglin 胡应麟. *Shi sou* 诗薮 (Thickets of Criticism). Shaihai: Shanghai Classics Publishing House, 1979.

8. Huang, Ziyun 黄子云. "Yehong shidi" 野鸿诗的 (The Yardsticks by Yehong for Critique of Poetry). In *Qing shihua* 清诗话 (The Poetic Discourses of the Qing Dynasty), edited by Fuzhi Wang 王夫之. Shanghai: Shanghai Classics Publishing House, 1978.
9. Hui Jiao 慧皎. *Gaoseng zhuan* 高僧传 (The Biographies of the Eminent and Learned Monks). Beijing: Zhonghua Book Company, 1992.
10. Ji, Kang 嵇康. "Sheng wu aile lun" 声无哀乐论 (On the Absence of Sentiments in Music). In *Quan sanguo wen* 全三国文 (An Encyclopedia of the Literature before the Tang Dynasty), edited by Kejun Yan 严可均. Beijing: Zhonghua Book Company, 1962.
11. Jiang, Kui 姜夔. "Baishidaoren shi shuo" 白石道人诗说 (Baishidaoren's Poetic Discourse). In *Lidai shihua* 历代诗话 (The Commentaries by the Critics of the Past Dynasties on Poetry), edited by Wenhuan He 何文焕. Beijing: Zhonghua Book Company, 1981.
12. Kayser, Wolfgang. *Yuyan de yishu zuopin* 语言的艺术作品 (Das Sprachliche Kunstwerk-Eine Einführungin die Literaturwis-senschaft), translated by Quan Chen 陈铨. Shanghai: Shanghai Translation Publishing House, 1984.
13. Kobo, Daishi. *Wen jin mi fu lun* 文镜秘府论 (Treatise on the Secret Treasury of Literary Mirror). Beijing: People's Literature Publishing House, 1980.
14. Li, Dashi 李大师 and Li Yanshou 李延寿. *Nanshi* 南史 (The Biography of Lu Jue of The History of the Southern Dynasties). Beijing: Zhonghua Book Company, 1975.
15. Luo, Dajing 罗大经. *Helin yulu* 鹤林玉露 (Jade Dew in the Crane's Forest or Tales of the Men of Letters of the Song Dynasty). Beijing: Zhonghua Book Company, 1983.
16. Mao, Chunrong 冒春荣. "Shenyuan shihua" 葚园诗话 (Shenyuan's Poetic Discourse). In *Qing shihua xubian* 清诗话续编 (A Sequel to the Poetic Discourses of the Qing Dynasty), edited by Shaoyu Guo 郭绍虞. Shanghai: Shanghai Classics Publishing House, 1983.
17. Ouyang, Xiu 欧阳修. "Song Zhiwen zhuan" 宋之问传 (The Biography of Song Zhiwen). In *Xin tangshu* 新唐书 (The New Tang Book). Beijing: Zhonghua Book Company, 1975.
18. Ouyang, Xiu 欧阳修. *Xin tangshu* 新唐书 (The New Tang Book). Beijing: Zhonghua Book Company, 1975.
19. Ruan, Ji 阮籍. "Yueji" 乐记 (On Music). In *Ruanji jijiaozhu* 阮籍集校注 (Collation of and Annotation on the Collection of the Works by Ruanji), edited by Bojun Chen 陈伯君. Beijing: Zhonghua Book Company, 1987.
20. Shen, Yue 沈约. *Songshu* 宋书 (The History of the Song Period of the Southern Dynasties). Beijing: Zhonghua Book Company, 1974.
21. Wang, Li 王力. *Hanyu shilüxue* 汉语诗律学 (The Chinese Prosody). Shanghai: Shanghai Educational Publishing House, 1979.
22. Wang, Shizhen 王世贞. "Yiyuan zhiyan" 艺苑卮言 (Random Talk from the Garden of Art). In *Lidai shihua xubian* 历代诗话续编 (A Sequel to the Commentaries by the Critics of the Past Dynasties on Poetry), edited by Fubao Ding 丁福保. Beijing: Zhonghua Book Company, 1983.
23. Wang, Yingkui 王应奎. *Liunan suibi* 柳南随笔 (Liunan's Desultory Notes). Beijing: Zhonghua Book Company, 1983.
24. Wei, Qingzhi 魏庆之. *Shiren yu xie* 诗人玉屑 (Chips of Precious Jade Collected from the Treasury of Remarks on Poetry). Shanghai: Shanghai Classics Publishing House, 1978.
25. Wen, Yiduo 闻一多. "Shi de gelü" 诗的格律 (The Tonal and Metrical Schemes of Poetry). In *Wen Yiduo Quanji* 闻一多全集 (A Complete Edition of Wen Yiduo's Works). Beijing: SDX Joint Publishing Company, 1982.
26. Wu, Ke 吴可. "Canghai shihua" 藏海诗话 (Canghai's Commentaries on Poetry). In *Lidai shihua xubian* 历代诗话续编 (A Sequel to the Commentaries by the Critics of

the Past Dynasties on Poetry), edited by Fubao Ding 丁福保. Beijing: Zhonghua Book Company, 1983.
27. Xiao, Zixian 萧子显. *Nanqishu* 南齐书 (The History of the Qi Period of the Southern Dynasties). Beijing: Zhonghua Book Company, 1972.
28. Xiao, Tong 萧统. *Wenxuan* 文选 (Selections of Refined Literature). Beijing: Zhonghua Book Company, 1977.
29. Xie, Zhen 谢榛. "Siming shuhua" 四溟诗话 (A Sea-in-the-Four-Direction Recluse's Remarks on Poetry). In *Lidai shihua xubian* 历代诗话续编 (A Sequel to the Commentaries by the Critics of the Past Dynasties on Poetry), edited by Fubao Ding 丁福保. Beijing: Zhonghua Book Company, 1983.
30. Yang, Zai 杨载. "Shifa jiashu" 诗法家数 (Techniques of Versification). In *Lidai shihua* 历代诗话 (The Commentaries by the Critics of the Past Dynasties on Poetry), edited by Wenhuan He 何文焕. Beijing: Zhonghua Book Company, 1981.
31. Ye, Mengde 叶梦得. *Shilin shihua* 石林诗话 (Tales and Critique of Poetry at Shilin). In *Lidai shihua* 历代诗话 (The Commentaries by the Critics of the Past Dynasties on Poetry), edited by Wenhuan He 何文焕. Beijing: Zhonghua Book Company, 1981.
32. Ye, Xie 叶燮. *Yuan shi* 原诗 (A Probe into the Essence of Versification). Beijing: People's Literature Publishing House, 1979.
33. Yin, Fan 殷璠. "Heyue yinglingji" 河岳英灵集 (A Collection of the Poems by the Quintessential Poets of the High Tang Dynasty). In *Tangren xuan tangshi shizhong* 唐人选唐诗十种 (Ten Tang Versions of an Anthology of the Tang Poetry), edited by Jie Yuan 元结. Shanghai: Shanghai Classics Publishing House, 1958.
34. Zhang, Biaochen 张表臣. "Shanhugou shihua" 珊瑚钩诗话 (A Miscellany of Insightful Remarks on Poetry and Other Subjects). In *Lidai shihua* 历代诗话 (The Commentaries by the Critics of the Past Dynasties on Poetry), edited by Wenhuan He 何文焕. Beijing: Zhonghua Book Company, 1981.
35. Zhong, Rong 钟嵘. "Shipin" 诗品 (Critique of Poetry). In *Lidai shihua* 历代诗话 (The Commentaries by the Critics of the Past Dynasties on Poetry), edited by Wenhuan He 何文焕. Beijing: Zhonghua Book Company, 1981.
36. Zhu, Guangqian 朱光潜. *Xifang meixue shi* 西方美学史 (A History of the Western Aesthetics). Beijing: People's Literature Publishing House, 1963.
37. Zhu, Tinzhen 朱庭珍. "Xiaoyuan shihua" 筱园诗话 (Xiaoyuan's Remarks on Poetry). In *Qing shihua xubian* 清诗话续编 (A Sequel to the Poetic Discourses of the Qing Dynasty), edited by Shaoyu Guo 郭绍虞. Shanghai: Shanghai Classics Publishing House, 1983.

5 Allusion

One special aspect of ancient Chinese poetry

In the eighteenth chapter of *The Story of the Stone*, subtitled "Yuanchun Visits Her Parents on the Feast of Lanterns/Daiyu Helps Her True Love by Passing Him a Poem", Baoyu is asked to improvise a poem, one of whose verses reads "lv yu chun you juan (Jade green leaves in spring are yet furled tight)". Glancing at it, Baochai nudges him into replacing "green jade" with another allusion, because Yuanchun would not like the former:

> At this, wiping his sweating forehead, Baoyu said: "But for the moment I can't think of anyone". Baochai, smiling, taught him: "Just change 'green jade' into 'green wax.'" "But is this an allusion?" With a mocking smile and a smack of her lips, she nodded and said: "If you're in such a state tonight, by the time you sit the Palace Examinations I dare say you'll even forget the first primer you've ever read. Have you forgotten the opening verse of that poem on plantain leaves by the Tang poet Qian Yi, which is 'leng zhu wu yan lv la gan (The smokeless cold candles look like green wax that has dried)'?" This instantly made Baoyu feel as if a veil had been lifted from his eyes.

This is a funny part where Baoyu is stupefied by Baochai, who sounds complacent although she herself mistook Han Yi for Qian Yi. But the issue of an allusion in question is serious. Usage of allusions was a target of deprecation by some ancient Chinese poetry critics, on the one hand, but, on the other, ancient Chinese poets were inclined to use allusions in their poetry. In reality, contrary to the low appraisal by those poetry critics, allusions were preferred by ancient Chinese poets, even to the point of being associated, for example, by Baochai with "the first primer", which is one of the three most important books for education of children in ancient China. Academic and more substantial evidence of the status of allusions and their history is found in sources such as Liu Xie's *The Literary Mind and the Carving of Dragons*, which asserts that "Since Yang Xiong and Liu Xiang (both of the Han Dynasty) allusions and quotations have been utilized to facilitate composition of either prose or poetry", which indicates the long tradition of use of allusions, and Zhang Jie's *Notes on Poetry Written in the Pine and Cypress Studio*, which concludes that

> Yan Yannian (of the Song period of the Southern Dynasties) should be the first poet who used allusions in his poems to show his erudition and Du Fu should be the one whose exploitation of allusion in his poems should have reached the acme of perfection.

which tells how great poets greatly valued allusions. Since the Tang Dynasty, ancient Chinese poets developed the habit of exploiting allusions whenever they could in their poetry. On record in this regard are poems by such poets as Li Shangyin, whose poetry is rife with allusions; the Xikun Style poets, who were obsessed with what Wang Fuzhi dismissed as "enigmatic stuff"; Huang Tingjian of the Song Dynasty, who took a fancy to studying and quoting the classics of wonderment; and even Yang Wanli, also known as Chengzhai, of the Song Dynasty, who, though self-assured in his unrivalled prosodic excellence, still could not resist the temptation to intersperse his characteristically brisk poetry with veiled allusions. For example, Song Changbai of the Qing Dynasty unveiled an allusion used by Yang in one of his two series poems entitled "Visiting the Terrace on Which the Duke of the State of Yue Once Set Foot on the Last Day of the Third Lunar Month", alleging that it actually was an unobtrusive rewriting of Li He's verse "yi hong hai shui bei zhong xie (The sea looks as if a pool of limpid water were pouring from a cup)"; Zha Shenxing of the Qing Dynasty also detected an allusion used by Yang in his poem "Winter Sweet", affirming that its two words "ta yang (by another name)" alluded to Yang Xiong, the aforementioned eminent scholar of the Western Han Dynasty, to whom *The History of the Han Dynasty* devotes a chapter. In fact, whether an allusion is used is by no means a yardstick for measuring the quality of a poem. For example, Li Shangyin crammed his "Titleless" poem series with allusions, which was not just well accepted but inspired meticulous annotations by his admirers. But, then, imitation by Yang Yi and Qian Weiyan, both of the Song Dynasty, of Li Shangyin's practice in their own poems was deprecated for being worthless. Here arise two questions: why do those ancient Chinese poetry critics who upheld the banner of naturalness deny a role to allusions in poetry, repudiating them with vengeance for being simply exhibitive, ornate, encrypted, disharmonizing, and so on, on the one hand, while, on the other, ancient Chinese poets so loved using allusions, so that their annotators spared no effort, even just for allusions' sake, to identify the allusions in their poems, especially their popularly acclaimed poems, which can lead an ordinary reader to suspect that he or she can be ambushed anywhere in an ancient Chinese poem by this or that metaphorical or symbolic allusion? And how can one look at the role of allusion in, generally speaking, ancient Chinese poetry or, specifically speaking, for example, Recent Style poetry?

This chapter attempts to discuss allusion as an idiosyncratic idiom regardless of its status, high or low, in the traditional scale of Chinese literature. Then, let us first define allusion from two contradictory perspectives as follows:

On the one hand:

> As a poetic idiom, an allusion is the result of abstraction from whatever is about moral and has its aesthetic value. In the course of being used, improved, and passed around, it will, through absorption and accumulation, gain more meaning

than what it originally had. This enables it, like an emblem, to exert influence over one's aesthetic appreciation. On the strength of it, though concise in form, a poem thus becomes concise, compact, richly profound, and subtly nuanced.

On the other hand:

It is due to the addition of new meanings, over a long time, to what it originally means that an allusion can become very involved and impenetrable, much like a pill whose insoluble coating prevents it from working on a patient. Given this, an allusion is nothing but an abstruse emblem that cannot appeal aesthetically. Thus, embedded in a poem, it not only clogs the natural and smooth movement of verses but encrypts their meanings. A poem like this is an unnatural enigmatic contrivance.

5.1. Cultural affinity between the poet and the reader: a key to decoding an allusion

In translating an ancient Chinese poem, a Western translator often has this headache: how to translate an allusion. For the translation to be understood by Western readers, he or she will have to annotate it with many extra words, which will have distracted the reader's attention, which should have been concentrated on the poem itself; if he or she does not translate it, he or she will lose the subtleties and profundities that the writer intends to give to the poem, which can be likened to casting off a valuable pearl in a jewellery box or an extract of decoction. Angus Charles Graham, an English sinologist, suggested, regardless of this loss, that it was better to let an allusion pass than to distract the reader by an annotation on it. (See his *The Translation of Chinese Poetry*.) This virtually echoes the opinion of Arthur Waley, an earlier English sinologist, who, even though he knew what an allusion could mean to an ancient Chinese poem, feared that annotation on the allusion(s) of a poem would devalue the latter itself, which thus would have turned out to be something like a piece of corroboration to the reader, whose otherwise burning interest would have been dampened, even if he or she could have grasped the meaning of an allusion with the aid of annotation. (See his *Yuan Mei: Eighteenth Century Chinese Poet*.) Either Graham's blunt suggestion or Waley's circuitous opinion is by no means a solution to how to deal with an ancient Chinese poem that contains one or more allusions when it is being rendered into a Western language. In a sense, translation of an allusion is like cracking a code; with a linguistic barrier (which, for the most part, is about culture), a translator who attempts to deal with an allusion in the source language can be frustrated as a decoder who is desperate yet cannot find any way to decrypt it.

This is interesting: a language is a vehicle to communication, on the one hand, but, on the other, it can be a barrier to it. Those who use the same native language usually communicate with and understand one another as easily as two people standing face to face reach out to hold the other by the hand. For those from different linguistic backgrounds, however, their communication can be blocked by what can be compared to soundproof glass erected between them, and the result is that, whatever is being verbally and gesticulatively expressed by one, it feels like a baffling pantomime in the eyes of the other, a spectator who, deaf to it, is altogether confused. In reality, linguistic barriers exist not only between peoples from different nations but also between people of the same nation due to discrepancies in their knowledge of local history, their social strata, their personal education, and the like, thus also posing other problems. For example, those in the Middle Tang Dynasty would think the words of *The Book of History*, one of the earliest Chinese classics, hard to pronounce, in terms of phonology, and comprehend, in terms of content; to the modern Chinese reader, Fan Zongshi of the Middle Tang Dynasty's poem entitled "A Poem about the Yuewang Tower of Mianzhou in Shu" (note: Yuewang was the rank title conferred by Emperor Taizong of the Tang Dynasty on his eighth son Li Zhen, who built the tower when he governed Mianzhou of Shu, i.e., the present-day Sichuan province) and such verses as "long tou suo jun chun (The head of the dragon recoils into the shape of a mushroom)/shi fu zhang peng heng (The belly of the swine distends like a rounded mound)" by Fan's contemporary Xuanyuan Miming, a Taoist priest, may as well be Greek; Jia Baoyu of *The Story of the Stone* could not catch the hint of "pa hui [incest between a man and his daughter-in-law]" in the jargon of Jiao Da, one of his servants, who in turn could not understand what the former and the girls around him talked about when they recited poems either. This is more the case in comprehension of an allusion in an ancient Chinese poem. An allusion not only has a long history but is a condensed idiom, so it is much harder to decode. When annotating an allusion, even ancient Chinese poetry annotators, much less their modern Chinese counterparts, would be befuddled and make mistakes. In his annotation on "gu ren jian zhu xi chuang yu (When would my old friend chat with me, together trimming the candlewick at the window facing west)" in Zhou Bangyan of the Song Dynasty's *Suo Chuang Han (Cold Engraved Window)/Han Shi (Cold Food)*, Chen Yuanlong, also of the Song Dynasty, sourced it to Wen Tingyun's poem entitled "An Elegy Inspired by a Dancer's Performance", one of whose verses reads "hui pin xiao yu xi chuang ke (You smiled and turned to me at the west window, recollecting)" "jian zhu xi chuang (trimming the candlewick at the window facing west)", which actually was derived from Li Shangyin's poem entitled "Writing to My Kin and Friends in the North at a Rainy Night"; thus Zhou's verse, which actually was about poignancy, was mistaken for describing a sunny mood; "meng gong (Menggong)" in "meng gong bu zai zi (Around me there is no one like Menggong)/zhong yi yi wu qing (With whom I am free to share my feelings)" in the sixteenth of Tao Yuanming's twenty poems under the title "A Series Composed after Drinking Rice Wine" was referred to by the poet himself as the "Menggong", by the name of Liu Gong, in *The History of the Latter Han Dynasty* who was said to have a keen eye for talent but then was mistaken by Tao Shu, a reputed textualist of the Qing Dynasty, for another "Menggong" by the name of Chen Zun, of the Western Han Dynasty, who was notorious for gluttony; hence Tao Yuanming's lamentation over want of a soul mate was misinterpreted as his lamentation over poverty and ensuing suffering, to choose just a few examples. Confusion of this nature also occurs in the West. In his *Das Sprachliche Kunstwerk*, Wolfgang Kayser, after comparing two poems by a German poet and a Portuguese poet, observes that even modern Occidental readers, much less their modern Oriental counterparts, if they have little or no knowledge of symbology, cannot understand the emblematic significance (i.e., fidelity) of palm trees, for a palm tree, they feel, is no more than a green tree; thus the palm tree becomes an impediment to communication. Given this, the German poet's verse "a palm tree sustains two anchors" feels to them like a grotesque image, and the Portuguese poet's personification of a palm tree, which is devised by the poet so that it will listen to him baring his heart, to, for example, a modern Chinese reader, may evoke, rather than what the poet intended, just a Chinese myth, wherein a man named Dong Yong and his wife, one of the young female immortals from Heaven, named the Seventh Sister, pled with a deified old Chinese scholar tree to help them out of a predicament.

An allusion is a barrier to one but access to another, like a locked house, which stops a stranger from entering but which its occupant with the key is free to enter, or like those cases in the history of Zen Buddhism, which are, to laymen, too erratic to make any sense but to its practitioners are as natural and intelligible as a hen hatching an egg, a cat catching a rat, or one wanting to eat in hunger or drink in thirst, or, again, as Wolfgang Kayser, in his *Das Sprachliche Kunstwerk*, says of the poets of the Baroque period and well-educated people, they knew symbology so well as to be capable of capturing any symbolic innuendo in any work of literature and art. To ancient Chinese readers, contrary to modern Chinese readers, the allusions permeating, for example, poems by Li Shangyin might not be arcane at all. Incidentally, Li's poetry, just because of its uncanny allusions, is said to have been modelled by such poets as Yanqian of the Tang Dynasty, who ended up having learned no more than Li's "delicateness and poignancy". Yang Yi, Qian Weiyan, Liu Yun, and others of the Song Dynasty viewed Li's poetry as subtly nuanced, expressive, and fluid, and, to follow suit, they also used many allusions in their own poems, which drew accolades from their contemporary admirers and followers. (See *Ge Lifang's Commentaries on Poetry*.) Even Ouyang Xiu spoke highly of them, for "their allusions not compromise but enhance the qualities of their poems". (See his *Liuyi's Commentaries on Poetry*.) Su Shi and Wang Anshi seemed to have surpassed Li Shangyin and were recognized masters of using allusions. For example, "hu tian" and "pai ta" in Wang's "yi shui *hu tian* jiang lv rao (The rivulet surrounds patches of verdant fields)/liang shan *pai ta* song qing lai (Two ranges of mounts seem to have opened the door to deliver greenness)" were derived from *The History of the Han Dynasty*, and "a lan re (araṇya) and "su du bo (*stūpa*)" in his "zhou yu zhai zai *a lan re* (Zhou Yu resides at araṇya)/lou yue shen sui *su du bo* (Lou Yue rests inside *stūpa*"), two place denotations in Sanskrit, are placed in antithesis, and this usage was praised for its rigid precision and natural symmetry. (See Ye Mengde's *Tales and Critique of Poetry at Shilin*.) Huang Tingjian, renowned for his knack for "turning a piece of crude writing into a genius work of art" and "emulating but surpassing his predecessors", virtually crammed his poems with allusions, but his poems were thought by his contemporaries to deserve such epithets as "unique', "lofty", "ethereal", "genuine", and "natural". (See Hu Zi, also known as Tiaoxi Yuyin [i.e., a reclusive angler at Tiaoxi], of the Song Dynasty's *Poetic Remarks from the Fisherman Recluse at the Trumpet-Creeper Creek*.) But, at the same time, his acclaimed mastery of allusion should be highlighted and

104 *Allusion*

naturally was counterattacked by his admirers, like Weng Fanggang, who defended Huang's use of allusions as well thought out and his allusions as so encyclopaedic as to concern Confucianist canons, Buddhist scriptures, guidebooks about how to practice alchemy and attain immortality, unorthodox historical records, fictitious tales, traditions of fishing and hunting, and so on, so they would confound those who were not well read, but they, not from what was far removed from what one ought to have read, should not at all be thought to be hard nuts to crack. (See his *The Collection of the Works at the Fufang Study*.)

Thus it should be evident that whether an allusion, as a poetic emblem, is easy to understand relies totally on whether there is an affinity, which generally is cultural, between the poet and the reader. Ivor Armstrong Richards, an English literary critic, uses "the qualified reader" to refer what to the reader and the poet should have in common or similarity such as their times, their nation, their culture, and their interests or to a reader who, lacking such commonalities or similarities, should at least be knowledgeable about the origin, evolution, and denotations and connotations of the allusions the poet has used in his poems. These requirements of "the qualified reader" are termed a "competence system". In the case of the allusions in a poem, it is this competence system that aids the reader in grasping their true and deep meanings; otherwise, the reader is most likely to be confused. Take, for instance, one of Li Shangyin's two poems under the title of "The Huaqing Palace":

> hua qing en xing gu wu lun /
> (The Huaqing Palace witnessed His Majesty's graces unrivalled ever since the remotest antiquity /)
> you kong e mei bu sheng ren.
> (Still, she feared someone would outshine her in charming beauty.)
> wei mian bei ta bao nv xiao /
> (Baosi, if alive, would knowingly sneer at her uneasiness /)
> zhi jiao tian zi zan meng chen.
> (She would have His Majesty temporarily afflicted with pain of fleeing for refuge)

For the ancient Chinese reader who was familiar with the allusions herein, it was easy to understand them. The modern Chinese reader, however, before fully appreciating this poem, will have to find out about what is behind "hua qing en xing (graces from His Majesty at the Huaqing Palace)"; the concubine by the name of Baosi; what happened to Sovereign You of the Zhou Dynasty and his darling Baosi; what Emperor Xuanzong of the Tang Dynasty experienced fleeing to Shu (i.e., present-day Sichuan); what Baosi's sneer implies; and what the irony of such a sneer is; on top of this, to be fully qualified, the reader will have to learn about what occurred during the middle and latter periods of the Tang Dynasty, as well as the other poems dedicated to the Huaqing Palace and Lady Yang, the favourite concubine of Emperor Xuanzong. Otherwise, a barrier of communication will erupt between the reader and the poet.

Allusions used by ancient Chinese poets were derived mainly from the ancient Chinese classics. Such allusions not only enrich the meanings of their poems but also demonstrate their erudition. As Kobo Daishi discovered, poets at the time would note down what they judged the quintessence of past or contemporary verses and carry with them notes called "an attendant scroll" that would save them the labour of searching for proper allusions. This practice became the vogue of the day. Kobo Daishi himself, at the end of his *Treatise on the Secret Treasury of Literary Mirror*, listed the reign titles of the past monarchs and the anecdotes about their virtues and accomplishments, which may well also be regarded as a kind of "an attendant scroll". It is said that whenever composing a poem, Li Shangyin would draw from his scrolls of quotations arrayed in catalogue to hand, reminiscent of an otter instinctively spreading the fish it has caught along a bank. (See Yang Yi's *The Garden of Sayings by Yang Wengong*.) Huang Tingjian would readily make notes concerning the Han and Jin dynasties, rectifying or underlining them with a red writing brush, in case they were used in versification. Tang Geng of the Song Dynasty confessed that he could not compose a poem without utilizing what he had collected by reading. (See Hu Zi's *Poetic Remarks from the Fisherman Recluse at the Trumpet-Creeper Creek*.) So, even for an ancient Chinese reader, if he did not read enough about, for example, these allusions, they could be esoteric. This is not to mention a modern Chinese reader who has presumably learned little about them. Jürgen Habermas thinks that the meaning of a text can only be understood within certain parameters; his parameters include prior cognition or rather the context that was shaped by the historical heritage and grammar that linguistically governed the text, as well as the cultural conventions of the time. In the case of a poem, the former circumscribe what the contemporaries of its author would have to take account of, and the latter requires readers of later generations to acquaint themselves with linguistic and cultural customs, the prerequisites for a deep, comprehensive, and accurate interpretation, in terms of logical semantics, of the allusion(s) of and the motivation behind them. An allusion used by a poet, to his contemporary reader, due to their affinity, which results from what they share in terms of time and space, linguistic rules, and the like, constitutes no barrier; rather, just as chocolate melts soon in its eater's mouth, so the meaning of the allusion is easily grasped. But the same allusion, to the later reader, due to the communication gap which results from the lapse of a long time, can be a tough nut to crack before he or she gains its kernel.

5.2. Does an allusion disrupt the process of appreciation?

Most ancient Chinese poems, and all ancient Chinese scenery poems, are the frames of meaningful pictures of words. Integration of the tone, form, and meaning that should be particular to a Chinese word, which both Ernest Fenollosa and Ezra Pound touched upon, ending with their conclusions, which happen to conform with the traits of a Chinese word, enables the words of an ancient Chinese poem to produce both visual and aural effects. This explains why an ancient Chinese poem is a display of imagery. Indeed, when reading an ancient Chinese poem, one appreciates not just its words but the images that its words project, feels the emotions not just in its words but in its images, and pulsates with the cadence of its tonally schemed procession of juxtaposed images so that one will have a deep understanding of it. This is, on the part of the reader, a particular, and also a holistic, process of telepathic correspondence and aesthetic appreciation.

For example:

tai yi jin tian du /
(Mount Taiyi stands near the celestial capital /)
lian shan jie hai yu.
(It extends, range after range, to seashores.)
bai yun hui wang he /
(I looked back to see white clouds gathering into a mass /)
qing ai ru kan wu.
(I lost myself in the mists emerging from the mount.)
fen ye zhong feng bian /
(The peak divides the region into two areas, east and west /)
yin qing zhong he shu.
(One has its own climate in its own valleys, different than the other.)
yu tou ren chu su /
(I was keen to find a household where I'd put up for a night /)
ge shui wen qiao fu.
(Across a rivulet was a woodcutter from whom I'd ask for information.)
("Mount Zhongnan" by Wang Wei)

Its first and second verses depict the grandeur of the mountain, whose range stretches hyperbolically as far as to the coastline; its third and fourth verses picture capriciously rolling white clouds and looming mists; its fifth and sixth verses bring forth the geographic impact of the grand mountain range on the shades of its area and the ensuing disparities in climate; and it concludes with the two verses which reconstruct the scene where the poet or rather the wayfarer solicits from a woodcutter information about accommodation. Throughout the poem, the poet's perspective shifts, or rather the poet shows his reader, segment by segment, a panoramic view of Mount Zhongnan—from overall to particular, from far to near, from near to far, and from high to low, from outside to inside, and so on—in a distinctive, smooth, natural cadence.

jun wen gui qi wei you qi /
(I can't answer your inquiry about the date of my return /)
ba shan ye yu zhang qiu chi.
(With the autumnal ponds at Mount Daba inundated with night rain.)
he dang gong jian xi chuang zhu /
(When shall I trim with you the candlewick at that west window /)
que hua ba shan ye yv shi.
(Recollecting how I was feeling every rainy night back here?)
("Writing to my Kin and Friends in the North at a Rainy Night" by Li Shangyin)

This poem runs, vividly and grippingly, with three images presented in an uninterrupted cadence: the actual image of "ba shan ye yu (night rain at the Mount Daba)" and the imagined vista of "jian zhu xi chuang (trimming the candlewick at that west window)" and, again, the actual image of "ba shan ye yu (night rain at Mount Daba)". They, however they are retained by the poet, are thus etched by the poet on the mind of the reader, who, in the process, is moved to sympathize with the poet from poignancy to longing to poignancy.

Even one verse, for example, "hei yun fan mo wei zhe shan" (Dark clouds, like a spill of black ink, are billowing yet leaving a section of the mountains unenveloped), the first verse in Su Shi's "A Poem Scribbled in Drunk at the Wanghu (Lakeview) Tower on the 27th Day of the 6th Lunar Month", brings to the reader's mind the images, both in juxtaposition and in succession and, more importantly, smoothly, of the billowing dark clouds and the mountains that were not yet clouded.

Smooth cadence in particular, in a verse, let alone in a poem, is necessary for the reader's uninterrupted aesthetic appreciation of the verse and, more importantly, the poem. Imagine how the viewers of a movie would react if the scenes were shown in broken succession.

Zhu Guangqian, in his *Correspondence on Aesthetics*, says that, when one involves both his or her mental and physical faculties in aesthetic appreciation of an object, he or she relishes the harmony between the cadence at which the object is represented and that at which the mental and physical faculties respond; otherwise, either "awkwardness" or "clumsiness" will result, which in turn adversely affects their mood. This also applies to appreciation of poetry. The smooth poetic cadence felt in succession of juxtaposed imagery occasions naturalness and ease to the reader, who thus immerses himself or herself, heart and soul, in the poetic world, or else unnaturalness and unease ensue, which certainly pose a hindrance to the reader's otherwise keen immersion. Compare this with what the American aesthetician Rudolf Arnheim says: insertion of a motionless scene in a succession of motion ones in a movie will cause the sensation of stiffness and inanimateness. (See his *Art and Visual Perception*.)

In the case of the allusion(s) in a poem, as a result of a lack of cultural affinity between the poet and the reader, their presence is most likely to disrupt the latter's otherwise smooth process of appreciation of the former's poem. In his *Remarks on Ci Poetry in the Human World*, Wang Guowei, a modern Chinese scholar, opposes the overuse of allusions. To justify his opposition, he cites "gui hua liu wa (Moonlight feels like water spreading down the roof tiles)", a verse in *Jieyuhua* [a speaking flower or a belle] *Shangyuan (Lantern Festival)* by Zhou Bangyan, saying its "gui hua (osmanthus tree flowers or moonlight; 'hua' hereof refers to either light or flower")", an allusion, is one case, for it disrupts the otherwise fluid appreciation process, and the reader is compelled to associate it first with the legendary *osmanthus tree* (pronounced in Chinese pinyin as "gui shu" or "gui hua shu") on the moon and then with the moonlight. Wang calls this "disharmonization", which also occurs in, for example, the four verses of the second of five allegorical poems by Li He: "du men jia sheng mu (Jia Yi's tomb lies outside the entrance to the capital)/ qing ying jiu duan jue (Even the ghost of 'qing ying' has not been seen for ages)/ han shi yao yang tian (On Cold Food Day white poplar trees are being swayed by winds)/fen jing chang su sha (How saddened and resented I feel at such long forlorn desolateness)". To the "qualified reader" who has adequately information about the outskirts, Jia Yi's tomb, no ghost of "qing ying", and white poplar trees being swayed by winds on Cold Food Day, he or she can follow the poet's thought flow in succession and feel what the poet felt at the sight of the forsaken desolation, which contrasted starkly with the unending procession of mourners and ever-rising wisps of incense smoke by Jia Yi's tomb in the past. But to the reader without the aforementioned "competence system", who has no idea that "qing ying" alluded to mourners (according to *The Biography of Yu Fan* in *The History of the Three Kingdoms*, Yu Fan, a scholar of the Kingdom of Wu, lamented over his being exiled: "There is no one I can bare my soul when I am alive; only after I die will 'qing ying' come and pay their respects to me"; Li He's contemporary Liu Yuxi's poem "Bemoaning afar the Death of Grandee Qiu" contains a pair of verses: "he ren wei diao ke [Who will go and pay their respects to him]/wei shi you 'qing ying' [It will be only those mourners who are bemoaning his death]", so "qing ying" here refers to a mourner or mourners), the use of "qing ying" will certainly disrupt the process of appreciation of the poem, and this disruption will impair not only the cadence but also the readability of the poem as a whole. Worse, it can cause misinterpretation. For example, Wang Qi, allegedly the most erudite annotator of the Qing Dynasty, mistook Li He's "qing ying" for the "qing ying" in *The Book of Songs*, which refers to "a slanderer", so "qing ying jiu duan jue" was misinterpreted by Wang Qi as the vanishing of those like ancient slanderers, an occasion for celebration. But why did the poet moodily react, as expressed in the last two verses? To resolve the contradiction, Wang Qi strained to explain that, although the existence of such slanderers was ephemeral, hatred of them persisted, without abatement, over generations, in light of which Li He did not react poignantly to what faced him at the moment but held a grudge against those past slanderers. (See Wang Qi's *Annotation on the Selected Annotations on Li He's Poems*.)

This disruption in ancient Chinese scenery poems has a worse effect on them. For example, in Wang Anshi's two verses: "xiao xiao bo shu sheng zhong ri (Orioles are heard chirping incessantly in the sunshine)/Mo mo chong chu ying wai tian (The figures of egrets are seen flying far up in the air)", "xiao xiao" are two onomatopoeic words for orioles' chirping, "bo shu" is otherwise known as an oriole, "sheng zhong ri" means that orioles in the sunshine are chirping, "mo mo" describes an ambience of distance and faintness, "chong chu" is another name for an egret, and "ying wai tian" depicts flying egrets afar against the distant horizon. Wang's two verses should have epitomized a consummate match between colour and sound and between boisterousness and stillness and fascinated the reader without the interspersion of "bo shu" and "chong chu", two unfamiliar allusions, both of which break the otherwise unbroken cadence. In contrast, Du Fu's "liang ge huang li ming cui niao (two orioles perched on green willows keep chirping)/yi hang bai lu shang qing tian (A flight of egrets are soaring up to the azure)", which is similar, in terms of embedment of bird names, to Wang's two verses, is judged to have produced desirable visual and aural effects. For "huang li (oriole)" and "bai lu (egret)", unlike "bo shu" and "chong chu", are two familiar bird names; thus they do not disrupt the process of appreciation on the part of the reader. What if "huang li" and "bai lu" were replaced respectively with "bo shu" and "chong chu"? Doubtless that would repel a great many readers.

Needless to say, poetic allusions, to the reader who knows about them, cause no disruption or disharmony, as earlier discussed. Rather, they inspire association and imagination, which need a caesura. This caesura, not like the stopping of operation of a recording gadget as a result of a power cut but like a purposeful caesura in performance of a symphony, allows the reader to stop for a moment to ponder their subtle nuances, so, in this sense, it is actually a continuation in the guise of disruption. It is virtually the opinion of Rudolf Arnheim that there is an essential difference between a lifeless pause and an animate one; the former is a disruption, a damage to a smooth cadence, whereas the latter is an inspiration, an enhancement of cadence (see his *Art and Visual Perception*).

Let us look at Su Shi's two pairs of verses, respectively, from his two poems "po yi hu lu yuan yan dao (How I'd need a companion like Yuan Yan dao, that notorious gambler)/nan yao ma zuo guan jiang jun (It can be hard to seek a crony like General Guan, that reviler at a banquet)" and "jun jia zi you yuan he jiao (You should boast your inheritance of your ancestral calligraphy)/mo yan jia ji geng wen ren (Never and ever deprecate your inheritance to learn from other styles)", cited by the anonymous author(s) of *An Unconstrained Old Man's Remarks on Poetry* of the Song Dynasty. Allusions like "hu lu (gamble)", "ma zuo (revile someone at a banquet)", and "yuan he jiao (a style of calligraphy formed during the reign of Yuanhe of the Tang Dynasty)", which will perplex those who have no idea what they mean, could not be more apt in usage, more plain in meaning, more natural in cadence, and more ingenious in craft, in the eyes of those who understand them (see Guo Shaoyu's *A Collection of Song Poetry*), and they will move further not just to associate them with their origins and the other verses embedded with them but bring forth what they can mean metaphorically and sentimentally. Doing so certainly will subtilize the meanings of these verses. Allen Tate of New Criticism calls the result a kind of "tension", the deepening and broadening, on the strength of the reader's pertinent knowledge, of the extension and the intension of the meaning of an allusion. In the words of Yang Yi, "the further a poetic allusion is delved into, the more meanings it has" (see *Ge Lifang's Commentaries on Poetry*), or it can be likened to chewing an olive: the longer it is chewed, the more flavour. Allusions are to a poem as distant mountains, blue skies, or flying birds are to a garden laid out with ponds and galleries: a visitor will take into view those externalities, which will lend charm to the garden.

Take Huang Tingjian's pairs of verses, for instance:

an de yi chan wu yu lao /
(How can I own an abode where I will spend the rest of my life /)
Jun ting zhuang xi bing shi yin.
(You shall still hear me moaning in my native dialect although I live away from home.)

110 *Allusion*

The reader who is familiar with the story of Zhuang Xi will understand that "zhuang xi bing shi yin" means literally that Zhuang Xi, who was originally a humble, low-status man and later became a high-ranking official of the state of Chu during the Warring States Period, was moaning still in the dialect of the state of Yue, his home country, when he fell ill and that it was used to allegorize Huang Tingjian reclusive sentiments, and, furthermore, will associate it with Wang Can's "zhuang xi xian er yue yin (Although Zhuang Xi prospered in the State of Chu, he moaned, when ill, in the dialect of the State of Yue, his home country)", by which Wang Can expressed his despondency about the vicissitudes of the human world, with Du Fu's "ai shi fei wang can (Wang Can was not alone to lament over the human world)/ zhong ran xue yue yin (I'll end up following Zhuang Xi by moaning in my native dialect though far away from home)", which vents his distress about his thwarted aspirations, with Yang Yi's "zhi yi dong yue ou (My chin rests on my hands, homesickness surging up)", a sketch of Yang engrossed in homesickness, with Su Shi's "yue yin zhi ting fou (Is any attention paid to the murmurs of homesickness?)/ shei nian bing zhuang xi (Who remembers Zhuang Xi, their folk, in ailment?)", which strikes one as desolate, and so on. Thus the reader will have felt, in Huang's pair of verses, a mixture of being forlorn, lonesome, befuddled, wretched, and downcast, to name just a few, and learned what they teach about ephemeral human life against the eternal universe and aloofness in resignation for one's remaining years.

An emblem will lose its charm once it can explicitly be illustrated. (See Carl Gustav Jung's *Psychological Types or the Psychology of Individuation*.) A poetic allusion, in a sense, is a fascinating "emblem" in its own right: it conveys more than what it literally carries, which inspires the reader in many ways, thus having tension, comparable to something that needs masticating for full-bodied flavour, which in turn enhances the verse in depth, breadth, and subtlety.

"Poems can either be hard or easy to understand. A hard poem has its peculiarity, with the acme of splendour as seen in lofty mountains and deep valleys. An easy poem has its beauty, with its plain naturalness as seen in unfurling clouds and gurgling streams". This is what Lu Shiyong of the Ming Dynasty said about ancient Chinese poems. (See Lu Shiyong's *A Comprehensive Digest of Good Ancient Poems*.) It can also apply to each allusion-embedded verse of an ancient Chinese poem.

5.3. How to use an allusion in a verse

"It is allusions that make a poem". This seemingly simple statement actually was a criticism by Tu Long of the Ming Dynasty of the poetry of the Song Dynasty. In Tu's opinion, an allusion could only be used in prose rather than in poetry. Is this opinion justified? Or, metaphorically, does the idea that a banquet serving dishes of not beef but fish is not a banquet in its truest sense hold water? An allusion, like any other word or phrase, is an emblem, so, if the latter is allowed in versification, why should the former be prohibited? As Formalism theorists such as R. Jakobson and J. Mukarovsky say, poetic language is the result of organized defamiliarization of the conventionalized language that has long been used in poetry. (See Lung-hsi

Chang's *A Review of the Twentieth Century Western Literary Theories*.) Poetic allusions are part of this kind of poetic language. As mentioned, Li Shangyin took a fancy to poetic allusions. For example, allusions punctuate the third, fourth, fifth, and sixth verses of his "The Adorned Zither", and who can deny that his poem is poetic? Wang Shimao was unbiased in this regard: "Any allusion itself is not to blame. How to use it in poetry is the concern". (See his *To Glean in the Field of Poetry*.) Indeed, and metaphorically again, it does not matter whether a banquet serves dishes of beef or of fish; what matters is how they are cooked by what chef.

As to how to use an allusion in a poem, ancient Chinese poets and poetry critics proposed their approaches, such as blending an allusion into a verse to leave no trace (see Yang Zai's *Techniques of Versification*), like salt dissolving in water (see Wei Qingzhi's *Chips of Precious Jade Collected from the Treasury of Remarks on Poetry*), treatment of an allusion unfamiliar to the reader in a formal way and of an allusion familiar to the reader in a casual way (see again Yang Zai's *Techniques of Versification*), and deriving allusions from ancient Chinese classics (see Fan Peng of the Yuan Dynasty's *Mu Tian Jin Yu* [a compilation of remarks by the preeminent members of the Imperial Academy since the reign of Kaiyuan of the Tang Dynasty on secrets to creating a consummate poem]), to choose just a few. But these propositions seem not quite practicable: an allusion itself can be involved and abstruse, so simply untraceable fusion of an allusion into a verse can make the allusion more so; treating an unfamiliar allusion formally and a familiar one casually, which may help the reader better understand them, may not add to the subtlety and appeal of a poem; and allusions derived from classics, though elegant, can strike the reader as clownishly supercilious.

So, to learn what is (are) more practicable way(s) of using one or more than one allusion in a poem, let us study a few examples that could be enlightening in this direction.

Poetic allusions like the aforementioned "gui hua", "bo shu", and "chong chu" are simply substitutions: "gui hua" for moon or moonlight, "bo shu" for oriole, and "chong chu" for egret. Such substitution does not change a poem in intension or extension. So an allusion is a simple metonymy, which, in the eyes of Fan Peng, was the same as a trite comparison of women to flowers and vice versa, which did not enhance a poem in terms of expression of emotions, subtilizing meanings, and construction of a transcendental world.

Another case in point is Liu Yun's poem entitled "A Veteran General" in *The Collection of Poems in Exchanges from the West Kunlun*:

zhang ba she mao zhan xue gan /
(The blood that smeared his formidable spear has dried up /)
zi sun jin yi lie cai guan.
(His sons and grandsons are now registered for the militia.)
qing yan bi wa kai xin di /
(His newly built blue-tile-roofed mansion stands in the smoky nimbus /)
bai cao huang yun fei jiu tan.
(The rallying terrace has gone to waste afar in the bleak frontier.)

lao bo ke gan xian lin she /
(His military exploits humble the most competent civilian officials hitherto /)
jue gao hai xu dai liu guan.
(His high status allows him to enjoy the exclusive privilege bestowed by His Majesty.)
qiu lai cong lie chang yang xie /
(In autumn he will accompany His Majesty on the hunting excursions in the royal garden /)
jue shuo you neng yi ju an.
(So sprightly, he can still ride his horse on an expedition for His Majesty.)

"chang yang xie (referring to a royal garden known for its willows as well as for its royal hunting activities)", "gan lin she" (alluding to the feats of General Lian Po of the State of Zhao toward the end of the Warring States Period)", "dai liu guan" (originating from an anecdote about Liu Bang, the founder of the Han Dynasty, who loved wearing a styled hat made of bamboo strips and later standing for a royal privilege), and "jue shuo . . . ju an (referring to Liu Xiang, of the Eastern Han Dynasty, who, though aged, could still ride a horse and who pleaded with his monarch to send him on a mission; here praising an aged general for his vivacity)", they were used to, metonymically ("chang yang xie") or a little more than metonymically ("gan lin she", "dai liu guan", and "jue shuo . . . ju an"), mean no more than an imperial honour, great military exploits, a high rank in officialdom, and defiance of advancement in age, respectively. True, these allusions have a little more than what they literally carry to chew on, but, still, they are specific and explicit. Allusions of this nature take up a large proportion in ancient Chinese poetry, such as "weng bian li lang" (Bi Zhuo, of the Jin Dynasty, who was responsible for selecting and recommending officials, once drank furtively from his neighbour's wine urn and ended up in a drunk sleep by it; a drunkard), "wang xiang wo bing" (it is said that, in ancient China, a young man named Wang Xiang once melted the ice frozen over a rivulet with his warm body to catch two carp for his sick mother; a filial love or person)", and "ban ji yong shan" (Ban Jieyu, a concubine of Emperor Cheng of the Han Dynasty, lamented over her painted full-moon–shaped fan; lamentation over loss of favour). Of those who felt an aversion to such allusions, Zhu Chengjue of the Ming Dynasty, in his *Critique of Poetry in Cunyu Study* ("cunyu study" means study where classics are preserved), repudiated a pair of verses, "sun kang ying xue han chuang xia (At cold winter night penurious Sun Kang would have to sit outside the window to make use of the luminescence of snow to read)/che yin shou ying bai xu zhong (Destitute, Che Yin had no alternative but to get a white gauze bag of live glowworms for illumination when learning in the evening)", for usage of such allusions, questioning contemptuously: "True, there *were* such two studious academic pursuers in the Jin Dynasty; and the two verses *are* antithetically symmetrized. But what is the good of such allusions?" His reason could be that they do not at all add to or, in western literary theorists' terms, give tension to the verses where they appear. In his *The Aristos*, John Robert Fowles argues thus: "Science is, legitimately, precision at all cost; and poetry, legitimately, inclusion at all cost". But these allusions, a mere condensation of tales of past personalities, are neither inclusive nor tensive, except that they almost literally and explicitly communicate specific meanings, just as Wang Anshi said: metonymic allusions could be taken totally on their face, for they told no more than tales, so, even if they were perfectly embedded in verses in antithetical symmetry, what was the point of it? (See *A Collection of the Song Dynasty Poetry* published by Zhonghua Book Company.) Moreover, embedment of such allusions in verses leads to loss of what Hans Hermann Frankel attributes, in terms of meaning, to ancient Chinese poetry: open-endedness or equivocality.

But there should be a solution to this problem.

In his *Chips of Precious Jade Collected from the Treasury of Remarks on Poetry*, Wei Qingzhi suggests two ways of using poetic allusions: one is for conveyance of literal meanings and the other for conveyance of feelings. The former is the subject of general linguistics whereas the latter is that of what I would call poetic linguistics. As you may have read, some ancient Chinese poets used allusions not just to convey certain meanings but, more importantly, to express their feelings. Such feelings are universally shared regardless of time and space. As the feelings of a poet are part of his poems, so the allusions used by him to express his feelings blend into his poems. Such allusions seem to have lost their idiosyncrasies, insofar as they are not to be seen as independent of his poems and cannot be replaced by any other words or phrases.

A case in point is the four verses of Li Shangyin's "The Adorned Zither":

zhuang sheng xiao meng mi hu die /
(A butterfly fascinates Zhuang Zhou: whether he is awake or asleep /)
wang di chun xin tuo du juan.
(Wangdi's attachment finds expression in the touching call of a cuckoo.)
cang hai yue ming zhu you lei /
(The bright moon reflected in the sea, tears shed by Jiaoren transform into pearls /)
lan tian ri nuan yu sheng yan.
(With warm sunshine, the fine jade of Mount Lantian issues wisps of smoke.)

Of these four verses, the first is derived from a tale about Zhuangzi's puzzlement or rather about his questions: "Which is a real life?" "Which is a dream? Is his life just his dream?" "Is his dream just his life?" "Why does a person suffer so much in a real life?" and "Why does a person enjoy so much freedom in a dream?" Thus the allusion here could be intended to communicate the poet's feel of confusion. Wangdi in the second one is said to be a monarch over a state called Shu; he abdicated his throne to one of his subjects to pursue immortality, and he finally metamorphosed into a cuckoo, who would, in spring, keep calling, heart-wrenchingly, until its bill was bleeding. The allusive image of a cuckoo also appears in lines like "zhong you yi niao ming du juan (Among them there is a bird named cuckoo)/yan shi gu shi shu di hun (It is said to be the soul of the king of Shu, an ancient state)/ sheng yin ai ku ming bu xi (Whose endless call sounds heart-wrenching)/yu mao qiao cui si ren kun (Plumage deprivation makes it look as if a man were deprived of his hair)" (from the seventh of Bao Zhao of the Southern Dynasties' eighteen-poem series under the title of "After the Style of the Ballads Entitled 'A Hard Journey'"); "du juan mu chun zhi (Towards the end of spring flew hither a cuckoo)/ai ai jiao qi jian (It kept calling in a sad tune)/wo jian chang zai bai (Each time I saw it, I stooped in awe and respect)/chong shi gu di hun (The king of remote antiquity is incarnated as a cuckoo)"(from Du Fu's "A Cuckoo"); "shu ke chun cheng wen shu niao (I, stuck at a town of Shu in spring, heard a homesick cuckoo)/Si gui sheng yin wei gui xin (whose call was touching a chord with me, its empathizer)" (from Yong Tao of the Tang Dynasty's second of his two poems entitled "Two Poems Inspired by the Call of a Cuckoo"); and "qi jian dan mu wen he wu (What, out here, would come to my ears from dawn to dusk?)/Du juan ti xue yuan ai ming (The bleeding call of cuckoos and the woeful cry of apes)" (from Bai Juyi's "To a Chinese Lute Player"). Evidently, the cuckoo as an allusion, as a result of its having been used over a long time, gains more meaning than its original reference. So does the allusive meaning of Legendary Wangdi or King Wang incarnated as a cuckoo after death, as in the second verse of Li's poem: the dejection of an unsettled traveller and the bitterness of an assiduous yet unrequited pursuit of a goal. "cang hai yue ming zhu you lei (The bright moon reflected in the sea, tears shed by Jiaoren transform into pearls)" draws from the tale of Jiaoren, a mythical sea creature, who shed tears which would turn into pearls, to describe a heart laden with endless gnawing woe. As to "lan tian ri nuan yu sheng yan (With warm sunshine, the fine jade of Mount Lantian issues wisps of smoke)", its definite source is hard to determine, but it is likely to come from *The History of the Han Dynasty*, which says that "The mountain Lantian produced fine jade" and/or from Sikong Tu's *A Letter to Jipu*, which quotes Dai Shulun of the Middle Tang Dynasty as saying "A poetic vision, likened to that of the jade of Mountain Lantian emitting wisps of smoke in tepid sunshine, looks like an unreachable mirage before one's eyes", so it must be used to symbolize a kind of perplexed mood. So interpreted, the four verses of Li's "The Adorned Zither" could, generally, describe an actually indescribable psychological uncertainty and unsettledness, a mix of befuddlement, desolation, poignancy, and dreaminess. Such a mood, consonant with what can be felt in "wu duan (I wonder why . . .) " of its first verse, "jin se wu duan wu shi xian (I wonder why the adorned zither had fifty strings)", and in "wang ran (in stupor)" of the last one, "zhi shi dang shi yi wang ran (what a shame that I, then in stupor, did not cherish it", forms a sentimental ambience, which should grip the "qualified reader", who should, in empathetic immersion, feel no "dis-harmonization". The "qualified reader" of Li's poem may care less about the exact meaning of these allusions. In fact, it is likely that "The Adorned Zither" was intended to communicate not specific meanings but one's sensibilities at the moment of recollection. As Liang Qichao, a modern Chinese scholar, said, poems like "The Adorned Zither" defied his interpretation of it verse by verse; even so, as a whole, it had an aesthetic impact on him insofar as he would always find pleasure and feel mentally refreshed whenever reading it. (See his *Sentiments in Ancient Chinese Poetry*.) He could have voiced what could be on the minds of the other readers of this poem. After all, poems are not commodities.

Allusion 115

The charm of a poem lies in its striking a chord with the reader by way of, best of all, its sentiment. And this could be a particular, workable, effective approach to using an allusion in an ancient Chinese poem.

But, if allusions, for example, again, "zhuang sheng meng die (Zhuang Zhou was dreaming of a butterfly)" and "wang di du juan (Wangdi, a legendary king who ruled over an ancient state called shu, metamorphosed into a cuckoo)", are not symbolically, as in "Adorned Zither", but literally used, as in this pair of verses "zhuang meng duan shi deng yu jin (When I awoke from a Zhuang Zhou dream, the lamp was going out)/Shu hun ti chu jiu chu xing (The call of a cuckoo incarnating Wangdi aroused me from drunkenness.)" (from Li Zhong of the Five Dynasties and the Ten States period's poem "Reflection in Later Spring in Memory of Yao Duan, my Revered Predecessor"), which specifically refer to a mere dream and a mere cuckoo, respectively, then this usage is inferior to the mentioned verses of "The Adorned Zither", as the former are much less evocative than the latter. So it is with Lu You's "jing hui meng die zui chu xing (Startled awake from my Zhuang Zhou dream, a drunk me gained a degree of sobriety)" (from his "An Inspired Impromptu"). True, one shall read melancholy into the verse, because of the allusion "Zhuang Zhou dream", as mentioned. But it functions here more as a concretely denotative phrase, that is, a mere dream from which the inebriated poet was awakened, than as an associative trigger, due to a lack of the sentimental ambience resulting from it that should have permeated not only the verse itself but the poem.

All in all, of the two approaches to using one or more than one allusion in a poem, the better one is to use it or them for a sentimental effect. But not all allusions are sentimental. For example, "er qian dan" (the chief of a prefecture in ancient China)", "san gong (the three predominant posts in the hierarchy of officialdom that allegedly originated in the Zhou Dynasty of ancient China)", "yue fa san zhang (the three-point law on which Liu Bang, the founder of the Han Dynasty, and his people reached a consensus)", "zhao gong tang zheng (a eulogy dedicated to Zhaogong, a minister of the Zhou Dynasty in ancient China for his loyal and successful service in dynastic governance)", and "da bi ru chuan (a writing brush that is big in the size of a rafter; commendation for someone's powerful writing)", because of their specific explicit literal references, lack what is needed for a sentimental or enlightening effect: "tension". So allusions as such do not fall under the sentimental category.

A sentimental and/or enlightening allusion has to:

1 give a beautiful visual impression, such as "gu luan wu jing (A luan, a bird in the Chinese myth, bereft of its mate, is said to keep wailing and flopping to death after it saw its image in a mirror; this myth alludes to fidelity)", "qiu feng lu kuai (Rise of autumnal winds evoked one's memory of delicious pork fillets far back home so that he would resign his office and return to his native land; this allusion implies mainly homesickness and, incidentally, indifference to governmental office)", and "qin gao kong li (Legend has it that Qin Gao, an immortal and musician, could travel, as he wished, in and out of the Zhuo River by riding

116 *Allusion*

a carp; this legend expresses a yearning for supernatural prowess and absolute freedom)".

2 be sentimentally tinged, such as "su men chang xiao (literally a lasting chorus-like whistle produced by a Taoist practitioner at the Mountain Sumen, which figuratively expresses one's aloofness)", "dui chuang ye yu (literally, at night two persons have a heart-to-heart chat across their beds; figuratively, it refers to complete leisure and happiness in reunion)", and "liu ruan tian tai (A Rip-Van-Winkle-like Chinese myth about two men named Liu Chen and Ruan Zhao meeting and enjoying a wonderful time with two fairies among mountains; this myth tells people's dream of being free from worldly concerns and having a consummate well-being)".

3 concern things like life; love; and the relationships between man and nature, society and individual, and a social person and a person's ego, which are universal subjects for humankind across time and space, because they will strike a chord deeply with the reader, who shall thus empathize deeply with what is in such allusions, just as Carl Gustav Jung notes: the reader, in that moment, is not an individual; rather, he or she represents humankind, for at the depth of his or her heart resonates the voice of humankind.

5.4. How to annotate an allusion

As to annotation on an allusion, what should be done first and foremost is annotate how it originated and how it has developed into what it is. Knowledge of this process is one of the most important prerequisites for understanding its intension and extension or, in other words, what is in and beyond it, more or less similar to what H.G. Gadamer posits:

> The hermeneutics developed here is not, therefore, a methodology of the human sciences, but an attempt to understand what the human sciences truly are, beyond their methodological self-consciousness, and what connects them with the totality of our experience of world.

(See Joachim Ritter's *Historisches Woerterbuch der Philosophie*.)

In the case of ancient Chinese annotators, they were both proud of and acclaimed for their minuteness, meticulousness, and comprehensiveness, but, at the same time, their annotation, even to the point of being pedantic, was derided. Their annotations could have shed at least some light on allusion, given plenty of substantial, allegedly pertinent evidence collected from past Chinese literature in this regard. But the reality is a different story. This is because they either focused too much on the so-called "origin" of an allusion to ignore its evolution or were too keen to show their erudition by displaying how much they knew to consider whether their knowledge was pertinent or simply deviated from the poem where it was embedded, to name just a few accusations. Thus their annotations could befuddle or even mislead the reader. For example, in an annotation on "yu zhou chang wan (Towards evening fishermen are singing their songs while oaring their boats)" and "yan zhen jing han (Flights of wild geese seem to be perturbed by currents of cold air)" in "A Rhapsody Improvised for the Banquet at Tengwang Tower" by Wang Bo of the Tang Dynasty, Jiang Qingyi of the Qing Dynasty sourced them respectively to "wu yuan zhi tuo yu zhou (Wu Zixu trusted himself with a fisherman)" mentioned in *The Family Instructions of Master Yan* by Yan Zhitui of the Southern Dynasties, which is about how a fisherman helped Wu Zixu, a military strategist of the Spring and Autumn Period, by hiding him in his boat to ferry across a river and flee from the State of Chu, and "jiu yan lie zhen (Nine wild geese fly in a formation)", contained in *Forest of Changes* by Jiao Yanshou of the Western Han Dynasty. But Jiang's sourcing is highly specious. (See *Annotations on "Wang Bo's Works"*.) Wu Zhaoyi of the Qing Dynasty, in his annotation on the verse "qing shan wang duan he (My wish should be likened to that that the dis-joined Mount Hua range would join again to stop the flow of the Yellow River)" of the seventh of the twenty-seven-poem series by Yu Xin, related Yu's "qing shan (the Hua Mount)" to "qing shan (the green mounts)" in Jiang Zong's "qing shan qu qu chou (The farther the green mounts are receding, the more grieved I am feeling)", but, in fact, this association is groundless and thus arbitrary and unhelpful. (See Jin Kaicheng and Ge Zhaoguang's *Detailed Annotations on Quintessential Ancient Chinese Poems*.)

The previously mentioned practices of annotation on an allusion, to be fair, have their own merits to speak of, for example, their abundant evidence concerning the development, in many ways, of an allusion, except for their deficiencies, as mentioned. Then how can one avoid these annotative deficiencies? Annotating allusions in ancient Chinese poems, one should be aware that they have their origins, that they develop through use over a long time, thus meaning more than what they originally meant, and that they must contextually be annotated. This should be the principle for annotation on any allusion in any ancient Chinese poem. One exemplary case in point is *Annotations on the Selected Poetry of the Song Dynasty* by Qian Zhongshu, an eminent modern Chinese scholar. He seems to have followed his pedantic predecessors in this respect, but, essentially, differs from them in that his annotation on an allusion is neither merely for discovering where it originated nor for showing off how learned he is but mainly for facilitating the reader's appreciation of it from an aesthetic perspective, so all his evidence for his annotation is not just pertinent but as close as possible to the evolution of it as a poetic idiom, and he proceeds, in this direction, to find out about the evolution of an allusion: how and for what it has been used and what effect it has had on the reader over time. Thus his annotation is not a pedantic show of learnedness but a purposeful aesthetic hermeneutic. Qian's art of annotation demands that an annotator of the allusions in ancient Chinese poems should not be pedantic, perfunctory, and aesthetically insensitive; otherwise, he or she is not in a position to claim that he or she has delved rightly into them.

An ancient Chinese allusion is also called an ancient Chinese tale. Using "tale" in place of "allusion" is not merely nominal. It signifies that an allusion is about what happened, and the happening was recorded in an ancient Chinese classic. For example, "liao dong he", contained in *More Records of the Search for the Supernatural*, allegedly by Tao Yuanming, is about a man by the name of Ding

118 *Allusion*

Lingwei from Liaodong, a Taoist self-cultivation practitioner, who later metamorphosed into a crane; "he shi bi" in *Han Fei Tzu* by Han Fei, a thinker of the State of Han during the Waring States Period, tells how a discoverer of a chunk of crude jade, a man surnamed He, persisted with its authentication and recognition of his tribute by the lords of the state of Chu despite having been mercilessly tortured successively by two of the lords; "ou niao wang ji" in *Liezi*, allegedly by Lie Yukou, a Taoist thinker of the Warring States Period, describes a flock of seagulls who, unwary of any human concerns, played with a man; "huang ting huan e", in *The History of the Eastern Jin Dynasty* by He Fasheng of the Song period of the Southern Dynasties, is an anecdote about Wang Xizhi, a calligrapher of the Eastern Jin Dynasty, who was cajoled by a Taoist priest, who used a white goose as bait, into handwriting a copy of Huangting, a canon of the doctrines of a Taoist sect for self-cultivation; and "shan ji wu jing", in *A Collection of Bizarre Stories* by Liu Jingshu of the Song period of the Southern Dynasties, narrates how a pheasant danced in front of an large mirror. These allusions originally were only tales.

There are other allusions that, from the very beginning, meant more than they as tales did. For example, in annotation on *The History of the Three Kingdoms* by Chen Shou of the Western Jin Dynasty, Pei Songzhi of the Song period of the Southern Dynasties turned to *The History of the Kingdom of Wei* by Sun Sheng of the Eastern Jin Dynasty for an allusion, or rather Ruan Ji of the Kingdom of Wei's utterance, which is "shi wu ying cai, shu zi cheng ming (At that moment, a lack of the true heroes on the land led to the success of such a villain as Liu Bang)", and this allusion was imbued, from the very beginning, with the implication of either one resenting at having no opportunity to show his talent or one sighing over the caprices of life; "tong tuo jing ji (a camel of bronze and a thicket of thistles)" in *The History of the Jin Dynasty* by a cohort of scholars, led by Fang Xuanling, of the Tang Dynasty, is a euphemistic prophecy by Suo Jing, a Jin Dynasty official, of the destiny of his colleagues while pointing at a bronze camel set at the entrance to the imperial palace inside Luoyang, then the capital, that he would soon see them prostrating themselves servilely in a thicket of thistles, an undertone of his abhorrence of the decadence and strife of the Western Jin Dynasty; and "kua fu zhui ri (Kuafu, a mythic man, chased after the sun)" originally signified a heroic spirit but then deviated from its original significance to mean an overestimation of one's own power, to choose just a few.

As the previous shows, two aspects are clear: an allusion usually is the most succinct description of a tale mostly in four Chinese words; an allusion usually means more than it initially and literally did, as a result of its use in various ways by ancient Chinese poets and the addition of the new meanings to it over a long time. To further illustrate especially the second aspect, let us look at two more examples:

"Lu qiong er ku (Ruan Ji once wailed because there was no way ahead for his cart and he had to return)" originally meant that Ruan Ji vented his subdued bitter emotions. As it was used by more and more ancient Chinese poets, apart from its original meaning, it came to mean one's lamentation over the destiny of a hero who had been pushed to the limit or, conversely, one's scorn at one who was wailing, as in the case of Du Fu's "cang mang bu bing ku (Despairing of continuation of his journey ahead, Ruan Ji wailed)" and "qiong tu ruan ji ji shi xing (When would a wailing Ruan Ji be relieved of his despairs and stay sober?)", by which Du Fu expressed his sympathy with Ruan Ji, contrary to his contempt at Ruan Ji in his "shei fen ku qiong tu (Who would expect me to become a wailing Ran Ji?)" and "she cun chi zuo qiong tu ku (Well-read and capable, it is beneath my dignity to behave like a wailing Ruan Ji)".

Wangdi is also a typical allusion in this regard. It originally had almost no tinge of sadness. According to *The Biographies of the Kings of Shu*, allegedly by Yang Xiong, not a resourceful king, Wangdi failed to control a deluge. But Bie Ling succeeded in his stead, so he chose to abdicate his throne in dignity to Bie Ling. Incidentally, he even had an affair with Bie Ling's wife during the days when Bie Ling was away on the deluge control mission. How could it then be that Wangdi should arouse sympathy? Henceforth, *Species of Birds*, whose author and date are disputable, quoted what *The History of Yizhou*, allegedly by Li Ying of the Liang period of the Southern Dynasties, said of Wangdi: "[he] metamorphosed into a cuckoo, who, into spring, would call plaintively", which began to tinge Wangdi with tragic colouring. *Additions to the Compilation of Medicinal Herbs* by Chen Cangqi, a herbalist of the Tang Dynasty, added a sadder touch to Wangdi: "it would allegedly not stop its woeful call until its bill was bleeding" and "Wangdi fled. Later, he struggled to reclaim his usurped throne, only to fail and die in agony. He then metamorphosed into a cuckoo", in *The Map of the Territory of the Song Dynasty* by Le Shi of the Song Dynasty, portrayed not just a sad but an agonized, wrathful, and tragic Wangdi. This tragic hue was deepened by Bao Zhao and Du Fu in their previously mentioned pertinent poems. Also, new strains of meaning for "Wangdi", such as lonesomeness in dejection, pain of homesickness, a lament over the passing of one's prime, and a heartsick sensitiveness to the lapse of spring, were perceived respectively in "shu hun ti lai chun ji mo (The call of a cuckoo, the soul of Wangdi, tinges spring with loneliness)" by Lai Peng of the Tang Dynasty in his "Reflection on Cold Food Day in the Mountainous Dwelling", Yong Tao's "shu ke chun cheng wen shu niao (I, stuck at a town of Shu in spring, heard a homesick cuckoo)/Si gui sheng yin wei gui xin (whose call was touching a chord with me, its empathizer)", Li Shang-yin's "wang di chun xin tuo du juan (Wangdi's attachment finds expression in the touching call of a cuckoo)", and Wang Ling of the Song Dynasty's "zi gui ye ban you ti xue (The dead of night resounds with the shrill of a cuckoo with its bill bleeding)/bu xin dong feng huan bu hui (It is obsessed with the conviction that its shrill shall recall the vernal wind)" in his "Adieu to Spring".

So another way of annotating an allusion is to bring forth, in chronological order, everything that relates to it. This will provide a full and deep view of its literary and aesthetic significance, so the modern Chinese reader will also be able to appreciate all it signifies explicitly and implicitly as well as their well-read ancient predecessors did. And, more importantly, in the process of annotation, integration of the ancient Chinese way of annotation, the Western hermeneutic, modern aesthetics, modern psychology, and modern linguistics is most likely to take place.

References

1. Arnheim, Rudolf. *Yishu yu shizhijue* 艺术与视知觉 (Art and Visual Perception), translated by Shouyao Teng 滕守尧 and Jiangyuan Zhu 朱疆源. Beijing: Social Sciences Academic Press, 1984.
2. Chang, Lung-hsi 张隆溪. *Ershishiji xifang wenlun shuping* 二十世纪西方文论述评 (A Review of the Twentieth Century Western Literary Theories). Beijing: SDX Joint Publishing Company, 1986.
3. Fan, Peng 范梈. "Mu tian jin yu" 木天禁语 (A Compilation of the Remarks by the Preeminent Members of the Imperial Academy since the Reign of Kaiyuan of the Tang Dynasty on Secrets to Creating a Consummate Poem). In *Lidai shihua* 历代诗话 (The Commentaries by the Critics of the Past Dynasties on Poetry), edited by Wenhuan He 何文焕. Beijing: Zhonghua Book Company, 1981.
4. Fowles, John Robert. "Yalisituosi" 亚里斯托斯 (The Aristos). In *Yingguo zuojia lun wenxue* 英国作家论文学 (The Perspectives of the British Authors on Literature), translated by Guojun Lü 吕国军. Beijing: SDX Joint Publishing Company, 1985.
5. Ge, Lifang 葛立方. "Yunyu yangqiu" 韵语阳秋 (Ge Lifang's Commentaries on Poetry). In *Lidai shihua* 历代诗话 (The Commentaries by the Critics of the Past Dynasties on Poetry), edited by Wenhuan He 何文焕. Beijing: Zhonghua Book Company, 1981.
6. Graham, Angus Charles. "Zhongguoshi de fanyi" 中国诗的翻译 (The Translation of Chinese Poetry). In *Bijiaowenxue yiwenji* 比较文学译文集 (Translations of the Theses on Comparative Literature), edited by Lung-hsi Chang 张隆溪. Beijing: Peking University Press, 1982.
7. Guo, Shaoyu 郭绍虞. *Song shihua jiyi* 宋诗话辑佚 (The Recovery of Lost Song Dynasty Poems). Beijing: Zhonghua Book Company, 1980.
8. Hu, Zi 胡仔. *Tiaoxi yuyin conghua* 苕溪渔隐丛话 (Poetic Remarks from the Fisherman Recluse at the Trumpet-Creeper Creek). Beijing: People's Literature Publishing House, 1981.
9. Jung, Carl Gustav. "Xinli leixing" 心理类型 (Psychological Types or the Psychology of Individuation). In *Shenmei xinli miaoshu* 审美心理描述 (Description of Aesthetical Psychology), by Shouyao Teng 滕守尧 and Jiangyuan Zhu 朱疆源. Beijing: Social Sciences Academic Press, 1985.
10. Kobo, Daishi. *Wen jin mi fu lun* 文镜秘府论 (Treatise on the Secret Treasury of Literary Mirror). Beijing: People's Literature Publishing House, 1980.
11. Lu, Shiyong 陆时雍. "Shijing zonglun" 诗镜总论 (A Comprehensive Digest of Good Ancient Poems). In *Lidai shihua xubian* 历代诗话续编 (A Sequel to the Commentaries by the Critics of the Past Dynasties on Poetry), edited by Fubao Ding 丁福保. Beijing: Zhonghua Book Company, 1983.
12. Ouyang, Xiu 欧阳修. "Liuyi shihua" 六一诗话 (Liuyi's Commentaries on Poetry). In *Lidai shihua* 历代诗话 (The Commentaries by the Critics of the Past Dynasties on Poetry), edited by Wenhuan He 何文焕. Beijing: Zhonghua Book Company, 1981.
13. Sikong, Tu 司空图. "Yu jipu shu 与极浦书 (A Letter to Jipu). In *Quantangwen* 全唐文 (The Qing Dynasty's Authorized Edition of the Anthology of the Works During the Tang Dynasty and the Period of the Five Dynasties and the Ten States), edited by Gao Dong 董诰. Shanghai: Shanghai Classics Publishing House, 1990.
14. Waley, Arthur. *Yuan Mei: Eighteenth Century Chinese Poet*. London: Allen & Unwin, 1956.
15. Wang, Guowei 王国维. *Renjian cihua* 人间词话 (Remarks on Ci Poetry in the Human World), edited by Xianhui Teng 滕咸惠. Jinan: Shangdong Qilu Press, 1981.

16. Wang, Shimao 王世懋. "Yipu xieyu" 艺圃撷余 (To Glean in the Field of Poetry). In *Lidai shihua* 历代诗话 (The Commentaries by the Critics of the Past Dynasties on Poetry), edited by Wenhuan He 何文焕. Beijing: Zhonghua Book Company, 1981.
17. Wei, Qingzhi 魏庆之. *Shiren yu xie* 诗人玉屑 (Chips of Precious Jade Collected from the Treasury of Remarks on Poetry). Shanghai: Shanghai Classics Publishing House, 1978.
18. Weng, Fanggang 翁方纲. "Fuchuzhai wenji" 复初斋文集 (The Collection of the Works at the Fuchu Study). In *Huangtingjian he jiangxishipai juan* 黄庭坚和江西诗派卷 (Huang Tingjian and the Jiangxi Poetry Society), edited by Xuancong Fu 傅璇琮. Beijing: Zhonghua Book Company, 1978.
19. Yang, Yi 杨亿. *Yangwengong tanyuan* 杨文公谈苑 (The Garden of Sayings by Yang Wengong). Shanghai: Shanghai Classics Publishing House, 1993.
20. Yang, Zai 杨载. "Shifa jiashu" 诗法家数 (Techniques of Versification). In *Lidai shihua* 历代诗话 (The Commentaries by the Critics of the Past Dynasties on Poetry), edited by Wenhuan He 何文焕. Beijing: Zhonghua Book Company, 1981.
21. Ye, Mengde 叶梦得. *Shilin shihua* 石林诗话 (Tales and Critique of Poetry at Shilin). In *Lidai shihua* 历代诗话 (The Commentaries by the Critics of the Past Dynasties on Poetry), edited by Wenhuan He 何文焕. Beijing: Zhonghua Book Company, 1981.
22. Zhang, Jie 张戒. "Suihantang shihua" 岁寒堂诗话 (Notes on Poetry Written in the Pine and Cypress Studio). In *Lidai shihua xubian* 历代诗话续编 (A Sequel to the Commentaries by the Critics of the Past Dynasties on Poetry), edited by Fubao Ding 丁福保. Beijing: Zhonghua Book Company, 1983.
23. Zhu, Chengjue 朱承爵. "Cunyutang shihua" 存余堂诗话 (Critique of Poetry in Cunyu Study or My Study Where Classics Are Preserved). In *Lidai shihua* 历代诗话 (The Commentaries by the Critics of the Past Dynasties on Poetry), edited by Wenhua He 何文焕. Beijing: Zhonghua Book Company, 1981.
24. Zhu, Guangqian 朱光潜. *Tanmei shujian* 谈美书简 (Correspondence on Aesthetics). Beijing: People's Literature Publishing House, 2005.

6 "Xu zi" words or phrases
A second special aspect of ancient Chinese poetry

In the fifth chapter, I discussed nouns or noun phrases as allusions. I shall talk about "shi yan", mainly a special verb in a verse, in the seventh chapter. This chapter focuses on "xu zi" words or phrases, approximately the equivalent of function words in their modern sense. In ancient Chinese poetry, a "xu zi" word or phrase, if it means something, has to be used in collocation with a "shi zi" word, or a content word in its modern sense, such as a verb, an adjective, and a noun.

Antonymous to "shi (full or substantial)", "xu", on many occasions, means "nothingness". Its meaning is manifest in its collocation with "kong (void or emptiness)" or "wu (nonexistence)", as in such traditional Chinese four-word phrases as "xu xi yi dai (literally, to leave a chair vacant to await a person to take it; figuratively, to look for a talent who has the required capabilities to take the offered post)" and "xu xin qiu jiao (literally, to empty one's heart to seek advice from another; figuratively, for one to stay humble and learn from another)". "Xu" can also mean "unreal", and its meaning is evident in its collocation with "jia (feigned)" and "wei (sham)", as in such traditional Chinese four-word phrases as "xu qing jia yi (literally, ungenuine cordiality and solicitude; figuratively, hypocritical)" and "jia feng xu huang (literally, a pair of pretend male and female phoenixes; figuratively, a couple of pretend spouses)". Hitherto, one may have been led to assume that the "zi (word)" modified by "xu" is inconsequential. Indeed, contempt for "xu zi" words or phrases is not uncommon in the critique of poetry by ancient Chinese critics, whose representative, Xie Zhen, criticized, in his *A Sea-in-the-Four-Direction Recluse's Remarks on Poetry*:

> When a poem is composed of more content words (hereinafter referred to as "shi zi" words or phrases in contrast to "xu zi" words or phrases) than "xu zi" words or phrases, its meaning is conveyed more economically, more clearly, and more emphatically; otherwise, more lavishly, more cloudily, and more unemphatically.

Xie's criticism, though biased, found supporters in other Chinese poetry critics at the time and later. This bias not only persists but also seems to have been worsened by some one-sided modern Chinese poetry critics, so much that any "xu zi" word or phrase in a verse is judged to be of no help altogether. Both ancient

DOI: 10.4324/9781003405993-6

and modern Chinese poetry critics seem to agree that the merits of an ancient Chinese poem are just its juxtaposition of images and the attendant visual effect as a result of its usage of "shi zi" words or phrases. Consequently "xu zi" words or phrases see increasing prejudice against them, to the point of being abhorred. The abhorrers hate to grant any place in ancient Chinese poetry to any "xu zi" word or phrase and wish to expel them from ancient Chinese poetry once and for all. When it comes to the merits of "shi zi" words or phrases, Ma Zhiyuan's short aria-like poem entitled "Autumnal Thoughts" is frequently cited as one of the exemplars in this regard, due to its striking visual effect produced by "shi zi" words or phrases, to justify exclusion of any "xu zi" word or phrase. Moreover, there is even an argument for dismissal that these words cannot possibly have such an effect as that produced by Chinese inkwash scenery painting drawn with the near-far or scattered perspective technique or a montage in a motion picture. All in all, no "xu zi" word or phrase, or even a verb, in a verse is claimed to have characterized ancient Chinese poetry.

It is believed that there were poetry critics as early as during the period called the Five Dynasties immediately after the Tang Dynasty who began to advocate using few or even no "xu zi" words or phrases in versification. Among them was Lu Yanrang. But his opponents accused him of not knowing the nature of poetry well. (See *A Random All-Inclusive Record by the Owner of "Being Capable of Self-Rectification" Study* by Wu Zeng.) True, like wooden blocks, which, if not glued together, are free to take different shapes, a poem composed of nouns only, without the interspersion of any "xu zi" word or phrase, which is comparable to glue, or even without any verb, allows free juxtaposition of images as one sees fit. In fact, "xu zi" words or phrases are necessary for a poem if it is intended to be subtly nuanced. They are analogous to mortar that is needed to fasten the bricks of an arched bridge, which thus can reach the other side. In the case of an ancient Chinese poem, interspersion of "xu zi" words or phrases, which should not be redundant, can subtilize it.

Let us examine "自", a "xu zi" word, in its collocation.

6.1. The connotations of "自 (zi)", a "xu zi" word, in collocation within a verse

"Xu zi" words or phrases are common in ancient Chinese poetry prior to the emergence of Recent Style poetry. In Recent Style poetry, including "jue ju" and "lv shi" poems, especially in the middle two pairs of verses of a "lv shi" poem, which all are tonally and metrically schemed, interspersion of "xu zi" words or phrases is discouraged and thus reduced virtually to naught, as evidenced in Xie Zhen's *A Sea-in-the-Four-Direction Recluse's Remarks on Poetry*. Earlier evidence is seen in such works as *Poetic Remarks from the Fisherman Recluse at the Trumpet-Creeper Creek* by Hu Zi, which quotes Huang Tingjian as saying that "Only a poem without any 'xu zi' word or phrase can be considered to be solid", and *Records from Someone Who Stopped Farming in the Southern Village* by Tao Zongyi, a historian of the late Yuan and early Ming dynasties, contains the perspective of Zhao Mengfu

124 *"Xu zi" words or phrases*

of the late Song and early Yuan dynasties: "Any 'xu zi' word or phrase in a poem has nothing to recommend it".

But there are exceptions, for example, Du Fu's "jiang shan *you* ('有'[to have]) ba shu (Speaking of rivers and mounts, there are those across Bashu)/dong yu *zi* qi liang (The temple has been here since Qi or the Liang period of the Southern Dynasties)" in his poem "A Visit to Tushita Temple" and "gu qiang *you* ('犹'[still]) zhu se (The shadows of bamboo still dance on the time-honoured walls)/xu ge *zi* song sheng (The empty tower resounds defiantly with pines' ancient soughing)" in his "Reflection at the Tengwang Tower". The two pairs of verses, though interspersed with such 'xu zi" word as "zi", still received accolades from ancient Chinese poetry critics of later generations. In his *Tales and Critique of Poetry at Shilin*, Ye Mengde noted:

> It is well known that a poet will weigh even one word for a single verse of his poem. Still, Du Fu surpasses all other poets in that even his one word can lend much to the meaning of a verse, insofar as to be beyond the reader's anticipation. So let us not take his word for it.

He then exemplified his notion with Du Fu's two pairs of verses, claiming that "Thousands of miles in space and hundreds of years in time are encompassed separately in 'you' ('有'[to have]) and 'zi (自)'. And the poet's reflection on the grandeur of sceneries and passage of time can be felt beyond them". And he went on with the praise that

> It is owing to "you ('犹'[still])" and "zi (自)" that this pair of verses become so consummate, which demands extraordinary prowess. Omission of them would lead to loss of the peculiarity of the Tengwang Tower, as the other eight words could apply to any other towers.

This "zi (自)" in particular is magical. In the first pair (herein referred to as "zi1", which means, according to *Annotation on the Ancient Chinese* by Yang Shuda, a modern Chinese scholar, "from or since"), it indicates the long history of the temple; in the second pair (herein referred to as "zi2", which figuratively means "defiantly"), it is symmetrically antithetical to "you ('犹' [still])" in the preceding verse in terms of tonal and metrical scheme, highlighting the same sound of pine trees, despite a lapse of centuries. The function of "zi1" and "zi2", as Ye claimed, could prove that interspersion of "xu zi" words or phrases in a poem that may otherwise have been crammed with "shi zi" words or phrases can better add to and, what's more, subtilize the poem.

But what it is exactly about "zi1" and "zi2" that wins Ye Mengde's commendation is yet to be explored.

Let us look first at Du Fu's pentasyllabic "lv shi" poem "A Visit to the Tushita Temple" in its entirety:

> dou shuai zhi ming si /
> (The Tushita Temple is known far and near for centuries /)

zhen ru hui fa tang.
(Its hall is where the ontological truth is preached.)
jiang shan you ba shu /
(Speaking of rivers and mounts, there are those across Bashu /)
dong yu zi qi liang.
(The temple has been here since Qi or the Liang period of the Southern Dynasties.)
yu xin ai sui jiu /
(Yu Xin lamented long over those self-consciously impious times /)
zhou yong hao bu wang.
(Zhou Yong always cherished his faith in Buddhist tranquillity.)
bai niu che yuan jin /
(Riding on the White Ox one could embark on the long journey to bliss /)
qie yu shang ci hang.
(I pray that I shall be delivered on the raft of mercy to the Pure Land.)

Although it contains several allusions, this poem is easy to understand: the time-honoured Tushita Temple is not just a good vantage point but also a holy Buddhist place where the poet himself wished to be enlightened on the truth of eternity to alleviate his pain over the tumultuous times. Qiu Zhaoao said of the fifth and sixth verses that

> Association of "jiang shan (rivers and mountains or landscapes or sceneries)" with "ba shu (Bashu, a region name)" is to present a spectacular geography; setting "dong yu (temple)" in "qi liang" (the Qi and Liang periods of the Southern Dynasties) is to stress its long history.

His interpretation certainly is not erroneous, but he seems to have overlooked what "zi1" implies: passage of time over a spate of dynasties, which should naturally compel the reader to think about what happened to the weathered temple, whose every aspect could be likened to whatever is represented in a traditional Chinese painting, telling its experience from the long past to the present. So small wonder that, in his *Oubei's Discourse on Poets and their Poetry*, Zhao Yi, also known as Oubei, of the Qing Dynasty, regarded Du Fu's pair of verses as the cream of the cream in Du Fu's five-word-a-verse (pentasyllabic) eight-verse "lv shi" poetry, and he almost echoed Ye Mengde by saying that

> Thousands of li [a Chinese measurement unit of distance] from east to west, hundreds of years over a long history, they are totally encompassed just in two 'xu zi' words, i.e., 'you ('有' [to have])' and 'zi1'. Who else could achieve it but one who must be divinely talented?

In his *Exposition of Du-Xue-Shan-Fang (i.e., the-Mountainous-Residence-Where-Snowfall-Is-Appreciated)'s Anthology of the Tang Dynasty Poetry*, Guan Shiming likewise agrees with Ye, speaking highly of Du Fu's aptitude for calling "xu zi" words or phrases into full play in the pair of verses despite their alleged damage to the appeal of a poem, especially a five-word-a-verse eight-verse "lv shi" poem. (See *A Sequel to "The Criticisms by the Qing Dynasty Critics on Poetry"*). Indeed, if "dong yu zi qi liang (The temple has been here since Qi or the Liang period of the Southern Dynasties)" was changed into "qi liang dong yu liu (The Qi or Liang period of the Southern Dynasties witnessed the completion of construction of the temple)", the latter would read more like an account of a factual event and less like a review of a history.

Let us look then at Du Fu's pentasyllabic "lv shi" poem "Reflection at the Teng-wang Tower" in its entirety:

ji mo chun shan lu /
(The mountain path is seldom treaded even in spring /)
jun wang bu fu xing.
(Let alone by the duke who is already history.)
gu qiang you zhu se /
(The shadows of bamboo still dance on the time-honoured walls /)
xu ge zi song sheng.
(The empty tower resounds defiantly with pines' ancient soughing.)
niao que huang cun mu /
(Towards dusk, only birds are heard twittering in that desolate hamlet /)
yun xia guo ke qing.
(Like unattached wayfarers, clouds drift across to Heaven knows where.)
shang si ge chui ru /
(I cannot help imagining the announcement of the duke's arrival with great fanfare /)
qian ji yong ni jing.
(Followed by an army of his steed-riding attendants upholding the colourful banners.)

This poem at once recalls the past and laments the status quo. In sight of the poet was an empty tower in a desolate ambience, except for bamboo shadows upon its ancient wall and the same echo in it of winds blowing through pines as that during the days when it had been in the grace of the duke, which aroused the poet's nostalgia for its glorious past. This kind of sentiment is felt through "you (still)" and "zi2", two "xu zi" words embedded in the third and fourth verses, respectively. "You (still)" hints at what physically remains of the temple; "zi2" implies what the temple has atmospherically retained. Moreover, "you (still)" here evokes "mu you ru ci ren he yi kan (True, these willows are tall and big; still, they have grown old, alas, let alone us human beings)", a tearful sigh heaved by Huan Wen of the Eastern Jin Dynasty when he saw the willows that had been planted centuries earlier; "zi2" here may remind one of "ting cao wu ren sui yi lv (Grasses within an unoccupied court green as they please)" by Wang Zhou, who was allegedly murdered by Yang Guang, the second emperor of the Sui Dynasty, for his insolent verse; of "nian nian sui sui hua xiang si (Flowers still look alike, though year after year elapses)/sui sui nian nian ren bu tong (Yet year after year sees different flower appreciators)" by Liu Xiyi of the Tang Dynasty, who was said to have been killed by being buried in a cave by Song Zhiwen, his uncle, also a courtier-cum-poet, for Liu had refused to grant his request for a monopoly on the pair of verses; and of Cen Shen of the Tang Dynasty's "ting shu bu zhi ren qu jin (Those garden trees remain oblivious to the decease of their planter)/chun lai hai fa jiu shi hua (Springtime will see them flowering as they would when he was alive)".

Worthy of mention is another of Du Fu's pair of verses "ying jie bi cao *zi* chun se (The steps reflecting verdant grasses are naturally green with a spring tint/ge ye huang li kong hao yin (Orioles in trees are chirping through leaves but without audience)" in his heptasyllabic eight-verse "lv shi" poem "To Prime Minister of the Kingdom of Shu"; "zi" in the first verse, symmetrically antithetical to "kong" in the second verse, which connotes "without audience", should contextually be understood to connote "naturally", although it is a "xu zi" word. This instance further attests to the polysemy of "zi". Indeed, there is more to "zi" that Du Fu used in his poems. This was discerned by Ge Lifang. He pointed out that Du Fu's "zi" reflected his gloomy moods when he was stuck in a precarious situation and that, to express his gloomy moods, Du Fu used "zi" to animate an inanimate object, whose imagined carefree existence thus contrasted with his careworn survival and, by this contrastive proxy, highlighted his heartfelt distress. (See *Ge Lifang's Commentaries on Poetry*.)

In his *Chips of Precious Jade Collected from the Treasury of Remarks on Poetry*, Wei Qingzhi, it seems, obliquely criticized Recent Style poets for their use of "xu zi" words or phrases by comparing Zeng Jifu's "bai yu tang zhong ceng cao zhao (In the imperial academy I drafted decrees)/shui jing gong li jin ti shi (In the moonlight I just scribbled poems)" and Han Zicang's "bai yu tang shen ceng cao zhao (Deep is the imperial academy where I once drafted decrees)/shui jing gong leng jin ti shi (The chilly moonlight just saw me scribbling poems)", Han's revision of Zeng's original, remarking that he preferred Han's to Zeng's in that Han replaced "zhong (in)" and "li (under)", two "xu zi" words, respectively, with "shen (deep)" and "leng (chilly)", two "shi zi" words; thus Han's substitutions not just differentiated his revisions from Zeng's originals but focused the reader's attention on "shi yan", which is to be elaborated on in the seventh chapter. Wei's reason presumably is that the two "xu zi" words, which themselves have little meaning, should specify the spatial relationships only to further restrict the reader's imagination, whereas the two substituting "shi zi" words invoke a sense of depth and chilliness and rid the verses of any spatial restriction. Contrary to Wei, Wu Ke, in his *Canghai's Commentaries on Poetry*, argued for the bolstering effect of "xu zi" words or phrases on versification as in his own case where he had replaced "you xi" and "zong heng" in his "*you xi* mo chi chuan shi ti (Like a game player, you play with your inkstones to inherit and carry forward so many styles of calligraphy/*zong heng* bi zhen sao qian jun (Like a warrior thrashing his spear, you wield your writing brush near and far to subdue so many calligraphers)" with "*man xi*" and "*zhen cheng*", two pairs of ancient "xu zi" phrases, thus the revised "man xi mo chi chuan shi ti (How you play with your inkstones to inherit and carry forward so many styles of calligraphy)/zhen cheng bi zhen sao qian jun (Bravo, you wield your writing brush near and far to subdue so many calligraphers)", which were believed by Wu to have surpassed the originals in terms of impact and logicality.

In fact, opinions of either the merits or the demerits of "xu zi" words or phrases being used in poetry varied with various ancient Chinese poetry critics, and each held his own ground. Used poorly, a "xu zi" word or phrase would mar an ancient Chinese poem as a whole, but, well used, it would subtilize an ancient Chinese poem, as in Du Fu's two poems. Fan Xiwen of the Song Dynasty, in his *An Intimate Poetry Discourse across Beds at Night*, said that

> It is already an incredible challenge to make an animate "xu zi" word or phrase more so in a verse, not to mention to animate an inanimate "xu zi" word or phrase in a verse to the possible extremity. Inanimate as a "xu zi" word or phrase be, it will have to be animated, so imagine what a challenge this can be.

But Du Fu is a master of this art. That should explain why his two pairs of verses are still read today. Evidently, a "xu zi" word or phrase itself is not to blame, and how to use it in a verse matters.

6.2. A "xu zi" word or phrase, help in conveyance of subtle nuances

Description of various visible, audible, or tangible things in this physical world certainly needs "shi zi" words or phrases (content words). But there are many other things, such as spatial, temporal, sequential, and cause-and-effect relationships, that an observer, from his or her perspective, hopes to delineate so that certain logical links can be established and certain attendant sensations or feelings can be clearly expressed. In that case, "xu zi" words or phrases (function words) come into play. This is also the case in ancient Chinese poetry. Doubtless, imagery, for the ancient Chinese poet, especially for the ancient Recent Style poet, is the decisive vehicle of conveyance of the meanings of his poems. But these "meanings" are also ingrained with his sensations or feelings resulting from his perception or observation, which "shi zi" words or phrases cannot bring forth all by themselves. For example. "chuan (boat)", "zou (sail)", and "he (river)", three "shi zi" words together, can roughly describe what happens, just like the inarticulate utterance of a babbling toddler about the sight of a thing, but they cannot detail the occurrence. Usually a grown-up will describe what he or she wants to describe in a much more nuanced way. For example, he or she may say, "he zhong chuan zai zou (A boat is sailing in the middle of the river)", so "zhong (in the middle of)" and "zai (which expresses a continuous tense)", the two Chinese "xu zi" words, are needed. For another example, if one wants to arouse others' sympathy with distress, mere "shi zi" words, such as "shang xin (heartbroken) and "luo lei (to shed tears), may not achieve it, even if their meanings are explicit. One has to turn to "xu zi" words or phrases for rhetorical help because they can, in a nuanced way, tease the nerves of, say, the readers and have more touching impact upon them.

Back to ancient Chinese poetry. Let us look first at "qiu shui *cai* shen si wu chi (Into autumn the Jinjiang River is adequately as deep as four or five chi) (chi, a Chinese measurement unit of depth)/ye hang *qia* shou liang san ren (That boat at the open pier happens to ferry two or three people, no more and no less)" in Du Fu's poem entitled "A Neighbour South of My Home". This pair of verses expresses the poet's pleasant surprise, a feeling that defies conveyance by any "shi zi" word or phrase but can only come through in "cai (roughly 'just')" and "qia (roughly 'only')", two "xu zi" words. Then let us look at "luan hua *jian yu* mi ren yan (Flowers, one cluster after another, are almost about to dazzle my eyes)/qian cao *cai neng* mo ma ti (Sprouting grasses are high just enough to hide my horse's hooves)" in Bai Juyi's poem entitled "A Stroll in Spring around the Qian Tang Lake". The poet uses "jian yu (roughly 'almost about')" and "cai neng (roughly 'just enough')", two "xu zi" phrases, to express his feeling of ecstasy and fondness about the vying blossoms and growing grasses. What effect would this pair of verses produce on the reader should they be modified into "luan hua mi ren yan (Flowers, one cluster after another, dazzle my eyes)/qian cao mo ma ti (Sprouting grasses hide my horse's hooves)"?

As the previous shows, "xu zi" words or phrases aid in nuanced, impactful conveyance of certain sensations or feelings. Apart from this, "xu zi" words or phrases also help, in the case of an ancient Chinese poem, to make it run more smoothly, to subtilize it, and to vary it in cadence.

Ancient Chinese "xu zi" words or phrases are typed by their linguistic roles as "qi yu ci", that is, the words that initiate a sentence; "jie yu ci" that logically connect sentences; "zhuan yu ci" that contrast the meaning of a sentence and the one that immediately follows it; "chen yu ci" that, as auxiliaries, facilitate the making of a sentence and those that perform as a summarization tag (i.e., "shu yu ci"), an interjection tag (i.e., "tan yu ci"), or an ending tag (i.e., "xie yu ci"). (See *The Secret to Mastery of 'Xu Zi' Words or Phrases* by Wang Mingchang of the Qing Dynasty.) In fact, "xu zi" words or phrases such as "qi yu ci", "chen yu ci", "shu yu ci", "tan yu ci", and "xie yu ci" are seldom used in Recent Style poetry, except for the sake of cadence. But "jie yu ci" and "zhuan yu ci", because of their attributes, are frequently employed in Recent Style poetry to help convey the poet's deep, delicate feelings with more nuance. In his *Random Notes on Prose Writing*, Liu Dakui of the Qing Dynasty says that

> For a time since they were coined in the remotest past, Chinese words included far more "shi zi" words or phrases than "xu zi" words or phrases. That is a part of the reason that classics produced during that period were so laconic and so ungrammatical. By the days of Confucius, "xu zi" words or phrases were complete in type and sufficient in number. They remarkably aided a writer in expression of his otherwise inexpressible delicate sensibilities.

He is correct about the evolution, from simple to complex, of the Chinese glossary. Here is another quotation from Wang Yun of the Qing Dynasty's *Exegeses of*

"Xu zi" words or phrases

Texts: "The earliest coinage by ancient Chinese of words was not for embellishment but for content, so there were only 'shi zi' words or phrases for a time since then. Later, some of 'shi zi' words or phrases were turned into 'xu zi' ones". The reason for this conversion could also be what Liu Dakui says previously. In his *A Glossary of "Xu Zi" Words or Phrases*, Yuan Renlin of the Qing Dynasty asserts that

> In proportion to a multitude of Chinese words, "xu zi" words or phrases are just a few. Nonetheless, interspersed in a piece of writing, "xu zi" words or phrases can be magically and effectively helpful; "shi zi" words or phrases are many and used to describe many things. When it comes to expression of feelings, however, only "xu zi" words or phrases are capable of it, economically yet subtly.

An expert on "xu zi" words or phrases, Yuan understandably is discriminatively fond of them. But, on the other hand, this assertion holds water, as I have discussed.

In a word, description by a poet of something physical will simultaneously involve sensations or feelings. These sensations or feelings are so delicate and nuanced that only "shi zi" words or phrases cannot fully convey them. So "xu zi" words or phrases are used to play a due role where "shi zi" words have failed. Thus the world, a mix of physicality and spirituality, in a "deep linguistic structure", as previously discussed, will be presented, genuinely and minutely, through a poem.

The salient features of Recent Style poetry, by some ancient Chinese poetry critics' standards, are its juxtaposition of images and its equivocality. This is because, for one thing, it has no redundant word, as Wu Ke, in his *Canhai's Commentaries on Poetry*, says of "cao cao bei pan gong xiao yu (A banquet is hastily prepared for us to happily chat over)/hun hun deng huo hua ping sheng (In the lit yet caliginous atmosphere we are recollecting our good old days)" in Wang Anshi's poem "To my First Younger Sister", which, unlike other seven-word-a-verse eight-verse "lv shi" poems, which could be verbose, used no more than the necessary words. Likewise, in his *Litang's Remarks on Poetry*, Li Dongyang praises "ji sheng mao dian yue (verbatim: Rooster crow, thatched inn, moon) (The crow of roosters around the thatched inn in the moonlight)/ren ji ban qiao shuang (verbatim: Human footprints, plank bridge, frost) (A few human footprints in the frost covering the bridge of plank)", a pair of verses in Wen Tingyun's poem "Early Departure from the Inn at the Shang Mount", for being not verbally redundant except for the words that were necessary for both visual and aural effect. Discouraging redundancy should be encouraged. But it seems that their redundant words were all "xu zi" words or phrases, which they thought would not just occupy space but interrupt cadence in a poem. So any "xu zi" word or phrase should be denied even a minor role in a poem altogether. This notion is deplorable. As has previously been discussed, a "xu zi" word or phrase alone is meaningless, but, once in collocation with a "shi zi" one, it can help subtilize the meaning of an ancient Chinese poem.

Fang Dongshu, in his *Illuminating Chatters*, advocated compact yet meaningful versification. His advocacy actually echoed what some poetry critics in the Song Dynasty had promoted. For example, in his *Jade Dew in the Crane's Forest or Tales of the Men of Letters of the Song Dynasty*, Luo Dajing spoke highly of "wan li bei qiu chang zuo ke (The autumnal vistas saddened me, a traveller thousands of miles away from home)/bai nian duo bing du deng tai (I, suffering all my life from ailments, ascended a highly raised terrace by myself)" in Du Fu's poem "Ascending a Highly Raised Terrace", for "its economical fourteen words include as many as eight-fold meanings; moreover, they are symmetrically antithetical to perfection". Luo Dajing's praise should remind one of a telegram whose succinct yet meaningful message is believed to show its sender's ingenuity. In the case of an ancient Chinese poem, how does one achieve succinctness? An ancient Chinese poet seemed to have no alternative but to crowd out "xu zi" words or phrases with "shi zi" ones. Such examples are many. Wu Hang, in his *Poetic Commentaries at the Huanxi Quarters*, noted that the charm of Du Fu's poems was that his one verse contained multiple meanings, such as his "jing qi ri nuan long she dong (The rainbow banners in the warm sunlight kept unfurling like outstretching dragons or snakes)/gong dian feng wei yan que gao (Swallows in breezes are soaring up well above the imperial palaces)", into which as many as five meanings could be read, and such meaningful succinctness as in Du Fu's poetry should be ascribed to there being no weak "xu zi" words or phrases in it but robust "shi zi" ones and not the other way around. But meaningful succinctness as such is presumably not recommendable, for it seems to me that an ancient Chinese poem only turns out to be crammed with images. If a poem like this was deemed good, would the "Jijiu Rimes", a primer compiled under the auspices of Emperor Yuan of the Western Han Dynasty for children to learn to read in the shortest possible time, known for such cramming, be taken as the acme of the poetry of this nature? Absolutely not. Wang Yingkui's *A Sequel to "Liunan's Desultory Notes"* contains an impressive anecdote about Wang Dunweng of the Qing Dynasty: Wang was academically at variance with his contemporary Qian Qianyi. One day he challenged Yan Baiyun, one of Qian's disciples, with the question: "Since you have followed your master for a long time, can you explain the quintessence of writing?" Yan answered: "Composition both of poetry and of prose abides by the same precept that the more both in allusion and in implication, the better", thus not letting Wang Dunweng get the upper hand. Worthy of note is Yan's pronouncement on "the more in implication", the achievement of which, as discussed, needs the aid of "xu zi" words or phrases.

6.3. "Xu zi" words or phrases, help in subtilization of the meaning of ancient Chinese poems

In the case of say, a Recent Style poem, "shi zi" words or phrases can juxtapose its images but do not necessarily subtilize its meaning. To subtilize the meaning of a Recent Style poem, especially to convey its delicate sentiments, the use of "xu zi" words or phrases is the better approach, not to mention that there is the occasion where the charm of even a Recent Style poem lies not in its juxtaposed imagery but in its undercurrent of nuanced feelings. Yang Wanli, in his *Chengzhai's Commentaries on Poetry*, exemplified this with Du Fu's "dui shi *zan* can *hai* bu neng (Hardly did my appetite for food return when I lost it once more)" and Han Yu's "*yu* qu *wei* dao *xian* si hui (I was desirous but started to think of returning short of arrival at a flowery scene)". The former has a threefold meaning: "I" faced some food, "I" forced "myself" to eat it despite "my" sorrow, but, however "I" tried, the sorrow deprived "me" of "my" appetite. And "my" sentiments in the course are meticulously expressed through such "xu zi" words as "zan (barely)" and "hai (still)". The latter also has a threefold meaning: "I" desired to go there, "I" almost arrived there, but "I" hesitated and finally changed "my" mind and turned back. And "my" feelings are thoroughly bared through such "xu zi" words as "yu (desire)", "wei (not yet)", and "xian (before)". As the two instances show, these "xu zi" words enable the verses to offer more food for thought. There are many other verses in kind. For example, Chen Yuyi' s "wan li lai you *hai* wang yuan (I've travelled ten thousand li [li, a Chinese measurement unit of distance] but still look as far as to the horizon)/san nian duo nan *geng* ping wei (I, having endured through perils of war though, am keener to ascend the perilous height)", an imitation of the aforementioned Du Fu's verses about the ascent of an elevated terrace, in his poem entitled "My Ascent of the Yueyang Tower", was extolled by Fang Hui of the Yuan Dynasty and Ji Yun and Xu Yinfang of the Qing Dynasty for the contrastive effect produced through such "xu zi" words as "hai (but still)" and "geng (which does not appear in the English translation but can be felt through the comparative form of 'keener')", in line with the view of Pan Deyu in his *Remarks on Poetry at Yangyi Studio* that the orthodox versification emphasized transitional or rather contrastive relations even between the parts of a verse.

If the typicality of these three examples from Yang Wanli's *Chengzhai's Commentaries on Poetry* should merit doubt, let us move on to look at more typical examples.

In "*que* kan qi zi chou *he* zai (I turned only to see my already worriless wife and offspring)/*man* juan shi shu xi *yu* kuang (In ecstasy I hastily parcelled my books for departure)" of his poem entitled "Inspired at the News of the Imperial Army Having Recovered Youzhou and Jizhou", Du Fu expressed his surprise at a piece of incredibly exciting news through such two "xu zi" words, "que" and "he", and his frenzy of euphoria through two "xu zi" words, "man" and "yu", two contrasting and intensifying sentiments which vivify the whole poem. Li Shangyin used, in "chun can dao si si *fang* jin (Spring silkworms keep spinning silk till they die)/la ju cheng hui lei *shi* gan (Candles' tear-like melted wax starts to dry when they burn up)" in one of his poems collectively entitled "Titleless", such "xu zi" words as "fang" and "shi", respectively, in the first and second verses to lend to the poem persistence of a poignancy and acceptance of a predestination. What if these "xu zi" words were discarded for their alleged redundancy? True, their omission does not at all affect the juxtaposition of imagery, according to Li Dongyang' s *Litang's Remarks on Poetry*, but it does affect transmission of the poets' fine sentiments to the reader.

Juxtaposition of imagery, like "cavalier perspective" in the ancient Chinese painting term, one of the features of Recent Style poetry, was highly recommended;

Ma Zhiyuan's "ku teng lao shu hun ya (Dry veins, ancient trees, and crows in twilight)/gu dao xi feng shou ma (A hoary trail, a scrawny nag, both in the western wind)", which, strictly speaking, is not of poetic class, was often used to exemplify this feature. As noted, however, juxtaposition of imagery does not necessarily subtilize the meaning of a poem; subtilization of the meaning of a poem, in many instances, needs "xu zi" words or phrases. In his *Jade Dew in the Crane's Forest or Tales of the Men of Letters of the Song Dynasty*, Luo Dajing suggested that a poem as a whole should be sustained by robust words, while its movement within and across its verses should be facilitated by auxiliary words. To specify his "auxiliary words", he cited "he" and "qie", two "xu zi" words, in Du Fu's "sheng li *he* yan mian (How shameful I am incapable of feeding my family)/you duan *qie* shui shi (All the year round grief is gnawing at my heart)" and "qi" and "ying", also two "xu zi" words, also in Du Fu's "ming *qi* wen zhang zhu (How am I supposed to establish my renown on my poems)/guan *ying* bing lao xiu (As one who is sick or senile has to resign or retire)", saying that robust words (namely "shi zi" words) are to a poem what pillars are to houses, while auxiliary words (namely "xu zi" words) are to a poem what axles are to the wheels of carts. His point is that "xu zi" words or phrases could help to subtilize the meaning of a poem. And, in fact, subtilization of meaning is also typical of Recent Style poetry. Examples of this are useful. Wang Bo, in "*yi* jue shi chuan shang bie nian (Sight of the running river has already evoked my heartache over the departure of my friend)/*fu* kan jin shu yin li zhou (Worse, those dock trees should be so unsympathetic as to prevent me from seeing my friend's leaving boat)" from one of his two poems under the title of "An Early Autumnal Farewell at the River Dock", employed two "xu zi" words, "yi (already)" and "fu (furthermore or, here, worse)", to redouble the poet's mental anguish at the moment of separation from his friend. In his "liu lang *yi* hen peng shan yuan (A man named Liu Chen bemoaned the despairingly long journey to the nirvana/*geng* ge peng shan yi wan chong (But imagine how many times as far as that the journey from me to you can be)" from one of his "Titleless" four-poem series, Li Shangyin, by virtue of "yi (already)" and "geng (even farther than)", accentuated the huge distance that made it unrealizable for the two characters, though obscure in the poem, to reunite. Likewise, "geng (farther)" and "que (incredibly)", as well as "yi (so)" and "hai (worse)", the four "xu zi" words, used by Jia Dao in "wu duan *geng* du sang qian shui (For no good reason I shall be forced to move farther across the Sangqian River)/*que* wang bing zhou shi gu xiang (My homesickness is surging, incredibly, for none other than Bingzhou)" in his poem entitled "Ferrying across the Sangqian River" and by Li Gou of the Song Dynasty in "*yi* hen bi shan xiang zu ge (It so grieves me for my sight to be blocked by those green mountains)/bi shan *hai* bei mu yun zhe (Worse is that those green mountains should be obscured by clouds at dusk)" in his poem entitled "Homesick", also help to attain subtle nuances. Zhang Jiuling in "*que* ji cong lai yi (I already knew that there would be beauty in store for me to see along this leg of my journey/*fan* yi meng li you (Still I am so astounded as to have an illusion of travelling in a dreamland)" in his poem entitled "Enchanted Just at the Very Beginning of my Xiang River Tour", harnessed "que (already)" and "fan (still)" to aid in intensifying, by degree, his wonderment and admiration. Zhang's "fan" was imitated by Sikong Shu in "*zha jian fan yi meng* (Our sudden re-meeting seemed so illusionary as to feel like a dream" in his poem entitled "Bidding Adieu to Han Shen after Remeeting and Putting Up at an Inn with him in Yunyang", in correspondence with the preceding "zha (suddenly)", to describe his inner state of being first shocked, then incredulous, and finally chuffed; no wonder the rhetoric was so clever in the eyes of Fan Xiwen, who, in his *An Intimate Poetry Discourse across Beds at Night*, exclaimed that "The reader seems to be witnessing such an unexpected reunion after a long separation". The Northern Song Dynasty ci poet Yan Jidao replaced "fan" with "you (despite the fact)" in "jin xiao jin ba yin gang zhao (Let me, tonight, illuminate you with a silver lamp for a careful examination) (worthy of note is that '剩', the third original Chinese word of the verse, should be pronounced in pinyin not as 'sheng' but as 'jin')/*you* (a sub for 'fan') kong xiang feng zai meng zhong (Despite your real presence I still suspect that our reunion is not substantial but illusory)" in one of his ci poems entitled "A Colourfully Attired Singsong Girl Holding a Goblet Urged Partaking of Wine"; Yan's substitution could be more ingenious and could make the reader experience an inner state of discomposure, a mixture of doubt and assurance, for a longer duration, before feeling utter exhilaration, on the occasion of such reunion, as the poet did; thus the meaning of the two verses is much more subtle than without the substitutionary "you".

Mao Chunrong, in his *Shenyuan's Poetic Discourse*, said, quite to the point, of ancient Chinese poetry that it should be circuitous or rather subtle (by virtue of "xu zi" words or phrases). To substantiate his conception, he cited Song Zhiwen's "*bu ji* xi shan yao (If you do not send me the immortal elixir)/*he you* dong hai qi (How shall I live for eternity)", noting that the poet, instead of directly baring his heartfelt admiration of a Taoist priest for his transmutation into an immortal, indirectly urged the latter (as "he you", a "xu zi" phrase, implies) to send him the medicine; Cen Shen's "qin wang *gan* wen dao (I dare not bemoan the far expedition for His Majesty/si xiang meng zhong gui (All I shall do is return home secretly in my dream)", with an annotation that an expedition officer, that is, the poet himself, expressed his desperation of seeing no hope, after a seemingly infinite spate of time, of going back home by an ironical utterance of his so-called solace, even if in his dreams, of returning afar to his homeland, for the sake of His Majesty's military enterprise (which is implied by "gan", a "xu zi" word); and Zhang Jiuling's "*zi fei* chang xing mai (I do not dare to take a far excursion often/*shei neng* zhi ci yin (Otherwise how could it be to enjoy such natural melodies)", observing that the poet, who actually was tired of the long travel that he had done previously, should instead say that he relished the reward after his long hike, the musical sound of the creek running across turquoise ("zi fei" and "shei neng", two "xu zi" phrases, hint at the poet's feelings as such).

The preceding should have proved that "xu zi" words or phrases, if used appropriately, subtilize the meaning of a poem in many aspects. To appreciate a poem thus subtilized, the reader should take the cues given by its "xu zi" word(s) or phrase(s); in this way, the reader, according to Mao Chunrong, will feel what the poet felt and eventually crack the poetic "cases".

6.4. Use of "xu zi" words or phrases, a criterion for judgment of the poetry of the Tang and Song Dynasties

Those Tang Dynasty Recent Style poems interspersed with "xu zi" words or phrases were not endorsed by many ancient poetry critics, especially after the Song Dynasty. This actually was due to a criterion by which those poetry critics judged the poems of the Tang and Song dynasties. By this criterion, Tang Dynasty poetry was superior to that of the Song Dynasty in that the former uses many fewer "xu zi" words or phrases than the latter or simply no "xu zi" words or phrases at all. Utilization of "xu zi" words or phrases in ancient Chinese poems, which seemed to resume in the Song Dynasty, actually restarted in the Middle Tang Dynasty, according to Xie Zhen's *A Sea-in-the-Four-Direction Recluse's Remarks on Poetry*. With the resumption of "xu zi" words or phrases, the language of Recent Style poetry, since the Middle Tang Dynasty, began to change from literary incrementally back to, again, the vernacular. Vernacular language was believed to characterize the poetry of the Song Dynasty, although it still appeared in the Recent Style. Zhu Tingzhen, in his *Xiaoyuan's Commentaries on Poetry*, concluded that Song Dynasty poets had preferred to use "xu zi" words or phrases especially in their seven-word-a-verse eight-verse "lv shi" poems, and that this preference, without exception, had weakened the touch of their poems upon the reader. Zhu's conclusion, it should be pointed out, is not justified, for it is based not on objective linguistic analyses but on subjective bias: he is biased toward Tang, especially High Tang, poetry but against that of the Song Dynasty.

Those who claimed that Song Dynasty poets used more "xu zi" words or phrases than their Tang Dynasty predecessors, whose poems were composed mainly of "shi zi" words or phrases had no statistical evidence. In fact, their claim was based purely on their impression of the poetry of the Tang and Song dynasties. Admittedly, one's impression can be true. Generally, the poets of the Song Dynasty would often, out of preference, intersperse even their Recent Style poems with "xu zi" words or phrases. Examples of this are Qian Weiyan's "you hen *qi yin* yan feng qu (Grieved, but not by loss of her ex-lover)/wu yan *ning wei* xi hou wang (Wordless, but not caused by separation from her former spouse)", one of his three poems under the title of "Titleless"; Wang Anshi's "*shao* jue ye yun cheng wan ji (Clouds had hardly dissipated and the sky had hardly cleared up, by the time of twilight)/*que* yi shan yue shi zhao tun (When a moon was rising from behind mounts that gave an illusion of a sun starting to ascend)" in his "In Response to My Younger Brother's Poem at the Relish Pavilion", one of his two responsive poems; Su Shi's "wu shi *hui xu* cheng hao yin (When in leisure let's drink to our heart's content)/si gui *shi yi* fu deng lou (When in homesickness let's ascend a tower to compose a poem as a vent to it)" from one of his five poems identically entitled "In Response to the Poems by Bangzhi and Ziyou"; and Xu Fu's "*pian* wei zi jie wei er nian (It seems that it is expressing its accolades only for you)/*shi* shei yi zhong dai jun lai (I suspect that it must have been grown here for your appreciation)" from his poem entitled "Inspired by the Blossoming Plum Tree inside the Courtyard to Write after the Old Rhyme Scheme a Poem for Duanbai". These instances are a proof that those Song Dynasty poets who either modelled their poetry on that of their later Tang Dynasty predecessors or broke ground for Song Dynasty poetry with its own features did love using "xu zi" words or phrases, not to mention the argumentative new Confucianists of their time. True, their Tang Dynasty predecessors had been far more interested in "shi zi" words or phrases. But that does not necessarily mean that they had absolutely shunned "xu zi" words or phrases. In other words, there are, for example, Du Fu's "chi ri jiang shan li (verbatim: Longer and longer spring daylight rivers mountains beautiful) (The light of longer and longer spring days beautifies rivers and mountains)/chun feng hua cao xiang (verbatim: Vernal winds flowers grasses fragrant) (The vernal wind carries in the air the aroma of flowers and grasses)" from one of his "Two Jue Ju Poems"; Wei Yingwu's "lv yin sheng zhou jing (verbatim: Dense green shadows generate days tranquillity) (Shadows green in hue generate diurnal serenity)/gu hua biao chun yu (verbatim: Solitary flowers indicate spring remnant) (Few blossoms are indicative of the elapse of spring)" from his "A Tour of the Kaiyuan Temple"; Wang Wei's "yu pu nan ling guo (verbatim: Fishing bay outskirts Nanling Town) (Lo and behold, there stretches the fishing bay around the outskirts of Nanling Town)/ren jia chun gu xi (verbatim: Households spring ravine stream) (Along a ravine where runs a stream are scattered households)" from his "Seeing Zhang Wuyin Off Back to Xuancheng"; and Wen Tingyun's "ji sheng mao dian yue (verbatim: Rooster crow, thatched inn, moon) (The crow of roosters around the thatched inn in the moonlight)/ren ji ban qiao shuang (verbatim: Human footprints, plank bridge, frost) (A few human footprints in the frost covering the bridge of plank)" from his "Early Departure from the Inn at the Shang Mount", which all are composed purely of "shi zi" words or phrases like nouns and verbs, on the one hand; on the other hand, there are also other Tang Dynasty poems, even poems by Du Fu, which, not rarely, exploited "xu zi" words or phrases, such as Du Fu' s "hua jing *bu ceng* yuan ke sao (For you alone I have swept my flower-strewn path that was not swept ever before)/peng men *jin shi* wei jun kai (Also for you alone I have opened my wicker door that was shut to any other visitor)" from his poem entitled "To Welcome my Revered Visitor", wherein "bu ceng" and "jin shi", two "xu zi" phrases, were employed. So just because the poets of the Song Dynasty take more interest than their Tang Dynasty predecessors in interlacing their poems with "xu zi" words or phrases does not necessarily mean that their poems are thus inferior. When it comes to critique of the poetry of the Tang and Song dynasties, Chinese poetry critics, either in ancient or modern China, tend to use such catchphrases on the latter as "more meticulous", "more particular", "more in-depth" (see Weng Fanggang's *The Commentaries on Poetry at the Rocky Edge of an Islet*), and "advantageous in sinewy texture and sound reasoning" (see Qian Zhongshu's *On the Art of Poetry*). If these traits epitomize Song Dynasty poetry, should they be ascribed to use of more "xu zi" words or phrases than in Tang Dynasty poetry?

One may say that even some Song Dynasty poetry critics were not quite satisfied with their poetry, which, by their standards, was more prosaic than poetic. As for the prosaic traits of the poetry of the Song Dynasty, I shall discuss it in the eighth chapter of this book. But here we may well know one of the main differences between the poetry of the Song Dynasty and that of the Tang Dynasty, which is that, owing to the use of much more "xu zi" words or phrases in the former, its verses read as more vernacular, more syntactically intact, verbally equal in gravity, and more smoothly, so that there is almost no word in each of them that stands out as its "shi yan", which will be discussed in the seventh chapter of this book, and the images in the former are not as juxtaposed as in the latter. To those, for example, poetry critics of the Ming and Qing dynasties, who would judge any other ancient Chinese poems against Tang Dynasty poetry, which they felt was poetic in its truest sense, Song Dynasty poetry naturally was far more prosaic.

It should be pointed out that, just because of the use of "xu zi" words or phrases, the poetry of the Song Dynasty was enhanced in terms of, apart from what has been mentioned, legibility, sinuousness, and subtlety. As I understand, there are two milestones that mark the development of Chinese poetry. The first one marks the shift from ancient Chinese poetry before the Southern Dynasties to Recent Style poetry, which took shape in the Southern Dynasties and matured during the Tang Dynasty, and the second one from Recent Style poetry to the vernacular Song Dynasty poetry through to vernacular modern Chinese poetry. As a result of the first shift, poetic language changed from vernacular to literary. This is shown in poems by Xie Lingyun, his peers, and their followers, which are distinct mainly for their juxtaposition of images and their rigid tonal and metrical schemes, leading to the inevitable reduction and even elimination of "xu zi" words or phrases. As a result of the second shift, poetic language changes back again to the prosaic or simply vernacular, the inevitable reuse of "xu zi" words or phrases. This change starts as early as the poems by Du Fu, an old trend resumed first by Du Fu which gained more and more momentum and reached its highest gear in the Song Dynasty. Song Dynasty poets at once inherited Du Fu's legacy and broke the linguistic fetters of Tang Dynasty poetry altogether to establish their own prosaic or vernacular style, whose salient feature is the use of "xu zi" words or phrases that help in intermediation, intensification, transition, and so on for meticulous, nuanced, in-depth, natural expression.

Last but not least, we need to learn more about the significance of "shi zi" words or phrases and "xu zi" ones. In my opinion, the former only reflects changes in the external world, while the latter reveals changes in the way of thinking.

This is an ever-changing world. Its change can be perceived by, as far as this book is concerned, an astute poet. He will, in the form of new appellations, show it in his poems, as in the case of the poems by some liberal-minded poets of the latter Qing Dynasty about what was happening, especially in the Western world. They, including Liang Qichao, Tang Sitong, and Huang Zunxian, launched a campaign of so-called poetic revolution, which actually did not at all shake the ancient Chinese poetry to its foundations but only added a few exotic modern transliterations (see Liang Qichao's *The Remarks Made in Yinbing Library on Poetry* [note: "yinbing", i.e., "eating ice", implies that doing so can allay one's internal heat or anxieties]) to its glossary, such as "ba li men (parliament)", "di qiu (globe)", "liu sheng ji (a gramophone)", "dian deng (electric lamp)", "ka si de (caste)", and the like, which were introduced to China as late as at the end of the Qing Dynasty. Exemplary verses are "gang lun can yi *ka si de* (What could be more ruthless than the *caste* that governs this human world)/fa hui sheng yu *ba li men* (The assemblage for a Buddhist sermon can be compared to that of a *parliament* in zeal)" (from one of Tang Sitong's two poems entitled "Attendance at a Buddhist Sermon at Jinling") and "tang yi cheng cha zhong you ke (If the mythic raft did transport one up to heaven)/hui tou wang wo *di qiu* yuan (The passenger would see a *globe* down below, which is our world)" (from Huang Zunxian's poem entitled "Thoughts on a Journey at Sea"). Do these verses deviate from what is required of ancient Chinese ones except for their transliterated names? Not in the slightest. More similar examples are "ni chang zi ru *liu sheng ji* (Those beautiful melodies seem to have by themselves entered the gramophone/xian yue feng piao chu chu wen (From out of it such divine tunes breeze and permeate the air)" and "*dian deng* gao gua ming ru yue (The electric lamp high overhead gave an illusion of the bright moon)/ji wu gui tu xiao bu xiu (I kept laughing at myself for my departure for home was almost delayed by it)", wherein "liu sheng ji" and "dian deng", the two transliterated modern names, can be replaced respectively by, for example, "li yuan dui (a theatrical troupe)" and "bang zhu (a pearl)", if more flavour of antiquity is intended. So it is safe to say that new appellations, even if they are exotic, do not bring about a poetic revolution which could eventually modernize ancient Chinese poetry. Otherwise, such a revolution should taken place earlier, for Chinese versions of foreign appellations appeared in poetry as early as even the latter Ming Dynasty when Wang Zheng, also known as Master Duanjie, used the Chinese versions of Catholic denominations like "san chou (i.e., Three Enemies, which refer to the devil, the flesh, and the world), "shi jie (Ten Commandments)", and "sheng shui (Holy Water)" in his poem entitled "A Recital at the Mountainous Dwelling". During the early years of the Qing Dynasty, Chinese transliterations or versions like "ou luo ba zhou (Europe)", "ya xi ya zhou (Asia)", "ce yuan (caliper)", and "san jiao (triangle)", were introduced by Quan Zuwang in his poem entitled "A Song for the Sundial Erected by the Ming Dynasty Astronomer Tang Ruowang [Tang Ruowang was the Chinese name for Johann Adam Schall von Bell]". Embedding their poems with these Chinese transliterations or versions of foreign appellations did not at all lead to a poetic revolution in its truest sense. A true poetic revolution, or rather the emergence of vernacular modern Chinese poetry, would not happen until the grammatical rules that had governed the ancient Chinese poetry were broken altogether. Two of the most significant resulting indicators are unrestricted vernacularized syntactic structures and the use, in good numbers, of "xu zi" words or phrases in versification.

References

1. Fan, Xiwen 范晞文. "Dui chuang ye yu" 对床夜语 (An Intimate Poetry Discourse across Beds at Night). In *Lidai shihua xubian* 历代诗话续编 (A Sequel to the Commentaries by the Critics of the Past Dynasties on Poetry), edited by Fubao Ding 丁福保. Beijing: Zhonghua Book Company, 1983.
2. Fang, Dongshu 方东树. *Zhaomei zhan yan* 昭昧詹言 (Illuminating Chatters). Beijing: People's Literature Publishing House, 1961.
3. Ge, Lifang 葛立方. "Yunyu yangqiu" 韵语阳秋 (Ge Lifang's Commentaries on Poetry). In *Lidai shihua* 历代诗话 (The Commentaries by the Critics of the Past Dynasties on Poetry), edited by Wenhuan He 何文焕. Beijing: Zhonghua Book Company, 1981.

4. Hu, Zi 胡仔. *Tiaoxi yuyin conghua* 苕溪渔隐丛话 (Poetic Remarks from the Fisherman Recluse at the Trumpet-Creeper Creek). Beijing: People's Literature Publishing House, 1981.
5. Li, Dongyang 李东阳. "Litang shihua" 麓堂诗话 (Litang's Remarks on Poetry). In *Lidai shihua xubian* 历代诗话续编 (A Sequel to the Commentaries by the Critics of the Past Dynasties on Poetry), edited by Fubao Ding 丁福保. Beijing: Zhonghua Book Company, 1983.
6. Luo, Dajing 罗大经. *Helin yulu* 鹤林玉露 (Jade Dew in the Crane's Forest or Tales of the Men of Letters of the Song Dynasty). Beijing: Zhonghua Book Company, 1983.
7. Mao, Chunrong 冒春荣. "Shenyuan shihua" 葚园诗话 (Shenyuan's Poetic Discourse). In *Qing shihua xubian* 清诗话续编 (A Sequel to the Poetic Discourses of the Qing Dynasty), edited by Shaoyu Guo 郭绍虞. Shanghai: Shanghai Classics Publishing House, 1983.
8. Pan Deyu 潘德舆. "Yangyizhai shihua" 养一斋诗话 (Remarks on Poetry at Yangyi Studio). In *Qing shihua xubian* 清诗话续编 (A Sequel to the Poetic Discourses of the Qing Dynasty), edited by Shaoyu Guo 郭绍虞. Shanghai: Shanghai Classics Publishing House, 1983.
9. Wang, Mingchang 王鸣昌. "Bianzi jue" 辨字诀 (The Secret to Mastery of 'Xu Zi' Words or Phrases). In *Guhanyu yufaxue ziliao huibian* 古汉语语法学资料汇编 (A Corpus of Ancient Chinese Grammar Data), edited by Dian Zheng 郑奠 and Meiqiao Mai 麦梅翘. Beijing: Zhonghua Book Company, 1964.
10. Wang, Yun 王筠. *Shuowen shili* 说文释例 (Exegeses of Texts). Beijing: Zhonghua Book Company, 1987.
11. Wei, Qingzhi 魏庆之. *Shiren yu xie* 诗人玉屑 (Chips of Precious Jade Collected from the Treasury of Remarks on Poetry). Shanghai: Shanghai Classics Publishing House, 1978.
12. Weng, Fanggang 翁方纲. "Shizhou shihua" 石洲诗话 (The Commentaries on Poetry at the Rocky Edge of an Islet). In *Qing shihua xubian* 清诗话续编 (A Sequel to the Poetic Discourses of the Qing Dynasty), edited by Shaoyu Guo 郭绍虞. Shanghai: Shanghai Classics Publishing House, 1983.
13. Wu, Hang 吴沆. *Huanxi shihua* 环溪诗话 (Poetic Commentaries at the Huanxi Quarters). Beijing: Zhonghua Book Company, 1988.
14. Wu, Ke 吴可. "*Canghai shihua*" 藏海诗话 (Canghai's Commentaries on Poetry). In *Lidai shihua xubian* 历代诗话续编 (A Sequel to the Commentaries by the Critics of the Past Dynasties on Poetry), edited by Fubao Ding 丁福保. Beijing: Zhonghua Book Company, 1983.
15. Wu, Zeng 吴曾. *Nenggaizhai man lu* 能改斋漫录 (A Random All-Inclusive Record by the Owner of 'Being Capable of Self-Rectification' Study). Shanghai: Shanghai Classics Publishing House, 1979.
16. Xie, Zhen 谢榛. "Siming shuhua" 四溟诗话 (A Sea-in-the-Four-Direction Recluse's Remarks on Poetry). In *Lidai shihua xubian* 历代诗话续编 (A Sequel to the Commentaries by the Critics of the Past Dynasties on Poetry), edited by Fubao Ding 丁福保. Beijing: Zhonghua Book Company, 1983.
17. Ye, Mengde 叶梦得. *Shilin shihua* 石林诗话 (Tales and Critique of Poetry at Shilin). In *Lidai shihua* 历代诗话 (The Commentaries by the Critics of the Past Dynasties on Poetry), edited by Wenhuan He 何文焕. Beijing: Zhonghua Book Company, 1981.
18. Zhao, Yi 赵翼. "Oubei shihua" 瓯北诗话 (Oubei's Discourse on Poets and their Poetry). In *Qing shihua xubian* 清诗话续编 (A Sequel to the Poetic Discourses of the Qing Dynasty), edited by Shaoyu Guo 郭绍虞. Shanghai: Shanghai Classics Publishing House, 1983.
19. Zhu, Tinzhen 朱庭珍. "Xiaoyuan shihua" 筱园诗话 (Xiaoyuan's Remarks on Poetry). In *Qing shihua xubian* 清诗话续编 (A Sequel to the Poetic Discourses of the Qing Dynasty), edited by Shaoyu Guo 郭绍虞. Shanghai: Shanghai Classics Publishing House, 1983.

7 Shi yan

A third special aspect of ancient Chinese poetry

There is an anecdote about Gu Kaizhi, a painter of the Jin Dynasty, in which the acme of his portrait of a person, or rather the finishing touch, was the person's eyes ("eye" is pronounced, in Chinese pinyin, as "yan"). (See Liu Yiqing's *A New Account of Tales of the World*.) This is one proof that, a long time ago, ancient Chinese literati were aware of the aesthetic significance of "eye". Another proof is what *The Book of Songs* says about the eyes of a beauty: "Her beaming countenance is so fair; her bright eyes are so charming". Also, when Buddhists and Taoists consecrate the statue of a deity by performing the prescribed ritual, their final act is for the most revered monk in Buddhism or Taoist priest in Taoism, to finish the drawing of the eyes that are believed to give life and superpowers to the statue. And, today, one's eyes are believed to be the windows to one's soul, through which one's personality can be seen. All this points to one thing: awareness of what is in one's eyes or rather expressiveness in one's eyes and one's life.

So it is with the verse of a poem ("verse", "poem", or "poetry" is pronounced in Chinese pinyin as "shi"), whose most expressive word is considered its "eye" (yan) or rather its focal word: the word that focuses one's attention or attracts one's eyes. As to who first conceptualized the eye or the focal word of a verse, "shi yan" in Chinese, I have not yet investigated. Nonetheless, at least one thing is certain: the terminology of "shi yan" already appeared in Song Dynasty poetry critics' works. According to Shi Buhua's *A Garrison Secretary's Talk about Poetry*, Wang Anshi deemed it a must-do to refine words in five-word-a-verse eight-verse "lv shi" poetry to acquire what he called "shi yan". Shi Buhua actually echoed what Fan Wen said. (See his *Qianxi's Perspective on Poetry*.) Whether Wang Anshi first conceived "shi yan" is yet to be verified. But something like "shi yan" was also mentioned by poets or poetry critics of the Song Dynasty such as Huang Tingjian ("shi yi ju zhong you *yan* [The reader of Du Fu's poetry shall admire him for his usage of '*yan*', i.e., focal words])" (see his preface to his four poems under the title of "A Poem Dedicated to Gao Zimian") and Yang Zai ("The words for a verse need refining, which is a process of acquiring one word that most attracts the reader's '*yan*', i.e., eyes"). (See his *Techniques of Versification*.) In this sense, the conception of "shi yan" could have been formulated as far back as in the Southern Dynasties, when Liu Xie dedicated a chapter of his *The Literary Mind and the Carving of Dragons* to how to refine words until the consummate ones were acquired.

Just as in the game of *go*, one side must lay "yan" (i.e., snares) to check the other or how for one to open his "yan" (i.e., eyes) is associated with life, so "yan" in the verse of a poem can enliven the verse or even the poem. Then how does a "shi yan" word function? And what is it that justifies the role of a word eventually acquired through a process of refinement as the "shi yan" in a verse?

7.1. How to acquire a "shi yan"

Ancient Chinese poets back in the Han Dynasty and before had no notion of a word in a verse functioning as the "shi yan". A parable in *Zhuangzi*, one of the ancient Chinese philosophical classics, about the death of a mythic ruler over the middle part of the universe that was caused by the efforts of his two good-willed yet ignorant visitors, the two mythic rulers who ruled separately over the Southern Sea and the Northern Sea, to chisel seven apertures on their host to equip him with seven faculties, two of which were the *eyes* (yan), could, in a way, attest to this "no eye" or "no yan" argument. Ancient Chinese poetry before the Southern Dynasties was merely for the poet to narrate events for and communicate meanings and feelings to the reader. Its language as a sheer vehicle for such purposes was plain and lucid, somewhere close to colloquial, just as Kobo Daishi, in his *Treatise on the Secret Treasury of Literary Mirror*, pointed out: "having no vestige of human exertion and sounding like that used by commoners in their everyday life, thus striking one as genuine and natural", and as Xie Zhen, in his *A Sea-in-the-Four-Direction Recluse's Remarks on Poetry*, noted: "[words] running plainly and naturally without a deliberate emphasis on any single one of them". Here "human exertion" refers to the effort made by later poets to refine words. Its absence back then led to the absence of "a deliberate emphasis on any single one of them" or rather a striking "shi yan". Thus an ancient Chinese poem back then read, in terms of its language, like everyday interlocution: crude and plain, each word being inconspicuous.

More than the poets or poetry critics of the Tang and Song dynasties, those of the Ming and Qing dynasties, it is believed, saw more clearly how a "shi yan" had developed. Hu Yinglin found that

> poetry of the Han Dynasty was composed, in terms of words, in equilibrium, so that not a single would stand out to become a "shi yan". In fact, the "shi yan" word in a verse back then could be deemed a defect, not to mention the florid "shi yan" words used by the poets of the Qi and Liang periods of the Southern Dynasties and of the Early Tang Dynasty. So the poets during the flourishing period of the Tang Dynasty rejected it to pursue the poetic harmony. Only when Du Fu began to "shi yan" (allow me to use it as a transitive verb) his verses was it widely recognized, for it beat the reader's anticipation with its exquisiteness in plainness.

In his *A Desultory Discourse on Poetry*, Shen Deqian of the Qing Dynasty observed that

For those ancient poets, meaning took precedence over wording. It was just because of this that their poetic words, simple or plain or common or even hackneyed as they might be, still struck the reader as fabulous or bold or original or fresh. Unfortunately, later poets sought to use abstruse words to "shi yan" their verses in the hope of thus producing jaw-dropping effect.

To be fair, both Hu and Sheng noticed the presence and development of "shi yan". But they themselves seem not to have defined what could relate to it. As they show, Hu's findings are fairly contradictory as to whether a "shi yan" word is a defect: he extolled Du Fu for his unrivalled "shi yan" words, on the one hand but, on the other, did not quite endorse his application of "shi yan". Sheng's observations are somewhat confusing as to who were "ancient poets" and who were "later poets"; which, meaning or wording, should dominate; and when the conception of "shi yan" came into being. Relatively speaking, *An Outline of the Chinese Poetry* by Fei Xihuang of the Qing Dynasty is explicit about when a word in a verse was highlighted by ancient Chinese poets as the "shi yan":

> The poetry of the Han Dynasty is plain and natural, but its general meaning is not easy to grasp, not to mention the meaning of its particular word or verse; true, there are annotations on it; but they are neither reliable nor indispensable. The poets during the Song and Qi periods of the Southern Dynasties began to pursue the tonal and metrical schemes in versification. The eminent poets of the Tang Dynasty set forth the criteria by which poetic words were refined, thus "shi yan" came into being.

Let us pass the poetry of the Han Dynasty and look at the poetry of the Song and Qi periods of the Southern Dynasties. The two periods are a time of, in the words of Roman Jakobson, "defamiliarization" of the familiar past poetic language, somewhat analogous to the chiselling act in the aforementioned parable of *Zhuangzi*. As a result, ancient Chinese poetry began to differ linguistically from what it had been, which is vernacular, plain, and natural, and became literary, which is refined and elegant. Such poetic language facilitates scheming a poem both antithetically and symmetrically in terms of tone and cadence, which in turn leads to juxtaposition of imagery, on the one hand, and, on the other, reduction or simply removal of "xu zi" words or phrases.

Let us read what three different ancient Chinese poetry critics said:

> The Song period of the Southern Dynasties was when the ancient style poetry ended whereas the Recent Style poetry started.
> (*A Comprehensive Digest of Good Ancient Poems* by Lu Shiyong)

> Comparison of the poetry respectively by Lu Ji and Xie Lingyun shows that the verses by the former, in contrast to those by the latter, were not antithetically symmetrized.
> (*Thickets of Criticism* by Hu Yinglin)

The symmetrical antithesis in the poetry by Xie Lingyun and his peers gave birth to the "lv shi" poetry.
(*Oubei's Discourse on Poets and their Poetry* by Zhao Yi)

These three different quotations actually are about antithesis within a verse and antithetical symmetry between the pair of verses of an ancient Chinese poem, which certainly concerns the tone and cadence.

Here are a few such exemplary verses, set in three groups, from Xie Lingyun's poems:

(1)

hun dan bian qi hou (Weather varies from dawn to dusk)/shan shui han qing hui (Mounts and waters bask in shimmery effulgence)
yuan xi yi lv liu (On a large wet depression are shooting green willows)/xu you san hong tao (Within hamlets and gardens are scattered reddening peach trees)
chi tang sheng chun cao (The pond is lush with vernal grasses)/yuan liu bian ming qin (The garden willows nestle chirping birds)

(2)

ye kuang sha an jing (Lo and behold, the expansive plain, the unsoiled sandy strand)/tian gao qiu yue ming (The far-off skies, the brilliant autumnal moon)
chun wan lv ye xiu (Towards the end of spring green fields beautify)/yan gao bai yun tun (Over lofty crags white clouds gather)
jiong kuang sha dao kai (The sandy land stretches into a vast expanse)/wei yu shan jing zhe (The zigzag mountainous trail seems to snap here and there)"

(3)

chu gu ri shang zao (The sun was still high up in the sky when we went out of the valley)/ru zhou yang yi wei (By the time we got on board the boat the twilight had diffused)
lv dan wu zi qing (The less worried about gain or loss, the more indifferent to externalities)/yi qie li wu wei (The more satiation of one's heart, the less violation of the canon for longevity)

As is manifest, the distinct units both of meaning and cadence of a verse and the correspondence between such units separately in each verse of a couplet, which had been rare in poetry before the Southern Dynasties, were patterned. The patterns were mainly either two words (a unit of meaning and cadence) plus one word (a unit of meaning and cadence) plus two words (a unit of meaning and cadence), as in the first group, or two words plus two words plus one word, as in the second group, both of which fall generally under the two-plus-three pattern. Let us look further at the specific verses. For example, in "hun dan bian qi hou (Weather varies from dawn to dusk)/shan shui han qing hui (Mounts and waters bask in shimmery effulgence)", the first verse of this couplet is composed of "hun dan (dusk and dawn)" + "bian (change)" + "qi hou (weather or "climate")", to correspond with which the second one also runs in the pattern of "shan shui (mountains and waters)" + "han (embrace)" + "qing hui (shimmery effulgence)". "Ye kuang sha an jing (Lo and behold, the expansive plain, the unsoiled sandy strand)" and "tian gao qiu yue ming (The far-off skies, the brilliant autumnal moon)" are composed respectively of "ye kuang (expansive plain)" + "sha an (sandy strand)" + "jing (unsoiled)" and "tian gao (far-off skies)" + "qiu yue (autumnal moon)" + "ming (brilliant)", and the two verses also correspond in terms of their units of meaning and cadence. Such a pattern has no "xu zi" word or phrase but "shi zi" words or phrases; "shi zi" phrases, such as "hun dan (dusk and dawn)" and "ye kuang (expansive plain)", represent certain images while a single "shi zi" word, usually a verb or an adjective, such as "bian (change)" and "jing (unsoiled)", indicates a certain state of being. Thus organized, a verse is clear cut in meaning and cadence. Indeed, who would confuse "chi tang sheng chun cao (The pond is lush with vernal grasses)", which is composed so lucidly of "chi tang (the pond)" plus "sheng (grow)" plus "chun cao (vernal grass)" in terms of the units of both meaning and cadence or rather caesura? It is thanks to such patterns that, of each couplet of the five-word-a-verse poetry of the Song and Qi periods of the Southern Dynasties and henceforth, one verse parallels the other in meaning and cadence to synchronize harmoniously, the way one dances perfectly to musical beat, which also corresponds comfortably to the reader's physiological and psychological state in the course of such aesthetic appreciation.

Poetic language of this nature, as it is literary, is far removed or even poles apart from the vernacular and impregnates a poem with what is felt to be unnatural; Xie Zhen, in his *A Sea-in-the-Four-Direction Recluse's Remarks on Poetry*, said that "Once a poet learned to compose his poem in the literary language, his poem would feel affected". Indeed, the natural fluidness of ancient Chinese poetry before the Southern Dynasties thus gives way. But, at the same time, the alleged unnaturalness leads to an idiosyncratic poetic language, both in form and in content, and, after its merits are recognized, became popular with ancient Chinese poets, because, after all, the aesthetic charm, as a result of the striking formality of this poetic language eventually, including its tonal and metrical beauty, shines through and fascinates the reader. In the case of poets and readers during the Southern Dynasties and henceforth, after they accustomed themselves to this fascinating new poetic language, they found it not fascinating any more or even strangely uncomfortable to revert to the past vernacular poetic language, even if it, due to "xu zi" words or phrases, once read as colloquial as natural as speech, and chose to discard it, for they now felt that, for example, interspersion of "xu zi" words or phrases in a poem disrupted its smooth cadence, broke its antithetical symmetry, and compromised its poetic effect, as noted by Kobo Daishi in his *Treatise on the Secret Treasury of Literary Mirror*. To learn more about the new poetic language, let us look at a few more verses by the Southern Dynasties poets, such as Xie Tiao's "tian ji shi gui zhou (Returning boats on the distant horizon can still be distinguished)/ yun zhong bian jiang shu (So is the hazy trees afar on the river)" and "xuan niao fu chun zhou (In spring chirping birds are flapping all over the isle)/za ying man fang dian (Flowers in different colours dot the grassy outskirts)", Shen Yue's "yu lv gou dan yan (Precipitous should be the epithet for those reddish mountains)/leng ceng qi qing zhang (While towering for those luxuriant peaks that look upright huge screens)", and Yu Xin's "yang chang lian jiu ban (A tortuous path links bends and turns)/xiong er dui shuang feng (Two peaks like a bear's ears face each other)", which adopt the pattern of "two (words) + one (word) + two (words)", as well as Wang Rong's "wu shan cai yun mo (That mythic mount named Wu must be shrouded by rainbow clouds) (Wushan or Mount Wu, an euphemistic reference to the sexual affairs between men and women in romance)/qi shang lv tiao xi (The willows on the Qi River are thinning out)", and Yu Xin's "gao ge qian xun kua (The lofty tower stands a thousand *xun* in span) (xun, an ancient Chinese measurement unit of, here, width)/chong yan bai zhang qi (The tiered roofs taper a hundred zhang upward) (zhang, an ancient Chinese measurement unit of, here, height)", which take the pattern of "two (words) + two (words) + one (word).

And it is in these two patterns where a "shi yan" began to take shape. As we can see, "two (words)" in such patterns, which represent images, are not, as Lessing said in his *Laocoon*, animated; they are static, thus they, like the aforementioned statue of a deity which is not animated due to lack of its eyes, also lack animation such as "mi lin (dense woods)" and "yu qing (fresh air)" in "mi lin han yu qing (Dense woods are diffused with fresh air)", "gu yu (Mount Guyu)", "zhong chuan (the middle of the river)" in "gu yu mei zhong chuan (The reflection of Mount Guyu beautifies the middle of the river)", "ling shuang (frostiness)", "gui ying (the moonlight)" in "ling shuang gui ying han (Frost even chills the moonlight)", and "ye an" (an array of high mountains) and "ping sha (an expansive sandy land)" in "ye an ping sha he (That expansive sandy land seems to have merged with those adjacent high mounts in array)", which feel unenlivened unless they are collocated respectively with "one (word)", which can be an adjective or a verb, as in "han (diffuse)", "mei (beautify)", "han (chill)", and "he (merge)". These single words, in terms of animation, can be likened to the eyes of the statue of a deity mentioned previously. If "one word" of this kind were taken out, would not these verses be deprived of what could otherwise be the mind-boggling power of not just visual but emotional impact? Positively. For example, how would the charm lent by "gu yu" to "zhong chuan" and the poet's emotional affinity to the two objects be conveyed without "mei"? How would the moonlight be associated, in terms of chill, with frostiness, without "han"? Given the absence of "he", would the illusion of fusion into one of "ye an" and "ping sha" be represented as if it were so? The answer is no. Thus "one word", which injects life into two otherwise static images and thus the verse they make, plays a pivotal role as what is called a "shi yan" or, in other words, the soul of a verse.

7.2. How else does a "shi yan" function?

A "shi yan" in its truest sense enlivens static images in a surprising way. To achieve this demands a poet's creativity. In other words, only the word in the verse of an ancient Chinese poem that shows the poet's genius can be called a "shi yan". For example. "sheng (grow)" in "chi tang sheng chun cao (The pond is lush with vernal grasses)" (by Xie Lingyun) should not be deemed a "shi yan", because that "chun cao (vernal grasses)" "sheng (grow)" is a common natural phenomenon, whereas "sheng" in "lv yin sheng zhou jing (Shadows green in hue generate diurnal serenity)" (by Wei Yingwu) is a "shi yan", because that "lv yin (shadows green in hue)" should "sheng (generate)" "zhou jing (diurnal serenity)" is an unconventional, bold creation, insofar as the reader is compelled to contemplate how it could happen, feel what the poet then felt, and think about its implications. This tells us that a prerequisite for a word, either a verb or an adjective, in the verse of an ancient Chinese poem to be highlighted as a "shi yan" is that, owing to its unheard-of collocation with the rest of the verse, it not only astounds the reader but arouses his or her curiosity about why it should be so collocated. In this sense, a "shi yan" is where the reader's full attention is focused and their deep contemplation is started with respect to, usually, an adjective or a verb within a verse.

But Xie Lingyun and other poets of the Southern Dynasties, in versification, seemed to have valued imagery far more than the "shi yan", because it seems that they preferred those nouns whose features enabled them to best depict variegated sceneries to verbs and adjectives. True, such verses as "qiu an *cheng* xi yin (The twilight against the autumnal riverside looks refulgent)/huo min *tuan* zhao lu (Morning dews seem to have blotched the autumnal skies)" and "mi lin *han* yu qing (Dense woods are diffused with fresh air)"/"yuan feng *yin* ban gui (The distant mountains are hiding half of a setting sun)" (by Xie Lingyun), "xin hua *dui* bai ri (Newly sprouting roses face a shining sun)/gu rui *zhu* feng xing (Their withered petals are gone with winds)" (by Xie Tiao), "xuan ya *bao* qi jue (Protruding rocks overhang an abysmal depth)/jue bi *jia* leng ceng (A sheer cliff cuts a precipitous slop)" and "jie shu *yin* gao chan (A vast canopy of trees have concealed cicadas well above)/jiao zhi *cheng* luo ri (Tangles of branches seem to be bearing a setting sun)" (by He Xun), and "qing yun *ren* yuan xiu (Light clouds link distant peaks)/xi yu *mu* shan yi (Thread-wise rain moistens greenery-clad hills)" (by Wu Jun), did appear in their poems, where each italicized verb shows the effort made by those poets in wording. But such verses are few, in proportion to their other verses, and the verbs may not consciously be intended to function as "shi yan" words but happen to have met what is required of them. In fact, a verb or an adjective, apparently like a "shi yan", in most of their pairs of antithetically symmetrical verses, is by no means functionally a "shi yan" because it is only collocated common-sensically with the other word(s) within the verse, such as "xi (frolic)" and "nong (stir)" in Xie Lingyun's "hai ou *xi* chun an (Seagulls are frolicking over the vernal seaside)/tian ji *nong* he feng (The celestial rooster is stirring wave and wave of breezes)" and "xiu (beautify)"; "tun (gather)", also in Xie Lingyun's "chun wan lv ye *xiu* (Towards the end of spring green fields beautify)/yan gao bai yun *tun* (Over lofty crags white clouds gather)"; and "dong (shiver)" and "luo (drop)" in Xie Tiao's "yu xi xin he *dong* (Sporting fishes cause shivering of newly-grown lotus)/niao san yu hua *luo* (Dispersing birds induce dropping of withered flowers)", which are used as convention dictates without novelty of any kind and thus, like salt dissolving in water, lack conspicuousness, and are no more than words in verses.

It is not until the flourishing period of the Tang Dynasty that ancient Chinese poets began to consciously weigh words for a "shi yan". As for Du Fu, he may not necessarily, as his admirers claim, be the first one who pursued a mind-blowing "shi yan" in a creative way, but, just as *A Compilation by Lvzhai of Classics and their Exegeses for Posterity* (by Sun Yi of the Song Dynasty, also known as Lvzhai) applauded Du Fu for his adeptness at weighing words for a "shi yan", he should rank among the masters of this art. An example is given by Ouyang Xiu, in his *Liuyi's Commentaries on Poetry*: one of "guo (fleet)", "ji (rush)", "luo (land)", "qi (soar)", and "xia (descend)" best fits in the blank at the end of the verse "shen qing yi niao (How light a bird that) ___", and this is believed to say all about Du Fu's deliberation before determination of the word "guo (whose English rendition could be "[is] fleeting [across]")". But, actually, "guo" is not differentiated so much from the other four words or simply should not be regarded as a "shi yan", because it is, as said previously, common-sensically used, after all. That "guo" should be acclaimed could be credited to the idolatry of Du Fu's worshippers in the world of Chinese poetry. Du Fu's "shi yan" prowess only shows when he, rather than mulling over a word itself, creatively employs those otherwise common verbs or adjectives to establish uncommon if not far-out yet, by inference, well-founded relevance to their collocations. This is not what his choice of "guo", which is, at best, a mere proof of Du Fu's fine dictional discrimination, is about. Establishment by Du Fu of apparently illogical but naturally logical relevance can be analogized to construction of a poetic bridge, which leads the reader, not directly but zigzag, to the other side or simply obscures itself from the reader, who will then, while groping along, have to count both on his or her sensitivity to and empathy with the sensibilities of the poet, which is also a psychological process of poetic re-creation on the part of the reader, to reach the other side, that is, the subtle nuances of Du Fu's verse.

Let us read a few more verses by Du Fu to learn more about his mastery of the art of weighing words for a "shi yan" word.

"Juan lian *can* yue ying (The curtains shattered the otherwise pool-like moonlight)/gao zhen *yuan* jiang sheng (Supporting my head on an elevated pillow distanced me from the splashing river)" in his poem entitled "Reflection Far Away from Home on a Night View" draws the eyes of the reader to the "shi yan" words: "can (shatter)" and "yuan (distance)".

It is common sense that moonlight shines through the curtains and throws shadows on the floor. So a corresponding description of such a view should have been "juan lian *lai* yue ying (The moonlight came indoors through the curtains)" or "juan lian *ru* yue ying (The moonlight entered indoors through the curtains)", but "lai" or "ru", which is both vernacular and common sense, would deprive the verse of its poetic flavour, in contrast to the literary "can", which here insinuates:

1 that the moonlight and the spots of light, as if sifted by the curtains on the floor, in their poetic sense, are transformed from intangible optical phenomena into tangible substance;
2 that the curtains are thus analogized to a sieve;

3 that "can" here, in addition to the meaning of "shatter", also means "remain", which implies the poet's affinity to the moonlight; and
4 that the verse, because of "can", may also suggest the poet's homesickness and thus be ineluctably reminiscent of another verse also by the poet, which reads "yue shi gu xiang ming (No moon anywhere else shines more brightly than at home)".

Likewise, "yuan" has more than one implication. An elevated pillow itself certainly cannot possibly keep the disturbing noise of the river nearby at a distance. Nonetheless, it seemed to the poet to have had this effect because he felt that he would, with his head resting on the elevated pillow, slumber in peace, especially at the moment of the depth of his heart being unsettled with longing for home, as well as with some other cares, to gain composure even if the river was out there swashing and lapping. Also, the river that incessantly sounded outside reminded the poet of one far back home, both of which were running all the way to their own home, the sea, whereas the poet himself, an unsettled seeker, was stuck in a strange place distant from his own homeland. What word would be more apt than "yuan" to describe the poet's depression then and there? What if "can" were replaced by, for example, "wu (literally 'null'; figuratively 'overcome')"? On balance, the latter certainly is incapable of what the former does.

As has been discussed, both "can" and "yuan" mean far more than they do separately as a verb and as an adjective; in other words, in collocation with the other word(s) of their verses, they communicate not just what is objective but also what is subjective, which concerns the state of mind of the poet.

In "ye run yan guang *bo* (Fields in shiny filmy morning haze looked as if greased)/sha xuan ri se *chi* (Warm sandy land bathed in the glow of a lingering sun)" in his poem entitled "A Revisit", Du Fu selected "bo (literally 'thin')" and "chi (literally 'late')" for the "shi yan" words, which should arouse the reader's curiosity about how "bo" is associated with shiny morning haze and "chi" with sunlight. Du Fu's associations, at first glance, seem inconceivable. But the reader will be impressed after vicariously imagining what the poet perceived and felt—the images of glossy or rather heavily greasy fields which set off the gossamer morning mists and a stretch of warm sandy land in the persistent glow of a setting sun. That is why Zhang Shangruo of the Qing Dynasty said of "bo" and "chi" that the former must lead to "run (literally 'moist'; figuratively [of a surface] so lustrous, as a result of being moistened, as to appear glossy or greasy)" and the latter to "xuan" (literally "warm"), and vice versa, from another perspective. (See *A Mirror of the Meanings of Du Fu's Poems* by Yang Lun of the Qing Dynasty.) So "bo" and "chi" as the "shi yan" words signify more than what they as sheer adjectives do: a window on the poet's sensibilities that infuse his two verses.

The interesting caesurae concerning "bei" and "hao" employed by Du Fu as the "shi yan" words in "yong ye jiao sheng *bei* zi yu/zhong tian yue se *hao* shei kan" of his poem entitled "A Nocturnal Lamentation When Lodging at General Yan Wu's Quarters" once caused contention. For example, one argument was that the caesurae within each of the pair of verses should be (1) "yong ye jiao sheng *bei*/zi yu (A bugle horn sounding wistful all night long, I was murmuring to myself)" and "zhong tian yue se *hao*/shei kan (The moon high up in the sky looked spell-binding, but who would be spellbound?)", while the other was (2) "yong ye jiao sheng/*bei* zi yu (A bugle horn sounding all night sounded as if wistfully murmuring to itself)" and "zhong tian yue se/*hao* shei kan (Who would the spell-binding moon high up in the sky spellbind?)".

In my opinion, the caesurae of either (1) or (2), subject to syntactic rules, thus limit what the pair of verses can mean, which in turn saps "bei" and "hao" as the "shi yan" words of their diffusive effect, for both "bei" and "hao" characterize an ambience which results respectively both from the heart-rending bugle of the horn and the pensiveness of the poet, in the case of the first verse, and both from a bright yet saddening moon and the pensiveness of the poet, in the case of the second verse, so the pair of verses can be understood to respectively mean

> A bugle horn sounded so wistful all night, and its listener was touched and so felt too, knowing that the bugle horn had been murmuring to itself the wistfulness in the human world/The moon high up in the sky was spell-binding, but, however spell-binding it was, who was its appreciator and who would hail her spell-binding beauty?

Such diffusion of "shi yan" words, in terms of implication, to the other parts of a verse deepens and subtilizes the meaning of the verse. There are many more such verses in Du Fu's poems.

Sun Yi's *A Compilation by Lvzhai of Classics and Their Exegeses for Posterity* cited Du Fu verses such as "er yue yi *po* (break) san yue lai (The second lunar month *gave way to* the third lunar one)", "yi pian fei hua *jian* (reduce) que chun (A single one falling petal is enough to signal the *elapsing* of spring)", "chao ba xiang yan *xie* (carry) man xiu (Their garments' sleeves, at the end of the audience of His Majesty, were *imbued* with incense fragrance)", and "he yong fu ming *ban* (trip) ci shen (What is the point of *encaging* ourselves in vanity)". The italicized words, or rather "shi yan", mean more than they usually do, which is that they carry the poet's feelings. This further proves Du Fu's miraculous transformation of a common word into a "shi yan".

Other ancient Chinese poetry critics such as Luo Dajing and Ye Mengde also turned to Du Fu's verses for exemplification of "shi yan". In his *Jade Dew in the Crane's Forest or Tales of the Men of Letters of the Song Dynasty*, Luo said of "ru" and "gui" as the "shi yan" words in Du Fu's "hong *ru* tao hua nen (Pink is suffusing each petal of peach blossoms that will appear tenderer)/qing *gui* liu ye xin (Green is creeping back on each branch of willows that will look fresher)" that the poet had converted a stationary state—pink and green as colours are stationary—to a nonstationary one—the two colours seem to have been animated by "ru (enter)" and "gui (return)", and, moreover, like two pillars, they sustained their own verses. Ye, in his *Tales and Critique of Poetry at Shilin*, commented on the "shi yan" words in Du Fu's "jiang shan *you* ('有'[to have]) ba shu (Speaking of rivers and mounts, there are those across Bashu)/dong yu *zi* qi liang (The temple has been here since Qi or the Liang period of the Southern Dynasties)" (in his poem "A Visit to the Tushita Temple") and "gu qiang *you* ('犹'[still]) zhu se (The shadows of bamboo still dance on the time-honoured walls)/xu ge *zi* song sheng (The empty tower resounds defiantly with pines' ancient soughing)" (in his poem "Reflection at the Tengwang Tower"), saying that these otherwise inconspicuous words (in italics) had been turned by the poet into striking ones, or rather "shi yan" words, that, in the case of "jiang shan *you* ('有'[to have]) ba shu (Speaking of rivers and mounts, there are those across Bashu)/dong yu *zi* qi liang (The temple has been here since Qi or the Liang period of the Southern Dynasties)", evoked a historical image across time and space, which the poet had, from his vantage, examined, and that it was owing to them, in the case of "gu qiang *you* ('犹'[still]) zhu se (The shadows of bamboo still dance on the time-honoured walls)" and "xu ge *zi* song sheng (The empty tower resounds defiantly with pines' ancient soughing)", that the time-honoured weathered Tengwang Tower was thus distinguished from any other tower across the country, and they showed the poet's reflection on the succession of the eventful dynasties.

To use Du Fu's verses to exemplify "shi yan" does not mean that the development of "shi yan" is his alone. Its development should be ascribed to the collective endeavour in this direction and signal a trend in the development of the language of ancient Chinese poetry. In fact, even before Du Fu, there had been other ancient Chinese poets who had already paid attention to "shi yan" and thus produced their well-known verses, such as "ye (choke)" and "leng (chill)" in Wang Wei's "quan sheng *ye* wei shi (Spring water dropping upon steep rocks sounds as if choked with sobs)/ri se *leng* qing song (Dense pine trees can chill even rays of penetrating sunlight)" and "zhi (upright)" and "yuan (round)" in his "da mo gu yan *zhi* (A plum of smoke on a vast barren desert was rising like an upright column)/chang he luo ri *yuan* (A sun descending against a long river appeared even rounder)", "yin (induce)" and "xian (hold)" in Li Bai's "yan *yin* chou xin qu (A flight of wild geese southward induced my grief)/shan *xian* hao yue lai (A brilliant moon appeared as if held high by ranges of mounts)" and "han (chill)" and "lao (age)" in his "ren yan *han* ju you (Households in the recess of tangerine and shaddock forest feel chilly)/qiu se *lao* wu tong (Heavy autumnal colours tend to age phoenix trees)", and "di (low)" and "jin (close)" in Meng Haoran's "ye kuang tian *di* shu (The skies over the far horizon of such an expansive wilderness seem lower than near trees)/jiang qing yue *jin* ren (The moon reflected in such limpid river feels so close as an intimate companion)" and "dan (pale)" and "di (patter)" in his "wei yun *dan* he han (Clouds, in wisps though, faded the Milky Way)/shu yu *di* wu tong (Rain, in sparse drops, was falling upon phoenix trees)". Epithets like crafted, exquisite, and divine, to choose just a few, apply to these chefs d'oeuvre. And their appeal endures. In the forty-eighth chapter of *The Story of the Stone*, a young maidservant wondered at Wang Wei's utilization of "zhi (upright)" and "yuan (round)" in his verses in question, remarking that

> How could it be that a plum of smoke would be upright? And the sun certainly is already round. So, apparently, "zhi" seems implausible; "yuan" seems shoddy. But, after I have closed the book and thought them over, those

so depicted images should feel like leaping out at me, as large as life. And there should be no other words that could replace them.

And this is why the poets of, say, the Tang Dynasty set great store by a "shi yan". Again, let us listen to the maidservant, whose opinion was so interesting and insightful:

> There is something you may not be able to explain in words, but, after you turn it over in your mind, you shall understand why it should be as it is; there is something you may think unreasonable, but, after you turn it over in your mind, you shall find out that it can never be more reasonable.

Her opinion should be understood to refer to an anti-conventional "shi yan", which first strikes the reader apparently as queer, fallacious, and even altogether illogical. The "shi yan" word as an idiom of such a nature certainly does not belong in the natural ingenuous vernacular register, as the latter, though adopted by ancient Chinese poets, does not fit in the role of a "shi yan". To comprehend a "shi yan", in the process of appreciation, the reader should endeavour to imagine what the poet must have imagined and, at the same time, empathize with what the poet must have felt instead of resorting to reason for an explanation, which can only be perceived in a "shi yan" and its verse themselves. Thus what apparently is logically incongruous between the "shi yan" and other word(s) of a verse, for example, how "yan (geese)" "yin (induce)" the poet's "chou xin (grief)" in "yan *yin* chou xin qu (A flight of wild geese southward induced my grief)", how "shan (mountains)" "xian (hold high)" "hao yue (a brilliant moon)" in "shan *xian* hao yue lai (A brilliant moon appeared as if held high by ranges of mounts)", what could "ye (choke)" "quan sheng (the sound of spring water)" in "quan sheng *ye* wei shi (Spring water dropping upon steep rocks sounds as if choked with sobs)", and what could "leng (chill)" "ri se (sunlight)" in "ri se *leng* qing song (Dense pine trees can chill even rays of penetrating sunlight)", will eventually feel logically congruous in essence, and the epiphany on the part of the reader will come about as well. This explains why a "shi yan" can be so particular and fascinating in terms of logical coherence and psychological attachment.

7.3. Phasing out of the "shi yan"

Just because it could help so much, as previously discussed, in versification, the "shi yan" certainly became the darling of ancient Chinese poets, who in and since the flourishing period of the Tang Dynasty were even obsessed with acquiring it for their verses. A great many verses by poets during the middle and latter periods of the Tang Dynasty feature exquisite antithetical symmetry and consummate "shi yan" words, such as Wei Yingwu's "han yu *an* shen geng (Chilly rain further darkened the dead of the night)/liu ying *du* gao ge (Glowworms flying well above the temple made it look loftier)", Lang Shiyuan's "chan sheng *jing* kong guan (The singing of cicadae quietened the empty lodge)/yu se *ge* qiu yuan (The mist of rain screened the autumnal field)", Sikong Shu's "gu deng *han* zhao yu (The light of a lone lamp felt chilly through the chilly rain)/shen zhu *an* fu yan (The recess of a bamboo grove appeared mythic in the misty smoke)", Jia Dao's "guo qiao *fen* ye se (To cross a bridge is to cross two worlds of scenery)/yi shi *dong* yun gen (To move a rock is to move the legendary root of clouds)", Yuan Zhen's "yuan shan *long* xiu (su) wu (The distant mounts are enveloped in the overnight mists)/gao shu *ying* zhao hui (The tall trees are silhouetted against the morning sunlight)", Bai Juyi's "luan hua jian yu *mi* ren yan (Flowers, one cluster after another, are almost about to dazzle my eyes)/qian cao cai neng *mo* ma ti (Sprouting grasses are high just enough to hide my horse's hooves)", Ma Dai's "shu yu *can* hong ying (The rainbow did not altogether vanish in the sparse rain)/hui yun *bei* niao xing (Clouds drifted and birds flew in the opposite directions)", and Du Xunhe's "yuan shan *heng* luo ri (A setting sun was overhanging a far mount range)/gui niao *du* ping chuan (Returning birds were fleeting over a level plain)". There are also anecdotes about poets during this time who weighed words for a "shi yan" in their verses. For example, Jiao Dao once thought hard over which word, "tui (push)" or "qiao (tap)", better fitted in his verse "seng ___ yue xia men (A monk was [*tapping/pushing open*] a moonlit door)" before he eventually decided on "qiao", hence the Chinese phrase "tui qiao (literally 'push and tap')", which figuratively means weighing words; Zheng Gu is said to have improved another poet's verse on plum blossoms sprouting early in a cold winter by changing "shu (many)" in "zuo ye *shu* zhi kai (Last night saw many sprays of plum blossoms sprouting)" to "yi (one)", thus the revision "zuo ye *yi* zhi kai (Last night saw only a single spray of plum blossom sprouting)", more vividly and more exactly envisioning the earliness of the new growth of plum flowers. These anecdotes, in a way, prove that seeking a "shi yan" at the time enjoyed a vogue.

But there is a potential danger that focusing too much on a "shi yan" can damage a poem as a whole. After all, one word, even if it is a "shi yan", is far from enough to make the world of a poem, whose construction need other words, which are also indispensable, akin to a staged multi-character drama, of whose characters any one alone is incapable of sustaining the whole drama; analogous to a sumptuous banquet that has to be made up of a medley of dishes; or comparable to a movie that shows a sequence of scenes, one of which, though it is the climax, is just a part of the plot. During the middle and latter periods of the Tang Dynasty, however, there were certain minor poets who got addicted to a "shi yan" only to be oblivious of the verse where it was used, let alone the whole poem. Worse, they tended to copy other poets' fine words to "shi yan" their own flimsy verses in profusion, regardless of whether they were appropriate. Such self-complacent "shi yan" words actually are trite, or, as Song Dynasty poetry critics satirized, those otherwise live words had been deprived of life by these poets. For example, the previously discussed Du Fu "you" and "zi" in "jiang shan *you* ba shu (Speaking of rivers and mounts, there are those across Bashu)/dong yu *zi* qi liang (The temple has been here since Qi or the Liang period of the Southern Dynasties) and Jia Dao's favourite "duo" and "ban" were imitated by many poets of later generations, say, during the latter period of the Tang Dynasty, in an attempt to cobble together their own trite verses, only to corrupt the originators' reputed "shi yan" words. This was observed by certain ancient Chinese poetry critics, like Liu Xizai of the Qing Dynasty, who, in his *Generalizations about Arts*, said that "Only when a word lends glamour to the verse, as well as to the poem, which accommodates it can it be classed as a 'shi yan' in its truest sense; otherwise, the word is what 'shi yan' masters scorn as 'a dead word'".

This consequently gave rise to a new trend: more and more ancient Chinese poets began to feel more and more averse to any "shi yan" words for their strictures and, meanwhile, attached more and more importance to communication of meaning in a natural, lofty, and profound manner, which they believed should be the goal of versification.

Here are four quotations from Song Dynasty poetry critics:

Only when a poet aims lofty will he likely create a lofty poem. If he focuses on words or even on verses, such focus, however it can be, is still the lesser.
(Baishidaoren's Poetic Discourse by Jiang Kui)

Versification has to tackle three main aspects in the order of priority: how to start and end a poem, how to craft a verse, and how to weigh words for a "shi yan".
(Canglang's Criticism of Poetry by Yan Yu)

The essential crux of versification is about what meaning to convey, next to it is about how to craft a verse, and the last step is about how to refine words. This is where poetic craftsmanship manifests itself.
(A Miscellany of Insightful Remarks on Poetry and Other Subjects by Zhang Biaochen)

[When it comes to versification,] refining words should come after crafting verses; crafting verses should come after subliming an entire poem.
(*On Poetry* by Shi Puwen)

These four quotations point to one thing: that versification has three levels, which was echoed by Wang Shizhen in his *Random Talk from the Garden of Art*, and these are, in order of priority, the art of composing a poem, the art of crafting each of its verses, and the art of refining words for a "shi yan" in each verse. This order shows that the "shi yan", once in vogue, considerably diminished in gravity in the Song Dynasty. Even Liu Ban, otherwise known as Gongwen, a historian of the Song Dynasty, in his *Liu Gongwen's Commentaries on Poetry*, joined to make his pronouncement that "A poem should focus primarily on its meaning, with its verses and words being secondary".

Certainly, "Poetry should focus primarily on its meaning" does not necessarily mean that the "shi yan" must be discarded altogether. But then emphasis on one thing naturally leads to deemphasis on if not ignorance of the other, like one who fixes his eyes on one object is bound to bypass others. By the standards of an idealistic poetry critic, a poem should be perfect in every aspect. But how could it be so in reality? So, when the poetry critics of the Song Dynasty began to value the meanings and morals which they believed poetry had to communicate, they began to find fault with the wording, which was accused of having clogged the otherwise unclogged communication of what they so valued. Of course the ideal is that the gravity of a poem as a whole, of the verses as its components, and of the words as the constituents of its verses, should be balanced. But a scale can tip. This time it was the poem as a meaningful whole that tipped it, while wording was abased. Wei Qingzhi, in his *Chips of Precious Jade Collected from the Treasury of Remarks on Poetry*, compared the meaning of a poem to a master and its wording, rhyme, and the like to servants, a precursor in this respect to what Yuan Mei observed in his *A Sequel to "Critique of Poetry"*. In fact, as early as in the Tang Dynasty, Du Mu, in his *The Collection by Fanchuan of His Own Poetry*, had compared the meaning to a general, the vitality to his subordinates, and the wording and rhetoric to his soldiers in versification, which was echoed by Yang Wanli, in his *The Collection of the Works by Chengzhai*, and, into the Yuan Dynasty, Fan Peng reemphasized the status of the meaning of a poem as the commander who manoeuvred his troops deviously. Even Cao Xueqin, a novelist of the Qing Dynasty, through the mouth of a heroine by the name of Lin Daiyu, who educated a maidservant called Xiangling about versification, in his *The Story of the Stone*, voiced his opinion that

> After all, either words or verses should be the last for you to consider. The first and foremost is to conceive a main idea before you start to write a poem. Where a genuine main idea is, both words and verses will naturally follow appropriately.

Actually, Cao also derived his notion from what had been maintained by his predecessors, those staunch advocates of this belief.

"Ju yan duan neng qiao yi zi (By the time I could determine a 'shi yan' word from the words I've been chanting and weighing)/yin chang he chi zhuo qian nian (I feel as if my such chanting and weighing should have lasted more than a thousand years)" described how Fang Hui was labouring to determine a word as a "shi yan". This, on the other hand, raises a question: would a "shi yan" thus acquired or use of a "shi yan" result in disruption of a poet's thought flow in or conveyance of the meaning of his poem, thus depriving his poem, as the aforementioned parable of *Zhuangzi* allegorizes, of its vitality? So far there is no definite answer to it. But one thing is certain: in their pursuit of naturalness, meaningfulness, and sublimity, Song Dynasty poets began to marginalize any "shi yan" word in versification, and this rebellious practice was followed by more and more ancient Chinese poets, who were seeking smoothness and naturalness in their poems. To compromise the meaning of a poem as a whole just for the sake of a "shi yan" word was the last thing they would do. This is because they thought that a "shi yan" word did attract the eye of the reader, but, at the same time, it could frustrate the reader due to its illegibility and disrupt the process of appreciation. So, for fear of such ramifications, the pursuit of a word as a "shi yan" in versification was eventually abandoned. What did this augur, a blessing or a condemnation on Chinese poetry?

References

1. Fan, Wen 范温. "Qianxi shiyan" 潜溪诗眼 (Qianxi's Perspective on Poetry). In *Song shihua jiyi* 宋诗话辑佚 (The Recovery of Lost Song Dynasty Poems), edited by Shaoyu Guo 郭绍虞. Beijing: Zhonghua Book Company, 1980.
2. Hu, Yinglin 胡应麟. *Shi sou* 诗薮 (Thickets of Criticism). Shaihai: Shanghai Classics Publishing House, 1979.
3. Jiang, Kui 姜夔. "Baishidaoren shi shuo" 白石道人诗说 (Baishidaoren's Poetic Discourse). In *Lidai shihua* 历代诗话 (The Commentaries by the Critics of the Past Dynasties on Poetry), edited by Wenhuan He 何文焕. Beijing: Zhonghua Book Company, 1981.
4. Kobo, Daishi. *Wen jin mi fu lun* 文镜秘府论 (Treatise on the Secret Treasury of Literary Mirror). Beijing: People's Literature Publishing House, 1980.
5. Liu, Ban 刘攽. "Zhongshan shihua" 中山诗话 (Liu Gongwen's Commentaries on Poetry). In *Lidai shihua* 历代诗话 (The Commentaries by the Critics of the Past Dynasties on Poetry), edited by Wenhuan He 何文焕. Beijing: Zhonghua Book Company, 1981.
6. Liu, Xizai 刘熙载. *Yi gai* 艺概 (Generalizations about Arts). Shanghai: Shanghai Classics Publishing House, 1978.
7. Lu, Shiyong 陆时雍. "Shijing zonglun" 诗镜总论 (A Comprehensive Digest of Good Ancient Poems). In *Lidai shihua xubian* 历代诗话续编 (A Sequel to the Commentaries by the Critics of the Past Dynasties on Poetry), edited by Fubao Ding 丁福保. Beijing: Zhonghua Book Company, 1983.
8. Luo, Dajing 罗大经. *Helin yulu* 鹤林玉露 (Jade Dew in the Crane's Forest or Tales of the Men of Letters of the Song Dynasty). Beijing: Zhonghua Book Company, 1983.
9. Ouyang, Xiu 欧阳修. "Liuyi shihua" 六一诗话 (Liuyi's Commentaries on Poetry). In *Lidai shihua* 历代诗话 (The Commentaries by the Critics of the Past Dynasties on Poetry), edited by Wenhuan He 何文焕. Beijing: Zhonghua Book Company, 1981.
10. Shen, Deqian 沈德潜. *Shuoshi zuiyu* 说诗晬语 (A Desultory Discourse on Poetry). Beijing: People's Literature Publishing House, 1979.
11. Shi, Buhua 施补华. "Xian yong shuoshi" 岘佣说诗 (A Garrison Secretary's Talk about Poetry). In *Qing shihua* 清诗话 (The Poetic Discourses of the Qing Dynasty), edited by Fuzhi Wang 王夫之. Shanghai: Shanghai Classics Publishing House, 1978.
12. Wang, Shizhen 王世贞. "Yiyuan zhiyan" 艺苑卮言 (Random Talk from the Garden of Art). In *Lidai shihua xubian* 历代诗话续编 (A Sequel to the Commentaries by the Critics of the Past Dynasties on Poetry), edited by Fubao Ding 丁福保. Beijing: Zhonghua Book Company, 1983.
13. Wei, Qingzhi 魏庆之. *Shiren yu xie* 诗人玉屑 (Chips of Precious Jade Collected from the Treasury of Remarks on Poetry). Shanghai: Shanghai Classics Publishing House, 1978.
14. Xie, Zhen 谢榛. "Siming shuhua" 四溟诗话 (A Sea-in-the-Four-Direction Recluse's Remarks on Poetry). In *Lidai shihua xubian* 历代诗话续编 (A Sequel to the Commentaries by the Critics of the Past Dynasties on Poetry), edited by Fubao Ding 丁福保. Beijing: Zhonghua Book Company, 1983.
15. Yan, Yu 严羽. "Canglang shihua" 沧浪诗话 (Canglang's Criticism of Poetry). In *Lidai shihua* 历代诗话 (The Commentaries by the Critics of the Past Dynasties on Poetry), edited by Wenhuan He 何文焕. Beijing: Zhonghua Book Company, 1981.
16. Yang, Lun 杨伦. *Du shi jing quan* 杜诗镜铨 (A Mirror of the Meanings of Du Fu's Poems). Shanghai: Shanghai Classics Publishing House, 1980.

17. Yang, Zai 杨载. "Shifa jiashu" 诗法家数 (Techniques of Versification). In *Lidai shihua* 历代诗话 (The Commentaries by the Critics of the Past Dynasties on Poetry), edited by Wenhuan He 何文焕. Beijing: Zhonghua Book Company, 1981.
18. Ye, Mengde 叶梦得. *Shilin shihua* 石林诗话 (Tales and Critique of Poetry at Shilin). In *Lidai shihua* 历代诗话 (The Commentaries by the Critics of the Past Dynasties on Poetry), edited by Wenhuan He 何文焕. Beijing: Zhonghua Book Company, 1981.
19. Yuan, Mei 袁枚. "Xu shipin" 续诗品 (A Sequel to "Critique of Poetry"). In *Qing shihua* 清诗话 (The Poetic Discourses of the Qing Dynasty), edited by Fuzhi Wang 王夫之. Shanghai: Shanghai Classics Publishing House, 1978.
20. Zhang, Biaochen 张表臣. "Shanhugou shihua" 珊瑚钩诗话 (A Miscellany of Insightful Remarks on Poetry and Other Subjects). In *Lidai shihua* 历代诗话 (The Commentaries by the Critics of the Past Dynasties on Poetry), edited by Wenhuan He 何文焕. Beijing: Zhonghua Book Company, 1981.
21. Zhao, Yi 赵翼. "Oubei shihua" 瓯北诗话 (Oubei's Discourse on Poets and their Poetry). In *Qing shihua xubian* 清诗话续编 (A Sequel to the Poetic Discourses of the Qing Dynasty), edited by Shaoyu Guo 郭绍虞. Shanghai: Shanghai Classics Publishing House, 1983.

8 Development of Chinese poetry from vernacular Song Dynasty style to vernacular modern style

Inheritance of the spirit of vernacular Song Dynasty poetry

The development of Chinese poetry can be studied either from the perspective of time or from the perspective of style. For example, from the temporal perspective, there is the style before the Southern Dynasties; the style of the Qi and Liang periods of the Southern Dynasties; the style of the Tang Dynasty; which can be sub-divided into that of the early, flourishing, middle, and declining periods of the Tang Dynasty; the vernacular Song Dynasty style; the vernacular modern style; the obscure modern style; and even what is called the fifth-generation modern style. As to why a poetic style is deemed to epitomize a certain stage in the development of Chinese poetry, it may not be easy to elucidate. It may depend on the criteria against which Chinese poetry critics judge what style typically becomes the poetry of a certain period. But such criteria are inexplicable, and their constituents differ from different Chinese poetry critics. The bottom line of their criteria can either be poets' thought, poetic characteristics, poetic subjects, and so on, all for a good reason. But such differences can confuse the reader. In that case, we would do well to turn to the following argument, which should rightly direct the reader:

> My thesis is that the age's imprint in a poem is not to be traced to the poet but to the language. The real history of poetry is, I believe, the history of the changes in the kind of language in which successive poems have been written.
>
> (*Theory of Literature* by René Wellek and Austin Warren)

Indeed, we shall find out that when we, from the linguistic perspective, study how Chinese poetry develops, the stages of its development can never be more clear cut, for each stage is naturally the result of defamiliarization of past poetic language. Such development is an apparently cyclic yet essentially spirally progressive movement. In its course, Chinese poets at a certain point purposefully and methodically defamiliarize an overused, hackneyed, and thus old poetic language into a new and more apt poetic language. Defamiliarization of this nature, it should be pointed out, is not a "war" between a new poetic language and an old poetic language, as certain poetry critics tend to exaggerate; an utter "breakup" with an old poetic language; or, in other words, an utter "liberation" of a new poetic language, as certain Chinese poetry historians tend to overstate. In fact, no matter how defamiliarized old poetic language can be, a certain link between it and the new poetic language still exists one way or another, whether it be acknowledged or not, and, when the time comes, the old poetic language, though previously repellent because of its being "old", can be reused in a new way. And this is how the language of Chinese poetry changes relatively between "old" and "new" or rather between vernacular and literary. As to which poetic language, vernacular or literary, dominates what stage, it depends ultimately on how different Chinese poets at different stages think of the function of their poetry.

So, when we talk about the development of poetry, we actually talk about the development of poetic language. The development of Chinese poetry is marked mainly by two major linguistic changes: the first one happened when the language of ancient Chinese poetry was defamiliarized by the poets of the Qi and Liang periods of the Southern Dynasties, and this defamiliarized poetic language was perfected by the poets of the Tang Dynasty to become the language of Recent Style poetry; the second one happened when the poets of the Song Dynasty reverted to and drew from the linguistic style of ancient Chinese poetry before the Qi and Liang periods of the Southern Dynasties and developed the language of vernacular Song Dynasty poetry, which would be given a new lease on life by the poets of vernacular modern Chinese poetry.

8.1. From the poetry of the Tang Dynasty (the literary style) to that of the Song Dynasty (the vernacular style)

In the third chapter of this book, I discussed the linguistic defamiliarization of ancient Chinese poetry. Generally speaking, the language of ancient Chinese poetry before the Southern Dynasties, or rather of the Pre-Qin, Han, Wei, and Jin dynasties, approximated the vernacular; thus poetry composed in this language had a syntactically customary word order, used "xu zi" words or phrases, and was not rigidly schemed in tone and cadence. Into the Southern Dynasties, ancient Chinese poets such as Xie Lingyun, Xie Tiao, and Shen Yue started to defamiliarize past poetic language by using the literary one in their poems. In the process of this linguistic defamiliarization, Recent Style poetry took shape. In a poem of this style, both reduction or even elimination of "xu zi" words or phrases and syntactic ellipsis and transposition led to juxtaposition of its images, condensation of verses, and apparent disengagement of the poet's thought flow from the word order of the verses; one of the tonal and metrical schemes is a pattern of intratextual antithesis and intertextual antithetical symmetry; it offers, instead of the poet's one and only fixed perspective, more than one angle, and these shift one way or another; the allusions and "shi yan" words embedded in the verses subtilize the meaning, and the absence of "xu zi" words or phrases such as indicators of temporal or spatial relationships requires the reader to understand the poem by virtue of more intuitive perception than reasoning.

But everything has two sides. Opposite its merits, Recent Style poetry also has demerits. For example, the juxtaposition of imagery and syntactic ellipsis and transposition can mystify and subtilize a Recent Style poem, on the one hand but, on the other hand, can also confuse the reader with, say, the resultant equivocality, which can counteract the efforts made by the poet. Its rigid tonal and metrical scheme, which ensures the fabulous intratextual antithesis and intertextual antithetical symmetry, viewed from another angle, restrains the otherwise free poetic form, analogous to a musical beat that gives a rhythm but at the same time constrains a dancer's movement. The "shi yan" words inspire the reader's intuitive perception and imagination, but then risk calling attention to themselves at the cost of other words in the verses, only to disrupt the conveyance of the meanings of the verses, like an actor who steals the show and ruins a play. All in all, these untraditional linguistic aspects will engage the attention of the reader, who is accustomed to the language of past poetry, which reads as simple, plain, and natural as a chat, only to render unclear the meaning of a Recent Style poem as a whole, an outcome of the form outweighing the content.

Even so, the linguistic form of Recent Style poetry continued to develop and reached the acme of perfection during the flourishing and middle periods of the Tang Dynasty. Such an established allegedly perfect linguistic form must have been addictive to ancient Chinese poets at the time, who would be all too ready to use it in versification. To meet its formal requirements for a verse or even a word, they would rack their brains, as seen in "yin cheng wu zi ju (To chant five words into a verse)/yong po yi sheng xin (I'd drain my resources of all life)" (by Fang Gan of the Tang Dynasty) and "shi jin yin he ju (What are you striving to chant into a verse)?/zi xin bai ji jing (For a few more strands of your beard have turned grey)" (by Li Pin of the Tang Dynasty). In the event, they were fettered by the linguistic form which should have helped in conveyance of the meaning of a poem. That a new form of poetic language should be brought forth merely for the form's sake and end up yoking a poet certainly is not what "defamiliarization" of a past poetic language aims at. But this was the trend, which came to be the routine, back then, as stipulated in Jiaoran's *Styles of Poetry: Poets' Active and Strenuous Mental Work*, Wang Changling's *Rules of Poetry*, Kobo Daishi's *Treatise on the Secret Treasury of Literary Mirror*, Qi Ji's *The Quintessence of Poetry*, and Xu Yin's *The Beau Ideals for Versification*, which have one thing in common: their authors all standardized poetic language that should otherwise have been unrestrained, original, and spontaneous when it comes to "poetic style". The minor poets of the time created their Recent Style poems, especially their five-word-a-verse eight-verse "lv shi" poems, the way one does crossword puzzles, mechanically: the first pair of verses must introduce what a poem is about; each of its middle two pairs of verses, which must depict sceneries, must be arranged in the pattern of "two words (a meaningful unit) + one word (a meaningful unit) + two words (a meaningful unit)" and "two words + two words + one word", respectively, in which the "one word", either an adjective or a verb, must be a "shi yan"; and its last pair of verses must transcend. That binding routine was ridiculed by, for example, Yang Shen of the Ming Dynasty, also known as Shengan, who, in his *Shengan's Commentaries on Poetry*, said of poets during the latter period of the Tang Dynasty that they routinized their versification to the point of being unimaginative. Thus they did not have a larger picture of a poetic world but only saw and reflected on what was under their noses, which was expressed only in the form of an over-crafted five-word-a-verse eight-verse "lv shi" poem, so, even though they could drain their brains to conceive even a single five-word verse, their practice was ridiculous. In fact, earlier than Yang Shen, Hu Zi, in his *Poetic Remarks from the Fisherman Recluse at the Trumpet-Creeper Creek*, commented thus:

> Those minor poets during the latter period of the Tang Dynasty and the Five Dynasties and Ten States, who wished to seek fame through their poems, would legalize their so-called well-established routines by citing their predecessors' poems as evidence. And they would argue at length for their theory in an aggressive way. Even so, their viewpoint would make one sneer. Most of them modelled their linguistic style on that of Jia Dao's poetry.

Derogatory epithets were also levelled at minor poets, such as degraded, tasteless, shallow, vile, overwrought, torpid, debased, weak, and so forth. Besides, they were metaphorized even as fleas inhabiting one's underpants. (See Lu Shiyong's *A Comprehensive Digest of Good Ancient Poems*.)

In those circumstances, the movement of defamiliarizing the poetic language of the Recent Style that had been initiated by Du Fu and Han Yu and would be perfected by the poets of the Song Dynasty gained momentum, which would in turn lead to the formation of the poetry of the vernacular Song Dynasty style.

Judgments of Song Dynasty poetry vary with various ancient Chinese poetry critics: to some, it philosophizes the world; to some, it epitomizes meticulousness; to some, it is inadequate in analogy and association; to some, it is given to reasoning and argumentativeness; to some, it pivots on breadth and depth in meaning; and to some, it disvalues imagery, to name just a few. Such judgments are based either on those critics' intuitive perceptions or the content of the poetry, but essentially, though undeclared, are against the Recent Style poetry of the Tang Dynasty. Few of those poetry critics linguistically compare the poetry of the two dynasties. So, their judgments of the poetry of the Song Dynasty seem comprehensive but, in my opinion, fail to hit the nail on the head. In all fairness, however, Yan Yu's notion of Song Dynasty poetry being vernacular should be pointed. (See his *Canglang's Criticism of Poetry*.) This notion was accepted by other ancient Chinese poetry critics, who even justified it with evidence but stopped at that without probing into what exactly had driven the poets of the Song Dynasty to vernacularize their poetry, how they had conducted the vernacularization, and why their linguistic style should be dispraised.

To answer these questions, we should look first at the functions of poetic language. According to Roman Jakobson's *Linguistics and Poetics*, to discuss the functions of poetic language, one should take into account "I (i.e., the poet)", "you (i.e., the reader)", and "it (i.e., the object)". If the poet intends to communicate with the reader, then poetic language serves as the vehicle of communicating meanings, so it is required to be grammatically organized to ensure that the meanings to be communicated will be easily and unmistakably understood by the reader. Certainly, in the process, a relative emphasis either on the poet or on the reader may shift;

if it is on the former, then poetic language is relatively subjective; if it is on the latter, then poetic language is relatively objective. But, whatever may be, poetic language in this case functions as a communicative vehicle. On the other hand, if the poet intends to reflect on an object, then what he or she will care about is how he or she feels in such reflection and how he or she expresses such feelings, which is the content of his poem, in what he or she thinks is a workable linguistic form, even to the point of flouting grammatical rules, regardless of how well the reader can understand his poem, only if the poet can achieve this goal. In this case, poetic language functions as an expressive vehicle.

In summary, generally speaking, poetic language functions either as a communicative vehicle or as an expressive one.

The language of the Recent Style poetry of the Tang Dynasty is more expressive than communicative. Of the Tang Dynasty poets, some, such as Li Bai and Li He, would volubly express "my" feelings; some, such as Bai Juyi and Yuan Zhen, would be keen to narrate something for "you", but their poems, strictly speaking, fall under the category of ancient Chinese poetry prior to the emergence of Recent Style poetry. The "jue ju" and "lv shi" poems of the Recent Style of the Tang Dynasty in their truest sense are mainly expressive, in terms of language, of the poets' feelings and intuitive perception, as Wu Qiao, in his *Talks about Poetry around the Hearth*, discusses:

> The Tang Dynasty poets composed their poems only to express their own feelings, caring not about whether the reader would understand them or not, whether the reader would speak highly or lowly of them. Deep down were their feelings that they could neither suppress nor be ready to share explicitly with others. So they chose to chant their feelings in an expressive poetic language.

This is exemplified by "luan sheng sha shang shi (A rattle is being heard as if produced by boulders on the sandy land)/dao ying yun zhong shu (Reflected in the river are the trees that are being clouded)" (by Liu Changqing), "han yu an shen geng (Chilly rain further darkened the dead of the night)/liu ying du gao ge (Glow-worms flying well above the temple made it look loftier)" (by Wei Yingwu), "gu deng han zhao yu (The light of a lone lamp felt chilly through the chilly rain)/shen zhu an fu yan (The recess of a bamboo grove appeared mythic in the misty smoke)" (by Sikong Shu), "lou sheng lin xia jing (The woods grow more still with each dropping of the water from the timer)/ying se yue zhong wei (The glow of glow-worms are dimmed in the moonlight)" (by Yao He), "cang hai yue ming zhu you lei (The bright moon reflected in the sea, tears shed by Jiaoren transform into pearls)/lan tian ri nuan yu sheng yan (With warm sunshine, the fine jade of Mount Lantian issues wisps of smoke)" (by Li Shangyin), and so forth, wherein such pronouns as "wo (I)" and "ru" or "nong" or "jun" (all refer to "you") that are subjects, as well as "xu zi" words or phrases that indicate, for example, spatial relationships so as to make verses syntactically complete for unequivocality in meaning, such as "zai (at/in/on, etc.)", "yu (from/in/on, etc.)", "zhi (to/of/toward, etc.)", and "suo (of/with/

for, etc.)" are few and far between. Instead, ellipses, transpositions, and equivocal words predominate. This will thus obliterate the poet, whose presence as, say, a mentor or a narrator, could otherwise have been strongly felt in ancient Chinese poetry prior to Recent Style poetry. These Recent Style poets truly present the reader nothing but what originally impressed them, in juxtaposed imagery, whose subtle nuances will put to test the discernment and empathy on the part of the reader, which Yan Yu, in his *Canglang's Criticism of Poetry*, likens to an antelope who sleeps by hanging its horns on the branch of a tree, with its hooves lifted high so as not to leave any trace on the ground that a predator may spot, an analogy applicable to Recent Style poetry that is too elusive and too mysterious to understand, in stark contrast to Song Dynasty poetry, of which Wu Qiao, in his *Talks about Poetry around the Hearth*, says:

> The Song Dynasty poets were eager to make their poems as legible as possible to the reader. To achieve this, their poems were, in the main, plain, natural, and unequivocal.

Their pursuit led to replacement of expressive poetic language (of the Recent Style poetry of the Tang Dynasty) by communicative poetic language (of Song Dynasty poetry).

Such a consequence is inevitable. Since they were keen for the reader to comprehend what they intend to communicate by way of their poems, Song Dynasty poets were more than ready to give cues or simply unmistakable indications to the reader in this direction. This starkly contrasts to what Tang Dynasty poets did, which is being disposed to turn to externalities for the most delicate possible expression of their sensibilities. (See *A Preface to the Poetry by Wang Jiao* by Ye Shi of the Song Dynasty.) For poets of the Song Dynasty, how to share with the reader explicitly what was on their mind is the first and foremost mission, so they would have to remove any potential linguistic barriers to communication between them and the reader. To achieve this, they would have to vernacularize the literary language that prevailed in the Recent Style poetry of the Tang Dynasty. One of the aspects of this vernacularization is normalization of the otherwise asyntactic word order that featured in the Recent Style poetry of the Tang Dynasty.

Cases in point are the most popular "lv shi" poems of the Song Dynasty, such as Mei Yaochen's "A Walking Tour in the Mount Lu", Ouyang Xiu's "A Reply to Yuanzhen for Fun", and Su Shi's "A Response to Ziyou's Verse: Recollection of Our Lodging at Mianchi". Having read these poems, one will agree that, in their verses, the images are not so juxtaposed, and their thought flow is not so concealed and elusive, as in the Recent Style poetry of the Tang dynasty, due to the use of Chinese auxiliary words such as "shi yu (become)", "fu (alternately)", "sui chu (from vantage to vantage)", and "du (alone)" in Mei's poem; "yi (doubt)", "you (as if)", and "yu (inclined)" in Ouyang's poem; and "na fu (impossibly)", "wu you (by no means)", and "hai (still)" in Su's poem. In other words, the poems by these poets communicate far more smoothly and lucidly and the transition from verse to verse in their poems is logically coherent, thanks to intertextual consistency, as in Mei's "ren jia zai he xu (Is there any household in the mountains)?/yun wai yi sheng ji (The crow of a rooster beyond clouds has reached my ears)", Ouyang's "chun feng yi bu dao tian ya (I doubt that the vernal wind would blow from afar to such a remote area)/er yue shan cheng wei jian hua (It is already the second lunar month but no vestige of bloom is in sight)", and Su's "ren sheng dao chu zhi he si (What should one's unsettling life be likened to)?/ying si fei hong ta xue ni (It should be likened to a migrant swan who leaves its footprints on snow-covered ground here and there)". Incidentally, Ouyang Xiu was said to gloat a great deal about his pair of verses, saying that they complemented each other to the point of one being indispensable to the other and that whenever he recited them, they would amaze him without fail. This should be ascribed mainly to the symbiosis between the poet's perceivable thought flow and the uninterrupted movement of the verses composed in the customarily syntactical word order. So it is with Su's pair of verses. Worthy of note is that, in "ying si fei hong ta xue ni (It should be likened to a migrant swan who leaves its footprints on snow-covered ground here and there)", the succession of the images of the migrant swan in flight and its treading on and impressing the snow-covered ground violates one of the tenets for the "lv shi" poetry of the Tang Dynasty: "one verse is dispensable of the other in terms of representation of imagery and communication of meaning", which thus coheres the verses in a consistent and deepening way.

Verses like these in other poems by poets of the Song Dynasty are not uncommon. Just take, for instance, such well-known verses as "chun yin chui ye cao qing qing (Vernal grey clouds hung over the fields whose green grasses appeared greener)/*shi you* you hua yi shu ming (In sight came a flowery tree somewhere that was brightly set off)" (by Su Shunqin), "*wo yi qie ru* chang ri zui (I might as well drink my wine, as usual, till tipsy)/mo jiao xian guan zuo li sheng (No tune of sad departure was allowed to be played on the string and wind instruments)" (by Ouyang Xiu), "ye *lai* guo ling *hu* wen yu (A sudden rain was heard falling while I put up overnight at the mountainous inn)/jin ri man xi *ju shi* hua (The next morrow all over the brook were fallen petals afloat)" (by Zheng Xie), "xin yue *yi* sheng fei niao wai (A waxing crescent was already up to silhouette the flying birds)/luo xia *geng zai* xi yang xi (Evening clouds were glowing farther west of a setting sun)" (by Zhang Lei), "yu hua *you ke* zui (Still remain some flowers keeping company while I am drinking my wine to my heart's content)/hao niao *bu fang* mian (The birds' melodious chirping is a lullaby rather than an annoyance)" (by Tang Geng), Huang Tingjian's "*wei* dao jiang nan *xian* yi xiao (Keen to please myself first before arrival at my hometown in Jiangnan)/yue yang lou shang dui jun shan (I ascended the Yueyang Tower with the view of Junshan Islet opposite)" and "*dan* zhi jia li *ju* wu yang (If and only if all are going well with our family)/*bu yong* shu lai xi zuo hang (You need not write me any lengthy letter in detail)", and Su Shi's "yu ba xi hu bi xi zi (I'd like to compare the West Lake to Xizi [a beauty of the State of Yue during the Spring and Autumn Period])/dan zhuang nong mo *zong xiang yi* (Whose natural beauty, in any makeup, ever shines)", "ci sheng ci ye *bu chang* hao (A moment as enjoyable as tonight can be rare in our life)/ming yue ming nian he chu kan (Where may you and I be next year, with the view of the same bright moon)?", "ren si qiu hong lai you xin (A human being, akin to a wild goose, will leave some trace behind on the to-and-fro journey)/shi ru chun meng *liao* wu hen (Human happenings, comparable to vernal dreams, become altogether untraceable in a wink)", "hai tang *zhen* yi meng (Crab apple flowers, exactly like vanished dreams, are withered and gone)/mei zi *yu* chang xin (Greengages are ripening to stimulate one's yearning for a bite)", and "bu shi lu shan zhen mian mu (We fail to have a panoramic view of the Mount Lu)/*zhi yuan* shen zai ci shan zhong (Just because our vantage is not over but in it)". Owing to the "xu zi" words or phrases (in italic), these verses are structured as syntactically required; their images, if there are any, are no more juxtaposed and, as previously said, dispensable than one another; and all the words in the verses have equal gravity, so no word is spotlighted to become a "shi yan". So, compared with the literary language of the Recent Style poetry of the Tang Dynasty, the language of the poetry of the Song Dynasty, to those later Chinese poetry critics, read as far more vernacular. That is why Ye Mengde, in his *Tales and Critique of Poetry at Shilin*, said of Ouyang Xiu's "lv shi" poems that they were used by the poet as the mere media of conveying meanings, so, even if they were not as literary as the Recent Style poetry of the Tang Dynasty, the poet did not care about it altogether. More directly than Ye Mengde, Xie Zhen, in his *A Sea-in-the-Four-Direction Recluse's Remarks on Poetry*, pointed out that the interspersion of "xu zi" words or phrases in verses inclined such verses toward oral interlocution, which was rooted in Song Dynasty poetry. If Ye's remarks are his criticism of Song Dynasty poetry against that of the Tang Dynasty, then Xie's criticism sounds like a contemptuous debasement of Song Dynasty poetry to something like a chat. Besides, He Shang, in his *A Discourse on Poetry at Zaijiu Garden*, was prejudiced, especially against Ouyang Xiu, among the other poets of the Song Dynasty, and accused him of being a culprit of perverting literary language in favour of the vernacular in versification, which resulted in his poems lacking depth, subtlety, and ingeniousness, thus being no more than plain recountings without analogy and association and setting a hideous example to other poets of his time and later generations, despite his having been credited for his contribution to the vernacularization of the poetic language. His comments may go a little too far, to be fair, for to change a poetic language is not necessarily ruinous. On the contrary, from an evolutionary perspective, it needs changing to correspond to the function of poetry at a certain point of history; as the function of poetry changes, so a change to poetic language is inevitable.

To change poetic language is to defamiliarize it, consciously or unconsciously. When Du Fu utilized "xu zi" words or phrases in his poems, which led to his poetic language being at variance with that of the Recent Style at the time, when Han Yu and Meng Jiao also used so-called unorthodox, recondite words for powerful and impressive impact, they were launching a campaign of defamiliarizing past poetic language, which they might not have been conscious of, probably simply out of their intensifying aversion to the past orthodox yet banal poetic clichés. This could explain why Du Fu avowed his relentless pursuit, as he transposed his verses, of the most astounding possible anti-conventional poetic words, which actually were just vernacular rather than literary and thus contrary to the stylish poetic language of the time, unless he ceased to be and also why Han Yu had a predilection for

Chinese poetry from the Song Dynasty to modern style 165

arcane words and vernacular style, with a view to being original and creative so as to shun triteness in his poetry. Moreover, in terms of tonal and metrical scheme, their poems were not as rigid as required of Recent Style poetry, which could be ascribed to the interspersion of "xu zi" words or phrases and use of words at odds with the tonal and metrical schemes, and, in terms of the poet's thought flow, it could more clearly be discerned throughout the verses of their poems. Du Fu's verses that typify this include "*xing bu zhe lai* shang sui mu (Had you sent me a spray of plum flower at the already saddening year-end)/*ruo wei kan qu* luan xiang chou (How could I have looked at it without feeling agitated in homesickness)?", "qiu shui *cai* shen si wu chi (Into autumn the Jinjiang River is adequately as deep as four or five chi)/ye hang *qia* shou liang san ren (That boat at the open pier happens to ferry two or three people, no more and no less)", "cheng jian jing ze jing pei chou (Even the banners at the top of the town built up and down a mountain fear its precipitousness, as well as the steepness of its side steps)/du li piao miao *zhi* fei lou (Faintly lofty and far out there stands a single tower that looks as if ready to fly)", and "zhang li tan shi *zhe shei zi* (Who else can be the man on a cane of puncture vine who is heaving a sigh over the human world?)/qi xue beng kong hui bai tou (But a grey-haired ageing me weeping bloody tears that are spraying into the air at the turning of my head)", which are in the style of "lv shi" poetry. Let us compare them with these verses, also by Du Fu but in the style of ancient poetry before the Southern Dynasties: "gu ren chen shi *yi* (An ancient once sighed: 'It's time I should retreat')/wu dao bu zhong *yan* (Alas, I can foresee the end of my aspiration)" and "qu *yi* ying xiong shi (Gone are those heroic deeds)/huang *zai* ge ju xin (What a wreckage left by those separatists)". Clearly, the former linguistically approximate the latter just because of "xu zi" words or phrases (in italic) in the former, whose vernacularization of otherwise literary language leads to relaxation of the otherwise rigid tonal and metrical schemes. Besides, there are other Tang Dynasty poets' verses that are similar to these verses by Du Fu and linguistically styled after ancient Chinese poetry before the Southern Dynasties, such as Han Yu's "po wu shu jian *er yi yi* (To his name is no more than a shabby partitioned shed)", "bu cong *er* zhu wei wan *yi* (Why not mete out punishment till a breach of the laws)", and "hu hu *hu* yu wei zhi sheng *zhi* wei le *ye* (How lifetime fleets before I have a chance to savour its sweetness)"; Lu Tong's "*wu* (note: it is not a 'xu zi' word but a pronoun 'I'; use of a pronoun is also a feature of vernacularization) jian yin yang jia you shuo (I know that the School of Yin-Yang believes)" and "*you* kong zi shi lao zi yun (Also both Confucius and Laozi hold)"; Huangfu Shi's "sheng *dang* wei da zhang fu, duan ji luo, chu ni tu (When alive, be a great man to break free from mundane constraints and relieve his people of plight"; Liu Cha's "*shi* yi yu long xia jie lai ren shi (I start to suspect that the Dragon of Jade must have descended to the human world)/*qi xiang* mao yan bu zhao ya (Its claws, in the form of icicles, are gripping the eaves of the thatched houses)"; and Li He's "hei yun ya cheng cheng *yu* cui (Dust of battlefield, like dark clouds, was closing in upon the fort that seemed to be crushed)/jia guang *xiang* ri jin lin kai (The enemy's scale armours, glittering in the sunlight, looked like golden fish scales)", "*wo* (the same as '*wu*' in the preceding Lu Tong's verse) you mi hun zhao *bu de* (My soul has been lost in the dark and cannot be invoked)/xiong ji *yi* chang tian xia bai ([Till you light the way out and its horizon suddenly broadens as] day breaks at the crow of a rooster)", and "fei guang fei guang, quan *er* (you) yi bei jiu (Flying time, flying time, I urge you to toss down this cup of wine)". All these verses would naturally disconcert and astound the reader of the time, who had gotten used to the tonally, metrically, and linguistically stringent Recent Style poetry, on the one hand, but would, on the other hand, inspire those poets who were eager to break the fetters of Recent Style poetry. Since then, the long-established edifice of the orthodox Recent Style poetry began to be torn down. This paved the way for the eruption of vernacular Song Dynasty poetry.

In his *A Probe into the Essence of Versification*, Ye Xie observes

> Han Yu significantly changed the language of the Recent Style poetry of the Tang Dynasty. Such change was impactful; his motive behind it was great. He set a new linguistic trend, which was followed by such Song Dynasty poets as Su Shunqin, Mei Yaochen, Ouyang Xiu, Su Shi, Wang Anshi, and Huang Tingjian. Those poets were obliged to enshrine Han Yu as their forefather in this respect.
>
> Indeed, the reigns of Kaiyuan and Tianbao of the Tang Dynasty were when the Recent Style poetry prospered. Such prosperity continued over more than a century till the reigns of Dali, Zhenyuan and Yuanhe. The impact was significant. But few of the popular poems, not to mention the unpopular ones, during this long period were exceptional. In that case, creative poets were called for to rectify the trend and re-formation of the already trite poetic language was urged.

Well said, indeed. And he is right about the time of the start of defamiliarization of the language of Recent Style poetry. For it is true that, to the reader during the Reign of Yuanhe, the poems began to feel not quite like the Recent Style. But bestowal of the honour of being the forefather of the linguistic style of Song Dynasty poetry on Han Yu is unconvincing, for it seems that Du Fu should be more entitled to that honour. Huang Tingjian was shrewd and was quoted by Chen Shidao of the Song Dynasty, also known as Houshan Recluse, in his *Houshan's Understanding of Poetry*, as saying that both Han Yu and Du Fu vernacularized their poetry, by which he indirectly yet unmistakably conferred the honour of being the trendsetter for the linguistic style of Song Dynasty poetry equally on Du and Han. Nonetheless, Song Dynasty poetry critics still disputed who should claim the honour. For example, Zhanglei wanted to credit Huang Tingjian, one of his friends, saying that

> Being bound by the rigid tonal and metrical schemes in versification is not recommendable anymore. But, not just the poets back in the Tang Dynasty clung to them, but even the poets of our time are subject to their regulation. It is none other than Luzhi [another name for Huang Tingjian] who has given them up and started to set a new linguistic trend for versification.

But his argument is disputed by Hu Zi, who believed that

> Lu Zhi has emulated Revered Du [i.e., Du Fu], whose poems were not restrained by the stringent tonal and metrical schemes of the Recent Style poetry, evidence to which is his nine-"jue ju" poem series under the title of "Impromptus", two-"jue ju" poem series under the title of "Yellow River", seven-"jue ju" poem series under the title of "Sauntering on the Side of the River for Flowers", ten-"jue ju" poem series under the title of "Singing about Kuizhou", and two-"jue ju" poem series under the title of "Rising Waters in Springtime".

In addition, Du Fu was the first poet who used colloquial expressions, such as "jin dang (stop)" in his "shu ri bu ke geng jin dang (The waters cannot possibly be stopped if they keep rising for several days on end)" of his aforementioned "Rising Waters in Springtime" and "shei neng (who is likely to)" in his "shei neng zai jiu kai jin zhan (Who is likely to take wine and invite me to drink there with him?)" of his aforementioned "Sauntering on the Side of the River for Flowers", in poetry. Colloquial as they are, Zhang Jie, in his *Notes on Poetry Written in the Pine and Cypress Studio*, lauded Du Fu's verses, saying

> Du Fu's poems, in the eyes of average literati, are intolerably colloquial. They do not know that "colloquial" as in Du Fu's poems is the hardest to acquire. In truth, Du Fu's "colloquial" is not what an ordinary man understands to be vulgar; on the contrary, it stands for the supreme level of naturalness, plainness, and pristineness. Since the decease of Cao Zhi and Liu Zhen [two preeminent men of letters during the Han-Wei period], over nearly a millennium, has emerged no one but Zimei [another name for Du Fu], who is capable of poeticizing this kind of "colloquial".

Also, Luo Dajing, in his *Jade Dew in the Crane's Forest or Tales of the Men of Letters of the Song Dynasty*, referred to Du's poetic language, in contrast to the crafted literary language of Recent Style poetry, as "crude and unspoiled", claiming it was a demonstration of the Dao, or Way of Heaven. Flouting the rigid tonal and metrical schemes of Recent Style poetry and employing vernacular language signalled a purposeful divergence from the dominant Recent Style poetry language. As for this kind of divergence, we may well listen to Victor Shklovsky, who says: "New forms in art are created by the canonization of peripheral forms". (See his *Sentimental Journey*.)

The notion of the function of poetry changes with the times, which also leads to change in poetic language. Expression of aspirations or admonitions is the function of the earliest ancient Chinese poetry. This has been a legacy ever since for Chinese poets. Social turmoil, such as the An Lushan-Shi Siming Rebellion that shook the Tang Dynasty almost to its foundations, was a wake-up call to those self-centred ancient Chinese poets, not to mention many other social and political vicissitudes. So, poets, for example, during the latter period of the Tang Dynasty, were compelled to reconsider the function of their poems, which they finally realized should serve as the means of socially ethical rectitude, as practised by such poets as Yuan Jie, Bai Juyi, Liu Mian, and Han Yu, who were obliged to shift their focus from their inner worlds to their social environments by informing their poems with what concerned either social ethics or social politics. Besides, in ancient China, not just Neo-Confucianists but poets of the Song Dynasty, who were influenced by religious schools such as the Taoists and the Zen Buddhists and had a metaphysical mindset that was sensible and meticulous, in addition to their life experience, thus grew more and more philosophical and rational. So, they would scrutinize almost everything, including one's personality, bamboos, flowers, the Way of Heaven, and beliefs, no matter whether they were tangible or not, no matter whether they were important or not. They hoped to, by means of such scrutiny, grasp what they believed to be the ultimate truth. They held that poetry should reflect such scrutiny. Xie Yi, a scholar of the Song Dynasty, also known as Xitang, in his *The Collection of Xitang's Works*, wrote:

> Whether an object is active or inactive, scrutiny by one with the mind that is like an unstained mirror of it shall, without discrimination, reflect its nature, which shall eloquently be committed either to speech or to paper, with fidelity.

Hitherto, it should be clear that notions held by ancient Chinese poets or poetry critics of the function of poetry began to change during the latter period of the Tang Dynasty, let alone during the Song Dynasty, which is that their poetry should serve the purpose of unmistakably, deeply, and effectively communicating, for example, socially related messages rather than, as before, expressing their own sentiments. To digress, those ancient Chinese poets came to realize that their exertion in wording would not necessarily pay off due to the intrinsic inadequacies of words. Thus their centre of attention began to shift. They did not indulge their own sentiments or intuitive perception; instead, they endeavoured to communicate, as clear as day, to the reader what they intended to educate or enlighten him or her about. Here, let us see how some Song Dynasty poetry critics criticized Tang Dynasty poetry (see the Qing Dynasty edition of *The Collection of the Works by Wenqian* [Wenqian, i.e., Zhang Lei, of the Song Dynasty]), which is contrary to the opinion of other poetry critics of the Song Dynasty, who blindly stood in reverence and awe of the Tang Dynasty poets:

> The Tang Dynasty poets worked so hard on even a word, but their endeavours had little significance.
>
> The Tang Dynasty is admired for its abundance in talented literati. Back then, those who retreated to dwell in mountains could readily chant their own verses to vent their own sentiments. But, nonetheless, their verses to me can be likened to Shuangjing tea, which tastes sour, although it has received accolade for its so-called fine quality.
>
> Those poetry critics deplore the poetry of the Tang Dynasty, because all it is about are sceneries, without even touching upon the morals.

In versification, the Tang Dynasty poets would reflect on externalities and express their intuitive perception of them. This, to some, is the quintessence of the Tang Dynasty poetry, but, to others who are averse to it, is too trivial, thus not the right way of versification.

These criticisms or mockeries boil down to one point: deploring Tang Dynasty poets having focused too much on their own intuitive perception and sensibilities to communicate ideas, beliefs, morals, and the like to the reader. In that case, the poets and poetry critics of the Song Dynasty decided that it was time to highlight these subject matters. For example, Mei Yaochen maintained that a poem should be inspiring in content (by which he actually prized communication of meanings) and crafted in language, which can be suspected of striking a balance. Liu Ban (see his *Liu Gongwen's Commentaries on Poetry*), Bao Hui (see his *A Letter to Zeng Zihua on Poetry*"), and Xie Yi (see his *Perusal of the Collection of the Works by Tao Yuanming*) held that, in versification, a poet should value communication of his beliefs over formal elements such as wording, remembering that effective communication itself would naturally ensure good wording, or else nothing valuable would result, any more than a crooked post is expected to cast a straight shadow. And Lv Benzhong realized the importance of the communicative function of poetry when lamenting that "since I went astray and felt obsessed with wording/ My hair on the temples has grown grey but to no avail" (see his poem "To Chao Chongzhi"). Evidently, those poetry critics are keen to elevate the communicative function of ancient Chinese poetry while subduing its expressive one. And more evident is what Wei Liaoweng of the Song Dynasty, also known as Heshan, in *An Epilogue to the Poem by Kang Jie* of his *The Complete Collection of the Works by Heshan*, stated:

> In versification, when his meaning is unmistakable and pertinent, the words a poet uses, and the verses composed of them, naturally correspond and fit, and he need not exert himself in this respect. Otherwise, no matter how he weighs words for a verse, his verses as such, as a result of failing to communicate meanings, are, like the singing of a certain autumnal insect or the charm of a certain morning fungi, are ephemeral and pathetic. So he should be aware of what is more important for his poems.

This discussion is all about how vernacularization of the language of Song Dynasty poetry corresponds to the poets', as well as poetry critics', notion of poetry being a vehicle by virtue of which the poet ("I") communicates a belief, a moral, or an idea to the reader ("you"), rather than a channel of expressing the poet's ("my") intuitive perception and sentimentalities. The pursuit of such a correspondence is compelling.

Worthy of note here is that in the course of vernacularization of the language in their poems, Song Dynasty poets do not just revert, in the opinion of some ancient Chinese poetry critics, to the poetic language of ancient Chinese poetry prior to emergence of Recent Style poetry but also assimilate the vernacular language of their time. In fact, as is shown, when it comes to the former, some Song Dynasty poets, in order to break away from the constraints of hackneyed Tang Dynasty poetic language, tended to use it with a vengeance, insofar as it should turn out to be irksomely esoteric, which certainly would not facilitate but impede communication between "I" and "you", as in the case of some of the poems by Huang Tingjian. Comparatively, absorption of the vernacular language of their time in versification (another kind of linguistic defamiliarization) is the right alternative for Song Dynasty poets to effectively communicate their beliefs, morals, ideas, and so on to the reader. After all, the vernacular language feels much plainer and far more natural, which was also what Song Dynasty poets aesthetically sought, than language used a long time back in ancient Chinese poetry before the Southern Dynasties, despite its being vernacular by the then-current standards. Thus Song Dynasty poems were imbued with verve, intimacy, and appeal, which were thought to have been lost in Recent Style poetry. To support this argument, let us read three Song Dynasty poems as follows:

mo yan xia ling bian wu nan /
(Do not say that once descending, a mountain climber then begins an effortless leg /)
zhuan de xing ren cuo xi huan.
(Many mountain climbers are so happily beguiled but end in pains.) zheng ru wan shan quan zi li /
(Once you place yourselves among ranges and ranges of mountains /)
yi shan fang guo yi shan lan.
(There will be one after another mountain in the way ahead that you have to overcome)

(Yang Wanli)

you si hao dang sui chun guang /
(Numerous ethereal gossamers glint in the vernal light /)
yi lai wei feng gu gu chang.
(They are often seen stretching out by virtue of gentle breezes.)
ji du ying sheng liu yu zhu /
(Several times invitation from chirping orioles seems to have stayed them /)
you sui fei xu guo dong qiang.
(Finally they choose to float away, with catkins, over the eastern walls)

(Zhang Shi)

ban mu fang tang yi jian kai /
(A half-mu pond [mu, a Chinese measurement unit of area], like a square mirror, appears in sight /)
tian guang yun ying gong pai huai.
(Reflections of celestial light and clouds together keep undulating all the time.)
wen qu na de qing ru xu /
(How can the pond be this pure and crystal clear /)

wei you yuan tou huo shui lai.
(It is just that the welling source springs keep it so)

(Zhu Xi)

Who would mistake them for the poems by Tang Dynasty poets, even if their authors and titles were concealed?

8.2. From vernacular Song Dynasty poetry to vernacular modern Chinese poetry

Song Dynasty poetry seems much less than a rival with the poetry of the Tang Dynasty for glorious reputation.

The function of Song Dynasty poetry, as said previously, is communicating "my" (the poet's) beliefs, morals, ideas, and so on to correspond with the development of its vernacular language, which, due to its customarily syntactical word order as a result of the interspersion of "xu zi" words or phrases and thus clear legibility, outperforms the literary language of the Recent Style poetry of the Tang Dynasty in terms of meticulousness, lucidity, and smoothness. Consequently, in stark contrast to "tension"-charged Tang Dynasty poetry, whose juxtaposed imagery can dazzle the reader and whose equivocality can puzzle the reader, who thus has to deal with these aspects without the leisure of appreciating, bit by bit, what "I" (the poet) intends to communicate, Song Dynasty poetry, owing to its legible vernacularized language and clear-cut logical connections, communicates unequivocally what "I" (the poet) intends to, even including the subtle nuances, to the reader. That is why Weng Fanggang, in his *The Commentaries on Poetry at the Rocky Edge of an Islet*, observed:

> Into the Song Dynasty, the Chinese poetry became more logical and meticulous, which should be attributed to the focus of the Song Dynasty poets on deliberate communication of their thoughts in a reasonable and legible manner. This is what the Tang Dynasty poets had failed to command.

But, on the other hand, Song Dynasty poetry, due to its transparency and lucidity simply for the sake of communication of meaning, thus loses the mystical appeal of the Recent Style poetry of the Tang Dynasty in terms of obscurity in meaning, the reader's considerable autonomy in imagination and association, non-abstract vivid yet involved depiction, and so on altogether. Therefore, not just in the Song Dynasty but henceforward, Song Dynasty poetry has often been denounced as anything but poetry. For example, Liu Kezhuang of the Song Dynasty, also known as Houzhuang, in his *Compendium of the Works by Houzhuang*, said:

> This Reign of His Majesty sees many more essayists than poets. This is because those who claim to have been composing poems have actually been writing essays, as their so-called poems reads like nothing but the rhymed essays about social or government issues.

More such harsh or harsher words are heard from later ancient Chinese poetry critics. Take some poetry critics of the Ming Dynasty, for instance. Li Mengyang, also known as Kongtongzi, asked: "Now that the Song Dynasty poets were interested mainly in promulgation of their beliefs. . . . Why did they then do so simply in essay instead of in poetry?" (See his *Collected Poems by Kongtongzi*.) I would say that he sounds somewhat euphemistic. He Jingming, also known as Dafu, bluntly concluded that the Song Dynasty was devoid of poetry of any kind. (See his *A Collection of the Works by He Dafu*.) Tu Long resented what he believed was a fact: "What have the poets, in the Song Dynasty and henceforth, done to poetry? They have decimated the soul of poetry". (See his *A Collection of my Works at the County of Youquan*.) True, there are also certain ancient Chinese poetry critics who recommended Song Dynasty poetry; even so, they failed to inform the reader about its intrinsic virtue and validate their recommendation. In that case, and ever eclipsed by Tang Dynasty poetry, Song Dynasty poetry would shine for a time but be dark most of the time, much less set a trend for the development of the Chinese poetry over hundreds of years to come. In contrast to Song Dynasty poetry, compared to the moon, Tang Dynasty poetry, likened to the sun, has ever been shining, and, overwhelmed by the brilliance of the latter, even allegedly revolutionary modern Chinese poets such as Huang Zunxian and Xia Zengyou did not go so far as to "revolutionize" the Recent Style to attain their goal of, in their words, "I am free to write what I want to speak"; rather, they did no more than deck the pattern of Recent Style poetry with certain foreign nouns or images.

It is not until the early years of the twentieth century, when a campaign of promoting vernacular modern Chinese poetry was launched by a cohort of modern Chinese poets in order to liberate versification from the yoke of archaic style, that the significance of vernacular Song Dynasty poetry was recognized and its spirit was revived. And this is an interesting, and historic, occurrence in the development of Chinese poetry.

What linguistically differentiates vernacular modern Chinese poetry from the Recent Style poetry of the Tang Dynasty? Kang Baiqing, a modern Chinese poetry critic, who upheld the banner of "Be a literary iconoclast", could never answer it more clearly than in his essay entitled "My View of the New Poetry":

In general, the poets of the old style poetry rigidly follow the tonal and metrical schemes, thus constrained by it; besides, they are particular about whatever concerns the elegant rhetoric. Conversely, the poets of the new style poetry are keen to be free in versification, so they hate to be bound by the rigid tonal and metrical schemes, they do not want to contrive rhymes, they discard the contrived rhetoric, and they use the vernacular instead of the literary language, in their poems.

Kang's remarks could also summarize the features of vernacular modern Chinese poetry of his time. Hu Shi, in a jocular way, once said of his early experiment with vernacular modern Chinese poetry that his poems could be likened to a Chinese woman's feet that were restored to what they should have been after being from the perennial binding in wraps (a gender-discriminatory custom in old China). His poems back then, such as "Two Butterflies" and "The Morning of the Hudson River: a Reply to Shuyong", unavoidably contained more or less the attributes of the Recent Style poetry of the Tang Dynasty, especially of the five-word-a-verse eight-verse "lv shi" poetry. Even so, unlike Huang Zunxian's some poems which had been embedded merely with certain transliterated outlandish names without truly metamorphosing into the vernacular modern Chinese ones, the said Hu Shi's poems were much closer to the prosaic style due to their vernacular language. This is exemplified by "bu zhi wei shen me (I didn't know why)/yi ge hu fei huan (One of them suddenly flew back)" and "ye wu xin shang tian (It didn't want to fly up either)/tian shang tai gu dan (It was so solitary in the sky)" in "Two Butterflies". Although apparently the said verses adopt the archaic five-word pattern, each of them, not restricted to the pattern of either "two words + two words + one word" or "two words + one word + two words", as previously discussed, is syntactically unrestricted, with the otherwise juxtaposed images in "shi zi" words or phrases separated at intervals by "xu zi" words or phrases, like "tai (so)", a sheer spoken "xu zi" word. In this way, the poet vividly describes his inner response to the externalities. The other case is his "ting wo gao su ni (Let me tell you)", "zhao xia jian san liao (Glowing morning clouds are gradually dispersing)", and "lao ren tang neng lai (If Lao Ren [Mr Ren; referring to 'you', i.e., Shuyong] should come over here)/he ni fen yi ban (I'd share them, fifty-fifty, with you)" in "The Morning of the Hudson River: a Reply to Shuyong"; in the same way, despite the sparse literary words thereof, these verses, almost in every aspect, such as tone, cadence, wording, and grammar, are vernacularized.

And this style was also adopted by other modern Chinese poets at the time who produced many such poems.

Cases in point are "wo *he* yi zhu *ding* gao *de* shu bing pai li *zhuo* (I'm standing, side by side, with an extremely tall tree)/*que* mei you kao *zhuo* (But not leaning on it)" (from Shen Yinmo's poem "A Moonlit Night"), "wu zi *li* long *zhuo* lu huo (Inside the room building up was the fire in a stove)/lao ye fen fu kai chuang mai shui guo (The master was ordering a servant to open the window to buy some fruits)/shuo 'tian qi bu len huo *tai* re (Complaining: 'It's not cold while the fire is too hot')/*bie ren* ta kao huai *liao* wo'('Don't let it be like this and scorch me')" (from Liu Bannong's poem "Divided Only by A Window Frame of Paper"), "ni kan, *na* qian qian *de* tian he (You look at that very shoal river across the skies)/*ding ran shi* bu *shen* kuan guang (It must be not very broad)/wo *xiang na* ge *zhuo* he *de* niu lang zhi nv (I suspect that the herd-boy and the weaving-girl [A Chinese myth has it that two lovers were separated by the celestial river, i.e., the Milky Way], though parted by it,)/*ding neng gou* qi *zhuo* niu er lai wang (sure can still visit with each other by riding their oxen)" (from Guo Moruo's "A Celestial Thoroughfare"), and "*ou ran* ting zhu *liao* yuan jian ([She] occasionally stopped the motion of her plump shoulders)/mo mo di di chui fen jing (And gently bent her tender nape)/*hao xiang zai* jie shui zhong jian (As if over a pool of water in the middle of the street)/zi gu ping ting de gu ying (to appreciate her own single slender reflection)" (from Tian Han's "A Tune for Spring Rain Falling on the Eastern Capital"). Notice the italicized words, which are either "xu zi" words or phrases that clearly indicate logical relationships in terms of time, space, and the like, or "shi zi" words or phrases that do not, as they do in the Recent Style poetry of the Tang Dynasty, depict images. Such words as these appear more and more in the verses of vernacular modern Chinese poetry, and they combine to unequivocally and minutely tell the reader how the poets mentally react to externalities and what they want to communicate.

Thus, in the case of these verses, their word order still approximates that of small talk; the poets' thought flow is transparent; the poetic images are like dots that can effortlessly be connected to convey the intended meanings; and the poems, both in particular and in general, are easy to grasp. To reinforce this argument, let us look at more examples such as two verses in Hu Shi's "A Whim": "wo ruo zhen ge hai ke gu de xiang si (If I should be afflicted with ingrained lovesickness)/bian yi fen zhong rao bian di qiu san qian wan zhuan (I would be orbiting the globe thirty million times a minute)", which read like the poet talking to himself or to the reader without a pause, and "re ji la (Too hot)! Geng mei you yi dian feng (Worse, there's not a slightest stir of wind)! na you qing you xi de ma ying hua xu (Those light thin tassels of rhododendron flowers over there)/dong ye bu dong yi dong (Show no sign at all of motion)" in Hu Shi's proudest poem, "An Arrested Star", "a truly brand-new style poem" in his words, whose salient features are repetition of the same word "dong [motion]", colloquial expressions such as "re ji la (too hot)", prosaic punctuation, and word order like that in a conversation, in which the poet starts with his sensation of heat, then describes a windless ambience outdoors to accentuate the sensation, and finally attests to it with the image of absolutely still flowers, all the way with each verse, and even almost each word, centring around the heat, without ellipsis or transposition that would interrupt the process of the reader's appreciation or cause ambiguity. A further example is "yi tiao xiao he (Here is a rivulet), wen wen de xiang qian liu dong (which is steadily flowing onward)/jing guo de di fang (Past sections), liang mian quan shi wu hei de tu (whose banks are covered with sheer pitch-black soil)/sheng man liao hong de hua (Overgrown with red flowers), bi lv de ye (green leaves), huang de guo shi (yellow fruits)" in "A rivulet" by another modern Chinese poet, Zhou Zuoren, a poem elevated to the status of the herald of the birth of the new poetry in its truest sense, which is thought to have epitomized vernacular modern Chinese poetry in every aspect, such as parts of speech like subject, predicate, object, attribute, complement, and adverb, each of which is in its right place as grammatically required from beginning to end, which is contrary to, say, the Recent Style poetry of the Tang Dynasty, whose verses, owing to ellipses and transpositions, turn out to be ungrammatically fragmented.

This is vernacular modern Chinese poetry. Apart from the previously mentioned, it discards altogether the rules of "jue ju" and "lv shi" poems, such as the number of words within a verse as well as verses within a poem, tonal and metrical schemes, patterns of antithetical symmetry, patterns of a verse like "two words plus one word plus two words" as previously discussed, any "shi yan" word, and the like. In a word, vernacular modern Chinese poetry in its truest sense, in defiance of the thousand-year-long established aesthetic principles for Chinese poetry, unrestrained almost in every aspect, reads like casual talk. (See Sun Zuoyun's *On the Poetry of the Modern School*.) It thus is regarded as historic liberation of the linguistic style of Chinese poetry. (See Hu Shi's *A Talk on the New Poetry: A Major Occurrence during the Past Eight Years*.) For further examples, let us read a part of Zhou Zuoren's "Two Snow Sweepers": "yin chen chen de tian qi (It was gloomy)/xiang fen yi ban bai xue (The powder-like snow)/xia de man tian bian di (Was swirling between Heaven and Earth, only to have covered the ground far and near)/tian an men wai bai mang mang de ma lu shang (On a snow-covered avenue outside of Tianan Gateway)/quan mei you che liang zong ying (Even the ghost of a vehicle of any kind was not in sight)/zhi you liang ge ren zai na li sao xue (Except for two persons who were sweeping snow over there)" and part of Hu Shi"s "A Rickshaw Puller": "ke wen che fu (The passenger asked the rickshaw puller): 'ni jin nian ji sui (how old are you)? La che la liao duo shao shi (and how long have you done this job)?'/ che fu da ke (The puller replied): 'jin nian shi liu (I'm sixteen now), la guo san nian che le (I've done the job for three years), ni lao bie duo yi (You're in the safe hands, sir)". Zhou's and Hu's verses are not musically rhythmic or rhymed, much less antithetically symmetric, in composition. So the reader may wonder whether they are poems or vernacular recounts. Their befuddlement is understandable. But Cheng Fangwu, a modern Chinese poet, was unpermissive; in his *Defence of Poetry*, he derided, for example, "Goodbye to My Peking University Classmates", a poem by Kang Baiqing, for being simply an essay in the guise of verse. The funniest case in point could be the publication of "Adorable", a lyrical essay by Xie Wanying, a modern woman Chinese writer (better known by her pen name "Bingxin"), by an editor responsible for the literary supplement of the *Morning Newspaper* who had it versified as a poem, which certainly was not what Bingxin had originally intended, but, curiously, she acquiesces to, and, more curiously, Bingxin decided, from then on, to set aside part of her time and energy for composing poems. The editor's mistake and Bingxin's acquiescence to it prove that what should be an essay and what should be a poem, at the time, could be hard to distinguish.

8.3 The common notion shared by the poets of the Song Dynasty and modern China of the function of poetry

Indeed, the language of vernacular modern Chinese poetry totally violates the linguistic rules for Recent Style poetry which started from the Qi and the Liang periods of the Southern Dynasties. But is such a violation "unprecedented"? To the revolutionary vernacular modern Chinese poetry experimenters at the beginning of the twentieth century, it was so in the history of Chinese poetry, and they believed it had shattered the linguistic chains that had bound past Chinese poets. So, understandably, they were so thrilled that they used overblown rhetoric to express their ecstasy with their liberation of poetic language and to strike wonderment in the public. But, to any rational Chinese poetry critic, a new poetic language relates, more or less, to an old one. So, the language of vernacular modern Chinese poetry cannot possibly emerge from nowhere; it must have its root somewhere. Those proud vernacular modern Chinese poetry experimenters, as well as their followers, however, are reluctant to admit or choose to simply ignore it; otherwise, they fear, their reputation of being the founders of an allegedly brand-new language for modern Chinese poetry can be compromised. But the fact that the language of their poetry has a precursor is undeniable. In that case, they try to identify the language of their poetry either with that of Chinese folk ditties or ballads, whose folksiness, they assume, makes their poetic language more revolutionary, or with that of Western poetry, such as the sonnet, rondeau, and blank verse, whose outlandishness, they assume, adds to the anti-traditionalness of their poetic language. They do so for a reason. After all, the language either of Chinese folk ditties or ballads or of Western poetry has more or less effect over that of vernacular modern Chinese poetry, but, it should be pointed out, not to the core. In fact, the de facto precursor, essentially, of the language of early modern Chinese poetry is that of vernacular Song Dynasty poetry. Then why do those early vernacular modern Chinese poetry experimenters so refuse to admit this kind of affinity? Is it just that vernacular Song Dynasty poetry is a part of ancient Chinese poetry, so they fear that to admit such affinity is to admit not cutting the umbilical cord of the language of their poetry attaching it to ancient Chinese poetry? Or is it just that Song Dynasty poetry is traditionally seen as inferior to that of the Tang Dynasty, so they fear that to admit indebtedness to the poets of the Song Dynasty in terms of poetic language is to admit the mediocrity of the language of their own poetry? Answers to these questions are yet to be known. But one thing is certain: however they attempt not to connect the language of their poetry with that of vernacular Song Dynasty poetry, their attempt surely is to no avail, on the ground that they themselves are immersed in the world of ancient Chinese poetry, especially of vernacular Song Dynasty poetry, which happens to come into vogue of their time, before being intent on experimenting with their vernacular modern Chinese poetry. So it is futile, even if they hate to admit the affinity. The truth is that vernacularization of the language of the modern Chinese poetry at the beginning of the twentieth century is rooted in such an affinity. So what should be done here is find out about what it is that is shared by poets of the two historical periods that are far removed from each other and compels both to vernacularize their poetic language, the characteristics of the time notwithstanding.

It is widely argued that because its language is vernacularized, early modern Chinese poetry reads as prosaic. Feiming, a modern Chinese literary researcher, in his *A Lecture on the New Poetry*, said that "We are writing poems, but in the language of prose. They are what is called 'free poetry'". In his *On the Content and the Form of the New Poetry*, Li Guangtian, Fei's contemporary, judged that "(A common feature of today's new poems is that) they are prosified". But only Hu Shi candidly admitted that the language of vernacular modern Chinese poetry should be traced back to that of vernacular Song Dynasty poetry:

The Song Dynasty poems read simply like vernacular interlocutions.
(*The History of the Vernacular Literature*)

I firmly believe that the development from the Recent Style poetry of the Tang Dynasty to the vernacular Song Dynasty poetry in the history of ancient Chinese poetry is just the change from one linguistic style to another, which is that the latter reads more like an essay or a speech.... The most significant contribution by those prominent Song Dynasty poets to the Chinese poetry is that they broke the fetters of the tonal and metrical schemes that had constrained the poets ever since the Southern Dynasties and vernacularized the language for their poetry.

(Driven to Rebel: Initiation of the Revolutionization of the Chinese Literature)

Hu confessed that, influenced as early as in 1915 by the vernacularized language of Song Dynasty poetry that he had read, he thus proposed use of vernacular language and removal of any ornate wording in versification. His proposal is encompassed in this poem, which can be understood to be his declaration of reformation of the language of the poetry of his time: "shi guo ge ming he zi shi (What should revolutionization of the ancient Chinese poetry start with)/yao xu zuo shi ru zuo wen (The first and foremost is to vernacularize its language)/zuo lou fen shi sang yuan qi (Ornateness can reduce the power of poetry to nil)/mao si wei bi shi zhi chun (True versification is about not form but content)/xiao ren xing wen po da dan (Forgive me, a humble man, for such a bold proposal)/zhu gong yi yi jie ren ying (Each one of you, respected gentlemen, the cream of the cream)/yuan gong lu li mo xiang xiao (Let's strive together rather than laugh at each other)/wo bei bu zuo fu ru sheng (Not to be bound by the archaic poetic language)". He proposes this absolutely not off the top of his head; on the contrary, he bases his proposal on then-ignored fact. At the time, although its impact had considerably diminished by the 1910s, Song Dynasty poetry was still emulated by a good many modern Chinese poets, to the point that even Du Fu's poems, by comparison, were dismissed as "decadent". (See the modern Chinese poet Liu Yazi's *Preface to the Poetry by Hu Jichen*.) Such zeal was perceived by Hu Shi, who, in his *The History of Literature in the Mandarin*, said that

> In the recent decades, the Song Dynasty poetry has been enthusiastically discussed and emulated . . . til today when most of the Chinese poets are promoting what characterize the Song Dynasty poetry.

Hu's perspective, as well as his aforementioned proposal, points to the affinity between vernacular Song Dynasty poetry and vernacular modern Chinese poetry, which thus dictates the role of the former as the precursor of the latter. This is the case indeed to any Chinese poetry critic only if he or she fair-mindedly and objectively evaluates the contribution of Song Dynasty poets to the development of the language of ancient Chinese poetry and scrutinizes the function and linguistic style of vernacular Song Dynasty and modern Chinese poetry.

The affinity in question certainly refers to their vernacularized language. But worthy of special note is what compels them to vernacularize the poetic language: their common notion of the function of poetry. Like their predecessors in vernacular Song Dynasty poetry, the founders of vernacular modern Chinese poetry also valued clear communication to the reader of their beliefs, their morals, their ideas, and so on. One of their deep-rooted beliefs is what Maodun, a modern Chinese novelist, in his *On the Early Vernacular Modern Chinese Poetry*, advocated: "substantialism", which, much more inclusive than "realism", means what Hu Shi suggests: "The content should be substantial". In 1916, Hu Shi, in his *A Letter to Chen Duxiu* (Chen Duxie, one of the torchbearers for the then *New Literary Campaign*), proposed eight points for the campaign of literary revolution, the fifth, seventh, and eighth of which touch respectively on revolutionizing the grammatical structure, using "my own" language to create "my own" poems without imitating ancient ones, and substantializing content. In 1917, in his actually well-thought-out *My Ill-Considered Proposals for Literary Reform*, he had these points reordered as follows:

1. substantializing the content;
2. using "my own" language to create "my own" poems without imitating ancient ones;
3. revolutionizing the grammatical structure.

Re-ordering this way clearly shows that the content, to those vernacular modern Chinese poetry experimenters, must take precedence over the form. To second Hu Shi's proposals, Chen Duxiu published his *On Revolutionizing Literature* to radically promulgate what he summed up as three –isms, which specifically are about, in the case of vernacular modern Chinese poetry, how to offer each and every Chinese citizen poems that feel intimate to them and touch their heart; how to substantialize the content from a new perspective and in a genuine manner; and how to create simple, plain, and popular poems that concern the social issues of the time. And, doubtless, the main concern is how to substantialize the content of a poem.

In the case of early vernacular modern Chinese poetry, to substantialize its content is not simply to make a poem out of a tale, expose social issues, or propound philosophical –isms by virtue of a poem. The presence of "I", the poet, in the guise of sentiment, aspiration, belief, ethos, perception, and so on in his poem must also be strongly and distinctly felt. This starkly contrasts what Recent Style poetry of the Tang Dynasty does with "I": in the case of the latter, whatever concerns "I" is, as previously discussed, overshadowed or, at best, embodied, but allegorically, associatively or symbolically, in its juxtaposed images, regardless of whether the reader is frustrated with its being obscure, equivocal, elusive, or simply abstruse. A modern Chinese scholar, Yu Pingbo, through his *The Opinions Held by Four Main Schools of the New Poetry*, proclaimed that

> For a poet of our time, a certain ism constitutes the soul of his poetry. . . .
> A poem of our time will, if devoid of its soul, be an embellished empty, which neither offers food for thought nor inspires the reader. A poem as such is a mere meaningless entertainment.

Again, in his *Driven to Rebel: Initiation of the Revolutionization of the Chinese Literature*, Hu Shi condemned the archaic poetry of his time for its defects as having a body without a soul and having a florid form without substantial content, which result in meaningless resonance and rhetoric. Thus poetry in a new language was called for so that the experimenters' notion of the function of poetry as a vehicle of effectively and efficiently communicating content to the reader could be realized. In these circumstances, early twentieth-century vernacular modern Chinese poems appeared by such avant-garde poets as Hu Shi (see his "A Rickshaw Puller" about a low-class labourer's hardships, "Two Butterflies" about a solitary life journey, and "Pigeons" about humans' heteronomy contrary to pigeons' freedom), Liu Bannong (see his "Divided Only by a Window Frame of Paper" about the inequality between the rich in cosy warmth and the deprived out in the deadly cold, "An Enslaved Apprentice" about a sorrowful apprenticeship, "Fallen Leaves" about the ephemerality of life, and "A Lass by the River" about romantic love), Zheng Zhenduo (see his "Mother" about our indebtedness to our mothers for their unselfish maternal love), Lu Xun (see his "Cupid" about mismatched lovers and "Humans and Time" about what past, now, and future mean), Zhou Zuoren (see his "My Bygone Life" about the lapse of a part of lifetime), and Yu Pingbo (see his "Mournful" about nostalgic inspiration). "I", almost omnipresent in those poems, keeps communicating "I"'s sense and sensibility or rather what "I" has experienced, felt, and contemplated *both* about and *for* the human world, in an educative manner, to the reader, who certainly is expected to empathize with "I". This is what Recent Style poetry of the Tang Dynasty lacks, and it is criticized by Hu Shi, who points out that it fails to establish the necessary communion between the poet and reader (see his *The History of Literature in the Mandarin*), which, in contrast, is just what the avant-garde modern Chinese poets strive for. And, back then, if they hoped to succeed in this respect, they would certainly have to vernacularize their poetic language. For that poetic language, due to its plainness, naturalness, and friendliness, has easy access to the reader's heart.

Here, let us see first what Liu Bannong, in his *My View of How to Reform Literature*, says:

> Words that are alleged to be soulless actually have their soul, only that it is felt not through themselves but through what they represent. Therefore, we need not . . . contrive words only to compromise what they represent. A work of literature has its soul which lives in its writer's mind, so its writer has to primarily inject into his words which make his work of literature his genuine thoughts, genuine emotions, and genuine aspirations. His work of literature as such can then be deemed genuine and worthy. . . . If his work of literature is soulless, however crafted its wording can be, it still is nonsensical. In that case, how can he claim to have created a work of literature?

Then let us quote Maodun, again from his *On the Early Vernacular Modern Chinese Poetry*:

> Content determines form. . . . The poetic form must be as free as possible. It is there not for the sake of a show-off. If a poem takes any form, its form

must not be artificial but natural. For a sound substantialized poem does not allow for any formal show-off. In a word, the poetic form must not become a barrier.

What both Liu Bannong and Maodun argue for or against is, apart from what has been discussed, in Hu Shi's words, to "shatter the shackles put on the muse and give her full freedom to compose her poetry out of whatever is at hand and to express whatever she wants to", which is "liberation of the poetic style" in its truest sense.

What compels this kind of liberation, as I have discussed, is the vernacular modern Chinese poetry experimenters' notion of the function of poetry of communicating the substantialized content, which is not just a revival but also the acme of the spirit of the poets of vernacular Song Dynasty poetry. No wonder that, from the perspective of Hu Shi, Qian Xuantong, and Chen Duxiu, Song Dynasty poets play the intermediary role of inheriting their predecessors' poetic legacy and, more importantly, inspiring, for example, poets of early vernacular modern Chinese poetry, in the history of Chinese poetry. On that score, they are insightful indeed.

8.4. Refinement by emulating the rhetoric of Recent Style poetry in early vernacular modern Chinese poetry

In the history of China, the May 4th Movement (1919) is a far-reaching event on many fronts. For example, it brought about a change in the mindset of Chinese literary society, which, in the words of Lu Xun (see his speech *A China without a True Voice*), was:

> We must speak the modern language. This language is our own language. It lives. We must use it to express our thoughts and feelings, directly and plainly.

Poets back then felt that they shouldered a great responsibility, by way of their vernacular modern poetry, of publicizing the new beliefs, educating the public about the new social ethics, voicing their resentment of outdated and reactionary institutions, and rallying the public under their banner. So they were compelled to write their poems in a simple, plain, and familiar language, which was to the taste of the public at the time, to achieve these goals. This called for liberation of poetic language from archaic constraints, hence vernacular modern Chinese poetry, which was believed to cover more subject matter and embody much acuter observations, much loftier aspirations, and much more complicated sentiments. (See Hu Shi's *A Talk on the New Poetry: A Major Occurrence during the Past Eight Years*.) But, on the other hand, the merits of which Hu Shi spoke highly would turn out to be responsible for diminishing the poetic flair of vernacular modern Chinese poetry. This is because a vernacular modern Chinese poem is tasked with too much to afford to take care with, for example, refinement and subtlety, like an already tired, out-of-breath hiker who cannot afford to take in the views around him or her.

Indeed, all that the vernacular modern Chinese poetry pioneers did is let the readers unmistakably know what they wanted them to know, immediately, giving little or even no consideration to what should be required of a poem in its truest sense. That is why Du Heng, one of the poets of the time, in his *Preface to the Poetry by Dai Wangshu*, recollects thus: "At the time . . . we as poets would speak or simply roar out each and every one of our poems, in a candid and torrential way. Such was the hallmark of our poems".

So, understandably, when crude and shallow were two epithets for early modern vernacular Chinese poetry, it would naturally be criticized even by contemporary poets themselves, such as Cheng Fangwu and Mu Mutian. In his *Defense of Poetry*, Cheng Fangwu harshly ridiculed poems by such poets as Hu Shi (like his "He", "My Son", and "Unkillable")", Kang Baiqing (like his "Goodbye to my Peking University Classmates"), Yu Pingbo (like his "Poems Written at Random while Staying at a Mountain" and "A Fool in the Sea"), Zhou Zuoren (like his "A Scene on a Road"), and Xu Yunuo (like his "The Future Flowery Garden", a collection of his poems), calling for "defense of the royal palace of Chinese poetry". Mu Mutian, in his *A Talk on Poetry: A Letter to Moruo*, acidly accused Hu Shi of being the chief culprit of plunging Chinese poetry into disaster because of his dogma, "The language of today's Chinese poetry must be vernacularized", for vernacular modern Chinese poetry. Their condemnations exerted due impact. When they felt less burdened by their social and moral responsibilities than ever before, when they finally became level headed, the Chinese poets of the time began to re-think the nature of their poetry as a literary art. Consequently, as a significant part of their poetry, its language regained its due status in versification. This is evinced by those poets' endeavouring to reform their poetic language by both maintaining the lucidity and intimacy of the vernacular language and reviving the aesthetic appeal in terms of techniques like tone, cadence, form, imagery, and subtle nuances. In this context, the linguistic merits of, say, Recent Style poetry of the Tang Dynasty were, undeclaredly, reintroduced in composition of vernacular modern Chinese poetry. This, ironically, seemed to have redressed the wrong done to Hu Xiansu, a staunch opponent of vernacular modern poetry, who, in his *On Reforming Chinese Literature*, had argued, "A poet ought not to write his poem totally in the vernacular language. The evidence for my argument can be found not just in the Chinese but also the Western poems". Indeed, the situation is that, in retrospect, even some of the poets of vernacular modern poetry began to take Hu Xiansu's stance. For example, Yu Pingbo came to realize that "The vernacular language must not be seen as the absolutely right linguistic device for versification" (see his *The Opinions Held by Four Main Schools of the New Poetry*); Guo Moruo, in his *On Rhythm*, acknowledged that "The good of the Recent Style poetry is that, on top of its poeticalness, it produces a musical effect"; Wen Yiduo, in his *The Tonal and Metrical Schemes of Poetry*, conceded to recognize and recommend "the beauty of the antithetical symmetry both between verses and between stanzas"; and Xu Zhimo, in his *To Suspend Publication of 'Poetry' Supplement*, simply "confess[ed] that we have accepted the practices by the Recent Style poets". As a result, the status of language in Recent Style poetry was, albeit sheepishly, reinstated, with a view to ameliorating

182 *Chinese poetry from the Song Dynasty to modern style*

the language of vernacular modern Chinese poetry. There thus emerged, for example, the Crescent School, whose poets sought to refine and musicalize their poems through tonal and metrical schemes, and the Symbolism School, whose poets enhanced their poetic images by tapping into the connotations of words to vivify their symbolic poems. Worthy of special note in their efforts is that the linguistic style of vernacular modern Chinese poetry inclined more and more to the literary. Literary language, or rather ingeniously contrived words instead of plain, insipid everyday words, was reused, with a view to deepening and subtilizing the otherwise overly obvious vernacular modern Chinese poems, which, just as Zhou Zuoren said in a preface written for a collection of Liu Bannong's poems "Cracking the Whip", is comparable to a crystal-clear marble, too transparent where cloudiness is preferable and hence lacking enticing mysteriousness. Zhou's observation can also be understood to have evinced poets' retrospection on the damage done as a result of usage of crude colloquial language to vernacular modern Chinese poetry.

To exemplify this reversion to the rhetoric of Recent Style poetry, here are several extracts from vernacular modern Chinese poems that were published in the wake of this retrospection:

ben xiang zai dong tian jiu wang diao ni /
(It did occur to me that I'd have put you out of my mind /)
xiang shu zhi wang diao ta de ye zi /
(As branches disremember ever having their leaves that have fallen /) /
ye zi ye jiu yong yuan hua cheng ni.
(Those leaves will have decomposed into soil.)

                                                          ("A Year" by Fang Weide)

tian tian xia yu /
(Raining on and on, each day /)
zi cong ni zou le.
(Since you departed.)
zi cong ni lai le /
(Since you came here /)
tian tian xia yu.
(Raining on and on, each day.)
liang di you ren yu wo le yi fu ze /
(I'm all too ready to relieve my friends caught in rain even away in two places /)
di san chu mei xiao xi ji yi ba san qu.
(To my friend afar in another place whom I haven't heard from I'll send an umbrella.)

                                                    ("Rain and Me" by Bian Zhilin)

you shi can ye meng hui /
(Haunted, again, by a homesick dream when night was nearing its end /)
zhen pan de shu shou sun le.

(My book by my pillow appeared emaciated.)
Yuan chu zhi lai yi pian gou fei /
(From afar seemed slung here canine barks /)
ji po chen ji de ye wang.
(Only to shatter the mesh of nocturnal stillness)
   ("A Snowy Night" by Wu Qiushan)

gu xian lu hua kai de shi hou /
(The reeds back at my home-place are flowering /)
lv ren de xie gen ran zhuo zheng ni /
(While I, a traveller, have my shoe soles soiled with the mud on the journey /)
nian zhu liao xie gen /
(It is sticking not just to my shoe soles /)
nian zhu liao xin de zheng ni /
(but to my heart /)
ji shi jing ke ai de shou fu shi?
(When will it be wiped away by her fond hands?)
   ("A Traveller's Homesickness" by Dai Wangshu)

xun meng?
(To pursue my dream?)
cheng yi zhi chang gao /
(Pushed by a long pole /)
xiang qing cao geng qing chu man shuo /
(My boat is rowing upstream where the lush grass is a verdant green /)
man zai yi chuan xing hui /
(Carrying a boatful of star luster /)
zai xing hui ban lan li fang ge.
(How I want to sing a song in the glittering luster of stars.)
   ("Adieu, River Cam" by Xu Zhimo)

These verses are composed, at first glance, in seemingly sheer vernacular language without any surprises. This actually is deceiving, for close scrutiny will show the poets' ingenious metaphorization via carefully weighed words, as in the separation of leaves from branches and decomposition of leaves into culturing soil; the symbolism of umbrellas as solicitude for distant friends; an "emaciated" book lying in place of the "emaciated" poet resting his head on a pillow; the barking of dogs and its imagined impact on an imagined net of the dense darkness of a soundless night; adherence of road mud to, literally, a traveller's shoe soles and, figuratively, the poet's heart and his eagerness for his far lover's affectionate hands that would wipe it off; and objectification of a dream that the poet wished to locate by rowing a boat that was being pushed against a long pole. What genius conceits! The reader has to harness his or her faculty of imagination and association to grasp their metaphoric or symbolic innuendoes and nuances.

Such conceits and the attendant subtleties, as a result of emulation of the rhetoric of Recent Style poetry, successfully rectify the defects in early vernacular modern Chinese poetry, whose new features manifest themselves as follows.

First, in the case of these verses, the one and only perspective of "I", the poet, throughout a poem, is replaced by shifting multi-observer perspectives; thus "I" has been discarded, as in Recent Style poetry.

Yet another example is Bian Zhilin's poem "A Snippet" (which originally was an extract from one of his long poems but later taken as a poem independent of its origin):

ni zhan zai qiao shang kan feng jing /
(You're, on the bridge, appreciating the view /)
kan feng jing de ren zai lou shang kan ni /
(Whilst, on the upstairs of a house, a person who was also appreciating the view is appreciating you /)
ming yue zhuang shi liao ni de chuang zi /
(The moon has decked out your window with brilliance /)
ni zhuang shi liao bie ren de meng.
(While you have decked out a person's dream)"

In this poem, the subjects keep changing—"you" (on the bridge), "a person" (on the upstairs of a house), "the moon" (up in the sky), and, again "you" (on the bridge)—and so do the perspectives and the views, with "I", the poet himself, utterly obscured, which shows that the poet could have lost his self, ending up in a state of daze and uncertainty. This poem may easily be associated with Li Shang-yin's "Writing to My Kin and Friends in the North at a Rainy Night". Incidentally, the two poems differ in that although both lack "I", such a lack does not necessarily obliterate the presence of Li as the subject in his poem nor prevent the reader from discerning Li's mind and attitude, whereas, in the case of Bian's poem, absence of "I" as the subject and the multiple other perspectives lead to loss of the poet's self and his attendant bewilderment, which contradicts the practice of highlighting "I" in early vernacular modern Chinese poetry and echoes, in a way, the metaphysical question of whether Zhuangzi has metamorphosed into a butterfly or a butterfly into Zhuangzi in a dream. Besides, the reader of Bian's poem may ask: Who is "I"? What is "I" doing there? And *is* there "I"? The answers will depend on the reader him- or herself to find through intuitive perception and empathy because "I" has been occulted.

To learn more about this respect, we can look at more such verses such as "ren zai hua li (There's me in flowers)/ren zai feng li (There's me in winds)/feng que zai ren xin li (while there're winds in my heart" (from "*Tear-Stain: A Poem Series*" by Liu Daibai), "hua ban er zai tan li (Petals' re afloat on a pond)/ren zai jing li (A mirror reflects a person)/ta zai wo de xin li (She has occupied my heart)/zhi chou wo bu zai ta de xin li (I ruefully wonder if she has ever cherished me at heart)" (from one of "My Poems Entitled Questions" by Kang Baiqing), and "yun zai tian shang (Clouds are in the sky)/ren zai di shang (Human beings are on the land)/ying zai shui shang (Reflections are in the water/ying zai yun shang (And over reflected clouds)" (from "Riverside" by Guo Shaoyu). These verses also show changes in subject and perspective and confusion of spatial and directional relationships, as if on a wild plain that is endless in all directions. This may well be associated with Zen Buddhism's trenchant paradox of the relationship between the image of bamboo and the vision of a person or of which is real, either a beautiful young lady or her disembodied soul, as in *Record of Buddhist Zen Monks, Dharm Talks, and Anecdotes* by Shi Daoyuan, a monk during the Reign of Jingde of the Song Dynasty. Moreover, they could have foretold such Chinese poems as enjoyed a vogue around the end of 1970s and the beginning of 1980s and were notorious for their obscurity, whose verses read, for example "wo jue de (I feel)/ni kan wo shi hen yuan (You are so distant whenever you look at me)/ni kan yun shi hen jin (You are so close whenever you look up at clouds)" (from "Distant and Close" by Gu Cheng, a modern Chinese obscure poet).

All in all, later vernacular modern Chinese poems, through emulation of the rhetoric of Recent Style poetry, are neither restrained to "I" 's perspective nor to a plain and direct way of preaching ideas such as beliefs, thus allowing the reader to construct, mainly by their own intuitive perception and aesthetic sensibility, their own poetic worlds out of them. In this sense, they approximate Recent Style poetry.

This rhetoric is still harnessed by today's poets, who are keen to have the world know their lost state of mind, such as Fei Mo and Zheng Chouyu. Zhuangzi's metaphysical riddle inspiring Fei Mo's "A Daisy·A Butterfly·Zhuangzi", a part of which runs: "die zai xiang ju (A butterfly is missing a daisy)/die guan bu liao hen duo de shi (Not much has ever preoccupied the butterfly)/yi ge bu ting di fei (It is flying, incessantly)/yi ge que na me an jing di kai fang (While it is blossoming, so well in peace) . . . er ju zai guan kan shuang mu wei qi de zhuang zi (But the daisy is watching Zhuangzi whose eyes are opened just slightly)/ju de gan jue yi pian chun bai (Pure white is how the daisy feels) . . . ta wei shen me bu shi yi zhu ju (Why has he not transformed into a daisy)/zhong zai qiu tian de yuan zi li (to be grown in an autumnal garden)/er wo shi ta (While I'd turn into him)/zuo zai yi bian (Sitting close by)/kan die de xi xi (To watch a butterfly frolicking)". An extract from Zheng Chouyu's "A Land of Dream" reads: "yun zai wo de lu shang (Clouds hang over my journey)/zai wo de yi shang (Upon my garment)/wo zai yi ge yin yin de si nian shang (I am living on a certain undefined nostalgia)/gao chu mei you niao hou (High up there is neither any bird's twittering)/mei you hua ye (Nor any flowery dimple)/wo zai yi pian leng leng de meng tu shang (I am living on a cold land of dream)". What should have been predicated change in Fei's verses, so do the perspectives. This indicates the poet's unsettled soul, which roams in no certain direction. Likewise, in Zheng's verses, "I", the poet, is situated in an unrealistic dream, where "I" separates into the flesh and the soul. Thus the otherwise commanding presence of "I" as the one entity is not felt altogether.

Secondly, the logical coherence between verses in the later vernacular modern Chinese poetry is disrupted, such disruption creates missing logical links, and such missing links depend on the reader to use his imagination and association to place where they should have been, thus "tension" as previously discussed develops.

Worthy of mention here is that such vernacular modern Chinese poems do not fall under this category as Xu Zhimo's "A View I Saw on my Train from Shanghai to Hangzhou" ("yi juan yan [A wisp of smoke]/yi pian shan [A cluster of mountains]/ji dian yun cai [a few touches of clouds]/yi dao shui [A meandering river]/yi tiao qiao [A crossing bridge]/yi zhi lu sheng [A rowing oar's sound]/yi lin song [A grove of pine trees]/yi cong zhu [A clump of bamboos], hong ye fen fen [A rain of red leaves])" and Dai Wangshu's "A Traveller's Homesickness" ("zhan shi xing fan de sui yue [What a period when I would rest on the level surface of a rock and eat some food in starlight]/zhou shan zhou shui de xing cheng [What a journey which would be punctuated by mountains and waters by turns])", whose images are juxtaposed and which lack "xu zi" words that indicate either intratextual or intertextual logical relationships, so that they can be identified, in this respect, with the Recent Style, but which are not typical of the vernacular modern Chinese poetry, not to mention that they are few in number. What we are discussing here refer to such vernacular modern Chinese poems as are logically coherent within a verse but seem not so between verses. For example:

ji yue mian jiang di /
(At the moment the moon is slumbering at the bed of the river /)
hai neng yu zi se de lin wei xiao /
(Fancy smiling with the purple woods as well /)
ye su jiao tu zhi ling /
(Those spirits of Jesus' disciples /)
yu (Woe) /
tai duo qing le.
(Too sentimental.)
 ("A Self-Portrait Poem" by Li Jinfa)

yi lv yi lv de xing xiang /
(One waft after another of smelly odor /)
shui bin ku cao huang jing de jin pang /
(Close to a forsaken trail flanked by withered weeds on a waterside /)
... xian nian de bei ai yong jiu de chong jing xin shang /
(The past griefs the persistent longing the young dead before their time /)
ting yi sheng yi sheng de huang liang /
(Hark to one cry after another across the desolation /)
cong gu zhong piao dang piao dang bu zhi na li meng long zhi xiang /
(From an age-old bell drifting away and on to God knows where an unnameable land is /)
cong gu zhong xiao san ru si dong de you yan /
(Its knell is dissipating into whiffs of smoke adrift in the air)
 (Mu Mutian's "The Pale Bong")

Each verse of the two extracts is easy to comprehend. But, when it comes to what relates one verse to the one that immediately follows it, it can be frustrating to work out their logical links, despite such "xu zi" words or phrases as "hai neng (as well)", "tai (too)", and "le (a Chinese tag that does not equate any English word but stands for perfect tense)". This is reminiscent of poems by Li Shangyin and Wen Tingyun, as well as Du Fu's seven-word-a-verse eight-verse "lv shi" poems that read like, according to Hu Shi, "poetic riddles". Poems of this kind are intended, in the main, not to tell the reader something or simply express what is on the author's mind but to build a certain particular ambience, which is beyond description, merely for the reader to sense. In the previously mentioned Li Jinfa and Mu Mutian verses, the seeming logical incoherencies between them, as if encrypted, challenge the reader's discernment to a considerable degree. And this is the case of many other vernacular modern Chinese poems at the time, such as the aforementioned Wu Qiushan's "A Snowy Night" and Bian Zhilin's "Rain and Me" (another extract from this poem reads "wo de you chou sui cao lv tian ya [As grasses are greening all the way to the corners of the world, so my griefs are abiding likewise]/niao an yu chao ma [Can a bird settle when in its nest]?/ren an yu ke zhen [Can a traveller settle when resting his head on a pillow but away from home]?"), as well as poems by contemporary Chinese poets such as Liu Zuci's "feng (Winds), xian dong shu ye (flipping the papers of your book)/li shi zai ni zhang xin (History is in your palms)/zi yu (Self-murmuring)" in his "A Historian" and Zheng Chouyu's "jing yin (A hidden path)/yuan yan (Swallows in a courtyard). li san (An interrupted fences)/yan qu (Curved eaves). zao xiao wei de liang ren (A small stove is warm just enough for two people)/shu xie hong guo san chuang (A tree in red hue slants across three windows)" from his "The Impromptus On an Spring Outing" series. Such verses, despite the images depicted in each of them, miss many intertextual logical links in terms of time, space, cause and effect: in a word, whatever concerns the thought flow of the poets, which are complete in the early vernacular modern Chinese poetry, that the reader will, on behalf of the poets, have to establish by virtue of their imagination. This could be ascribed to the aforementioned conceits or rather emulation of the rhetoric of Recent Style poetry.

Creative utilization of a word and deliberate collocation with other words within a verse poeticize an otherwise insipid, unpoetic vernacular modern Chinese poem. In the seventh chapter of this book, I discussed a verb or an adjective as a "shi yan" and its collocation. Actually, ancient Chinese poets had no idea of what is a part of speech and/or what is an unconventional collocation; they just placed what was supposed to be the right word where it was supposed to be in what was supposed to be a right collocation within a verse, so they had neither, for example, verbalized an adjective for the sake of a "shi yan" nor created a collocation purposefully. In the case of poets of vernacular modern Chinese poetry, this was a different story, for Chinese words were already classified by part of speech and verbal collocation was already conventionalized. So, when they used, for example, an adjective where a verb should have been used and/or collocated a word unconventionally with any other word or phrase within a verse and produced an impressive effect, it should be regarded as a manifestation of their creativity or conceit. For example, "qiao (strike)" in "si shang de yi sheng sheng wan zhong (One bong after another of the bell in the temple)/*qiao* jin liao wo xin fei de shen chu (*Striking* down at the depth of my heart)" (from "On the Walls of Taicheng" by Ma Zihua) (Taicheng, an ancient royal palace) and "qian (tie)" in "xi yu *qian* zhu xing zhou (Drizzles are *tying* the otherwise sailing boat)" (from "An Unnamed Canyon" by Li Jinfa), both of which, in the Chinese language, denote an act in its physical sense, are used here both to metaphorize and also visualize the relationships between the bell and the poet and between the drizzle and the sailing boat for psychological and emotional impact. Admittedly, their use, strictly speaking, did not transcend what the poets of Recent Style poetry had done. Nonetheless, modern Chinese poets, unlike their Tang Dynasty predecessors, who, as has been discussed, had done so unconsciously yet naturally, given the linguistic circumstances of their time, had to consciously bend the well-established linguistic rules to satisfy their needs for linguistic creation or else they could not have created such astounding effects.

Worthy of special mention is this kind of collocation. For example, in "rang meng xiang chui shang liao zheng yi (Let the aroma of dream be blown upon what we have put on for our trek)" (from "A Mountain Trek" by Dai Wangshu), "meng (dream)" is seemingly collocated absurdly with "xiang (aroma)", which should be "chui shang (blown upon) "zheng yi (what we have put on for our trek)"; in "gu zhong piao san zai shui bo zhi jiao jiao" (from "The Pale Bong" by Mu Mutian), the poet uses "gu zhong (an age-old bell)" instead of "zhong sheng (bong)" and, to the reader's amazement, collocates it with "piao san (dissipate)" to show, palpably, the bong fading out "zai shui bo zhi jiao jiao (over a stretch of unstained white waving waters)"; and in "wo jiang you ni de yi yao li/ning shi ta ming mei de shuang yan" (from "Lamplight" by Zhu Ziqing), the poet uses "ni de yi yao (your gleam)", lamplight, to symbolize "ta ming mei de shuang yan (her two bright charming eyes)" that "wo (I)" "jiang (would)" "you ni de yi yao (in your gleam)" "ning shi (gaze at)". Their incredible collocations naturally arouse curiosity in the reader, who in turn contemplates, by virtue not just of common sense but also empathy, what exactly can be in such seemingly nonsensical collocations and, by completing the possible logical links left out by the poets, eventually re-creates a poetic world, to some extent, of his or her own out of the verses.

To sum up, the otherwise rude, insipid early vernacular modern Chinese poetry, through these conceits, is thus more poeticized. Nonetheless, more poeticized vernacular modern Chinese poetry inherits the spirit not of Recent Style poetry but of Song Dynasty poetry, which focuses more on preaching ideas such as beliefs, morals, and revelations, for these conceits derive not from one's spontaneity but from one's rationality. Here we briefly review what characterizes the Recent Style poetry of the Tang Dynasty and vernacular Song Dynasty poetry, respectively. The former, salient for its equivocality and obscurity, mainly as a result of juxtaposition of images with the presence of "I" (the poet), and his exertions therein almost undetectable, is an impressionistic world, whose discovery demands the reader's intuitive perception. In contrast, the latter presents a definite world, even if it is cleverly fabricated of the words and thoughts of one who is superficially a layman but deeply a philosopher, and the reader, on the cues offered by the poet here and there, can access it, gratified by having revealed the world that can be ascribed to the poet's conceits, like wise metaphors, symbolic devices, and euphemisms, which are reminiscent of Zen Buddhists' paradoxes and ironies. A few more words about "conceits". They are the fruits of one's sharp wisdom and reflect, in the case of vernacular modern Chinese poetry, how quickly, coherently, and profoundly the poet can think. Such conceits are embodied in deliberately organized vernacular language. His apparently plain, simple, and even shallow poetic language, reinforced by the aforementioned rhetorical devices, actually carries his philosophical concerns about ideas such as life, society, and the universe, which can be grasped by the reader via inference. This is just what the poets of vernacular modern Chinese poetry in the 1920s and early 1930s pursued, although their cherry-picked words may be reminiscent of the rhetoric of Recent Style poetry, especially of the Tang Dynasty. Their endeavours in this direction set a trend towards contemporary Chinese poetry.

When we say that vernacular modern Chinese poetry should not be equated with contemporary Chinese poetry, it is just that, in terms of language, it was to the poets of that time not as it is to the contemporary poets: the former saw language not as an ontological entity that reflects what is in the universe but as a sheer vehicle or form of communicating their thoughts, their sentiments, and the like. This is understandable: after all, they were not equipped with what their contemporary successors are equipped with, such as the knowledge of the science of contemporary cultural psychology or contemporary philosophy. So, when they expressed their sense of confusion, their sense of being forsaken, their sense of being isolated, and so on, actually expressed their states of mind that were caused by what they had physically and/or mentally experienced, such as despairing of wooing the gentler sex for her love, despondency about the status quo of the society, and failing to have fulfilled a career, unlike their contemporary successors, who will instead look philosophically and transcendentally into, for example, relationships between humans and the universe; among humans themselves; and among the id, the ego, and the superego. Not to mention that development of vernacular modern Chinese poetry was disrupted, just when it was thriving in the middle of the 1930s, by China plunging into a life-and-death crisis. The poets were obliged to join the fight to save their country from perishing by using their poems as a clarion call to rally their compatriots against foreign invasion, and they thus cared about the direct impact rather than the rhetorical conceits of their poems. It was not until decades later, in the 1980s, that development was resumed. Even so, vernacular modern Chinese poetry, which should be deemed the acme of the second revolution of poetic language that had long before been launched by the poets of the Song Dynasty, should also be the overture for the formation of contemporary Chinese poetry as it is, shouldn't it?

References

1. Chen, Shidao 陈师道. "Houshan shihua" 后山诗话 (Houshan's Understanding of Poetry). In *Lidai shihua* 历代诗话 (The Commentaries by the Critics of the Past Dynasties on Poetry), edited by Wenhuan He 何文焕. Beijing: Zhonghua Book Company, 1981.

2. Du, Heng 杜衡. "Wangshucao xu" 望舒草序 (Preface to the Poetry by Wangshu Dai). In *Wangshucao* 望舒草 (The Poetry by Dai Wangshu), by Wangshu Dai 戴望舒. Shanghai: Shanghai Contemporary Book Company, 1933.
3. Fei, Xihuang 费锡璜. "Hanshi zongshuo" 汉诗总说 (An Outline of the Chinese Poetry). In *Qing shihua* 清诗话 (The Poetic Discourses of the Qing Dynasty), edited by Fuzhi Wang 王夫之. Shanghai: Shanghai Classics Publishing House, 1978.
4. Feng, Wenbing 冯文炳. *Tan xinshi* 谈新诗 (A Talk on New Poetry). Beiping: Beiping Xinmin Press, 1944.
5. Guo, Moruo 郭沫若. "Lun jiezou" 论节奏 (On Rhythm). *Chuangzao yuekan* 创造月刊 (Creation Monthly), 3, 1919.
6. He, Shang 贺裳. "Zaijiuyuan shihua" 载酒园诗话 (A Discourse on Poetry at Zaijiu Garden). In *Qing shihua xubian* 清诗话续编 (A Sequel to the Poetic Discourses of the Qing Dynasty), edited by Shaoyu Guo 郭绍虞. Shanghai: Shanghai Classics Publishing House, 1983.
7. Hu, Shi 胡适. *Baihua wenxueshi* 白话文学史 (The History of the Vernacular Literature). Shanghai: The Xinyue Bookstore, 1928.
8. Hu, Shi 胡适. "Bishangliangshan" 逼上梁山 (Driven to Rebel: Initiation of the Revolution in Literature). In *Zhongguo xinwenxue daxi jianshe lilun ji* 中国新文学大系·建设理论集 (The Theories Part of the Anthology of New Chinese Literature). Shanghai: Liangyou Book Company, 1935.
9. Hu, Shi 胡适. *Guoyu wenxueshi* 国语文学史 (The History of Literature in the Mandarin). Beijing: Beijing Wenhua Society, 1927.
10. Hu, Shi 胡适. "Ji Chenduxiu" 寄陈独秀 (A Letter to Chen Duxiu). *Xin Qingnian* 新青年 (The New Youth), 2(2), 1916.
11. Hu, Shi 胡适. "Wenxue gailiang chuyi" 文学改良刍议 (My Ill-Considered Proposals for Literary Reform). *Xinqingnian* 新青年 (The New Youth), 5(2), 1917.
12. Hu, Xiansu 胡先骕. "Zhongguo wenxue gailiang lun" 中国文学改良论 (On Reforming Chinese Literature). *Dongfangzazhi* 东方杂志 (Dongfang Journal), 16, 1919.
13. Hu, Zi 胡仔. *Tiaoxi yuyin conghua* 苕溪渔隐丛话 (Poetic Remarks from the Fisherman Recluse at the Trumpet-Creeper Creek). Beijing: People's Literature Publishing House, 1981.
14. Jakobson, Roman. "Yuyanxue yu shixue" 语言学与诗学 (Closing Statement: Linguistics and Poetics). In *Wenxue jiegouzhuyi* 文学结构主义 (Structuralism in Literature: An Introduction), edited by Robert Scholes, translated by Yu Liu 刘豫, Beijing: SDX Joint Publishing Company, 1988.
15. Kang, Baiqing 康白情. "Xinshi di wojian" 新诗底我见 (My View of the New Poetry). *Shaonian Zhongguo* 少年中国 (Young China), 9(1), 1920.
16. Kobo, Daishi. *Wen jin mi fu lun* 文镜秘府论 (Treatise on the Secret Treasury of Literary Mirror). Beijing: People's Literature Publishing House, 1980.
17. Li, Guangtian 李广田. "Tan xinshi de neirong yu xingshi" 谈新诗的内容与形式 (On the Content and the Form of the New Poetry). *Wenxue pinglun(chuangkanhao)* 文学评论·创刊号 (Literary Review/The First Issue), vol. 1; pp. 14–19, 1943.
18. Liu, Ban 刘攽. "Zhongshan shihua" 中山诗话 (Liu Gongwen's Commentaries on Poetry). In *Lidai shihua* 历代诗话 (The Commentaries by the Critics of the Past Dynasties on Poetry), edited by Wenhuan He 何文焕. Beijing: Zhonghua Book Company, 1981.
19. Liu, Bannong 刘半农. "Wozhi wenxue gailiangguan" 我之文学改良观 (My View of How to Reform Literature). In *Zhongguo xinwenxue daxi jianshe lilun ji* 中国新文学

大系·建设理论集 (The Theories Part of the Anthology of New Chinese Literature). Shanghai: Liangyou Book Company, 1935.
20. Liu, Yazi 柳亚子. "Hujichen shixu" 胡寄尘诗序 (Preface to the Poetry by Hu Jichen). *Nanshe* 南社 (The Southern Society), 4, 1912.
21. Lu, Shiyong 陆时雍. "Shijing zonglun" 诗镜总论 (A Comprehensive Digest of Good Ancient Poems). In *Lidai shihua xubian* 历代诗话续编 (A Sequel to the Commentaries by the Critics of the Past Dynasties on Poetry), edited by Fubao Ding 丁福保. Beijing: Zhonghua Book Company, 1983.
22. Lu, Xun 鲁迅. "Wushengde zhongguo" 无声的中国 (A China without a True Voice). In *San xian ji* 三闲集 (A Collection Entitled "Leisure, Leisure, and Still Leisure). Beijing: People's Literature Publishing House, 1973.
23. Luo, Dajing 罗大经. *Helin yulu* 鹤林玉露 (Jade Dew in the Crane's Forest or Tales of the Men of Letters of the Song Dynasty). Beijing: Zhonghua Book Company, 1983.
24. Mao, dun 茅盾. "Lun chuqi baihuashi" 论初期白话诗 (On the Early Vernacular Modern Chinese Poetry). *Wenxue* 文学 (Literature), 8, 1937.
25. Puji (Shi Daoyuan) 普济. *Wudeng huiyuan* 五灯会元 (Record of Buddhist Zen Monks, Dharm Talks and Anecdotes). Beijing: Zhonghua Book Company, 1984.
26. Sun, Zuoyun 孙作云. "Tan xiandaipaishi" 谈现代派诗 (On the Poetry of the Modern School). *Qinghua zhoukan* 清华周刊 (Tsinghua Weekly), 1, 1935.
27. Wellek, René and Austin Warren. *Wenxue lilun* 文学理论 (Theory of Literature), translated by Xiangyu Liu 刘象愚 et al. Beijing: SDX Joint Publishing Company, 1984.
28. Wen, Yiduo 闻一多. "Shi de gelü" 诗的格律 (The Tonal and Metrical Schemes of Poetry). In *Wen Yiduo Quanji* 闻一多全集 (A Complete Edition of Wen Yiduo's Works). Beijing: SDX Joint Publishing Company, 1982.
29. Weng, Fanggang 翁方纲. "Shizhou shihua" 石洲诗话 (The Commentaries on Poetry at the Rocky Edge of an Islet). In *Qing shihua xubian* 清诗话续编 (A Sequel to the Poetic Discourses of the Qing Dynasty), edited by Shaoyu Guo 郭绍虞. Shanghai: Shanghai Classics Publishing House, 1983.
30. Wu, Qiao 吴乔. "Weilu shihua" 围炉诗话 (Talks about Poetry around the Hearth). In *Qing shihua xubian* 清诗话续编 (A Sequel to the Poetic Discourses of the Qing Dynasty), edited by Shaoyu Guo 郭绍虞. Shanghai: Shanghai Classics Publishing House, 1983.
31. Xie, Zhen 谢榛. "Siming shuhua" 四溟诗话 (A Sea-in-the-Four-Direction Recluse's Remarks on Poetry). In *Lidai shihua xubian* 历代诗话续编 (A Sequel to the Commentaries by the Critics of the Past Dynasties on Poetry), edited by Fubao Ding 丁福保. Beijing: Zhonghua Book Company, 1983.
32. Yan, Yu 严羽. "Canglang shihua" 沧浪诗话 (Canglang's Criticism of Poetry). In *Lidai shihua* 历代诗话 (The Commentaries by the Critics of the Past Dynasties on Poetry), edited by Wenhuan He 何文焕. Beijing: Zhonghua Book Company, 1981.
33. Yang, Shen 杨慎. "Shengan shihua" 升庵诗话 (Shengan's Commentaries on Poetry). In *Lidai shihua xubian* 历代诗话续编 (A Sequel to the Commentaries by the Critics of the Past Dynasties on Poetry), edited by Fubao Ding 丁福保. Beijing: Zhonghua Book Company, 1983.
34. Ye, Mengde 叶梦得. *Shilin shihua* 石林诗话 (Tales and Critique of Poetry at Shilin). In *Lidai shihua* 历代诗话 (The Commentaries by the Critics of the Past Dynasties on Poetry), edited by Wenhuan He 何文焕. Beijing: Zhonghua Book Company, 1981.
35. Ye, Xie 叶燮. *Yuan shi* 原诗 (A Probe into the Essence of Versification). Beijing: People's Literature Publishing House, 1979.

36. Yu, Pingbo 俞平伯. "Shehuishang duiyu xinshi de gezhong xinliguan" 社会上对于新诗的各种心理观 (The Opinions Held by Four Main Schools of the New Poetry). *Xinchao* 新潮 (The New Trend), 2, 1919.
37. Zhang, Jie 张戒. "Suihantang shihua" 岁寒堂诗话 (Notes on Poetry Written in the Pine and Cypress Studio). In *Lidai shihua xubian* 历代诗话续编 (A Sequel to the Commentaries by the Critics of the Past Dynasties on Poetry), edited by Fubao Ding 丁福保. Beijing: Zhonghua Book Company, 1983.
38. Zhang, Lei 张耒. *Zhangwenqian wenji* 张文潜文集 (The Collection of the Works by Wenqian). Beijing: Zhonghua Book Company, 1990.

Index

"A Collection of Nineteen Ancient Poems" 47
Ackermann, M. K., *The German-Chinese Dictionary* 27
allusion 4, 99; aesthetic appreciation 105–110; annotation 101, 102, 116–119; "attendant scroll" 105; competence system 104, 108; definition 100–101; in Huang 103–104; in Li 103, 108, 111, 113–115; linguistic barriers 101–103, 104; in Liu 111–112; meaning 105, 118–119; misinterpretation 108; "qualified reader" 114; sentimental 115–116; in Su 103, 109; "tales" 117–118; tension 109, 110; translation 101–105; usage 110–116; Wangdi 119; in Zhou 107–108
An Lushan-Shi Siming Rebellion 2, 6, 14–15, 16, 18, 34, 167
ancient Chinese poetry 123, 141; allusion 100, 103; defamiliarization 158; poetic language 48–49; rhymed 64; subtilization of the meaning of 131–134; succinctness 131; tonal and metrical schemes 63–64; *see also* poetry; Song Dynasty poetry; Tang Dynasty poetry
annotation 7, 8–9; allusion 101, 102, 116–119
antithetical symmetry 73–75, 95–96, 113, 143; heterogenous 77–79, 80; homogenous 76–77; limiting the number of couplets in Recent Style poetry 85–88, 89–94; naturalizing 81–85; types 76; *see also* tonal and metrical scheme/s
approach 2–3, 17
architecture 62–63
Aristotle, *Poetics* 94–95
Arnheim, R. 43, 107, 109; *Visual Thinking* 42

asyntactical word order 42
"attendant scroll" 105
aural imagery 45, 62
auxiliary words 133, 162

background 1–2, 17, 23; and meaning 2, 3, 12; "the northern spirit" 4; politics 9, 10, 13, 14
background-based interpretation 2–3, 10; determinism 19; and intuitive perception 33–34; reconstruction of a certain background 8; specific 4–6; symbolism 16–17; verifying the background 6–7; versification 18–19
Bai, J. 34; "A Stroll in Spring around the Qian Tang Lake" 129
Beardsley, M. C. 9; *The Affective Fallacy* 23
Bian, Z.: "Rain and Me" 187; "A Snippet" 184
Book of Change, The 95
Book of History, The 102
Book of Rites, The 94–95
Book of Songs, The 27, 46
Brandes, G., *Introduction to Main Currents in the Nineteenth Century Literature* 1
Brooks, C., *The Well-Wrought Urn: Studies in the Structure of Poetry* 24

cadence 31, 64, 69, 94–95, 107, 108, 109, 143–144
Cai, J., *Cai Kuanfu's Remarks on Poetry* 77
Cai, M. 10
Canby, H. S. 27
Cao, X., *The Story of the Stone* 63, 99–100, 102, 150–151, 154
Chen, B. 9
Chen, D., *On Revolutionizing Literature* 178
Chen, J. 13
Chen, M., *A Selection of the Poems by the New Crescent School Poets* 95–96

Chen, S., *Houshan's Understanding of Poetry* 166
Chen, Y. 4; "My Ascent of the Yueyang Tower" 132; "Two Poems Composed on a Spring Day" 21
Cheng, F., *Defence of Poetry* 175, 181
chimes 30
Chinese language: suitability for Recent Style poetry 45; word order 40, 44–45
Chomsky, N. 40, 42–43
ci poem 16, 134; background 1–2
Clemen, W., *Development of Shakespeare's Imagery* 19
communication 101–102
competence system 104, 108
concepts 42
Confucianism, Neo- 168
Confucius, *The Analects* 12
contemporary Chinese poetry 189
content: and form 179–180; *see also* substantialism
context 29, 36
Crescent School 182
critique 7; annotations 7, 8–9; architecture 62–63; intuitive perception 21–25, 30; knowledge of a specific background 4–6; linguistic interpretation 23–24; reconstruction of a certain background 8; "shi yan" words 149–150, 153–154; Song Dynasty poetry 136–137; standards for judging poetry 53; syntactic analysis 28–29; Tang Dynasty poetry 168–169; taste 25–27; tone 31–33; wording 15, 16, 17, 21–23, 24; *see also* interpretation; intuitive perception

Dafang, L., *The Chronicle of Han Yu of the Tang Dynasty's Life* 4–5
Dai, W., "An Impression" 30
deep linguistic structure 42–44, 45, 57
defamiliarization 25, 48, 142, 157–158, 159–160, 164–165; *see also* poetic language
denomination 35–36
determinism 19
development of Chinese poetry: from the literary style to the vernacular style 158–171; poetic language 157–158; Recent Style poetry 158–159; from vernacular Song Dynasty poetry to vernacular modern Chinese poetry 171–175
Dezong, Emperor 9
disharmonization 107–108, 109; *see also* harmony

displacement 18
Donne, J., "The Canonization" 24, 28
Du, F. 4, 13, 14–15, 19, 23, 28, 30, 34, 40–41, 52, 54, 55, 82, 108, 165, 166, 187; allusions in 110; "Ascending a Highly Raised Terrace" 131; colloquial expressions 167; "Escorting Zhen Guangwen in a Tour of the He Clan's Forested Mountain" 26; "Inspired at the News of the Imperial Army Having Recovered Youzhou and Jizhou" 132; "Lament for the Princes" 5; "Looking at the Mounts Below" 2; "The Milky Way" 15; "A Neighbor South of My Home" 129; "A New Crescent" 9–10; "A Nocturnal Lamentation When Lodging at General Yan Wu''s Quarters" 148–149; "To Prime Minister of the Kingdom of Shu" 127; "Reflection at the Tengwang Tower" 126–127; "A Revisit" 148; "shi yan" 147–150; "Spring Outlook" 89–90; "Two Jue Ju Poems" 136; "A Visit to Tushita Temple" 124; "To Welcome a Revered Visitor" 136; "xu zi" words in 124–128, 164; "Yu Hua Gong (The Yuhua Palace)" 6–7
Du, H., *Preface to the Poetry by Dai Wangshu* 181
Du, M., *The Collection by Fanchuan of His Own Poetry* 154
Du, X. 52

Eastern Han Style poetry 47
"Eight Defects" 64–65, 66–67; "feng yao" 66, 68; "he xi" 67; *see also* tonal and metrical scheme/s
ellipsis 42, 43–44, 45, 49–50, 53, 56, 57, 58–59
emotion 27–29
"eye" 140, 141, 145; *see also* "shi yan"

Fan, P. 111
Fan, W.: *An Intimate Poetry Discourse across Beds at Night* 128; *Qianxi's Perspective on Poetry* 46, 62–63
Fan, X., *An Intimate Poetry Discourse across Beds at Night* 134
Fan, Y., *A Collection of the Poems by the Quintessential Poets of the High Tang Dynasty* 70
Fan, Z., "A Poem about the Yuewang Tower of Mianzhou in Shu" 102
Fang, D., *Illuminating Chatters* 52, 131
"fanqie" 65

feeling/s 22, 24, 25, 29–30, 31, 32; Chinese language 44; conveying through allusion 113–114; "xu zi" words or phrases 129, 130
Fei, G., *Notes of Liangxi* 46–47
Fei, M.: "A Daisy A Butterfly Zhuangzi" 185; *A Lecture on the New Poetry* 176
Fei, X., *An Outline of the Chinese Poetry* 142
Feng, B. 22
Feng, H., *Annotations on Yixisheng's Poems* 9
"feng yao" 65, 66, 68
Fenollosa, E. 105
Five Dynasties 123
form: antithetical symmetry 73–76, 77–79, 80; and content 179–180; "lv shi" poetry 93–94; *see also* antithetical symmetry
Formalism 31, 48, 110
Foucault, M. 8; *The Archaeology of Knowledge* 36
"Four Tones" 64–65, 66–68; *see also* tonal and metrical scheme/s
Fowles, J. R., *The Aristos* 112–113
Frankel, H. H. 113
function words 46–47, 49

Gadamer, H. G. 17, 116
Gao, Y. 69
Gao, Z., *The Anthology of the Poetry of the Resurgent Period of the Tang Dynasty* 77
Ge, L. 127; *Ge Lifang's Commentaries on Poetry* 82
Ginsberg, A. 42
Gong, X., "Learn to Compose a Poem" 21
Graham, A. C. 101
grammar 42
Gu, C. 1
Guan, S., *Exposition of Du-Xue-Shan-Fang's Anthology of the Tang Dynasty Poetry* 125–126
"gui" 27
Guo, M., *On Rhyme* 181

Habermas, J. 16, 105
Han, H., *Cold Food* 13–14
Han, Y.-F., "A Long Song" 47
Han, Z. 54
"Han Wu" 15
Hao, Y., *Annotations on the Classical Annotations on 'Conforming to or Nearing Elegance'* 31–32
harmony 95
Hawkes, T., *Structuralism and Semiotics* 24, 51

He, S.: *A Discourse on Poetry at Zaijiu Garden* 84, 164; *A Record of the Remarks by a Burning Lamp* 27
He, X. 50, 69
"he xi" 67
Heidegger, M.: *Being and Time* 17; *Hölderlin and the Essence of Poetry* 57–59
Herder, J. G. 42
hermeneutics 17; interpretation 16
heterogenous antithetical symmetry 77–79, 80
Hölderlin, F. 59
homogenous antithetical symmetry 76–77
Hong, M., *Five Notes from the Tolerant Studio* 46
Hoy, D. C., *The Critical Circle: Literature, History and Philosophical Hermeneutics* 16
Hu, S. 25, 172–173, 176–177; "An Arrested Star" 174; *Driven to Rebel: Initiation of the Revolutionization of the Chinese Literature* 178–179; *The History of Literature in the Mandarin* 177; *A Letter to Chen Duxiu* 178; *My Ill-Considered Proposals for Literary Reform* 178; "A Whim" 174
Hu, X.: *A Critical Look at Hu Shi's "Attempts at Composing Poetry in the Vernacular"* 73; *On Reforming Chinese Literature* 181
Hu, Y.: on "shi yan" words 141; *Thickets of Criticism* 93–94
Hu, Z., *Poetic Remarks from the Fisherman Recluse at the Trumpet-Creeper Creek* 123, 160
Huang, T. 105, 163; allusions in 103–104
Huang, X., *A Catalogue of Collected Li Bai's Poems in a Chronicle* 7
Huang, Z., *The Yardsticks by Yehong for Critique of Poetry* 22, 88
Hui, J., *The Biographies of the Eminent and Learned Monks* 69

"I" perspective 171, 178–179, 184, 185
iambus 31
imagery 62, 79, 105–106; aural 45; juxtaposition 53–55, 56–57, 132–133, 137, 158–159, 186
imagination 35–36, 109
Ingarden, R., *The Cognition of the Literary Work of Art* 53
intent-based intuitive perception 35–36
intention 84–85

interpretation 1, 3; approach 2–3, 17; background-based 2–6; context 29, 36; hermeneutics 16; intuitive perception 21–25, 30; linguistic 23–24, 31; linguistic devices 27–28; notion 39; politics 9, 10, 13, 14, 15; syntactic analysis 28–29; tone 31–33; transposition and 51; trusting 8–9; versification 18–19; and word order 42
intuitive perception 21–25, 26, 28, 30; and background-based interpretation 33–34; based on the poet's intent 35–36; based on the poet's personality 34–35; language-based 36; tone 31–33
Iser, W., *The Act of Reading: A Theory of Aesthetic Response* 53

Jakobson, R. 31, 110–111, 142; *Closing Statement: Linguistics and Poetics* 36; *Linguistics and Poetics* 160–161
Ji, X. 56
Ji, Y. 22–23
Jiang, K. 51–52
Jiang, S. 23
Jiang, Z. 50; "Using the Old Verse 'Hand in Hand upon the Venue of Departure' to Entitle the Poem Composed in Response to the Decree by His Majesty" 91–92
Jiao, R. 47
Jiaoran, *Styles of Poetry: Poets' Active and Strenuous Mental Work* 52, 68, 85
"Jijiu Rimes" 131
Jin Dynasty 1
"jue ju" 63, 90
Jung, C., *Psychology and Literature* 44
juxtaposition of imagery 53–55, 56–57, 58–59, 132–133, 137, 158–159, 186

Kang, B.: "Goodbye to My Peking University Classmates" 175; "My View of the New Poetry" 172
Kayser, W., *Das Sprachliche Kunstwerk-Eine Einführungin die Literaturwis-senschaft* 31, 62, 102–103
Kobo, D. 105; *Treatise on the Secret Treasury of Literary Mirror* 47, 66, 70, 76, 141, 144–145
Kristeva, J., *Sèméiotikè: Recherches pour une sémanalyse* 17

"l" and "d" tones 69–70, 71
landscape 1
language: -based intuitive perception 36; concepts 42; defamiliarization 48; grammatical rules 43; literary 49, 164, 172, 182; personality and 34–35; poetic 48, 49, 56, 57–58, 59, 110–111, 137, 144–145; principle of temporal sequence 40; refinement 25–27; temporal sequence 40–41; topicalization 40–41; vernacular 49, 53, 55, 56, 158; *see also* vernacular; wording and word order
Laozi 95
Lehmann, W. P., *Descriptive Linguistics: An Introduction* 31, 40
Levy-Bruhl, L., *Primitive Mentality* 44
Li, B. 4; "Bidding Farewell to Song Zhiti at Jiangxia" 7; "A Concubine Who Soon Lost Favour" 15; "Fifty-Nine Poems in Ancient Style" 13; "What a Trek to Shu" 34
Li, D. 45; *Classification in Order of the Five Musical Notes of the Initial Consonants of Chinese Words* 65–66; *The History of the Southern Dynasties* 64; *Litang's Remarks on Poetry* 52, 130; *Yucun's Remarks on Poetry* 15
Li, G.: *On the Content and Form of the New Poetry* 176–177; "Ferrying across the Sangquian River" 133; "Homesick" 133
Li, H.: "Extreme Northern Cold" 9; "Li Ping at the Vertical Harp" 2; "Southern Garden" 7
Li, J. 30, 44
Li, S. 28–29, 100, 105, 187; "The Adorned Zither" 111, 113–115; allusions in 103; "A Ballad on the Sea" 9; "The Huaqing Palace" 104; "Return from Hanzhong by Way of Fenshuiling to the North" 7; "Titleless" 18, 23–24, 100, 132, 133; "Writing to My Kin and Friends in the North at a Rainy Night" 102
Li, Y., *Spontaneous Glimpses in Leisure* 63
Liang, Q. 114
Lin, B. 30
linguistic approach 21–22; *see also* wording and word order
linguistic devices 23, 27–28
literary language 49, 164, 172, 182; *see also* vernacular
literature 31
Liu, B. 25; *Liu Gongwen's Commentaries on Poetry* 153
Liu, C., "A Poem Composed at a Riverside Pavilion in Late Autumn" 40–41
Liu, D.: *Random Notes on Prose Writing* 129; *Tear-Stain: A Poem Series* 184–185

Liu, S.: *The Gist of the Four Tones* 66; *A Partial Discourse on the Correspondence between Designation and Denotation* 32
Liu, X. 8–9; *Generalizations about Arts* 153; *The Literary Mind and the Carving of Dragons* 36, 46, 51, 62, 76, 99, 140
Liu, Y.: *A New Account of Tales of the World* 1; "A Veteran General" 111–112
love 15, 24; romantic 28
Lu, J., *Remarks in the Style of an Ode on Literary Creation* 18, 62
Lu, T. 26
Lu, Y. 30, 123
Lui, Z., "A Historian" 187
Luo, B., "A Prisoner's Reflection on Buzzing Cicadae" 72
Luo, D. 149; *Jade Dew in the Crane's Forest or Tales of the Men of Letters of the Song Dynasty* 131, 133, 167
Lv, J., *The Collection of the Second Vowels of Chinese Words* 66
"lv shi" poetry 46, 63, 89–92, 159–160, 162–163, 164, 187; form 93–94; "Reflection at the Tengwang Tower" 126–127; "shi yan" 140; *see also* "shi yan"

Ma, Z., "Autumnal Thoughts" 123
Madam Wei 30
Mao, C.: *Shenyuan's Poetic Discourse* 134; *Shenyuan's Remarks on Poetry* 27
Mao, D., *On the Early Vernacular Modern Chinese Poetry* 177–178, 179–180
meaning 6, 17, 21, 24, 53; of allusions 105, 118–119; and background 2, 3, 12; poetry 1–2, 154; subtilization 132–134; thought flow 39–40; transposition and 50–51; wording and 23–24; "xu" 122; *see also* thought flow
Mei, S. 51
melodic pattern 31
Mencius 33
Meng, J., "Reflection in Autumn" 32–33
metaphor 13, 15, 16, 24, 25, 26, 28, 55
metrical schemes *see* tonal and metrical scheme/s
Ming Dynasty 2
More Records of the Search for the Supernatural 117–118
mountains 1, 106–107
Mu, M., *A Talk on Poetry: A Letter to Moruo* 181
Mukarovsky, J. 110–111
musical notes 65–66

naturalness 110; allusion 100–101; in antithetical symmetry 81–85; poetic language 144
New Book of Tang, The 75
New Criticism 24, 109
Nietzsche, F., *The Use and Abuse of History* 18
"notion" 39–40

Olson, E. 24
Ouyang, X. 163; *The Biography of Song Zhiwen* 62; *Liuyi's Commentaries on Poetry* 51, 147

Pan, D., *Remarks on Poetry at Yangyi Studio* 33–34, 35, 132
Payne, J. H.: "Home, Sweet Home" 27
pentasyllabic poems 66–67
perception 22; *see also* intuitive perception
personality, and intuitive perception 34–35
personification 103
"ping tou" 64–65, 66–67
poetic language 48, 49, 56, 57–58, 59, 110–111, 137; defamiliarization 25, 48, 142, 157–158, 164–165; functions 160–161; Song Dynasty poetry 160, 162–164; Southern Dynasties 144–145; Tang Dynasty poetry 161–162, 167–168; vernacular modern Chinese poetry 172–176, 179; *see also* development of Chinese poetry; Recent Style poetry; Song Dynasty poetry; Tang Dynasty poetry
poetic revolution 137–138
poetic style, vernacular Song Dynasty 160; *see also* development of Chinese poetry; Recent Style poetry; vernacular
poetry 23, 31; architecture 62–63; background 3; *ci* 16; critic 2–3; defamiliarization 48; functions of 169, 175–180; interpretation 1–2; juxtaposition of imagery 53–55; meaning 1–2, 24, 154; melodic pattern 31; pattern 62; pentasyllabic 66–67; and prose 46–47, 48; Recent Style 31–32, 40; sentiment 115; tension 56–57; *see also* allusion; background; interpretation; meaning; tonal and metrical scheme/s
politics 9, 10, 13, 14, 15, 16, 33
Pope, A., "Essay on Criticism" 3
Pound, E. 105
Preface to the Book of Songs, A 12
principle of temporal sequence 40
process of displacement 18

prose 176; and poetry 46–47, 48; word order 47
Pu, Q.: *Assiduous Annotations on Du Fu's Poems* 6; *A Catalogue of the Chronicled Collection of the Poems by Du Fu* 8–9
pun 24

Qian, Q. 2, 5; *Appreciation, Like Smelling Aroma, of the Poetry by Xu Yuantan* 22
Qian, W., "Titleless" 135
Qian, X. 35; *Record of Motions* 16–17
Qian, Z., *Annotations on the Selected Poetry of the Song Dynasty* 117
Qing Dynasty 2
Qiu, Z. 55; *Copious Notes on Du Fu's Poetry* 2, 10
Quan, Z., "A Song for the Sundial Erected by the Ming Dynasty Astronomer Tang Ruowang" 138

Ransom, J. C., *The New Criticism* 56
Recent Style poetry 31–32, 43, 48, 58–59, 59, 158–159, 188; antithetical symmetry 73–76, 81; ellipsis 49–50; emulating in early vernacular modern Chinese poetry 180–189; juxtaposition of imagery 53–55, 56–57, 58–59, 132–133; "l" and "d" tones 69–70, 71; limitation of the number of couplets within a poem 85–88, 89–94; "lv shi" 46, 63; minor poets 159–160; pictorialness 44; subtilization of meaning 133; suitability of the Chinese language 45; Tang Dynasty 161–162; word meaning 44; word order 40–41, 45; "xu zi" words or phrases 123–124, 127, 129
refinement 25–27, 141, 142, 153; in early vernacular modern Chinese poetry 180–189; "shi yan" 140; "suoyinfa" 55
reform: literary 178; versification 49; *see also* defamiliarization; refinement
rhetoric 27–28, 29; Recent Style poetry 172, 182–187
rhyming 64, 95; terminal-word 72; transitional 71–72
Richards, I. A. 104; *The Philosophy of Rhetoric* 29; *Practical Criticism* 16
romantic love 28
Russian Formalism 24, 31, 48

Santayana, G., *The Sense of Beauty* 27
semantics 27, 40; word order 40
sentiment and sentimentality 56, 115–116, 126

Shakespeare, W. 4
"shang wei" 65
Shen, K. 42
Shen, Y. 66, 67–68; *The History of the Song Period of the Southern Dynasties* 64
Sheng, D., *A Desultory Discourse on Poetry* 141–142
Shi, B., *A Garrison Secretary's Talk about Poetry* 23, 26, 140
"shi yan" 140, 152, 159, 187–188; in Du Fu 147–150; Fei on 142; how to acquire 141–145; Hu on 141; overuse 152; Sheng on 142; in Tang Dynasty poetry 147–149; and thought flow 154; usage 145–151
"shi zi" words or phrases 122–123, 128, 137–138, 144; "Autumnal Thoughts" 123
Shizhen, W. 27; *Questions and Answers on Poetry at Gu Fu Yu Pavilion* 24
Shklovsky, V. 25; *Theory of Prose* 48
Sidney, P., *The Defence of Poetry* 31
Sikong, S., "Bidding Adieu to Han Shen after Remeeting and Putting Up at the Inn with him in Yunyang" 134
Sikong, T., *Twenty-Four Poems on Poetry* 51–52
Skiner, Q., *Hermeneutics and the Role of History* 2
Song, C. 100
Song, Z., "Ferrying across the Han River" 11, 34
Song and Qi periods of the Southern Dynasties 12, 13; poetic language 143–145
Song Dynasty poetry 2, 12–13, 142–144, 164, 172; linguistic style 166–167; "shi yan" 140; tonal and metrical schemes 165; vernacular style 160, 162–164, 169–171, 176–177, 188–189; "xu zi" words or phrases 135–138
Southern Dynasties: antithetical symmetry 74–75; linguistic reform 49; "shi yan" 146
specific background 4–6
speech 69; and thought flow 40
Stegmüller, W., *Hauptstromungen der gegenwartsphilosophie* 58
Steiner, G., *After Babel: Aspects of Language and Translation* 59
Su, S. 163–164; allusions in 103, 109; "In Response to the Poems by Bangzhi and Ziyou" 135; "On the Way to Xincheng" 26
substantialism 178–179
subtilization of the meaning of ancient Chinese poems 131–134

Sun, Y., *A Compilation by Lvzhai of Classics and Their Exegeses for Posterity* 149
"suoyinfa" 55
surface linguistic structure 43
Suzong, Emperor 9–10, 10
symbolism and symbology 16–17, 24, 103
Symbolism School 182
symmetrical antithesis *see* antithetical symmetry
syntactic analysis 28–29

Tai, J. 40
"tale" 117–118
Tang, G. 105
Tang Dynasty poetry 2, 6, 7, 9, 11, 13, 172; criticism 168–169; "Han Wu" 15; poetic language 161–162, 167–168; "shi yan" 147–149; tonal and metrical schemes 165–166; "xu zi" words or phrases 135–138; *see also* Recent Style poetry
Tao, Y. 16, 18, 27, 34; "Motionless Aggregated Clouds" 12–13; "Narration for Wine" 12; "A Series Composed after Drinking Rice Wine" 102; "A Song for King Ke" 19
Tao, Z., *Records from Someone Who Stopped Farming the the Southern Village* 123–124
taste 25–27
Tate, A. 109
temporal sequence 40
tension 56, 56–57, 80, 110; in allusion 109; vernacular modern Chinese poetry 185–186
terminal-word rhyme 71–72, 72
thought flow 39; ancient Chinese thinking 44; deep linguistic structure 42–44, 45; and "shi yan" words 154; and speech 40; surface linguistic structure 43; and word order 41–42, 51–59
Todorov, T. 18; *Critique de la critique: Un Roman D'apprentissage* 4
tonal and metrical scheme/s 31–33, 50, 62, 95–96; "Eight Defects" 64–65, 66–67; "fanqie" 65; "feng yao" 65, 66; "Four Tones" 64–65, 66–68; "he xi" 67; "jue ju" 63, 90; "l" and "d" tones 69–70, 71; limiting the number of couplets in Recent Style poetry 85–88, 89–94; "lv shi" 46, 63, 89–93; musical notes 65–66; "ping tou" 64–65, 66–67; rhyming 64; "shang wei" 65; Song Dynasty poetry 165; Tang Dynasty poetry 165–166; transitional rhymes 71–72

topicalization 40
transitional rhymes 71–72
translation of allusion 101–105
transposition 42, 43–44, 50, 50–51, 53, 56, 57, 58–59
tune 94–95

Valery, P. 53
vernacular 49, 53, 55, 56, 158; modern Chinese poetry 172–175, 176, 177–178, 179–180, 180–189; Song Dynasty poetry 160, 162–164, 166, 169–171, 176–177, 188–189; *see also* poetic language; prose
versification 18–19, 24, 58, 62, 153; "Eight Defects" 65–66; ellipsis 49–50; reform 49; *see also* antithetical symmetry; ellipsis; "shi yan"; tonal and metrical scheme/s; "xu zi" words or phrases
von Humboldt, W. 44–45

Waley, A. 101
Wang, A. 34, 113, 140; allusions in 103; "Ascending the Top of Mount Damao" 22; "To my First Younger Sister" 130; *New Discourses by Approaching Annoying Problems* 52; "In Response to My Younger Brother's Poem at the Relish Pavilion" 135
Wang, B.: "An Early Autumnal Farewell at the River Dock" 133; "A Rhapsody Improvised for the Banquet at Tengwang Tower" 117
Wang, C. 74; "Seeing Xin Jian Off at the Hibiscus Tower" 11; "Songs of the Noble Mansion" 34
Wang, D. 131; "A Discourse on Poetry" 29; *The Pale Toll* 29–30
Wang, F., *Jiangzhai's Commentaries on Poetry* 14–15, 22
Wang, G., *Remarks on Ci Poetry in the Human World* 107
Wang, J., *A Comprehensive Study of Arias and Dramas* 63
Wang, L. 23; *The Chinese Prosody* 71; *A Manuscript about the History of the Chinese Language* 32
Wang, Q. 108
Wang, S. 10, 26–27, 41–42, 55; *Explications of Du Fu's Intentions in His Poetry* 35; *Random Talk from the Garden of Art* 77, 94
Wang, W. 4, 56; "Birds Chirping in the Canyon" 18; *A Collection of Su Shi's Poems with Annotations* 5; "Mooring at

the Foot of Mount Beigu" 28; "Mount Zhongnan" 13–14, 106–107
Wang, Y.: *Exegeses of Texts* 129–130; *Liunan's Desultory Notes* 25, 62, 80; *A Sequel to "Liunan's Desultory Notes"* 131
Wang, Z. 2
Warren, A., *Theory of Literature* 48
Way of Heaven 94–96
Wei, L., *An Epilogue to the Poem by Kang Jie* 169
Wei, Q., *Chips of Precious Jade Collected from the Treasury of Remarks on Poetry* 54, 75–76, 111, 113, 127, 154
Wei, T., *Remarks on Poetry in Reclusion on the Han River* 22
Wei, Y., "A Tour of the Kaiyuan Temple" 136
Wellek, R. 24; *Theory of Literature* 48
Wen, T. 187; "Early Departure from the Inn at the Shang Mount" 45, 130, 136; "An Elegy Inspired by a Dancer's Performance" 102
Wen, Y., *The Tonal and Metrical Schemes of Poetry* 62
Weng, F. 26–27
White, H., *Tropics of Discourse* 8
Wimsatt, W. K. 9; *The Affective Fallacy* 23
Wo, H., "Reflection on Falling Flowery Petals" 14
wording and word order 15, 16, 17, 21–23, 24, 39–40; asyntactical 42; deep linguistic structure 42–44, 45, 57; denomination 35–36; ellipsis 42, 45, 49–50, 53, 56, 57; function words 46–47, 49; prose 47; rhetoric 29; surface linguistic structure 43; taste 27; temporal sequence 40–41; thought flow 41–42, 51–59; topicalization 40–41; transposition 42, 50–51, 53, 56, 57; vernacular modern Chinese poetry 174
Wu, H., *Poetic Commentaries at the Huanxi Quarters* 131
Wu, K., *Canghai's Commentaries on Poetry* 81–82, 127–128, 130
Wu, L., *A Discourse in Bits and Pieces on Poems* 10
Wu, R. 30
Wu, Z., *A Random All-Inclusive Record by the Owner of 'Being Capable of Self-Rectification' Study* 54

Xiao, S., *The Supplementary Categorical Annotations on Li Bai's Poems* 15
Xie, K. 1
Xie, L. 33, 47, 48, 137, 146; "Ascending the Pavilion by the Pond" 13; *History of the Southern Dynasties, The* 88
Xie, T. 146
Xie, W., "Adorable" 175
Xie, X., *A Sea-in-the-Four-Direction Recluse's Remarks on Poetry* 47
Xie, Y.: *The Collection of Xitang's Works* 168; *Rhymes and Tones vis-a-vis Literature* 32
Xie, Z.: *A Sea-in-the-Four-Direction Recluse's Remarks on Poetry* 32, 49, 53, 54–55, 74, 135, 141, 144, 164; on "xu zi" words 122–123
Xu, F.: "Inspired by the Blossoming Plum Tree inside the Courtyard to Write after the Old Rhyme Scheme a Poem for Duanbai" 135–136
Xu, S., *An Anthology of All-Time Critics' Remarks on Poetry* 73
Xu, Z.: *To Suspend Publication of 'Poetry' Supplement* 181; "A View I Saw on my Train from Shanghai to Hangzhou" 186
"xu zi" words or phrases 164; conveyance of subtle nuances 128–131; criterion for judgment of Tang and Song Dynasty poetry 135–138; in Du Fu 124–128; Liu on 129; in Recent Style poetry 123–124; subtilization of the meaning of ancient Chinese poems 131–134; Xie on 122–123; "xu" 122; Yuan on 130; "zi" 123–128
Xuantong, Q. 25
Xuanzong, Emperor 2, 5
Xue, X., *Yipiao's Remarks on Poetry* 10, 35

Yan, J., "A Colourfully Attired Singsong Girl Holding a Goblet Urged Partaking of Wine" 134
Yan, Y. 48
Yan, Z., *The Family Instructions of Master Yan* 117
Yang, S.: *Annotation on the Ancient Chinese* 124; *Shengan's Commentaries on Poetry* 159–160
Yang, W. 100; *Chengzhai's Commentaries on Poetry* 132
Yang, X. 100; *Exemplary Sayings* 34
Yang, Z., *Techniques of Versification* 93
Yao, W., *Annotated Li He's Poems* 2
Ye, G., *On New Poetry* 96
Ye, J. 9
Ye, M., *Tales and Critique of Poetry at Shilin* 62, 73, 82–84, 149–150, 164

Ye, X., *A Probe into the Essence of Versification* 63
Yeats, W. B. 24
Yiduo, W., *The Tonal and Metrical Schemes of Poetry* 181
Yin, F., *A Collection of the Poems by the Quintessential Poets of the High Tang Dynasty* 11–12, 68
Yin, K., "A Newly Completed Palace Named Tranquility and Peace" 68
Yin and Yang 73, 81, 95
Yongming Style 47–48; *see also* Recent Style poetry
Yu, F. 108
Yu, P., *The Opinions Held by Four Main Schools of the New Poetry* 178–179
Yu, X. 54
Yuan, M., *A Sequel to 'Critique of Poetry'* 22
Yuan, R., *A Glossary of "Xu Zi" Words or Phrases* 130
Yucun 15
Yun, J. 26

Zen Buddhism 16, 25, 103
Zha, S. 100
Zhan, Y., *A Collection of Li Bai's Poems in a Chronicle* 7
Zhang, C., *Annotations on the Chronicled Poems by Yuxisheng* 9
Zhang, J.: "Enchanged Just at the Very Beginning of my Xiang River Tour" 133–134; *Notes on Poetry Written in the Pine and Cypress Studio* 26, 99–100, 167
Zhang, Q., *Jianzhai's Remarks on Poetry* 24
Zhao, C. 2, 42
Zhao, Y., *Oubei's Discourse on Poets and their Poetry* 125
Zheng, C., "The Impromptus On a Spring Outing" 187
Zhong, R. 47; *Critique of Poetry* 55, 88
Zhong, X., *A Treatise on Poetry* 36
Zhou, B., *Jieyuhua Shangyuan (Lantern Festival)* 107–108
Zhou, L., *Epilogue to the Collection of Xu Zhimo's Poetry* 26
Zhou, Z. 27, 174; "Two Snow Sweepers" 175
Zhu, C., *Critique of Poetry in Cunyu Study* 112
Zhu, G., *Correspondence on Aesthetics* 107
Zhu, H., *Annotations on the Collected Poems of Li Yishan* 5, 9
Zhu, T.: *Xiaoyuan's Commentaries on Poetry* 80, 135; *Xiaoyuan's Remarks on Poetry* 78
Zhuangzi 141
Zuo, Q., *Zuo Qiuming's Commentaries on the Spring and Autumn Annals* 12

For Product Safety Concerns and Information please contact our EU
representative GPSR@taylorandfrancis.com
Taylor & Francis Verlag GmbH, Kaufingerstraße 24, 80331 München, Germany

www.ingramcontent.com/pod-product-compliance
Lightning Source LLC
Chambersburg PA
CBHW050535300426
44113CB00012B/2112